IFIP Advances in Information and Communication Technology

454

IFIP – The International Federation for Information Processing

IFIP was founded in 1960 under the auspices of UNESCO, following the First World Computer Congress held in Paris the previous year. An umbrella organization for societies working in information processing, IFIP's aim is two-fold: to support information processing within its member countries and to encourage technology transfer to developing nations. As its mission statement clearly states,

IFIP's mission is to be the leading, truly international, apolitical organization which encourages and assists in the development, exploitation and application of information technology for the benefit of all people.

IFIP is a non-profitmaking organization, run almost solely by 2500 volunteers. It operates through a number of technical committees, which organize events and publications. IFIP's events range from an international congress to local seminars, but the most important are:

- The IFIPWorld Computer Congress, held every second year;
- Open conferences;
- Working conferences.

The flagship event is the IFIP World Computer Congress, at which both invited and contributed papers are presented. Contributed papers are rigorously refereed and the rejection rate is high.

As with the Congress, participation in the open conferences is open to all and papers may be invited or submitted. Again, submitted papers are stringently refereed.

The working conferences are structured differently. They are usually run by a working group and attendance is small and by invitation only. Their purpose is to create an atmosphere conducive to innovation and development. Refereeing is also rigorous and papers are subjected to extensive group discussion.

Publications arising from IFIP events vary. The papers presented at the IFIP World Computer Congress and at open conferences are published as conference proceedings, while the results of the working conferences are often published as collections of selected and edited papers.

Any national society whose primary activity is about information processing may apply to become a full member of IFIP, although full membership is restricted to one society per country. Full members are entitled to vote at the annual General Assembly, National societies preferring a less committed involvement may apply for associate or corresponding membership. Associate members enjoy the same benefits as full members, but without voting rights. Corresponding members are not represented in IFIP bodies. Affiliated membership is open to non-national societies, and individual and honorary membership schemes are also offered.

More information about this series at http://www.springer.com/series/6102

Christian Damsgaard Jensen · Stephen Marsh
Theo Dimitrakos · Yuko Murayama (Eds.)

Trust Management IX

9th IFIP WG 11.11
International Conference, IFIPTM 2015
Hamburg, Germany, May 26–28, 2015
Proceedings

 Springer

Editors
Christian Damsgaard Jensen
Technical University of Denmark
Lyngby
Denmark

Theo Dimitrakos
BT Research & Innovation
Ipswich
UK

Stephen Marsh
University of Ontario
Oshawa, ON
Canada

Yuko Murayama
Iwate Prefectural University
Takizawa
Japan

ISSN 1868-4238   ISSN 1868-422X   (electronic)
IFIP Advances in Information and Communication Technology
ISBN 978-3-319-38708-6   ISBN 978-3-319-18491-3   (eBook)
DOI 10.1007/978-3-319-18491-3

Springer International Publishing AG Switzerland is part of Springer Science+Business Media
(www.springer.com)

Preface

Dear Reader

Welcome to the IFIPTM 2015 Proceedings!

This volume contains the proceedings of the 9th IFIP Working Group 11.11 International Conference on Trust Management. The conference was held in Hamburg, Germany, May 26–28, 2015.

IFIPTM is a truly global conference, spanning research, development, policy, and practice for the increasingly important areas of trust management and computational trust. Given the breadth of application of these areas, and true to our historical underpinnings established at the first IFIPTM conference in 2007, IFIPTM 2015 focused on several areas, including trust and reputation and models thereof, the relationship between trust and security, socio-technical aspects of trust, reputation, and privacy, trust in the cloud, and behavioral models of trust.

The conference received 28 submissions from a wide variety of countries, including France, Germany, The Netherlands, UK, Algeria, Norway, Singapore, Greece, Denmark, China, Japan, Malaysia, Luxembourg, Romania, China, USA, Australia, and Canada. Every submission was subjected to a thorough peer review process, with at least three and most often four reviews per paper. Following these we accepted eight long and five short papers (an acceptance rate for long papers of 32%). In addition, since IFIPTM was colocated with the IFIP SEC conference, we solicited two papers from SEC that were more suitable for the Trust Management area, each of which was also reviewed by IFIPTM Program Committee members. The resulting program is broad and we hope stimulating for the attendees and yourself.

IFIPTM also hosts every year the William Winsborough Commemorative Address in memoriam of our esteemed colleague Prof. William Winsborough. The award is given to an individual who has significantly contributed to the areas of computational trust and trust management. In 2015, the Working Group was pleased to host Prof. Ehud Gudes of Ben-Gurion University of the Negev, who keynoted the conference and provided an extended abstract which can be found in these proceedings.

In addition to papers and keynote address, IFIPTM hosted a tutorial on identity and access management by Prof. Audun Jøsang of the University of Oslo, a special session on Data Protection, Privacy, and Transparency organized by Dr. Rehab Alnemr from HP Labs and Dr. Carmen Fernández-Gago from University of Málaga and keynoted by Marit Hansen, Deputy Chief of Unabhängiges Landeszentrum für Datenschutz, Germany. Finally, the conference hosted a special session on Trusted Cloud Ecosystems organized and chaired by Dr. Theo Dimitrakos of BT, from which papers and a message from Dr. Dimitrakos are included in these proceedings.

Conferences are multiheaded beasts, and as such require a team of dedicated people to tame them. To our Program Committee and associated reviewers, who delivered thoughtful, insightful and very much on time reviews, our thanks. This year we have been lucky to work with truly professional and helpful Workshop, tutorial, Poster and

Demonstration, Publicity, and Liaison Chairs. Since IFIPTM is colocated with IFIP SEC, the task of local organization and registration fell on the IFIP SEC team, notably Dr. Dominik Herrmann of the University of Hamburg, to whom, special thanks for putting up with our frailties. Thanks also to the University of Hamburg for providing the facilities.

No conference would succeed without authors. To all of those who submitted, our thanks and congratulations for being part of a growing, important, and vibrant research area. There are many, many conferences for which trust is listed as either a key or an associated area of interest, and we are keenly aware of the applicability of trust and trust management to a great many aspects of computer security, Human Computer Interaction, privacy, the social sciences, and beyond. We continue to try to build IFIPTM as a cross-disciplinary conference of choice, and appreciate your support.

For more information on the working group, please visit http://www.ifiptm.org/.

We hope you enjoy the conference and the proceedings.

March 2015   Stephen Marsh
                                                        Christian Damsgaard Jensen

IFIP Trust Management IX

9th IFIP WG 11.11 International Conference on Trust Management, 2015
Hamburg, Germany

May 26–28, 2015

General Chairs

Theo Dimitrakos   Security Research Centre, BT Group CTO
                   and University of Kent, UK
Yuko Murayama   Iwate Prefectural University, Japan

Program Chairs

Christian Damsgaard Jensen   Technical University of Denmark, Denmark
Stephen Marsh   University of Ontario Institute of Technology, Canada

Workshop and Tutorial Chairs

Sheikh Mahbub Habib   Technische Universität Darmstadt, Germany
Jan-Philipp Steghöfer   Göteborg University, Sweden

Poster and Demonstration Chairs

Dhiren Patel   NIT Surat, India
Audun Jøsang   University of Oslo, Norway

Panel and Special Session Chairs

Jean-Marc Seigneur   University of Geneva, Switzerland
Masakatsu Nishigaki   Shizuoka University, Japan

Publicity Chairs

Tim Muller   Nanyang Technological University, Singapore
Anirban Basu   KDDI R&D Laboratories, Japan

Graduate Symposium Chairs

Nurit Gal-Oz   Sapir Academic College, Israel
Jie Zhang   Nanyang Technological University, Singapore

Local Organization Chair

Dominik Herrmann   University of Hamburg, Germany

Program Committee

Rehab Alnemr	HP Labs Bristol, UK
Man Ho Au	Hong Kong Polytechnic University, Hong Kong
Anirban Basu	KDDI R&D Laboratories, Japan
Elisa Bertino	Purdue University, USA
Pamela Briggs	Northumbria University, UK
David Chadwick	University of Kent, UK
Piotr Cofta	
Lynne Coventry	Northumbria University, UK
Frédéric Cuppens	TELECOM Bretagne, France
Theo Dimitrakos	Security Research Centre, BT Group CTO and University of Kent, UK
Natasha Dwyer	Victoria University, Australia
Babak Esfandiari	Carleton University, Canada
Rino Falcone	Institute of Cognitive Sciences and Technologies, Italy
Hui Fang	Nanyang Technological University, Singapore
Carmen Fernández-Gago	University of Málaga, Spain
Josep Ferrer	Universitat de les Illes Balears, Spain
Simone Fischer-Hübner	Karlstad University, Sweden
Sara Foresti	Università degli Studi di Milano, Italy
Nurit Gal-Oz	Sapir Academic College, Israel
Dieter Gollmann	Hamburg University of Technology, Germany
Stefanos Gritzalis	University of the Aegean, Greece
Ehud Gudes	Ben-Gurion University of the Negev, Israel
Sheikh Mahbub Habib	CASED/Technische Universität Darmstadt, Germany
Omar Hasan	University of Lyon, France
Peter Herrmann	NTNU Trondheim, Norway
Xinyi Huang	Fujian Normal University, China
Roslan Ismail	Universiti Tenaga Nasional, Malaysia
Valerie Issarny	Inria, France
Christian Damsgaard Jensen	Technical University of Denmark, Denmark
Audun Jøsang	University of Oslo, Norway
Yuecel Karabulut	VMware, USA
Tracy Ann Kosa	University of Ontario Institute of Technology, Canada
Costas Lambrinoudakis	University of Piraeus, Greece
Gabriele Lenzini	SnT/University of Luxembourg, Luxembourg
Joseph Liu	Monash University, Australia

Yang Liu	Nanyang Technological University, Singapore
Javier Lopez	University of Málaga, Spain
Stephen Marsh	University of Ontario Institute of Technology, Canada
Fabio Martinelli	IIT-CNR, Italy
Sjouke Mauw	University of Luxembourg, Luxembourg
Weizhi Meng	Institute for Infocomm Research (I2R), Singapore
Max Mühlhäuser	Technische Universität Darmstadt, Germany
Tim Muller	Nanyang Technological University, Singapore
Yuko Murayama	Iwate Prefectural University, Japan
Wee Keong Ng	Nanyang Technological University, Singapore
Masakatsu Nishigaki	Shizuoka University, Japan
Zeinab Noorian	University of Saskatchewan, Canada
Dhiren Patel	NIT Surat, India
Günther Pernul	Universität Regensburg, Germany
Sini Ruohomaa	University of Helsinki, Finland
Pierangela Samarati	Università degli Studi di Milano, Italy
Jean-Marc Seigneur	University of Geneva, Switzerland
Murat Sensoy	Özyeğin University, Turkey
Ketil Stølen	SINTEF, Norway
Tim Storer	University of Glasgow, UK
Mahesh Tripunitara	The University of Waterloo, Canada
Claire Vishik	Intel Corporation, UK
Ian Wakeman	University of Sussex, UK
Shouhuai Xu	University of Texas at San Antonio, USA
Jie Zhang	Nanyang Technological University, Singapore
Jianying Zhou	Institute for Infocomm Research (I2R), Singapore

External Reviewers

Naipeng Dong	National University of Singapore, Singapore
Ida Maria Haugstveit	SINTEF, Norway
Ravi Jhawar	University of Luxembourg, Luxembourg
Spyros Kokolakis	University of the Aegean, Greece
Francisco Moyano	University of Málaga, Spain
Aida Omerovic	SINTEF, Norway
Ruben Rios	University of Málaga, Spain
Aggeliki Tsohou	Ionian University, Greece
Dongxia Wang	Nanyang Technological University, Singapore
Yang Zhang	University of Luxembourg, Luxembourg

Contents

Winsborough Award Invited Paper

Reputation - from Social Perception to Internet Security 3
   Ehud Gudes

Full Papers

Mathematical Modelling of Trust Issues in Federated Identity Management. . . . 13
   Md. Sadek Ferdous, Gethin Norman, Audun Jøsang, and Ron Poet

Simple and Practical Integrity Models for Binaries and Files 30
   Yongzheng Wu and Roland H.C. Yap

Enabling NAME-Based Security and Trust. 47
   Nikos Fotiou and George C. Polyzos

Trust Driven Strategies for Privacy by Design 60
   Thibaud Antignac and Daniel Le Métayer

Lightweight Practical Private One-Way Anonymous Messaging 76
   Anirban Basu, Juan Camilo Corena, Jaideep Vaidya, Jon Crowcroft,
   Shinsaku Kiyomoto, Stephen Marsh, Yung Shin Van Der Sype,
   and Toru Nakamura

Privacy-Preserving Reputation Mechanism: A Usable Solution Handling
Negative Ratings. 92
   Paul Lajoie-Mazenc, Emmanuelle Anceaume, Gilles Guette,
   Thomas Sirvent, and Valérie Viet Triem Tong

Obscuring Provenance Confidential Information via Graph Transformation. . . 109
   Jamal Hussein, Luc Moreau, and Vladimiro Sassone

Social Network Culture Needs the Lens of Critical Trust Research 126
   Natasha Dwyer and Stephen Marsh

Predicting Quality of Crowdsourced Annotations Using Graph Kernels 134
   Archana Nottamkandath, Jasper Oosterman, Davide Ceolin,
   Gerben Klaas Dirk de Vries, and Wan Fokkink

An Architecture for Trustworthy Open Data Services. 149
   Andrew Wong, Vicky Liu, William Caelli, and Tony Sahama

Short Papers

1,2, Pause: Lets Start by Meaningfully Navigating the Current Online
Authentication Solutions Space   165
  Ijlal Loutfi and Audun Jøsang

Data Confidentiality in Cloud Storage Protocol Based on Secret
Sharing Scheme: A Brute Force Attack Evaluation   177
  Alexandru Butoi, Mircea Moca, and Nicolae Tomai

The Detail of Trusted Messages: Retweets in a Context of Health
and Fitness   185
  Natasha Dwyer and Stephen Marsh

Reusable Defense Components for Online Reputation Systems   195
  Johannes Sänger, Christian Richthammer, Artur Rösch,
  and Günther Pernul

Continuous Context-Aware Device Comfort Evaluation Method   203
  Jingjing Guo, Christian Damsgaard Jensen, and Jianfeng Ma

Special Session: Toward Trusted Cloud Ecosystems

Foreword: Towards Trusted Cloud Ecosystems   215
  Theo Dimitrakos

A Cloud Orchestrator for Deploying Public Services on the Cloud – The Case
of STRATEGIC Project   217
  Panagiotis Gouvas, Konstantinos Kalaboukas, Giannis Ledakis,
  Theo Dimitrakos, Joshua Daniel, Géry Ducatel,
  and Nuria Rodriguez Dominguez

Integrating Security Services in Cloud Service Stores   226
  Joshua Daniel, Fadi El-Moussa, Géry Ducatel, Pramod Pawar,
  Ali Sajjad, Robert Rowlingson, and Theo Dimitrakos

Building an Eco-System of Trusted Services via User Control
and Transparency on Personal Data   240
  Michele Vescovi, Corrado Moiso, Mattia Pasolli, Lorenzo Cordin,
  and Fabrizio Antonelli

Security-as-a-Service in Multi-cloud and Federated Cloud Environments   251
  Pramod S. Pawar, Ali Sajjad, Theo Dimitrakos, and David W. Chadwick

The Role of SLAs in Building a Trusted Cloud for Europe   262
  Ana Juan Ferrer and Enric Pages i Montanera

Author Index   277

Winsborough Award Invited Paper

Reputation - from Social Perception to Internet Security

Ehud Gudes[✉]

Ben-Gurion University, 84105 Beer-Sheva, Israel
ehud@cs.bgu.ac.il

Abstract. Reputation is a concept that we use in many aspects of our social life and as part of our decision making process. We use reputation in our interaction with people or companies we do not know and we use it when we buy merchandize or reserve a room in a hotel. However, reputation plays also an important role in the internet society and enables us to establish trust which is essential for interaction in the virtual world. Reputation has several important aspects such as Aggregation, Identity and Transitivity which make it applicable in completely different domains. In this presentation we show the use of these aspects in several different domains and demonstrate it with our own previous and current research on reputation.

A good name is more desirable than great riches;
to be esteemed is better than silver or gold.
Proverbs 22:1

1 Introduction

Reputation is a key concept in our social life. Many of our day to day decisions such as which book to buy or which physician to consult with are based on Trust. This trust is based either on our own direct experience or when such direct experience is lacking, on other people (whose opinion we value) direct experience. However when no such direct or indirect experience is available we tend to rely on an aggregated opinion of a large set of people or a community which is manifested as Reputation. Reputation plays also a major role in virtual communities and social networks. Attempts to tarnish reputation in social networks have caused much damage to people in recent years (several cases of suicide have been reported as a result of tarnished reputation). So maintaining a good online reputation becomes a critical issue for both people and businesses. The existence of easily accessible virtual communities makes it both possible and legitimate to communicate with total strangers. Such interaction however must be based on trust which is usually based on personal experience. When such experience is not readily available, one often relies on reputation. Thus, computing reputation to capture a community's viewpoint is an important challenge.

Reputation has become a key component of several commercial systems such as E-bay [3]. Also, quite a few models for trust and reputation were developed.

© IFIP International Federation for Information Processing 2015
C.D. Jensen et al. (Eds.): IFIPTM 2015, IFIP AICT 454, pp. 3–10, 2015.
DOI: 10.1007/978-3-319-18491-3_1

Different models use different conceptual frameworks including simple average of ratings, bayesian systems, belief models [11] which enable the representation of uncertainty in rating, flow models in which the concept of transitive trust is central such as Eigen-trust [13] and Page-rank [16] and group-based models such as the Knot model [7]. In this presentation we discuss three important aspects of reputation and show how they are used in different domains. While the first two domains we discuss involve reputation of real-life users, the third domain deals with abstract entities, internet domains, yet computing and using reputation in this domain is similar to its use in the social domain.

The first aspect we deal with is the use of reputation as part of an **Identity**. In the social domains, reputation is an important part of a person identity, and the identity of a person determines its permitted actions. An expert programmer may gain more access rights to an open source code managed by some company, as her reputation increases. Such rights may be review or modify code at different levels. Our first domain then is the Authorization domain and the use of reputation for fine-grained access control. In Sect. 2 we present some models which use reputation as part of a user identity and consider it in making access control decisions.

The second aspect we examine is **Aggregation**. Most reputation computational models use some form of aggregation of ratings to compute the reputation [12]. However, such aggregation is usually done within a single community. In real-life, users may be active in several communities and to protect their privacy, users may use different identities in different communities. A major shortcomings is that user efforts to gain a good reputation in one community are not utilized in other communities they are active in. Another shortcoming is the inability of one community to learn about the dishonest behavior of some member as identified by other communities. Thus the need arises to aggregate reputation from multiple communities. We developed the Cross-Community Reputation (CCR) model for the sharing of reputation knowledge across virtual communities [5, 6, 9]. The CCR model is aimed at leveraging reputation data from multiple communities to obtain more accurate reputation. It enables new virtual communities to rapidly mature by importing reputation data from related communities. The use of Aggregation in the CCR model is discussed in Sect. 3.

The third aspect we discuss is **Transitivity**, an important property of trust which has implications on the computation of reputation. It enables us to compute reputation not only from our own experience or our friends experience but also from our "friends of friends" experience, etc. Several flow models for computing reputation while practicing the transitivity property, have been published, including Eigen-trust [13] and Page-rank [16]. Our unique contribution here is in transferring these ideas to the computation of Internet domains reputation. Today's internet world is full of threats and malware. Hackers often use various domains to spread and control their malware. The detection of these misbehaving domains is difficult since there is no time to collect and analyze traffic data in real-time, thus their identification ahead of time is very important. We use the term *domain reputation* to express a measure of our belief that a domain is benign or malicious. Computing domain reputation by using the Transitivity property and a Flow algorithm was investigated by us [15] and will be discussed in Sect. 3.

2 Identity-Reputation and Access Control

Conventional access control models like role based access control are suitable for regulating access to resources by known users. However, these models have often found to be inadequate for open and decentralized multi-centric systems where the user population is dynamic and the identity of all users are not known in advance. For such systems, there must be, in addition to user authentication, some trust measure associated with the user. Such trust measure can be represented by the user reputation as one attribute of its identity. Chakraborty and Ray [2] presented TrustBAC, a trust based access control model. It extends the conventional role based access control model with the notion of trust levels. Users are assigned to trust levels instead of roles based on a number of factors like user credentials, user behavior history, user recommendation etc. Trust levels are assigned to roles which are assigned to permissions as in role based access control. In Trustbac, when the reputation of a user decreases because of past actions, its assignment to the original role may not be valid anymore and a new role with less permissions is assigned by the system. An example of such scenario in the digital library domain is given in [2]. The switching of roles may not be desirable in all cases. In a medical domain for example, a physician with less reputation may not lose its role as "doctor" but may lose instead some of her permissions. This dynamic assignment of permissions for the same role, based on the user reputation may be much more flexible and can prevent the proliferation of too many roles. In [14] we define this dynamic model formally and show a detailed example of its operation in the software development domain. The main observation of this is that when one considers reputation as part of the user identity, one can support much more flexible role-based models without the need to increase significantly the number of roles in the system.

3 Aggregation and Cross Community Reputation

In this section we briefly describe the way reputation is aggregated from several communities using the CCR model [5,9]. The CCR model defines the major stages required to aggregate the reputation of a community member with the reputation of that member in other communities. The first stage determines the confidence one community has in another as a precondition for receiving reputation information from the latter. The second stage involves the conversion of reputation values from the domain values of one community to those of the other. In the third stage, a matching procedure is carried out between the sets of attributes used by the participating communities to describe reputation. As an example, suppose there are two sport communities in which a commentator is active, one for Basketball, the other for Football. Assume that Bob a commentator likes to import (and aggregate) his reputation from the football community into the basketball community. The first stage considers the general confidence that basketball community members have for reputation computed in the football community. The second stage considers the statistical distribution of reputation values in the two communities and apply the required transformation (e.g., a very good rating in one community may only be considered "good" in the other). The third stage maps the specific attributes that are used to compute the reputation in the two communities (e.g., the attribute "prediction accuracy" in the football community may be partially mapped to the attribute "general reliability" in the basketball community). A detailed mathematical model which explains the process of the mapping and aggregation of CCR, is described in [5]. The CCR model was implemented as the TRIC software. TRIC is concerned primarily with aggregating different reputation mechanisms across communities and with protecting user rights to privacy and control over data during this aggregation. The CCR computation process [5] begins when a *requesting community* that wishes to receive CCR data regarding one of its users, sends a request to relevant *responding communities*. Communities that have reputation data of the user and are willing to share the information reply with the relevant reputation data. The received data is aggregated and assembled into an object containing the CCR data of the user in the context of the requesting community. This process is illustrated in Fig. 1.

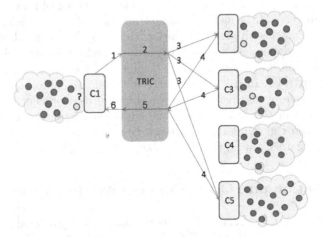

Fig. 1. Request for CCR scenario: (1): A requesting community sends TRIC a request for the CCR of a community member; (2): TRIC compiles a request and (3) submits it to all potential responding communities; (4): Responding communities submit a reputation object of the member at subject; (5): TRIC processes all reputation objects and compiles a CCR object; (6): TRIC sends the CCR object to the requesting community

One of the important goals associated with sharing reputation between communities is dealing with privacy. Within the CCR model, we identified three major privacy concerns that are not present or that are less significant in single community domains. First Unlinkability is a primary concern raised by the CCR model. Although we aim to compute a user's CCR from several communities, we provide the means to do so without compromising the user's anonymity in each community and while upholding the requirement of unlinkability between the communities. Controlling the dissemination of reputation information is another privacy requirement. We present a policy-based approach that enables both the users and the communities to have control over the dissemination of reputation data. The third privacy issue we address is the tradeoff between privacy and trust. We suggest the transparency measure for evaluating CCR objects. To attain a high transparency rank, members are encouraged to disclose their reputation-related information whenever it is clear that disclosing their information is preferable and more valuable to them than the potential impairment of their privacy. The issue of Privacy within the CCR model is discussed in [8].

4   Transitivity and Computing Domains Reputation

As was discussed earlier, computing domain reputation and identifying suspicious domains is a very important problem in Internet security today. Our approach to the problem [15] uses a graph of domains and IPs which is constructed from mapping information available in DNS log records. The Domain Name Service (DNS) maps domain names to IP addresses and provides an essential service to applications on the internet. Many botnets use a DNS service to locate their next Command and Control (C&C) site. Therefore, DNS logs have been used by several researchers to detect suspicious domains and filter their traffic if necessary. We take the famous expression *Tell me who your friends are and I will tell you who you are*, motivating many social trust models, into the internet domains world. Thus a domain that is related to malicious domains is more likely to be malicious as well. This Transitivity property motivates the use of a Flow algorithm. Although DNS data was used by several researchers before to compute domain reputation (see [1]), in [15] we present a new approach by applying a flow algorithm on the DNS graph to obtain the reputation of domains and identify potentially malicious ones. Computing reputation for domains raises several new difficulties:

- Rating information if exists, is sparse and usually binary, a domain is labeled either "white" or "black".
- Static sources like blacklists and whitelists are often not up-to-date.
- There is no explicit concept of trust between domains which makes it difficult to apply a flow or a transitive trust algorithm.
- Reputation of domains is dynamic and changes very fast.

These difficulties make the selection of an adequate computational model for computing domain reputation a challenging task. Our approach is based on a flow algorithm, commonly used for computing trust in social networks and virtual communities. We are mainly inspired by two models: the Eigentrust model [4] which computes trust and reputation by transitive iteration through chains of trusting users and the model by Guha et al. [10] which combines the flow of trust and distrust. The motivation for using a flow algorithm is the assumption that IPs and domains which are neighbors of malware generating IPs and domains, are more likely to become malware generating as well. We construct a graph which reflects the topology of domains and IPs and their mappings and relationships and use a flow model to propagate the knowledge received in the form of black list, to label domains in the graph as malicious or suspected domains. Although we do not claim that every domain (or IP) connected to a malicious domain in our graph is malicious, our research hypothesis is that such domains(IPs) have a higher probability to become malicious. Our preliminary experimental results support this hypothesis.

The main input to the flow algorithm is the Domains/IPs graph. This graph is built from the following sources: (1) A-records: a database of successful mappings between IPs and domains, collected from a large ISP over several months. These mapping basically construct the edges between Domains and IPs. (2) Whois: a query and response protocol that is widely used for querying databases that store the registered users or assigners of an Internet resource. This database groups IPs which have similar characteristics and is therefore the base for IP to IP edges. In addition there are Domain to Domain edges which are related to similarity between domain names. (3) Feed-framework: a list of malicious domains which is collected over the same period of time as the collected A-records. This list is used as the initial "malicious" domains set. (4) Alexa: Alexa database ranks websites based on a combined measure of page views and unique site users. The initial "benign" domains is derived from this list. (5) VirustTotal: a website that provides free checking of domains for viruses and other malware. We use it to test our results as will be described below. The most difficult part in constructing the Domain/IP graph is assigning the weight on the edges, since the weight is proportional to the amount of flow on the edge. We tested several methods to assign weights which consider topologies of the graph and other factors, see [15]. Once the DNS graph is built and the sets of "benign" and "malicious" domains are extracted, the algorithm can be performed. The entire process is depicted in Fig. 2.

The flow algorithm models the idea that every IP and domain distribute their reputation to IPs or domains connected to them. This is done iteratively and the reputation in each iteration is added to the total reputation of a domain or IP, with some attenuation factor. The attenuation factor is a means to reduce the amount of reputation one vertex can gain from a vertex that is not directly connected to it by transitivity. The flow algorithm is executed separately to propagate good reputation and bad reputation and then the two reputation values are combined in several manners resulting with several variations of the algorithm (see details in [15].)

The important contribution of these algorithms is their ability to correctly predict future malicious domains. Although not all maliciouse domains are identified, a significant amount is discovered. In one of the experiments we used DNS logs over a 3 months period from which a large Domain-IP graph was

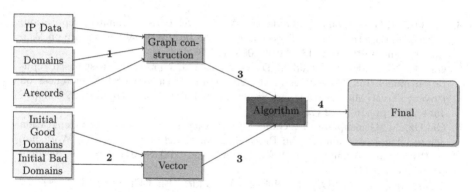

Fig. 2. The process for computing the score: (1) Create the graph and assign weights represented as matrix; (2) Create the initial vector used for propagation; (3) Combine the matrix and the vector to execute the flow algorithm; (4) Get the final scores.

constructed with nearly one million nodes, and the flow algorithm was applied to it. The results were that out of the top 1000 highly suspected domains, 30 % were found to be known malicious (using VirusTotal), while in a random set of 1000 domains only 0.9 % were known as malicious.

5 Conclusions

Reputation is a key concept in making decisions in our social life. In this paper we have discussed three key aspects of reputation: Identity, Aggregation and Transitivity which are important when migrating the concept of reputation from one domain to another. This was shown by briefly reviewing several research papers of ours. The main conclusion is that reputation plays a major role in a wide range of domains beside the social arena domain.

References

1. Antonakakis, M., Perdisc, R., Dagon, D., Lee, W., Feamster, N.: Building a dynamic reputation model for DNS. In: USENIX Security Symposium, pp. 273–290 (2010)
2. Chakraborty, S., Ray, I.: TrustBAC: integrating trust relationships into the RBAC model for access control in open systems. In: Proceedings of the 11th ACM symposium on Access Control Models and Technologies (SACMAT 2006), pp. 49–58. ACM, New York (2006)
3. Dellarocas, C.: Analyzing the economic efficiency of ebay-like online reputation reporting mechanisms. In: ACM Conference on Electronic Commerce, pp. 171–179 (2001)
4. Kamvar, S.D., Schlosser, M.T., Garcia-Molina, H.: The eigentrust algorithm for reputation management in P2P networks. In: WWW, pp. 640–651 (2003)
5. Gal-Oz, N., Grinshpoun, T., Gudes, E.: Sharing reputation across virtual communities. J. Theor. Appl. Electr. Commer. Res. **5**(2), 1–25 (2010)

6. Gal-Oz, N., Grinshpoun, T., Gudes, E., Meisels, A.: Cross-community reputation: policies and alternatives. In: Proceedings of the International Conference on Web Based Communities (IADIS - WBC2008) (2008)
7. Gal-Oz, N., Gudes, E., Hendler, D.: A robust and knot-aware trust-based reputation model. In: Proceedings of the 2nd Joint iTrust and PST Conferences on Privacy, Trust Management and Security (IFIPTM 2008), Trondheim, Norway, June 2008, pp. 167–182 (2008)
8. Gal-Oz, N., Grinshpoun, T., Gudes, E.: Privacy issues with sharing reputation across virtual communities. In: Proceedings of the 2011 International Workshop on Privacy and Anonymity in Information Society, PAIS 2011, Uppsala, Sweden, p. 3. March 2011
9. Grinshpoun, T., Gal-Oz, N., Meisels, A., Gudes, E.: CCR: a model for sharing reputation knowledge across virtual communities. In: Proceedings of the IEEE/WIC/ACM International Conference on Web Intelligence and Intelligent Agent Technology (WI 2009), pp. 34–41. IEEE (2009)
10. Guha, R., Kumar, R., Raghavan, P., Tomkins, A.: Propagation of trust and distrus. In: WWW, pp. 403–412 (2004)
11. Jøsang, A., Ismail, R.: The beta reputation system. In: Proceedings of the 15th Bled Electronic Commerce Conference, vol. 160, pp. 17–19 (2002)
12. Jøsang, A., Ismail, R., Boyd, C.: A survey of trust and reputation systems for online service provision. Decis. Support Syst. **43**(2), 618–644 (2007)
13. Kamvar, S., Schlosser, M., Garcia-Molina, H.: The eigentrust algorithm for reputation management in P2P networks. In: Proceedings of the 12th International Conference on World Wide Web (WWW 2003), pp. 640–651. ACM (2003)
14. Lavi, T., Gudes, E.: A dynamic reputation based RBAC model. Report, The Open University Raanana Israel (2015)
15. Mishsky, I., Gal-Oz, N., Gudes, E.: A flow based domain reputation model. Report, Ben-Gurion University, Beer-Sheva, Israel (2015)
16. Parreira, J.X., Donato, D., Michel, S., Weikum, G.: Efficient and decentralized pagerank approximation in a peer-to-peer web search network. In: Proceedings of the 32nd International Conference on Very Large Data Bases, pp. 415–426 (2006)

Full Papers

Mathematical Modelling of Trust Issues in Federated Identity Management

Md. Sadek Ferdous[1](✉), Gethin Norman[1], Audun Jøsang[2], and Ron Poet[1]

[1] School of Computing Science, University of Glasgow,
Glasgow G12 8QQ, Scotland
{sadek.ferdous,gethin.norman,ron.poet}@glasgow.ac.uk
[2] Department of Informatics, University of Oslo, 0316 Oslo, Norway
josang@mn.uio.no

Abstract. With the absence of physical evidence, the concept of trust plays a crucial role in the proliferation and popularisation of online services. In fact, trust is the inherent quality that binds together all involved entities and provides the underlying confidence that allows them to interact in an online setting. The concept of Federated Identity Management (FIM) has been introduced with the aim of allowing users to access online services in a secure and privacy-friendly way and has gained considerable popularities in recent years. Being a technology targeted for online services, FIM is also bound by a set of trust requirements. Even though there have been numerous studies on the mathematical representation, modelling and analysis of trust issues in online services, a comprehensive study focusing on the mathematical modelling and analysis of trust issues in FIM is still absent. In this paper we aim to address this issue by presenting a mathematical framework to model trust issues in FIM. We show how our framework can help to represent complex trust issues in a convenient way and how it can be used to analyse and calculate trust among different entities qualitatively as well as quantitatively.

Keywords: Trust · Federated Identity Management · Mathematical modelling

1 Introduction

Unlike the brick and mortar world, the physical evidence and visual cues that can be used to establish trust and gain confidence are largely absent in online services. Despite this, the popularity of online services has grown exponentially in the last decade or so. The concept of trust played a crucial role in popularising online services. In fact, trust is the inherent quality that binds together all involved entities and provides the underlying confidence that allows them to interact in an online service. The mathematical modelling and analysis of different trust requirements in online services are abound and is a well established research area. Such a model helps to express and to reason with trust issues in a

© IFIP International Federation for Information Processing 2015
C.D. Jensen et al. (Eds.): IFIPTM 2015, IFIP AICT 454, pp. 13–29, 2015.
DOI: 10.1007/978-3-319-18491-3_2

formal way which can ultimately help to create novel ways for determining trust among involved entities.

The concept of Federated Identity Management (FIM) has been introduced to ease the burden of managing different online identities and to allow users to access online services in a secure and privacy-friendly way [1]. FIM offers an array of advantages to different stakeholders and has gained considerable popularities in recent years. Being a technology targeted for the online setting, FIM is also bound by a set of trust requirements. Surprisingly, the mathematical representation, modelling and analysis of different trust requirements of FIM have received little attention so far. The aim of this paper is to fill this gap.

Here, we present a comprehensive mathematical framework considering different trust aspects targeted for FIM. In doing so, we show how our framework can formally express trust in FIM and how such expressions can be used to analyse and evaluate trust qualitatively and quantitatively. The main contributions of the paper are:

1. Inspired by the notation of trust presented in [14], we present a notation to express trust between different entities in FIM.
2. We use this notation to develop the first mathematical framework to model, analyse and derive trust in different types of identity federations.
3. We explore trust transformations resulting from interactions in FIM.
4. Finally, we present a simple method to evaluate trust quantitatively in FIM.

The paper is structured as follows. Section 2 provides a brief introduction to FIM and the required trust issues in this setting. Section 3 introduces the notation and the interaction model that will be used in our framework. The trust issues in different types of identity federations are modelled in Sects. 4 and 5. We show how trust transformations occur within different federations using our framework in Sect. 6 and how trust can be calculated quantitatively in Sect. 7. Section 8 discusses the related work and finally Sect. 9 concludes the paper.

2   Background

In this section, we provide a brief introduction to FIM, to different aspects of trust in general and to trust issues in FIM specifically.

Federated Identity Management. Identity Management consists of technologies and policies for representing and recognising entities using digital identifiers within a specific context [7]. A system that is used for managing the identity of users is called an Identity Management System (IMS). Each IMS includes the following types of parties: **Service Providers (SPs)** or **Relying Parties (RPs)** - entities that provides services to users or other SPs, **Identity Providers (IdPs)** - entities that provides identities to users to enable them to receive services from SPs and **Clients/Users** - entities that receive services from SPs. Among different IMS, the Federated Identity Management (FIM) has gained much attention and popularity.

The Federated Identity Management is based on the concept of Identity Federation. A federation with respect to Identity Management is a business model in which a group of two or more trusted parties legally bind themselves with a business and technical contract [1,17]. It allows a user to access restricted resources seamlessly and securely from other partners residing in different Identity Domains. An identity domain is the virtual boundary, context or environment in which an identity of a user is valid [17]. Single Sign On (SSO) is the capability that allows users to login to one system and then access other related but autonomous systems without further logins. It alleviates the need to login every time a user needs to access those related systems. A good example is the Google Single Sign On service which allows users to login a Google service, e.g., Gmail, and then allows them to access other Google services such as Calendar, Documents, YouTube, Blogs and so on.

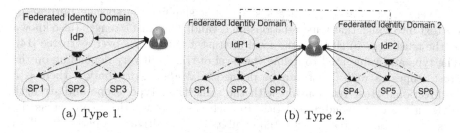

(a) Type 1.   (b) Type 2.

Fig. 1. Federated identity domain.

A federated identity domain can be formed by one IdP in an identity domain and a number of SPs with each SP residing in a separate identity domain (Type 1 in Fig. 1(a)). Several federated identity domains can be combined to form a larger federated identity domain where each smaller federated domain is of Type 1 (Type 2 in Fig. 1(b)). A Type 2 federation allows an IdP of a Type 1 federation to delegate the authentication task to another IdP in a different Type 1 federation. To enable this, both IdPs need to act as both IdPs and SPs. The issue of trust is a fundamental concept in FIM as different autonomous bodies need to trust each other inside the federation. Such parties inside a federation are said to form the so-called Circle of Trust (CoT).

A federation can be of two types depending on how it is created. The traditional federation, also called a *Static Federation*, is where the federation is created at the admin level and is bound with a legal contract using a specified set of administrative procedures. On the other hand, in a *Dynamic Federation* any user, not only administrators, can create the federation in a dynamic fashion without administrative intervention or a legally binding contract [3].

Trust. The concept of trust and trust management in the setting of online services is a widely studied topic and has been defined in numerous ways. For the purpose of this paper, we use the following definition taken from [11] which was originally inspired by [13].

"Trust is the extent to which one party is willing to depend on something or somebody in a given situation with a feeling of relative security, even though negative consequences are possible."

The definition gives a directional relationship between two entities: the first is regarded as the *Trustor* and the second the *Trustee*. The trustor and trustee can be any entity, however, in the scope of this paper, only those involved in FIM will be considered (i.e. users, IdPs and SPs). The pairwise trust relations we consider are user-IdP, user-SP, IdP-SP and IdP-IdP which is inline with current IMS setting and the relationships that occur inside a federation.

Trust can be of two types: Direct Trust (DT) and Indirect Trust (IT) [12]. Direct trust signifies that there exists a trust relationship between the entities based on first hand experience and evidence. On the other hand, indirect trust, also known as Transitive Trust, is a trust relationship between two entities based on referral from one or more intermediate third parties.

Every trust relationship has a scope that signifies the specific purpose or context into which that trust relationship is valid. The trust strength (also known as the trust degree) signifies the level of trust a trustor has over a trustee [14]. The type and value used to define the level of trust will vary depending on the trust scopes as well. Trust can be defined as *Mutual Trust* only if there is a bi-directional trust relationship with the same trust type, scope and strength between the corresponding entities. In such case, both entities can act as the trustor and the trustee. Trust often exhibits the transitivity property [11]: if an entity A trusts another entity B and B trust another entity C, a trust relation can be derived between A and C. To derive such a transitive trust relation, the trust scope must be same. The trust transformation is the process when a trust relationship between two entities changes due to the change of trust strength while the trust type remains the same. Such a transformation occurs normally for two reasons: (i) when the trust is derived following the transitivity property and (ii) when one entity interacts with another entity to perform a certain action which ultimately triggers the change in the trust strength. The transformation can be positive, meaning the new trust strength is higher than what was before, or can be negative, meaning the new trust strength is lower than what was before.

A trust with a single scope can be defined as atomic trust. Compound trust can be defined as the combined trust of several different atomic trusts where the trustor, trustee and the trust direction and strength between them remain the same. The compound trust will also have the same trust direction and strength.

Trust Issues in Identity Management. The issue of trust is a fundamental concept in FIM as different participating organisations need to trust each other inside the federation at a sufficient level to allow them to exchange and trust user information. We will consider such trust issues using two separate instances.

The first, called *High Level* trust, is the abstract level of trust that is assumed between federated entities (IdPs and SPs) in a federation. This level of trust is common in the existing literature on FIM. For example, it is common to express that two entities trust each other if they belong to the same CoT. In such an expression, the trust is treated at an abstract level and is used mostly to signify their architectural relation inside a federation.

The second, called *Fine-grained* trust, is a detailed expression of trust including the scope between entities (including users) in a federation. The expression may (optionally) include a trust type or strength. Inspired by the requirements outlined in [8,12], the authors in [2] have outlined a set of fine-grained trust requirements in the traditional federation which are applicable for both Type 1 and Type 2 federations. We will use their requirements to represent fine-grained trusts in Sect. 4.

Trust in a dynamic federation is modelled using three classes of entities [3]: **Fully Trusted** entities are IdPs and SPs in the traditional SAML (Security Assertion Markup Language) federation which have a legal contract between them [18]; **Semi-trusted** entities are SPs in a dynamic federation that have been added dynamically to an IdP inside the federation under **some conditions** without a contract and to whom any user of the IdP has agreed to release a subset of her attributes and **Untrusted** entities are IdPs and SPs in a dynamic federation which have been added dynamically under **some conditions** without a contract. A detailed discussion of these classes can be found in [3].

3   Notation

In this section we will introduce the notation that will be used to build up the model. We use E to denote the set of entities, with U the set of users, SP the set of service providers and IDP the set of identity providers. Since each user, SP and IdP is also an entity, we have $E = U \cup IDP \cup SP$. In addition, $\mathcal{F}$ denotes the set of federations and will use subscript from $\mathcal{F}$ to define the contexts of entities (i.e. the federation in which they belong). For example, E_f will be used to denote the sets of entities in a federation f. We use T to denote the set of trust types. As explained above, we consider two types of trust: direct trust (denoted by DT) and indirect trust (denoted by IT). Therefore, $T = \{DT, IT\}$.

We use S for the set of trust scopes. Different trust scopes can be defined depending on the trust requirements. We consider the following trust scopes for FIM based on the fine-grained trust requirements of [2]:

- *REG* is trust in the implementation of the registration process;
- *STO* is trust in secure attribute storage;
- *AUTHN* is trust in the implementation of the authentication mechanism;
- *AP* is trust in allowing the use of anonymous or pseudonymous identifiers;
- *CONSENT* is trust in the release of only those attributes consented to;
- *ABU* is the trust that an entity will not abuse attributes released to it;
- *CARE* is the trust an entity handles her attributes with adequate care;
- *HON* is the trust that an entity provides attribute values honestly;
- *ACDA* is the trust that an entity adheres to the agreed policies and procedures during access control and delegated access;
- *SRV* is the trust in service provisioning;
- *MIN-ATT* is the trust that an entity requests only minimal attributes;

- *REL* is the trust in an entity correctly releasing attributes;
- *ND* is the trust in an entity adhering to the non-disclosure of attributes;
- *FED* is trust between federated entities.

We consider the following types of trust strengths in FIM.

Subjective Trust. This defines the subjective trust a user may have in IdPs and SPs in a federation and will be denoted with *conf*. It can have different levels, however, we have opted for three levels: *LOW (L), MED (M), HIGH (H)*.

Level of Assurance (LoA). This defines the trust strength between federated IdPs and SPs and is used during service provisioning. It is based on the NIST LoA guidance of 1 to 4 where Level 1 can be used to model the lowest trust and Level 4 the highest [15]. It will be denoted as *loa* with values from 1 to 4.

Federation Trust. The last type concerns the trust strength between federated IdPs and SPs with respect to their architectural relations. It is denoted with *fed-trust* and can take four different values: *UNTRUSTED (UT), SEMI-TRUSTED (ST), RESTRICTED-TRUSTED (RT)* and *FULLY-TRUSTED (FT)*. The lowest trust strength *UT* means a trustor does not trust a trustee at all and is associated between entities federated in a dynamic fashion or between entities in a transitive trust in static federations (see below). The strength *ST* means a trustor trusts a trustee upto a certain level. An example is the trust strength between a dynamically federated IdP and an SP and the fact that the IdP may not want release sensitive attributes to the SP as there are no formal agreement between them. The strength *RT* is higher than *ST*, but lower than *FT*. Such a strength is exhibited when the trust relationship between a trustor and trustee is derived using transitivity and the trustor may not fully trust the trustee as there are no formal agreements between them. The strength *FT* signifies the highest strength and is exhibited when the trustor and trustee are part of a traditional federation. The federation trust strengths are ranked:

$$UT < ST < RT < FT .$$

To indicate an entity $e_1 \in E_f$ (the trustor) has $t \in T$ trust over an entity $e_2 \in E_f$ (the trustee) in a federation $f \in \mathcal{F}$ with a trust scope of $s \in S$ and the trust strength of v, we will use the following notation, inspired by [14]:

$$e_1 \xrightarrow{\; t \; : \; s \;}{v} e_2$$

where v represents the trust strength (either *conf*, *loa* or *fed-trust*). To express the same trust t between two entities e_1 and e_2 with same trust strength v in a number of different scopes, $s_1, \ldots, s_n$, we extend the notation to:

$$e_1 \xrightarrow{\; t \; : \; \{s_1, \ldots, s_n\} \;}{v} e_2$$

If there exists a mutual trust (t) between two entities in the same trust scope (s) with the same trust strength (v), we use the notation:

$$e_1 \xleftrightarrow{\; t \; : \; s \;}{v} e_2$$

3.1   Interaction Model

To enable a protocol flow in a federation, each entity interacts with another entity in order to perform an action at another entity. A user interacting with an IdP to authenticate herself by providing an identifier (e.g. username) and a credential (e.g. password) is example of an interaction. Interaction between entities to perform an action can cause the trust between the involved entities to transform. The interaction model consists of the actions that an entity can perform at another entity in a federation. Such interactions must be carried out using a communication channel. We will use the notation $CHANNEL$ to define the set of channels. Two types of channels will be considered: secure channels, denoted SC, model secure HTTPS connections whereas unsecured channels, denoted UC, model unsecured HTTP connections.

To denote an interaction that represents an entity e_1 performs action a at entity e_2 using communication channel c, we will use the following notation: $c(e_1 \overset{a}{\rightsquigarrow} e_2)$. There could be many interactions in a federation, however, to the scope of this paper, we restrict attention to the following interactions:

- $c(u \overset{RG}{\rightsquigarrow} idp)$ representing user u registering at IdP idp through channel c;
- $c(u \overset{A}{\rightsquigarrow} idp)$ representing user u authenticating herself at IdP idp through channel c;
- $c(idp \overset{AP}{\rightsquigarrow} u)$ representing IdP idp allowing user u to use anonymous or pseudonymous identifiers through channel c;
- $c(idp \overset{C}{\rightsquigarrow} u)$ representing IdP idp providing user u with the opportunity to provide consent for releasing selected attributes through channel c;
- $c(idp \overset{RL}{\rightsquigarrow} sp)$ representing IdP idp releasing user u's selected attributes to the SP sp through channel c.

4   Trust Modelling in Traditional (Static) Federations

In this section, we model trust between different entities in traditional federations. We will consider first high level trust and then fine-grained trust.

4.1   High Level Trust Modelling

We can express the high level trust in a Type 1 federation $f \in \mathcal{F}$ between an IdP $idp \in IDP_f$ and an SP $sp \in SP_f$ by:

$$idp \xleftarrow{\quad \frac{DT:FED}{FT} \quad} sp$$

This signifies that idp and sp have a mutual direct trust in the scope of the federation. Since it is a Type 1 federation, the entities trust each other fully, hence the trust strength is fully trusted (FT).

Let us now consider a Type 2 Federation consisting of two Type 1 federations, say $f_1, f_2 \in \mathcal{F}$. Since f_1 and f_2 are Type 1 federations, we have for $i \in \{1, 2\}$, $idp_i \in IDP_{f_i}$ and $sp_i \in SP_{f_i}$:

$$idp_i \xleftarrow[\;\;FT\;\;]{DT:FED} sp_i$$

Trust between an IdP $idp_1 \in f_1$ and an IdP $idp_2 \in f_2$ deserves further attention. Since they are in a Type 2 federation, these IdPs will act as both IdPs and SPs depending on the use-cases. Without specifying which entity acts as what, we can model the underlying trust relations between these IdPs as follows:

$$idp_1 \xleftarrow[\;\;FT\;\;]{DT:FED} idp_2$$

Next we model the trust transitivity property of [11] by introducing the following rules to derive a transitive trust between entities in a Type 2 Federation.

Rule 1 (Trust Type in a Transitive Trust). *A derived transitive trust between entities in a traditional Type 2 Federation must be of indirect trust type.*

Rule 2 (Trust Strength in a Transitive Trust). *The strength of the derived trust is that immediately below the lowest value of the intermediate trusts except when no such value exists, in which case the strength will be the lowest value.*

The trust type between the entities changes in a transitive trust since they are not directly connected with each other. Changes in the trust strength between entities in a transitive trust is because there need not exist a formal agreement between the entities, and hence the rule ensures that the derived level of trust is the lowest among (or lower than) any intermediate trust levels in the transitive path. The rule also includes a limiting condition to ensure that the trust strength does not reduce to an undetermined value as it is reduced along a transitive path of trust.

Next, let us consider a Type 2 Federation consisting of two Type 1 federations $f_1, f_2 \in \mathcal{F}$. For $sp_1 \in SP_{f_1}$, $idp_1 \in IDP_{f_1}$ and $idp_2 \in IDP_{f_2}$ the transitive trust between sp_1 and idp_2 can be derived using Rule 1 and 2 as follows:

$$\frac{\left[sp_1 \xleftarrow[\;\;FT\;\;]{DT:FED} idp_1 \right] \quad \left[idp_1 \xleftarrow[\;\;FT\;\;]{DT\;:\;FED} idp_2 \right]}{\left[sp_1 \xleftarrow[\;\;RT\;\;]{IT\;:\;FED} idp_2 \right]}$$

We can use these rules to derive trust between any number of entities in a Type 2 federation. For example, consider three federations $f_1, f_2, f_3 \in \mathcal{F}$ with three different IdPs $idp_1 \in IDP_{f_1}$, $idp_2 \in IDP_{f_2}$ and $idp_3 \in IDP_{f_1}$. Furthermore, suppose there is a Type 2 federation between f_1 and f_2 and another between f_2 and f_3, and hence both idp_1 and idp_2, and idp_2 and idp_3 are directly connected.

For an SP sp_1 in federation f_1 we can derive the trust relations between sp_1 and idp_3 using Rule 1 and 2 and the following proof tree:

$$\frac{\left[sp_1 \xleftarrow{\frac{DT:FED}{FT}} idp_1\right] \quad \left[idp_1 \xleftarrow{\frac{DT:FED}{FT}} idp_2\right]}{\dfrac{\left[sp_1 \xleftarrow{\frac{IT:FED}{RT}} idp_2\right] \quad \left[idp_2 \xleftarrow{\frac{DT:FED}{FT}} idp_3\right]}{\left[sp_1 \xleftarrow{\frac{IT:FED}{ST}} idp_3\right]}}$$

4.2   Fine-Grained Trust Modelling

Now, we model fine-grained trust for a Type-1 Federation as outlined in [2]. In the following scenarios, each trust will include a strength *conf* or level of assurance *loa* in a Type 1 federation $f \in \mathcal{F}$ between a user $u \in U_f$, IdP $idp \in IDP_f$ or SP $sp \in SP_f$. The trust strength *conf* is assumed when one of the entities is a user and *loa* when the trust is between an IdP and SP.

User Trust in the IdP

T1. The user trusts that the IdP has correctly implemented user registration procedures and authentication mechanisms (denoted *T2* in [8]):

$$u \xrightarrow{\dfrac{DT \ : \ \{REG, AUTHN\}}{conf}} idp$$

Note the direction between the said entities. Since it is not a mutual trust, the direction of trust is from the user to the IdP. Also, as there are two trust scopes (registration and authentication).

T2. The user trusts that the IdP allows the user to utilise anonymous or pseudonymous identifiers (denoted *T1* in [8]):

$$u \xrightarrow{\dfrac{DT \ : \ AP}{conf}} idp$$

T3. The user trusts that the IdP will release only those attributes to the SP that the user has consented to:

$$u \xrightarrow{\dfrac{DT \ : \ CONSENT}{conf}} idp$$

T2 and **T3** can be combined to denote the user trusting the IdP to protect the privacy of the user through the following rule for compound trust of privacy.

Rule 3 (Compound Trust of Privacy). *A compound trust of Privacy (PRIV) is a user's trust in the IdP to preserve its privacy to an SP using anonymous or pseudonymous identifiers (**T2**) and trust in allowing the user to* *choose and provide consent regarding the attributes that it wants to release to the SP (**T3**). Formally we have:*

$$\frac{\left[u \xrightarrow[\text{conf}]{DT \; : \; AP} idp\right] \quad \left[u \xrightarrow[\text{conf}]{DT \; : \; CONSENT} idp\right]}{\left[u \xrightarrow[\text{conf}]{DT \; : \; PRIV} idp\right]}$$

As mentioned earlier, the trust direction and strength must be same in **T2** and **T3** and the compound trust will inherit these values.

T4. The user trusts that the IdP has satisfactory mechanisms to store user attributes safely and securely:

$$u \xrightarrow[\text{conf}]{DT \; : \; STO} idp$$

User Trust in the SP

T5. The user trusts that the SP will ask only for the minimum number of user attributes that are required to access any of its services:

$$u \xrightarrow[\text{conf}]{DT \; : \; MIN\text{-}ATT} sp$$

T6. The user trusts that the SP will not abuse the released user attributes and will use them only for the stated purpose(s):

$$u \xrightarrow[\text{conf}]{DT \; : \; ABU} sp$$

IdP and SP Trust in the User

T7. The IdP trusts that the user handles their authentication credentials with adequate care (denoted as *T3* in [8]):

$$idp \xrightarrow[\text{conf}]{DT \; : \; CARE} u$$

T8. The SP trusts that the user is honest while providing attributes to an IdP:

$$sp \xrightarrow[\text{conf}]{DT \; : \; HON} u$$

IdP Trust in the SP

T9. The IdP trusts that the SP adheres to the agreed privacy policies regarding non-disclosure of user data (denoted as *IdP-T.1* in [12]):

$$idp \xrightarrow[\text{conf}]{DT \; : \; \{ND,ABU\}} sp$$

In other words, the SP will not abuse the released user attributes and will use them only for the stated purpose(s). The policy might include that the SP will not cache any user-attributes other than those which are absolutely necessary. This is to ensure that the IdP can always provide the updated attributes regarding the user. In cases where the SP needs to cache any attributes (e.g. IdP-supplied identifiers), the SP must inform the IdP.

T10. The IdP trusts that the SP adheres to the agreed policies and procedures, if they are available regarding access control and delegated access:

$$idp \xrightarrow[conf]{DT \ : \ ACDA} sp$$

If there are no such policies or procedures, this requirement is ignored.

Like Rule 3, we can combine **T9** and **T10** to define a compound trust through the following rule.

Rule 4 (Compound Trust of Policy). *A compound trust of Policy, denoted as POL, is an IdP trust in a SP adhering to the non-disclosure of attributes and not abusing the released attributes (**T9**) and maintaining the agreed policies and procedures regarding access control and delegated access (**T10**). Formally:*

$$\frac{\left[idp \xrightarrow[conf]{DT \ : \ \{ND,ABU\}} sp\right] \quad \left[idp \xrightarrow[conf]{DT \ : \ ACDA} sp\right]}{\left[idp \xrightarrow[conf]{DT \ : \ POL} sp\right]}$$

As before, the trust direction and strength must be same in **T9** and **T10** and the compound trust also will have that same trust direction and trust strength.

SP Trust in the IdP.

T11. The SP trusts that the IdP has implemented adequate procedures for registering users and for issuing credentials (denoted as $T7$ in [8]):

$$sp \xrightarrow[loa]{DT \ : \ REG} idp$$

This captures the realistic scenarios where a LoA value, determined and released by the IdP, is used by the SP to evaluate the level of trust it can have on the IdP in a specific trust scope. A lower LoA value may influence the SP to place a lower trust and similarly a higher LoA value may influence the SP to have a higher trust on the IdP for a particular scope.

T12. The SP trusts that the IdP will authenticate the user appropriately as per the requirement and will release user attributes securely:

$$sp \xrightarrow[loa]{DT \ : \ AUTHN} idp$$

We combine **T11** and **T12** to define a compound trust using the following rule.

Rule 5 (Compound Trust of Registration-Authentication). *A compound trust of Registration-Authentication, denoted as RAUTH, outlines the SP trust that the IdP registers users securely (**T11**) and authenticates users and releases attributes as per the requirement (**T12**). Formally, we have:*

$$\frac{\left[sp \xrightarrow[loa]{DT \ : \ REG} idp\right] \quad \left[sp \xrightarrow[loa]{DT \ : \ AUTHN} idp\right]}{\left[sp \xrightarrow[loa]{DT \ : \ RAUTH} idp\right]}$$

5   Trust Modelling in Dynamic Federations

In this section, we model trust between different entities in traditional federations. We only consider high level trust as the fine-grained trust for this federation is similar to traditional federations.

Type 1 Federation. Here, we have two different types of trust. To an SP, each dynamically added IdP will be treated as *untrusted*. Formally, in a Type 1 federation $f \in \mathcal{F}$ for $sp \in SP_f$ and dynamically added $idp \in IDP_f$:

$$sp \xrightarrow[UT]{DT \ : \ FED} idp$$

However, to the IdP, the SP can be *untrusted* or *semi-trusted* depending to conditions discussed previously:

$$idp \xrightarrow[\{UT,ST\}]{DT \ : \ FED} sp$$

Type 2 Federation. This is similar to the traditional Type 2 federation as discussed previously, except there is no mutual trust between dynamically added entities and static entities, hence we consider each trust direction separately.

Using Rule 1 and 2 we can derive a transitive trust between any two entities in a dynamic federation as follows. For $f_1, f_2 \in \mathcal{F}$, $sp_1 \in SP_{f_1}$, $sp_2 \in IDP_{f_2}$, $idp_1 \in IDP_{f_1}$, $idp_2 \in IDP_{f_2}$ and where idp_2 has been added dynamically into federation f_1 and sp_2 has been added dynamically into federation f_2:

$$\frac{\left[sp_1 \xleftarrow[FT]{DT \ : \ FED} idp_1\right] \quad \left[idp_1 \xrightarrow[UT]{DT \ : \ FED} idp_2\right]}{\left[sp_1 \xrightarrow[UT]{IT \ : \ FED} idp_2\right]}$$

Since, idp_1 acts as the SP to idp_2 and a dynamically added IdP is always treated as an *untrusted* entity to a SP, the trust from idp_1 to the idp_2 is regarded as untrusted. A few more derivation are given below:

$$\dfrac{\left[idp_2 \xrightarrow[UT]{DT\ :\ FED} idp_1\right] \quad \left[idp_1 \xleftarrow[FT]{DT\ :\ FED} sp_1\right]}{\left[idp_2 \xrightarrow[UT]{IT\ :\ FED} sp_1\right]}$$

This derives the transitive trust between idp_2 and sp_1.

$$\dfrac{\left[sp_2 \xrightarrow[UT]{DT\ :\ FED} idp_2\right] \quad \left[idp_2 \xrightarrow[UT]{DT\ :\ FED} idp_1\right]}{\left[sp_2 \xrightarrow[UT]{IT\ :\ FED} idp_1\right]}$$

This derives the transitive trust between sp_2 and idp_1 and below we derive the transitive trust between idp_1 and sp_2.

$$\dfrac{\left[idp_1 \xrightarrow[UT]{DT\ :\ FED} idp_2\right] \quad \left[idp_2 \xrightarrow[\{UT,ST\}]{DT\ :\ FED} sp_2\right]}{\left[idp_1 \xrightarrow[UT]{IT\ :\ FED} sp_2\right]}$$

6 Trust Transformation with Interactions

We have seen how trust is transformed due to transitivity. Next, we explore how it is transformed due to interactions. We use the following notation to denote a change of trust from T_1 to T_2 for an interaction A: $T_1 \stackrel{A}{\Rightarrow} T_2$. Sometimes, we logically join (using the "$\wedge$" operator) more than one interaction to signify the fact that more than one interaction is required to trigger a trust transformation.

Trust Transformation in Static Federations. Our first example explores how the trust can be transformed between a user (the trustor) and an IdP (the trustee). At the initial stage, the confidence (trust strength) of the user could be low. Once the user is registered and authenticated using a secure communication channel (e.g. HTTPS), the trust strength could increase to medium since it reflects that the IdP is careful to maintain the confidentiality and integrity of her data. For a federation $f \in \mathcal{F}$, $u \in U_f$ and $idp \in IDP_f$, this is modelled by:

$$\left[u \xrightarrow[L]{DT:\ RAuth} idp\right] \xRightarrow{\{SC(u \stackrel{RG}{\rightsquigarrow} idp)\} \wedge \{SC(u \stackrel{A}{\rightsquigarrow} idp)\}} \left[u \xrightarrow[M]{DT\ :\ RAuth} idp\right]$$

The user may have another boost in trust when she has a positive interaction with the IdP for a period. One example is the use of a consent form that allows the user to select the attributes that she wants to release to an SP, and thus allows her the option to provide consent to release data to the SP. Formally:

$$\left[u \xrightarrow[M]{DT:\ SRV} idp\right] \xRightarrow{\{SC(idp \stackrel{c}{\rightsquigarrow} u)\}} \left[u \xrightarrow[H]{DT\ :\ SRV} idp\right]$$

Our second example involves transforming privacy trust with interactions. The involved interactions are the IdP allowing the user to use anonymous or pseudonymous identifiers and offering the opportunity to provide consent regarding attributes. The trust strength will initially be low and will transform to either medium or high depending on different factors. Example factors are a user-friendly interface that makes it easier for the user to choose anonymous or pseudonymous identifiers or allows the user to choose attributes and provide consent. The trust transformation is modelled by:

$$\left[u \xrightarrow{\quad DT \ : \ PRIV \quad}_{L} idp \right] \xrightarrow{\{SC(idp \overset{AP}{\leadsto} u)\} \wedge \{SC(idp \overset{C}{\leadsto} u)\}} \left[u \xrightarrow{\quad DT \ : \ PRIV \quad}_{\{M,H\}} idp \right]$$

Trust Transformation in Dynamic Federations. For federation $f \in \mathcal{F}$, $u \in U_f$, $idp \in IDP_f$ dynamically added by u and $sp \in SP_f$, the trust transformation occurs only if u has agreed to release her attributes from idp to sp:

$$\left[idp \xrightarrow{\quad DT \ : \ FED \quad}_{UT} sp \right] \xrightarrow{\{SC(u \overset{C}{\leadsto} idp)\} \wedge \{SC(idp \overset{RL}{\leadsto} sp)\}} \left[idp \xrightarrow{\quad DT \ : \ FED \quad}_{ST} sp \right]$$

7   Quantifying Trust

In real life, trust is an analogue property, and hence it is difficult to represent with discrete values. However, it might be useful to compute the trust between involved entities using discrete values when the entities belong to a computational system and require a discrete value to represent the trust in that system. Among three pieces of information used to represent trust (type, scope and strength), we only use type and strength to compute a trust value. This is because scope only represents a context, a qualitative attribute, in which trust holds, while both type and strength can be represented numerically. For example, direct trust represents a higher confidence as it is based on first-hand experience, unlike indirect trust. We introduce the following formula to quantify trust in a federation $f \in \mathcal{F}$ between entities $e_1, e_2 \in E_f$ for trust scope s where e_1 is the trustor and e_2 is the trustee:

$$QT_{e_1}^{e_2}(s) = t_{e_1}^{e_2}(s) \cdot v_{e_1}^{e_2}(s)$$

where $QT_{e_1}^{e_2}(s)$, $t_{e_1}^{e_2}(s)$ and $v_{e_1}^{e_2}(s)$ represent the quantified trust, trust type and strength of e_1 over e_2 in the scope s for federation f.

In the formula the trust strength quantifies how much trust one entity may have over another entity and the trust type signifies the confidence on that quantification. Trust type can be thought as the weight of the trust strength. Note that, this is one way of quantifying a trust and there are other possibilities.

We now consider a few examples. As stated above to quantify trust we need to give values to trust types and strengths. Regarding types, we assign 1 and 2 to indirect and direct trust respectively, and for strength, we assign 1, 2 and 3 to *conf* and 1, 2, 3 and 4 to *fed-trust*.

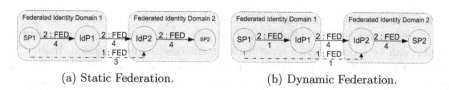

(a) Static Federation.   (b) Dynamic Federation.

Fig. 2. Quantifying trust example.

We can now quantify trust in the federations illustrated in Fig. 2. The left box of Fig. 2(a) illustrates a Type 1 static federation while Fig. 2(a) and (b) illustrate a Type 2 static and dynamic federations respectively. The direct trust between sp_1 and idp_1 for the Type 1 static federation is given by:

$$QT_{sp_1}^{idp_1}(FED) = 2 \cdot 4 = 8$$

since the entities have direct trust between them $(t_{sp_1}^{idp_1}(FED) = 2)$ and they fully trust each other $(v_{sp_1}^{idp_1}(FED) = 4)$.

For the static Type 2 federation in Fig. 2(a), the indirect trust between sp_1 and the idp_2 is given by:

$$QT_{sp_1}^{idp_2}(FED) = 1 \cdot 3 = 3$$

This is because the entities have indirect trust between them $(t_{sp_1}^{idp_2}(FED) = 1)$ and according to Rule 2, the trust strength between them $(v_{sp_1}^{idp_2}(FED) = 3)$.

Similarly, for the dynamic Type 2 federation in Fig. 2(b) and calculating the indirect trust between sp_1 (the trustor) and the idp_2 (the trustee), where the trust strength between the transitive entities are not same, we have:

$$QT_{sp_1}^{idp_2}(FED) = 1 \cdot 1 = 1$$

8 Related Work

A few major papers on the general topic of trust and trust management can be found in [5,9–11,16]. These works mainly concentrated on the discussion and analysis of trust and trust management and the discussion of trust regarding identity management was mainly absent.

A comprehensive taxonomy of trust requirements for the FIM can be found in [2]. Unfortunately, the requirements have been outlined in textual formats and none of requirements has been modelled and analysed mathematically. The authors in [14] have presented an integrated trust management model with respect to context-aware services. The model is based on different trust relationships which have been analysed using mathematical notations. The paper did not consider the underlying trust requirements that hold together the involved entities in that trust relationship. In this paper we have adopted their notation to illustrate the trust relationship. Huang et al. [6] have presented a trust calculus targeted for the PKI (Public Key Infrastructure) and have shown how the calculus can be used to derive trust between entities in a certification chain. The focus of their work is quite different than ours in the sense that they did not deal with any underlying trust requirements in the FIM. The authors in [4] have presented a formalisation of authentication trust for the FIM. The authors did not consider any other trust requirements, and hence their formal representation is not comprehensive in nature.

9 Conclusions

Trust in the traditional Type 1 Federation is a complex issue with the involvement of several different autonomous parties and their disparate security domains. The complexity increases with the introduction of a Type 2 Federation. The advent of the dynamic federation adds up another layer of complexity. Even though there exist numerous works on the mathematical modelling of trust in the online setting, there is a gap on the mathematical modelling and analysis of trust in the setting of FIM. In this paper we have introduced a mathematical framework to represent and analyse complex trust issues in FIM. We have used our model to represent trust in different settings. We have introduced a model of interactions for FIM and have shown how interactions and the trust transitivity can transform trust. Finally, we have proposed a simple formula to quantify trust. Our model can be used in a wide range of applications. It can be used to express and derive trust between any number of entities in any type of federations. A larger federation where there are many IdPs and SPs that exhibit a highly dynamic nature where changes are common. Trust transformation using interactions can be the ideal way to represent trust in such a dynamic environment. Finally, the way we have evaluated trust can be used to assess trust between any entities in a federation or to assess the quality of service provided by an IdP or an SP. Next, we plan to use our model to analyse other aspects of identity management such as attribute aggregation and mobile identity management.

References

1. Chadwick, D.W.: Federated identity management. In: Aldini, A., Barthe, G., Gorrieri, R. (eds.) FOSAD 2008/2009. LNCS, vol. 5705, pp. 96–120. Springer, Heidelberg (2009)
2. Sadek Ferdous, M., Poet, R.: Analysing attribute aggregation models in federated identity management. In: SIN 2013, pp. 181–188. ACM (2013)
3. Ferdous, M.S., Poet, R.: Dynamic identity federation using security assertion markup language (SAML). In: Fischer-Hübner, S., de Leeuw, E., Mitchell, C. (eds.) IDMAN 2013. IFIP AICT, vol. 396, pp. 131–146. Springer, Heidelberg (2013)
4. Gomi, H.: An authentication trust metric for federated identity management systems. In: Cuellar, J., Lopez, J., Barthe, G., Pretschner, A. (eds.) STM 2010. LNCS, vol. 6710, pp. 116–131. Springer, Heidelberg (2011)

5. Grandison, T., Sloman, M.: Trust management tools for internet applications. In: Nixon, P., Terzis, S. (eds.) iTrust 2003. LNCS, vol. 2692, pp. 91–107. Springer, Heidelberg (2003)
6. Huang, J., Nicol, D.: A calculus of trust and its application to PKI and identity management. In: IDtrust 2009, pp. 23–37. ACM (2009)
7. Jøsang, A., Al Zomai, M., Suriadi, S.: Usability and privacy in identity management architectures. In: ACSW 2007, pp. 143–152 (2007)
8. Jøsang, A., Fabre, J., Hay, B., Dalziel, J., Pope, S.: Trust requirements in identity management. In: ACSW Frontiers 2005, pp. 99–108. Australian Computer Society Inc. (2005)
9. Jøsang, A., Ismail, R., Boyd, C.: A survey of trust and reputation systems for online service provision. Decision Support Syst. **43**(2), 618–644 (2007)
10. Jøsang, A., Keser, C., Dimitrakos, T.: Can we manage trust? In: Herrmann, P., Issarny, V., Shiu, S.C.K. (eds.) iTrust 2005. LNCS, vol. 3477, pp. 93–107. Springer, Heidelberg (2005)
11. Jøsang, A., Gray, E., Kinateder, M.: Simplification and analysis of transitive trust networks. Web Intel. Agent Syst. **4**(2), 139–161 (2006)
12. Kylau, U., Thomas, I., Menzel, M., Meine, C.: Trust requirements in identity federation topologies. In: AINA 2009, pp. 137–145 (2009)
13. McKnight, D.H., Chervany, N.L.: The meanings of trust (1996)
14. Neisse, R., Wegdam, M., van Sinderen, M., Lenzini, G.: Trust management model and architecture for context-aware service platforms. In: Meersman, R. (ed.) OTM 2007, Part II. LNCS, vol. 4804, pp. 1803–1820. Springer, Heidelberg (2007)
15. NISTWP. Electronic Authentication Guideline: INFORMATION SECURITY, April 2006. http://csrc.nist.gov/publications/nistpubs/800-63/SP800-63V1_0_2.pdf
16. Ruohomaa, S., Kutvonen, L.: Trust management survey. In: Herrmann, P., Issarny, V., Shiu, S.C.K. (eds.) iTrust 2005. LNCS, vol. 3477, pp. 77–92. Springer, Heidelberg (2005)
17. Sadek Ferdous, M., Chowdhury, M., Jabed, M., Moniruzzaman, M., Chowdhury, F.: Identity federations: a new perspective for Bangladesh. In: ICIEV 2012, pp. 219–224. IEEE (2012)
18. OASIS Standard. Assertions and Protocols for the OASIS Security Assertion Markup Language (SAML) V2.0, 15 March 2005. http://docs.oasis-open.org/security/saml/v2.0/saml-core-2.0-os.pdf

Simple and Practical Integrity Models
for Binaries and Files

Yongzheng Wu[1] and Roland H.C. Yap[2]($\boxtimes$)

[1] Huawei, Singapore, Singapore
Wu.Yongzheng@huawei.com
[2] National University of Singapore, Singapore, Singapore
ryap@comp.nus.edu.sg

Abstract. Software environments typically depend on implicit sharing
of binaries where binaries are created, loaded/executed and updated
dynamically which we call the *binary lifecycle*. Windows is one example where many attacks exploit vulnerabilities in the binary lifecycle of
software. In this paper, we propose a family of binary integrity models
with a simple and easy to use trust model, to help protect against such
attacks. We implement a prototype in Windows which protects against
a variety of common binary attacks. Our models are easy to use while
maintaining existing software compatibility, i.e. work with the implicit
binary lifecycle requirements of the software and assumptions on binary
sharing. We also propose a conservative extension to protect critical non-
binary files.

1 Introduction

It is typical in software environments that the software consists of a collection of
software components in the form binaries such as executables, dynamically linked
libraries (DLLs), plugins, drivers, etc., e.g. this is the case in Windows. Binaries may be shared and used (executed/loaded) by many software, e.g. Windows
Office software components are shared by programs in the Office suite. Binaries
are usually created when a software is installed. Software updates modify/delete
existing binaries or create new ones. Software uninstall usually deletes binaries. We call the creation, usage, sharing, modification and deletion of binaries
associated with software, the *lifecycle of binaries*.

Binaries often have a complex and dynamic lifecycle with many kinds of interactions (arising from functionality, usability and software development reasons).
However, the binary lifecycle is also exploited in attacks, e.g. a Java malware
(EUR:Backdoor.Java.Agent.a [1]) exploits a vulnerability (CVE-2013-2465) to
copy itself to the user home directory and launch on system startup. This attack

This research is supported in part by the National Research Foundation, Prime
Minister's Office, Singapore under its National Cybersecurity R&D Program (Award
No. NRF2014NCR-NCR001-21) and administered by the National Cybersecurity
R&D Directorate.

C.D. Jensen et al. (Eds.): IFIPTM 2015, IFIP AICT 454, pp. 30–46, 2015.
DOI: 10.1007/978-3-319-18491-3_3

shows exploitation of the binary lifecycle in two ways: (a) it uses operating system mechanisms which can load or execute binaries; and (b) the malware uses binaries so that it becomes persistent.

Windows is a primary target for binary attacks. It has mostly implicit sharing of binaries and co-dependencies between binaries, e.g. Firefox uses other software plugins, Windows Explorer uses third party codecs, etc. Windows also has a large attack surface [12,14] with many mechanisms for running executables or loading binaries which is used both in the binary lifecycle but also exploited in attacks.

Many security models and mechanisms [10,11,13,15,16,21] have been proposed to protect against binary attacks. They may not be practical in a Windows context and mostly not designed for a dynamic and closed-source binary lifecycle. Furthermore, policy-based mechanisms may be less practical as it assumes users can create and maintain complex policies. This is not realistic in commodity operating systems like Windows. Thus, a good tradeoff between security and usability is needed.

Our goal is to increase security in the binary lifecycle. We propose and formalize a family of security models, *BInt*, which provides binary integrity and protection by incorporating an easy-to-use trust labelling mechanism. We also propose FInt which extends to protecting other critical files. We apply BInt by implementing a Windows prototype which protects against common binary attacks while giving good compatibility with existing software and deals with binary lifecycle issues. It is fairly easy to use without the need for complex administration or policy specification.

1.1   Related Work

The Biba model [11], is an early security policy to secure information flows. Data integrity is achieved by preventing information flow from low to higher levels (labels). However, Biba style models are not suitable for the binary lifecycle problem and it is unclear whether binaries are data or subjects.

Domain and Type Enforcement (DTE) [10] is representative of MAC access control approaches where a policy specifies what access is allowed by domains (states of processes) and types (resources). DTE and also other policy based approaches, e.g. Biba, have usability challenges – how to create and maintain policies dealing with the binary lifecycle given that the software and lifecycle details may be unknown and not under one's control, e.g. Windows.

Signed binaries only allow signed binaries to be loaded or executed [9,13] However, signing is primarily about establishing trust relationships. It only ensures that the signed binaries are from a party having the key. Requiring all software to be signed is best under a closed ecosystem, e.g. iOS, but less practical in an open ecosystem like Windows.

The Windows binary lifecycle also requires updates – creating new problems for trust management. The security of signing is based on trusting the signing keys, e.g. the Stuxnet worm has a driver signed by a Realtek key, thus, is implicitly trusted by Windows. Revocation checking is expensive as it cannot be done locally and may not be timely. Bit9 [3] a binary whitelisting system was attacked to compromise systems protected by Bit9 signatures [2].

Self-signed executables [21] is proposed for easier management of software updates for signed binaries. While it protects binary integrity for updates, it does not prevent new malware from being introduced. Deletions cause a problem – the file stubs increasing monotonically over time. It also modifies the normal POSIX file semantics which may break compatibility.

Isolation lets untrusted programs read the trusted system while confining the modifications [15,16]. Some processes can be executed in isolation domains while others are executed normally in the base system. This may not be practical in the binary lifecycle for software on Windows and the implicit "all" sharing.

While these works provide integrity or restrict binary usage, they are less suited for complex, dynamic and closed-source binary lifecycle environments.

2   BInt Integrity Models

When a program executes, typically, it runs a binary (the executable) which may load other binaries implicitly (dynamic loading of binaries) or explicitly load binaries during execution. We want to protect "unwanted" binaries from being executed or loaded, i.e. protect against the large binary attack surface of Windows [12,14,19]. In the binary lifecycle of software, binaries are loaded/created/ modified/deleted. Securing binaries requires preventing arbitrary modification/ deletion of binaries while allowing some software in the lifecycle to do so.

An important consideration is that many security mechanisms rely on explicit policy specification, e.g. Biba [11] or DTE [10] assume someone creates and maintains the policy. In practice, this assumption may not be workable – users cannot be expected to deal with complex policies. The software environment is often dynamic. Users expect to be able to install, update and uninstall (arbitrary) software (within limits). Software updates and auto-updates must be handled. With closed-source software, the workings of the dynamic lifecycle is not known making policies requiring such details problematic. In practice, an implicit requirement is also compatibility with existing software and its lifecycle.

We propose *BInt* (Binary INTegrity) which is a family of security models for binary usage and integrity to protect against attacks on the binary lifecycle which takes into account the above considerations.[1] The following examples illustrate the problems BInt models handle. In the Safari Carpetbomb attack [8]: the Safari browser automatically downloaded files onto the user desktop, while Internet Explorer by default allowed DLLs to be loaded by filename instead of a full path. A malicious website can then perform a "binary planting attack" [7] where Safari downloads a malicious DLL which Internet Explorer loads. However, running or loading binaries from the desktop is normal behavior in Windows, preventing this also breaks normal functionality. In the PDF embedded executable attack [5], a malicious PDF file contains an embedded executable, viewing the PDF runs

---

[1]   A short paper briefly describes a basic form of BInt [20].

Table 1. The BInt model (**R1-14**) and BInt+tr (**R8**$_{tr\lor}$, **11**$_{tr\lor}$, **8**$_{tr\land}$, **11**$_{tr\land}$) where $T(f)$ means f is signed by the trusted signature repositories.

Action	$L_m(p)$	Requires	Result	Rule
The BInt Model and Rules				
p create f	d-mode	true	$L_d(f) := \perp$	1
	t-mode	true	$L_d(f) := \perp$	2
	i-mode	true	$L_d(f) := L_d(p)$	3
p read f		true		4
p write or delete f	d-mode	$L_d(f) = \perp$		5
	t-mode	$L_d(f) = \perp$		6
	i-mode	$L_d(f) = \perp \lor$ $L_d(f) = L_d(p)$	$L_d(f) := L_d(p)$	7
p load f	d-mode	$L_d(f) \neq \perp$		8
	t-mode	true		9
	i-mode	true		10
p execute f	d-mode	$L_d(f) \neq \perp$	$L_m(p') :=$ d-mode	11
	t-mode	true	$L_m(p') :=$ t-mode	12
	i-mode	true	$L_m(p') :=$ i-mode; $L_d(p') := L_d(p)$	13
p modetrans		authentication	change $L_d(p)$ and $L_m(p)$	14
Rules for BInt+tr$\lor$ and BInt+tr$\land$				
p load f	d-mode	$L_d(f) \neq \perp \lor T(f)$		8$_{tr\lor}$
p execute f	d-mode	$L_d(f) \neq \perp \lor T(f)$	$L_m(p') :=$ d-mode	11$_{tr\lor}$
p load f	d-mode	$L_d(f) \neq \perp \land T(f)$		8$_{tr\land}$
p execute f	d-mode	$L_d(f) \neq \perp \land T(f)$	$L_m(p') :=$ d-mode	11$_{tr\land}$

Javascript to write out an executable which can be run from the PDF. However, a legitimate installer also behaves in this fashion.

We start with a basic BInt model using the following abstractions. We denote in an operating system, the following system entities: processes by p and files by f. Each process and file has associated security labels which represent information associated with the process/file – the notation $L(o)$ denotes the security label of the system entity o.[2]

Processes interact with files and other processes through the actions: *create, read, write, delete, execute,* and *load* a file. The *load* action denotes that a process loads a binary file to be used as a DLL. For Windows, we can use our abstraction to model process creation as follows: a process p *executes* a binary to create a new process p'.

BInt uses two kinds of labels, L_m and L_d. A process has a state which we call an *execution mode*. The execution mode label of process p is denoted by $L_m(p)$

---

[2] For simplicity, directories and threads are not modelled but are easy to add.

which can take three values: *d-mode* (*default mode*); *i-mode* (*install mode*); or *t-mode* (*temporary trusted mode*). Intuitively, d-mode corresponds to the normal (default) execution mode for running software and processes start in d-mode. Installing/updating software occurs in i-mode. For special cases, t-mode handles scenarios when we want to run software which needs to dynamically create and load binaries but is not meant to be software installation, e.g. building binaries in an IDE or for dynamic temporary binaries created by a process.

The second kind of label on a process p or file f, denoted by $L_d(p)$ or $L_d(f)$ respectively, can be thought of as a *software domain*. Intuitively, a particular software domain labels all the processes and files related to a particular installed software. For example, the software domain could denote the name of a particular software or the software vendor. There is a distinguished software domain $\perp$ denoting binaries which do not have a valid software domain, we call such binaries *b-invalid*, otherwise a binary is *b-valid*. The only relation among software domains is equality ($=$).

Our first BInt model is formalized in rules 1–14 from Table 1. Each rule specifies the requirement and result of an operation on binaries for a given mode. An actual implementation would distinguish binary files from other files (see Sect. 3) but we omit binary tests to avoid cluttering up the model. Throughout the paper, for brevity, we refer to rule i as **R**i.

A b-valid binary can only be created in i-mode with the software domain of the process creating the binary (**R3**), otherwise only b-invalid binaries are created (**R1–2**). File reads are not affected by BInt (**R4**). This helps compatibility. Rules **R5–7** deal with binary integrity. To ensure binary integrity, a binary can only be written to or deleted in i-mode if it is b-valid with the same software domain or if it is b-invalid (**R7**). The integrity of b-invalid binaries is not maintained, so there are no restrictions in d/t-mode as long as it is b-invalid (**R5–6**).

Rules **R8–13** deal with the use of binaries (load/execute). In d-mode, only b-valid binaries can be loaded/executed (**R8,11**). In t-mode and i-mode, any binary can be loaded (**R9, 10**) and executed. In our abstraction (as in Windows), executing a binary creates a new process. The execution mode of process p is preserved in the new process p' (**R11-13**) and in i-mode, the software domain of p carries to p' (**R13**).

A process changes its execution mode from d-mode to either i-mode or t-mode through a special operation, called *modetrans*. Changing d-mode to i-mode changes both the mode and software domain of the process, while changing to t-mode only changes $L_m(p)$ as the domain is not used (**R14**). Modetrans is a privileged operation, for example, it could be implemented with a secure authentication mechanism requiring a password to the operating system. Sudo in Unix or UAC in Windows also require secure authentication but they elevate privileges which modetrans does not.

Unlike policies where labels are explicitly specified, our labels on processes and files are implicit. In d-mode and t-mode, file labels are implicitly created as $\perp$ and its process label is not relevant. Modetrans allows d-mode to go into i-mode. When switching to i-mode, a label is specified which is the software domain used to label the process. File labels in i-mode come from the software domain obtained from modetrans. In terms of user interaction, the user only specifies the software domain once when performing the privileged modetrans operation. Modetrans can be thought of as a simple way of associating trust relationships between binaries and its label where the labelling is automatic using just the software domain label from the d-mode to i-mode transition.

Installing and updating software in i-mode assumes that the installer/updater process(es) are part of the process tree hierarchy from the original process in i-mode for that software domain. While this is reasonable for a generic model, it needs to be customized for a particular operating system – in Windows, we handle the Windows MSI installer and provide an execution mode policy for auto-updaters (see Sect. 3).

2.1 Using BInt

We use a life-cycle of the Firefox web browser to illustrate how BInt works. The user first downloads the Firefox installer ($f_{installer}$) using some other web browser or downloader ($p_{downloader}$), which runs in d-mode ($L_m(p_{downloader}) =$ d-mode). By **R1**, $L_d(f_{installer}) = \perp$. The user then uses the privileged *modetrans* operation to run the installer in i-mode specifying its software domain as firefox. The installer process ($p_{installer}$) and its child processes run in i-mode with the firefox domain, $L_m(p_{installer}) =$ i-mode $\wedge L_d(p_{installer}) =$ firefox. The installer installs a number of binaries, which are in the firefox domain according to **R3**. After installation finishes, the user executes Firefox from the Windows start menu or desktop shortcut. At this point, the Firefox process runs in d-mode due to **R11**.[3] Suppose that Firefox is exploited by a malicious website, e.g. a drive-by-download downloads and runs a malicious executable (f_{mal}). However, the binary f_{mal} has $L_d(f_{mal}) = \perp$ by **R1**, thus, f_{mal} cannot execute by **R11** and the attack fails.

In order for Firefox's auto-update to work, the updater is specified in the execution mode policy (see Sect. 3) so that it automatically runs in i-mode with firefox domain. To uninstall, the user uses modetrans to execute the uninstaller, which then deletes the Firefox binaries without affecting other binaries by **R7**.

A different scenario occurs during software development – the programmer is often creating binaries which may be transient. The IDE can be run in t-mode allowing the software developed to be temporarily executed (**R9**, **R12**).

2.2 BInt+tr: Adding Further Trust

BInt focuses on maintaining integrity of binary files. Which binaries to trust is an orthogonal issue. In accordance with defence in depth, we extend BInt with an

---

[3] We assume the user is familiar with the usage and principles of BInt. The user should not launch Firefox from the installer since normal software execution should be in d-mode. However, similar to Windows UAC prompts, warnings can be issued when executing a new binary in i-mode.

additional source of trust. We assume an external trusted signature repository publishing signatures of vetted binaries, e.g. such as Bit9 [3], but alternative mechanisms are also possible. The binary signature is used (additionally) to certify that a binary and associated software domain is trusted.

We describe two alternative models, BInt+tr$\lor$ and BInt+tr$\land$ presented in Table 1 from $\mathbf{R8}_{tr\lor}$ to $\mathbf{R11}_{tr\land}$. BInt+tr$\lor$ is a more permissive model which allows binary f to be loaded/executed in d-mode if f is b-valid *or* if it is certified by the trusted signature repository ($\mathbf{R8}_{tr\lor},\mathbf{11}_{tr\lor}$). For example, third parties can certify a list of trusted software, a user can use the list to avoid switching to i-mode to install software in the list. This allows for broader software compatibility without compromising the integrity of other binaries. It also reduces the use of i-mode but requires a trusted service.

A restrictive policy is BInt+tr$\land$ which requires both signature verification and b-validity ($\mathbf{R8}_{tr\land},\mathbf{11}_{tr\land}$). For example, in an organization, this can enforce that only specified software can be used and exceptions only occur through t-mode. Variations of the signing requirements for t-mode are also possible. The whitelist approach of BInt+tr$\land$ may be too restrictive for general use since only binaries on the whitelist can be executed. A practical incarnation may only require the verification for certain pathnames of software domains. Incorporating an external trust mechanism allows to add MAC policies and also an ecosystem of security providers which provide whitelists of vetted binaries, e.g. similar to Bit9 [3].

An even more restrictive form of BInt+tr$\land$ is to require that binaries created in i-mode must pass the signature verification, otherwise, the creation and subsequent writing of the binary has no effect.[4] We call this variant, BInt+tr$\land$W.

2.3 Analysis of BInt Models

The binary protection from BInt arises in three ways. First is whether execution or loading of binaries is prevented. Note that this does not prevent all malware code execution, e.g. code injection, we focus on attacks employing binary mechanisms. Second is it provides integrity guarantees for binaries, preventing malware from modifying binaries. Thirdly, in order for malware to persist on the system, it will normally need to be in files (binaries), otherwise the vulnerability must be one which can reoccur on the same system which we do not deal with.[5] We remark that without tailoring BInt for a particular operating system, execution/loading/reading/writing of binaries are the only relevant operations in our model when dealing with binary files so the discussion focuses on these operations and also `modetrans`.

---

[4] This changes the semantics of file write so that changes behave like a shadow file until it can be verified when the file is closed. Self-signing [21] also needs to work in a similar way.

[5] E.g. a vulnerability in the network code in the operating system might allow an attacker to gain arbitrary code execution within the kernel with an external network request, however, this is not a binary vulnerability or exploit.

Security of **d-mode:** Most processes run in d-mode, thus its security is critical. The threat model is whether a process in d-mode can execute/load an undesired binary (b-invalid binary) or modify existing (b-valid) binaries.

The guarantees in d-mode are: b-invalid binaries cannot be loaded (**R8**); b-valid binaries cannot be modified (**R5**); and binaries created are b-invalid (**R1**). Thus, a d-mode process is unable to introduce new binaries to d-mode processes including itself which prevents common attacks which use execution or binary loading. This prevents both the example attacks (Safari Carpetbomb and PDF embedded executables). The integrity guarantee is that existing binary files which are b-valid cannot be modified by the attacker. It is also not possible to delete b-valid binaries. As d-mode is orthogonal from other privileges, i.e. system administrator privileges, these guarantees apply even for privileged processes in d-mode. An important consequence is that even if a software running in d-mode is successfully attacked, the attack cannot be made *persistent* through binaries as it cannot write b-valid binaries nor can it modify any binaries. Since the operations considered on binaries are execution, loading and file operations, this completes the analysis of d-mode.

Security of **i-mode:** Changing from d-mode to i-mode using `modetrans` requires authenticated privileges for the operation (**R14**), thus, no processes in d-mode can enter i-mode by themselves. So the threat model is that an attacker needs to get the user to enter i-mode, e.g. a social engineering attack. However if BInt+tr∨ is used, then `modetrans` can be a rare and unusual operation making is more difficult to social engineer unlike UAC in Windows where the user is "trained to click allow".

There are two cases to consider whether the user installs the malware in a new software domain or existing domain. Firstly, if it is a new domain, as the malware installer cannot modify existing b-valid binaries, their integrity is assured. However, the malware can install new binaries which might be loaded into existing software, e.g. the Safari Carpetbomb DLL attack, if there is an exploitable vulnerability. The BInt+tr∧ model (and BInt+tr∧W) can prevent this since the malware should not be in the whitelist. Our prototype additionally keeps a *binary database* of binaries and their software domains and also logs of binary usage and loading relationships, allowing attacks to be detected and be removed more easily. Secondly, if it is an existing domain, the malware can modify binaries of the above BInt models except in the BInt+tr∧W model which only allows modification with another trusted binary of the same domain. Thus, BInt+tr∧W being the most restrictive model prevents binary integrity attack in both cases.

The damage that can be caused by the malware in the other BInt models depends on the domain. For critical domains such as `microsoft` (for all the system binaries), the malware can affect all software as programs use Windows system DLLs in the `microsoft` domain. To reduce the impact of such attacks, one approach is to require extra privileges such as a separate password for critical domains. Furthermore, unlike the Windows UAC privilege escalation, the binary database in the prototype can be used to explain whether a binary is relevant to the software domain.

The extensions discussed in Sect. 5 also reduce the threats from i-mode.

Security of **t-mode:** Like i-mode, t-mode also requires authentication for the privilege escalation. However, t-mode behaves like d-mode in terms of binary integrity, a t-mode process cannot modify b-valid binaries (**R6**). Thus, a malicious t-mode process cannot introduce new binaries to d-mode processes. However, t-mode processes can load b-invalid binaries (**R9**) which allows for binary attacks to these processes. T-mode is meant to be a special exception, it is like i-mode in that most software and processes do not run in this mode. Since in t-mode, any binary can be loaded, the threat model is whether the attacker can make the malware persist. However, in order to persist, it would need to be able to lure the user to authenticate and run it in t-mode every time, as it cannot execute/load in d-mode and t-mode does not affect binaries. We argue that unlike UAC, user authentication for i/t-mode is more controlled and without the problem that users tend to choose "always allow" [17]. The problem with UAC is that users do not know how to choose between allow or deny, they learn that deny just means the software fails, so they learn to click "allow".

3   A BInt Windows Prototype

We implemented a prototype in Windows XP of BInt models. We describe the implementation of basic BInt and mention differences for other models. We also discuss some implementation features for our models to deal with special features in Windows as BInt is generic and the model is not targeted for Windows. We use a kernel driver in Windows XP to intercept native calls (Windows system calls) for binary loading, file reading, file modification, process creation and some other operations.[6] It also maintains the labels of processes and binaries. As our implementation works inside the Windows kernel, it allows us to apply all the rules of BInt to all processes and binaries in Windows.

Our prototype is meant to be a proof of concept to show that BInt can be implemented efficiently, provide security against binary attacks and be compatible with existing software. Nevertheless, the prototype shows the viability of BInt and that it would be relatively easy for Microsoft to implement. It should be clear also that building a version of BInt in another operating system, e.g. Unix, is relatively straightforward.

For **R8–13** in Table 1, we intercept the NtCreateSection native call, which is necessary for binary loading. If the execution mode is d-mode and the binary is b-invalid, NtCreateSection fails resulting in the load/execute failing. For **R1–7**, we intercept the ZwCreateFile call, which opens or creates a file and returns a handle. For **R11–13**, we use the kernel API PsSetCreateProcessNotifyRoutine to inherit execution mode and software domain in the child process. For **R14**, we use IOCTL (I/O control) to implement the system call-like modetrans operation.

---

[6] We use Windows XP, later versions require signed drivers.

Most of the corresponding rules in BInt+tr are implemented in the same way as BInt. The $T(f)$ signature verification in BInt+tr is cached so that multiple loadings only need a single verification unless the binary is modified. This caching optimization is similar to that in [13] which has been shown to be efficient with negligible overhead for real applications. File writing, renaming and deletion are monitored through the `ZwCreateFile` and `ZwDeleteFile` kernel APIs.

We assume all file modifications are under the control of the operating system kernel. This assumption can be invalid in some cases. When the system mounts a network shared file system, (e.g. through SMB) an attacker can change the binaries outside the system. Similarly, files can be changed when the system is offline. We call such files, *unmonitorable files.* To prevent these attacks, we use file signatures to detect modification. A *binary database* stores information about files, signatures, modification history and other metadata. We also generate logs of how binaries were used which is useful for explanations and creating special exceptions, e.g. execution mode policy. Log maintenance is done outside the kernel. For unmonitorable b-valid files, their signatures are updated immediately after the file is modified. For binaries that just come online, we verify the signatures once for each binary and cache the result [13]. We optimize the signature verification with a lazy way of updating signatures to reduce the overhead of signature verification. We store normalized internal kernel paths to disambiguate Windows 8.3 filenames, long file names and symbolic links. For the NTFS filesystem, we use the object ID to disambiguate hard links.

In Windows, there is no distinguishing feature of a binary (the filetype is only a convention, i.e. an executable need not have file type `.exe` or `.com`), other than its format. We test whether or not the file is a binary by reading the file header. This makes i-mode more costly than other modes since only i-mode creates b-valid binaries. We modify the semantics of Windows slightly so that files opened for writing in i-mode are in exclusive mode to simplify signature creation. We do not expect this to be a major restriction as the installer is likely to be creating files sequentially. When p closes the file handle of f, the file contents is now complete and f's signature can be re-computed (lazily). In principle, signatures only need to be maintained for non-monitorable files. However, to reduce the impact of offline attacks, we choose to maintain signatures of all b-valid binaries and critical files.

Since a software installer may launch several helper programs to accomplish the installation, we need to ensure all helper processes are labelled with the same execution mode and software domain. This is accomplished by mode and domain inheritance (**R11–13**). BInt assumes that all helper processes are the child (or descendant) processes of the first installer process. While the assumption holds for most installers, there is an important exception. MSI (Windows Installer) is a generic installation engine for installing and updating software on Windows. It is used for both Microsoft and non-Microsoft software. MSI makes use of a service (daemon) process to perform installation. The service process is always running and is not part of the process hierarchy of the original installer. Dealing with MSI requires some minor extensions to how i-mode works. We monitor the communication channel, a named pipe \Pipe\Net\NtControlPipeX, between the installation process and the MSI service. When an i-mode process triggers the service to start installation, the service is switched to i-mode with the same domain as the triggering process. When the installation terminates, the service is switched back to d-mode. As the MSI service is used atomically, there is no interference between concurrent requests.

We now illustrate how BInt is used in our Windows prototype. When the system is booted, the initial process(es) run in d-mode, thus all subsequent processes run in d-mode unless modetrans is used. We have implemented a command-line modetrans utility which authenticates the user using a password and executes a user-specified program in a user-specified mode and domain.

Since auto-update program should always run in i-mode, we introduce an *execution mode policy* which simplifies system usage by predefining special cases where the operation of modetrans can be performed automatically. For example, Windows auto-update (wuauclt.exe), is specified to run in i-mode and the microsoft domain. Finally, the mechanisms also protect the BInt policy files, modifications to the policies require user authentication.

The execution mode policy is to make usage of BInt more transparent so that users do not need to explicitly go into i-mode. This policy is small and mostly for well-known cases with a few exceptions. Thus, it is much easier to deal with and maintain than more complex policy-based models.

3.1   Evaluating BInt on Windows

We evaluated our prototype with the basic BInt model as the other models would need additional external trusted third party providers. In terms of performance, the main mode is d-mode as other modes should only be used more rarely. As we employ caching to monitor binaries, once a binary signature has been checked, there is little overhead (as the implementation of signed binaries in [13]). Since many binaries are shared, we find that once the system has started and some binary has been loaded before, the overheads for real applications are negligible and we did not notice any significant difference between running our prototype and normal Windows.

We evaluated d-mode on the following common binary attack vectors: directly running a b-invalid executable from the GUI Windows Explorer shell (a social engineering attack) and the cmd shell; PDF attack on Acrobat Reader using a PDF embedded binary [5]; loading a b-invalid driver; starting a b-invalid service; loading b-invalid shell extensions and Browser Helper Objects (exploits a vulnerability where binaries could be loaded as a Windows help file [4]); and loading b-invalid DLLs by PATH manipulation (such as DLL planting attacks [7,8]). While our security analysis already shows that d-mode prevents these attacks in the abstract model, the evaluation confirms this for the prototype.

We tested compatibility with the binary lifecycle of common Windows software by installing, running and uninstalling the following applications: Internet Explorer (IE, highly integrated into Windows), Winamp (music player with 88 binaries), Yahoo Messenger (instant messaging client with 55 binaries), Firefox

(32 binaries), Google Chrome (137 binaries), Adobe Acrobat Reader (31 binaries) and Java Development Kit (229 binaries).

IE tests Microsoft software installation. The software domain is `microsoft` due to the highly integrated nature of Microsoft software in Windows. In fact, IE modifies several Windows system DLLs. No problems were observed during installing and running IE. Windows update handles the auto update of Windows related software including IE, this occurred transparently without problems.

The Winamp installer uses its own Nullsoft installer. No problem was observed during running and uninstalling Winamp. Yahoo Messenger uses a network-based install, the installer is an initial installer which downloads a much larger installer. The installer tries to upgrade the Flash ActiveX plugin `flash.ocx` if it is out of date. This action is blocked as the software domains do not match. However, this is not a problem as the Flash plugin can be updated separately. We noticed that a `YahooAUService.exe` service is created for auto-update. In order for the auto-update to work transparently, we should add `YahooAUService.exe` to the execution mode policy to run in i-mode with the `Yahoo` domain.

No problem was found during Firefox installation. Auto-updates are handled by `updater.exe` in the Firefox software domain. For transparent update, it is added to the execution mode policy. No problem was observed for Chrome. Reader and Java Development Kit use the MSI engine which is handled transparently without any user interaction.

We tested typical software which cover a range of mechanisms for installation, uninstall, and update. We found that usage scenarios for the software lifecycle aspects are usable with little effort needed. In some cases, the security policy achieves complete transparently. For full transparency, the execution mode policy is used with a minimal specification. This can be done manually immediately after installation if the user knows which program does the update. It can also be done at the first time the updater performs the updates. In this case, the user will be notified about the attempt to modify binaries. Information from the binary database and logs can then be used to set the execution mode policy. Alternatively, auto-updaters can be run manually in i-mode as a more secure alternative which does not rely on any execution mode policy specification. Naturally that requires a bit more effort on the part of the user. If a more secure policy is needed we should expect that it needs some information but it should be sufficiently easy to specify and maintain without extensive analysis and expert knowledge, which is how we designed BInt.

4 The FInt Model

BInt only covers binaries but the integrity of non-binaries may also be important for the security of the system. For example, the attacker can modify the Java class files used by the Java compiler to insert malicious bytecode even though neither the Java virtual machine nor compiler is compromised [18]. An attack can modify a good script (`.bat`) into a malicious one. Without modifying the web server binaries, the attacker can change the web server's configuration file or PHP script to steal data or modify the web site.

Table 2. Rules for FInt. Assumes the files are non-binary. α: Apply the FInt policy for pathnames. If the result is "verify", the condition is: $(L_d(f) \neq \perp$ (when owner flag is not set)) $\vee$ $(L_d(f) = L_d(p)$ (when owner flag is set))

Action	$L_{m'}(p)$	Requires	Result	Rule
p create f	d-mode'	true	$L_d(f) := \perp$	1_f
	t-mode'	true	$L_d(f) := \perp$	2_f
	i-mode'	true	$L_d(f) := L_d(p)$	3_f
p read f	d-mode'	α (see caption)		4_f
	t-mode'	true		5_f
	i-mode'	true		6_f
p write/delete f	d-mode'	$L_d(f) = \perp$		7_f
	t-mode'	$L_d(f) = \perp$		8_f
	i-mode'	$L_d(f) = \perp \vee L_d(f) = L_d(p)$	$L_d(f) := L_d(p)$	9_f
p modetrans		authentication	change $L_d(p)$ and $L_{m'}(p)$	10_f

We generalize BInt to protect integrity of any file. The use of files which are not binaries is quite different from binaries. Firstly, the operating system does not distinguish between an interpreter executing a script and reading a data file. Usually we only want to protect the integrity of the former. Secondly, while there are usually many more non-binaries than binaries, only a small fraction of the non-binaries is critical to security of the system. Thirdly, the semantics of non-binaries is program specific, unlike binaries which the operating system understands, e.g. a malicious Perl script is significant when opened by the Perl interpreter, but not when opened by a text editor.

Due to these differences, we adopt a different approach to protecting the integrity of non-binaries. Only files defined by a *FInt policy* are protected. Essentially the FInt policy specifies what pathnames are critical to certain software. This policy can be specified on a per-program or per-domain basis. We remark that other variants of FInt are possible, we present FInt as a conservative extension of BInt.

The FInt policy consists of a list of subjects. Each subject is associated with a list of objects (pathnames) and associated action. The subjects and objects correspond to processes and files in the operating system. The subject is defined by a pathname of a binary or a software domain; and the object is a rule for the subject defined by a regular expression for a pathname along with the following actions: *allow, deny,* or *verify*. *Allow* means the files are allowed to be read/loaded. Files matching the *allow* rule are considered to be not critical to the program. *Deny* means the files are denied from being read/loaded. *Verify* means that the reading/loading is allowed depending on the execution modes and software domains of the process and file. The FInt policy extends BInt (specifically, rules **R4, R11-R13**) by applying to all files including binaries.

More than one rule can be specified for a subject. The action specified by the first matching rule is taken. The default action (none of the regular expressions

match the path) is *verify* for binary and *allow* for non-binary. This is to make
FInt consistent with BInt when no FInt policy is specified.

In FInt, non-binaries are labeled with software domains similar to BInt. The
default label is $\perp$ for *all* files unless otherwise created with a different domain
which extends the notion of b-invalid $(L(f) = \perp)$ and b-valid $(L(f) \neq \perp)$ to
all files. We introduce file execution modes in FInt which add to those in BInt.
New file execution mode of a process p are denoted by $L_{m'}(p)$, namely: d-mode',
t-mode', and i-mode'. Table 2 formalizes FInt for non-binary files. We add a *file
execution mode policy* which specifies which programs should be automatically
executed in which file execution modes. For example, the Java compiler can run
automatically in i-mode' so that the compiled class file will be b-valid, and is
unmodified by anything else when used by the Java VM.

In order to prevent a program from (accidentally) reading files created by
other programs (e.g. malware), we introduce an optional flag *owner* for each
policy rule – the flag means that the file read/loaded must not only be b-valid,
but also have the same software domain as the process (see Ex3).

One motivation for FInt policies is that they can be used to construct specialized behavior for FInt. It can also be used to create special security policies
or restrictions. We give some examples of how to use FInt policies.

Ex1: The following simple policy protects all batch files for the CMD shell:

```
[c:\windows\system32\cmd.exe] verify .*\.bat
```

Ex2: The following policy verifies Java bytecode coming from .class and .jar
files except for a project directory. The purpose is to allow modification of the
Java code under development by non-JDK program such as IDEs. This policy
is shared by programs such as java.exe and javaw.exe (GUI version of java) in
the JDK software domain.

```
[jdk]
    allow  E:\\projects\\foo\\.*\.class
    allow  E:\\projects\\foo\\.*\.jar
    verify .*\.class
    verify .*\.jar
```

Ex3: The following policy prevents Firefox's built-in JavaScript modules and
extensions from being hijacked by third party program. It uses the "owner" flag.

```
[firefox]
    verify owner C:\\Program Files\\Firefox\\.*\.jar
    verify owner C:\\Program Files\\Firefox\\.*\.js
    verify owner C:\\Program Files\\Firefox\\.*\.xul
```

Ex4: In order to prevent the web server from being exploited to launch a cmd
shell, one may run the web server in a more restricted environment with cmd.exe
blacklisted by the following policy. Even without this policy, the web server is
already protected as binaries which are not b-valid cannot be executed. Thus, if
an attacker breaks in, they cannot run their own binaries but are restricted to

the existing b-valid binaries. This policy further reduces the allowed binaries by denying the cmd shell.

```
[apache] deny .*\\cmd.exe
```

5   Discussion and Conclusion

We discuss further extensions and possibilities for BInt for which there is lack of space to go into the details.

File Deletion: For simplicity, the uninstaller runs in the same execution mode, i-mode, as installer and updater. This allows the uninstaller to add new binaries. We can prevent this by introducing a *u-mode*, which is more powerful than d-mode and less powerful then i-mode. In u-mode, the process can delete binaries with the same software domain or ⊥, so that it can delete its binaries. Binaries created by a u-mode process are ⊥, so that it cannot introduce new binaries. We remark that as an alternative to deletion, the label can simply be downgraded to ⊥ if the binaries are to be retained but not executable or loadable.

Software Dependencies: In BInt, software domains are treated equally, i.e. a process running in one software domain can load a binary of another software domain. If a user accidentally installs a malicious binary, it can be loaded into all processes. To prevent this, we can incorporate software dependencies into BInt, so that a process can load a binary if the software group of the process depends on the group of the binary. This adds a partial order relation while BInt only needed equality. For example, the dependencies can specify a plugin of a web browser can only be loaded by the browser but not other software. The dependency information can either be specified during software installation or come from a trusted third party such as the software developers.

Sandboxed Domains: BInt requires i-mode to first install software before use, which may be considered troublesome to some users, i.e. users expect to be able to run a software immediately after downloading. We can use the idea of a *sandboxed domain* to allow immediate execution while still prevent the new binary from being loaded by other software. Binaries created by d-mode or t-mode process are assigned a new sandboxed software domain (instead of ⊥ in BInt) – the new domain is denoted by *newsb*. Any binary can be executed in d-mode but if the binary is from a sandboxed domain, the process label also becomes sandboxed (a modification of **R11**). Thus, a downloaded binary can be executed immediately. However, to prevent malware from automatically executing downloaded binaries, when a sandboxed domain is executed for the first time, a UI prompt (with the creator's software domain, creation time, binary path, etc.) will ask for permission.

In summary, we have proposed a flexible family of binary integrity models which are designed to handle dynamic creation, modification and deletion of binaries in their lifecycle. Our models combine integrity of the binaries together with trust to protect against typical attack vectors which exploit the use of binaries which is a major headache in Windows. Our models are suitable as a security enhancement for Windows since the large attack surface of Windows leads to many binary attacks which BInt models prevent. Our prototype demonstrates that these models are practical and easy to use. As binary attacks are commonplace in Windows, we believe what is needed are simple policy mechanisms which give a good tradeoff between usability and security. BInt does not deal with code injection attacks but it can be combined with other runtime security mechanisms which do that, e.g. ASLR, NX, etc.

While we have focused on Windows, the BInt models are general and can be applied to other operating systems. Although Windows is where BInt would have the biggest benefit, there are also documented attacks on Unix such as autorun-style USB attacks in Linux [6] and the Flashback and Mac Defender malware on Mac OSX. We also propose FInt as a conservative extension of BInt to protect the integrity of non-binary files. We believe that the recent ShellShock bug in bash (a script injection vulnerability regarded as critical in most Unix/Linux systems) can be mitigated with extensions to our models.

References

1. HEUR:Backdoor.Java.Agent.a. https://www.securelist.com/en/blog/8174/A_cross_platform_java_bot
2. http://www.computerworld.com/s/article/9237295/Researchers_link_latest_Java_zero_day_exploit_to_Bit9_hack
3. http://www.bit9.com
4. http://www.cve.mitre.org/cgi-bin/cvename.cgi?name=CVE-2010-0483
5. http://blog.didierstevens.com/2010/03/29/escape-from-pdf
6. USB Autorun Attacks in Linux. http://blogs.iss.net/archive/Shmoocon2011.html
7. http://www.microsoft.com/technet/security/advisory/2269637.mspx
8. http://www.oreillynet.com/onlamp/blog/2008/05/safari_carpet_bomb.html
9. Apvrille, A., Gordon, D., Hallyn, S., Pourzandi, M., Roy, V.: DigSig: run-time authentication of binaries at kernel level. In: USENIX LISA (2004)
10. Badger, L., Sterne, D.F., Sherman, D.L., Walker, K.M., Haghighat, S.A.: Practical domain and type enforcement for UNIX. In: IEEE S&P (1995)
11. Biba, K.: Integrity considerations for secure computer systems, ESD-TR-76-372, MITRE (1977)
12. Dai, T., Zhang, M., Yap, R.H.C., Liang, Z.: Understanding complex binary loading behaviors. In: ICECCS (2014)
13. Halim, F., Ramnath, R., Sufatrio Wu, Y., Yap, R.H.C.: A lightweight binary authentication system for windows. In: Karabulut, Y., Mitchell, J., Herrmann, P., Jensen, C.D. (eds.) Trust Management II. IFIP, vol. 263, pp. 295–310. Springer, Boston (2008)
14. Howard, M., Pincus, J., Wing, J.M.: Measuring relative attack surfaces. In: Workshop on Advanced Developments in Software and Systems Security (2003)
15. Kato, K., Oyama, Y.: SoftwarePot: an encapsulated transferable file system for secure software circulation. In: Okada, M., Babu, C., Scedrov, A., Tokuda, H. (eds.) ISSS 2002. LNCS, vol. 2609, pp. 112–132. Springer, Heidelberg (2003)
16. Liang, Z., Sun, W., Venkatakrishnan, V., Sekar, R.: Alcatraz: an isolated environment for experimenting with untrusted software. In: ACM TISS, **12**(3) (2009)

17. Motiee, S., Hawkey, K., Beznosov, K.: Do windows users follow the principle of least privilege?: investigating user account control practices. In: SOUPS (2010)
18. Thompson, K.: Reflections on trusting trust. In: CACM **27**, 761–763 (1984)
19. Wu, Y., Yap, R.H.C., Ramnath, R.: Comprehending module dependencies and sharing. In: ICSE (2010)
20. Wu, Y., Yap, R.H.C.: Towards a binary integrity system for windows. In: ASIACCS (2011)
21. Wurster, G., Oorschot, P.C.V.: Self-Signed Executables: restricting replacement of program binaries by malware. In: USENIX HotSec (2007)

Enabling NAME-Based Security and Trust

Nikos Fotiou$^{(\boxtimes)}$ and George C. Polyzos

Mobile Multimedia Laboratory, Department of Informatics
School of Information Sciences and Technology,
Athens University of Economics and Business,
Patision 76, 10 434 Athens, Greece
{fotiou,polyzos}@aueb.gr

Abstract. An integral component of almost any security and trust system is endpoint identity verification. The predominant identification primitive, used in most contemporary systems, is the digital certificate. A digital certificate binds a NAME (i.e., an "official way to refer to an entity") to a cryptographic public key, which is then used for the NAME verification. In this paper, we propose a NAME verification system that does not rely on digital certificates. Our solution uses Hierarchical Identity Based Encryption (HIBE) to allow fine-grained NAME verification, trust delegation and attribute-based access control. For the delivery of the necessary system parameters we propose an approach that leverages the NAME registration and resolution systems, eliminating the need for a Public-Key Infrastructure. As proof of concept, we implement and evaluate our system using the Lewko-Waters HIBE scheme and DANE-DNSSEC.

1 Introduction

Almost every entity in the Internet has at least one *NAME*, i.e., *an official way to indicate an entity uniquely* [11]. Examples of NAMEs are domain names, e-mail addresses, and electronic product codes. NAMEs can be bound to a cryptographic public key using a *Digital Certificate* (DC); DCs can then be used for NAME verification. This process is an essential component of many security and trust systems. In this paper, we postulate that security and trust systems can be built directly on NAMEs without relying on DCs. What is more, we argue that the NAME hierarchy can be used to implement trust delegation and access control mechanisms. To this end, we propose a solution in which NAMEs hold the role of public keys. In the following use case scenario we illuminate some of the advantages of the use of NAMEs as public keys.

Service A enables decentralized content sharing. Users of this service are registered using a short, memorable nickname. The organizers of *Conference B* use *Service A* in order to allow conference attendants to exchange files. A sponsor of *Conference B* has prepared an electronic gift card and it has encrypted it with the public key "Service A.Conference B.attendant". The gift card and the decryption key are "transmitted" to the conference attendants during the "welcome session". During the conference, a presenter wishes to share her slides with

© IFIP International Federation for Information Processing 2015
C.D. Jensen et al. (Eds.): IFIPTM 2015, IFIP AICT 454, pp. 47–59, 2015.
DOI: 10.1007/978-3-319-18491-3_4

the audience. She includes her nickname "nickname A" in her first slide and broadcasts a list of files and their location, digitally signed with the private key that corresponds to "Service A.nickname A". Moreover, the presenter has delegated the NAME "Service A.nickname A.presentation.live" to a video streaming service which is now authorized to stream her presentation.

Various features of NAME-based security and trust systems can be identified in this use case: it is possible to create a ciphertext using a public key (NAME) that will be generated in the future, NAMEs can be small and memorable and they can even be included in a presentation slide or a business card, NAME-based digital signatures can be easily verified, simply by using the NAME of the signer, and NAMEs can be structured and sub-NAMEs can be delegated to third parties, enabling them to act on behalf of the NAME owner.

In this paper we propose a solution that enables NAME-based security and trust systems. We take advantage of the structure of NAMEs and we design constructions for trust delegation and attribute-based access control. Our system uses Hierarchical Identity Based Encryption (HIBE). HIBE is selected since, compared to plain IBE, it facilitates (private) key generation and transitivity of trust. In our system, HIBE system parameters can be disseminated using the name resolution infrastructure. As a proof of concept we implement our system using the Lewko-Waters HIBE scheme [10].

This paper is organized as follows: In Sect. 2 we discuss related work in this area. In Sect. 3 we briefly present HIBE. In Sect. 4 we detail our construction, whereas in Sect. 5 we present its implementation and evaluation. Finally our conclusions are presented in Sect. 6.

2   Related Work

Related work in this area mostly concerns Identity Based Encryption (IBE). Despite using NAMEs as keys, IBE, is not as flexible as HIBE. The generation of a private key always involves communication with a third party and trust delegation is not straightforward. Moreover IBE schemes cannot be used for generating digital signatures and an additional Identity Based Signature (IBS) scheme is required in systems that use IBE.

Smetters and Durfee [13] utilized IBE encryption to provide secure email delivery and encrypted network traffic. In their scheme they used DNSSEC to deliver the system parameters (we detail these parameters in Sect. 3). Smart [12] used IBE in order to implement authenticated key agreement, whereas Green and Giuseppe [5] utilized IBE to implement proxy re-encryption (i.e., transformation of a ciphertext encrypted with key A to a ciphertext encrypted with key B). All these works consider a particular application of IBE, whereas our work proposes a holistic NAME-based trust enabler system.

The work of Zhang et al. [14] has very similar goals with our system. In their work, Zhang et al., utilized the IBE scheme proposed by Boneh and Franklin [3] and the IBS scheme proposed by Hess [6] in order to provide name-based security trust mechanisms for the NDN Information Centric Networking (ICN) architecture [7]. Moreover they used a legacy PKI in order to deliver system parameters.

Our work improves [14] in the following: (a) we utilize HIBE, therefore, (i) private key generation is faster, (ii) no separate signature scheme is required, and (iii) trust can be delegated and (b) we use the name resolution infrastructure to deliver system parameters which, as we argue, offers better fault isolation and easier security breach detection.

3 Background

An Identity Based Encryption (IBE) scheme is a public key encryption scheme in which an identity (i.e., an arbitrary string) can be used as a public key. An IBE scheme is specified by four algorithms, Setup, Extract, Encrypt and Decrypt.

- Setup: it is executed by a Private Key Generator (PKG). It takes as input a security parameter k and returns a master-secret key (MSK) and some system parameters (SP). The MSK is kept secret by the PKG, whereas SP are made publicly available.
- Extract: it is executed by a PKG. It takes as input SP, MSK, and an identity ID, and returns a secret key SK_{ID}.
- Encrypt: takes as input an identity ID, a message M, and SP, and returns a ciphertext C_{ID}.
- Decrypt: takes as input C_{ID}, the corresponding private decryption key SK_{ID}, and returns M.

HIBE schemes consider hierarchical identities and specify an additional algorithm: Delegate

- Delegate: takes as input SP, SK_{ID_1}, and an identity $ID_1.ID_2$ and outputs $SK_{ID_1.ID_2}$.

Delegate algorithm is of particular importance, as it enables the owner of in identity to generate SKs for its descendants in the identity hierarchy without the involvement of the PKG.[1] As a consequence, a message encrypted using an identity ID as the public key, can be decrypted by any of the ancestors of ID in the identity hierarchy. Figure 1 illustrates the main components and algorithms of HIBE.

Recent advances in HIBE have led to practical schemes, such as the solution proposed by Lewko and Waters [10]. This scheme supports arbitrary number of identities, it does not require the identity hierarchy depth to be known during Setup, and it has constant size SP.

4 System Design

Our system assumes that every *administrative domain* is identified by a NAME and maintains its own PKG (we discuss in Sect. 5.3 the granularity of administrative domains). All entities in an administrative domain are hierarchically organized. The position of an entity in the domain hierarchy is reflected in its NAME.

---

[1] On the contrary, key generation in IBE schemes always involves the PKG.

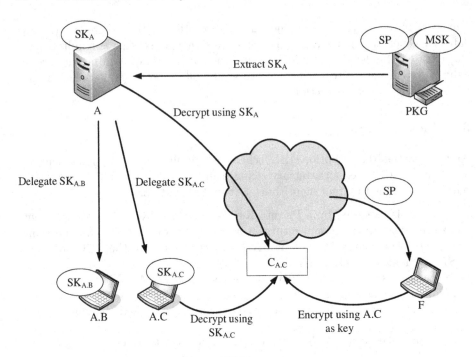

Fig. 1. HIBE overview

The NAME of an entity is used as a public key. The PKG generates the SKs of the "first level" entities, using the **Extract** algorithm, the "first level" entities generate the SKs of the "second level" entities, using the **Delegate** algorithm, and so forth. In the following we present some constructions that can be used to build security and trust systems.

4.1 Basic Constructions

Being public key encryption based, our construction supports the following constructions:

Digital Signature. A digital signature over a piece of content authenticates the identity of the signer and protects content integrity. Assuming that the underlay HIBE algorithm is CCA secure a digital signature scheme can be trivially constructed using the following two algorithms [3]:

- **Sign**: takes as input SP, a message M, a SK_{NAME}, a secure hash function H, and outputs a digital signature $Sign_M = SK_{NAME.H(M)}$. The digital signature $Sign_M$ is constructed by using the **Delegate** algorithm of the HIBE scheme with input SP, SK_{NAME}, $NAME.H(M)$
- **Verify**: takes as input SP, H, a message M, a digital signature $Sign_M$ and the $NAME$ of the signer. Then:

1. Selects a random number r
2. Encrypts r using the HIBE `Encrypt` algorithm with input $NAME.H(M)$, r, SP and produces a ciphertext C
3. Verifies that C can be decrypted using the HIBE `Decrypt` algorithm, with input C, $Sign_M$, SP

Only the entity that owns SK_{NAME} is able to generate $Sign_M$. Moreover since $Sign_M = SK_{NAME.H(M)}$ Step 3 of the verification algorithm is successful iff the digital signature is valid.

Authenticated Key Exchange. An authenticated key exchange protocol enables two parties to authenticate themselves and to establish a secure communication channel. In the following we describe a Diffie-Hellman (D-H) based authentication key exchange protocol between two entities with NAMEs N_1 and N_2. For the sake of simplicity we assume that both entities use the same SP. Let g, p be the public parameters of the D-H protocol, then:

1. N_1 selects a random number r_1, computes $u_1 = g^{r_1}$ (mod p), signs it using `Sign` algorithm–described previously–and sends u_1 and $Sign_{u_1}$ to N_2.
2. N_2 selects a random number r_2, computes $u_2 = g^{r_2}$ (mod p), signs it using `Sign` algorithm, and sends u_2 and $Sign_{u_2}$ to N_1.
3. Both users verify the signatures and if the verification is successful they compute $u = g^{r_1 * r_2}$ (mod p) which is used as the shared secret key.

4.2   Additional Constructions

The use of hierarchical NAMEs and HIBE in our system enables some additional constructions.

Trust Delegation. Suppose an entity with NAME N_1 that wants to use a content distribution network CDN_A to disseminate some files. Our system enables (i) CDN_A to digitally sign stored files on behalf of N_1, and (ii) users to verify that CDN_A has indeed been authorized by N_1 to store these files. This is achieved using the following process.

Let $N_1.files$ be the prefix of the NAME of the files. N_1 executes `Delegate` algorithm and generates $SK_{N_1.files}$ which is securely transmitted to CDN_A. CDN_A can digitally sign a file on behalf of N_1 using the `Sign` algorithm described previously, with input SP, the file, and $SK_{N_1.files}$. A user U_1 can "challenge" CDN_A to prove that it has been indeed authorized by N_1 to host $N_1.files$ using the following procedure:

1. U_1 selects a random number r_1 and sends it to CDN_A.
2. CDN_A computes $SK_{N_1.files.r_1}$, using the `Delegate` algorithm and sends the result back to U_1.
3. U_1 selects a random number r_2, encrypts r_2 using the HIBE `Encrypt` algorithm with input $N_1.files.r_1$, r_2, SP and produces a ciphertext C.
4. U_1 Verifies if C can be decrypted using the HIBE `Decrypt` algorithm, with input C, $SK_{N_1.files.r_1}$, SP.

Attribute-Based Access Control. Using HIBE it is possible to encrypt data in a way that only certain categories of users can decrypt it. Consider the example of a laboratory where the head of the lab should be able to decrypt data encrypted for lab members, but not vice versa. Moreover, each lab member should be able to decrypt only data encrypted for her. In this scenario the head of lab should be equipped with a SK that corresponds to the NAME of the lab (e.g., SK_{lab}), whereas lab members should have a SK that corresponds to a NAME prefixed with the lab NAME (e.g., $SK_{lab.member01}$). Data encrypted for *lab.member01* can be decrypted by both the head of the lab and member01. Moreover data encrypted for *lab* can only be decrypted by the head of the lab. Another interesting example is the case of a spam communication detection filter. By revealing to the filter the key SK_{lab}, it should be able to decrypt and inspect all messages, whereas users will be able to decrypt only their own.

4.3   Delivery of System Parameters

A crucial aspect of our system (and of any (H)IBE based scheme) is SP delivery. One solution that can be considered the use of the name resolution service. In this subsection we describe such an approach without binding it to a particular name resolution system. In the next section we detail our DNSSEC-based implementation.

It is assumed that the administrative domain NAMEs are of a hierarchical form. Moreover, it is assumed that these NAMEs are "registered" to a naming *registration* system, composed of reliable "brokers" which are also organized using the same hierarchical form. The root brokers are responsible for managing the root of the NAME space, the first level brokers are responsible for managing the first level of the NAME space and so forth. Every broker has a self-generated public/private key pair. The public keys of the root brokers are considered well-known and trusted, whereas the public keys of the rest of the brokers are digitally signed by their direct ancestor, i.e., the public keys of the first level brokers are signed by a root broker, the public keys of the second level brokers are signed by a first level broker, and so forth. The NAME of an administrative domain is registered to a leaf broker (the *registrar*). Each administrative domain NAME is associated with a public/private key pair. The public part of this key is signed by the NAME registrar, whereas the private part of this key is used for digitally signing SP.

We now distinguish two forms of NAME *resolution*: (i) the case in which the NAME resolution system is coupled to the naming registration system, and (ii) the case in which these systems are decoupled. The first case is the most commonly used (e.g., in DNS). In this case a name resolution request follows the brokers hierarchy and "collects" signed public keys and signed responses. For example, the NAME resolution of *.gr.edu.mmlab* will result in the collection of the public key of the broker that manages the *.gr.edu* NAME space, signed by a root broker and the public key of the broker that manages the *.gr.edu.mmlab* NAME space, signed by the *.gr.edu* broker. Since the public keys of the root brokers are well known, this chain of signatures can be trivially verified. Figure 2

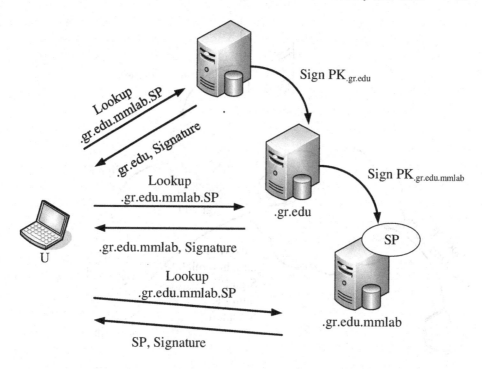

Fig. 2. Coupled NAME registration and NAME resolution systems

illustrates this case. The second case of naming resolution is used in contemporary architectures, such as ICN architectures, that either use other forms of naming resolution systems, e.g., DHT name resolutions systems–such as in [8], or they do not use a naming resolution system at all (e.g., [7] floods–in a controlled–way the NAMEs in the network). In this case the complete chain of signatures of the NAME registration system should be "advertised". Figure 3 illustrates this case.

4.4 Key Revocation

The loss of a SK means that the associated NAME can be hijacked, therefore it should be revoked. In order to prevent this event, our systems considers the usage of two NAMEs per entity: a NAME that identifies the entity and a NAME that is used as a public key of that entity. The latter NAME is constructed by appending to the former a *serial number* (e.g., the public key of lab.user01 can be lab.user01-0034 with 0034 being the serial number). Every time a new SK is required the serial number is incremented. In order to learn the current serial number of a NAME the following solutions can be applied: (i) use out of band mechanism (e.g., in the use case discussed in the Introduction the serial number could have been included in the first slide), (ii) resolve the serial number using the name resolution service (e.g., perform a NAME lookup for lab.user01.SN),

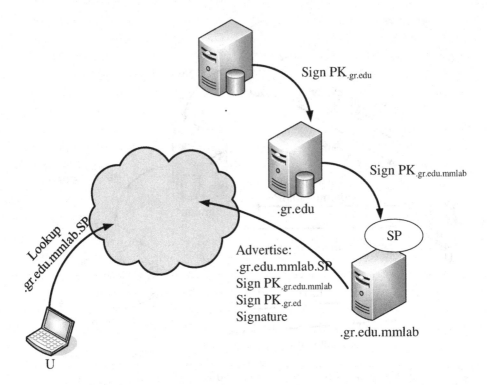

Fig. 3. Decoupled NAME registration and NAME resolution systems

(iii) have the communicating endpoints to agree out-of-band for a serial number (e.g., use as a serial number the current date). These solutions can be used in combination by applying each of them at different hierarchy levels.

An interesting application of dual NAMEs is *key expiration*, i.e., the ability to construct keys with certain lifetime. Supposed that it is desirable to create keys that are valid only for the current month: by creating SKs of the form $SK_{NAME||Current\_Month}$, where $||$ denotes concatenation, and by enforcing users to use $NAME||Current\_Month$ as the public key, the desired functionality can be achieved.

5   Evaluation

As a proof of concept we have implemented our system using the Lewko-Waters [10] HIBE scheme. The Lewko-Waters scheme is fully secure and it is based on bilinear maps applied over the elements of a group G of order p, where p is a prime number.[2] In our implementation G is a subset of the elements of a supersingular Elliptic Curve (EC). In this setup, public keys are elements of $\mathbb{Z}_p$, messages are elements of G (i.e., they are points of an EC), and ciphertexts are elements of $\mathbb{Z}_{p^a}$, where

---

[2] We have considered modification of the scheme for prime order settings [9].

a is a small number affected by the selection of G. The security of this scheme is based on the hardness of the Discrete Logarithm problem in $\mathbb{Z}_{p^a}$.

As a NAME registration and resolution service we consider DNSSEC. In DNSSEC all DNS servers are equipped with a public/private key pair. The private key is used for digitally signing DNS records. Moreover, a digest of the public key of a DNS server is stored as a signed record by its ancestor DNS server. Finally, all DNS-clients are pre-configured with the public keys of the root DNS servers. Following an approach similar to DANE TLSA [2], our implementation stores SP as a KEY record in the DNS zone of the administrative domain, using the alias SP. Therefore, supposing that the NAME of a domain is .gr.edu.mmlab, the resolution of the NAME .gr.edu.mmlab.SP, will result in the secure transmission of SP.

5.1   Performance Evaluation

The Lewko-Waters scheme for prime order settings has been implemented using the Charm-Crypto tool [1] in Python 2.7.[3] All measurements have been performed using an Ubuntu 12.04 PC, equipped with an Intel i5 processor and 2 GB RAM.

For our evaluation we have used a supersingular EC of order 512. The elements of this curve are mapped to $\mathbb{Z}_{p^2}$, i.e., $\mathbb{Z}_{1024}$. The size of the base64 encoding[4] of the SP for this particular setup is 5816 bytes. It should be reminded that the size of SP remains constant and that the scheme does not require any information regarding NAMEs in order to create SP.

One of the drawbacks of the Lewko-Waters scheme is that SK length and ciphertext size, as well as, the encryption and decryption times, are affected by the level of the NAME that is used as the public key. Table 1 shows the size of SK, the encryption time of a random number $r \in G$ (the hash of which can be used as they key to a symmetric encryption scheme) and the size of the ciphertext C_{NAME}, as a function of the level of the NAME used as the public key.

Table 1. SK size in bytes, encryption time in ms and ciphertext size in bytes, as a function of NAME level

NAME level	SK size	Enc. time	C_{NAME} size
0	6340	32	1172
1	7236	63	2068
2	8128	84	2964
3	9024	103	3848
4	9916	122	4744

[3] Source code available at: https://github.com/nikosft/HIBE_LW11.
[4] We are using base64 since SP are stored as a DNS record.

The decryption time of a ciphertext C_{NAME} does not depend on the level of the NAME used as the public key, it only depends on the level of the NAME that corresponds to the SK that is used for the decryption. As an example the decryption time using $SK_{lab.user}$ is the same for $C_{lab.user}$ and $C_{lab.user.file1}$. Table 2 shows the decryption time in ms, for decrypting a ciphertext C generated using a NAME of 4th level, as a function of the level of the NAME of the decrypting entity.

Table 2. Decryption time in ms as a function of NAME level

NAME level	Dec. time
0	47
1	83
2	119
3	153
4	186

The execution time of the `Delegate` algorithm also depends on the level of the NAME of the entity that performs the delegation. Table 3 shows the execution time of the `Delegate` algorithm measured in ms, as a function of the NAME level of entity that performs the delegation.

Table 3. Execution time of the `Delegate` algorithm, measured in ms

NAME level	Deleg. time
0	60
1	105
2	132
3	165

It should be noted here that in all algorithms the hash of a NAME is used (and not the NAME itself), therefore the length of a NAME does not affect the algorithms performance.

As it can be observed from the above results, the overhead introduced by our scheme it totally acceptable.

5.2   Security Evaluation

The security of the basic constructions of our system depends on the security of the underlay HIBE algorithm. Currently there are fully secure algorithms that can be safely used in our system.

When our system is used and providing that the SP that correspond to an endpoint NAME are known, it is possible to establish a secure communication channel with that endpoint without any additional information. This is a big improvement compared to legacy certificate based schemes. It should be noted here that knowing the SP that correspond to a NAME is not equivalent to knowing a security certificate, since SP are administrative domain wide. Therefore, by learning once the SP of an administrative domain, one can establish secure communication channels with any of the entities that belong to this domain.

The usage of the name resolution system for disseminating SP makes Man in the middle attacks harder, compared to Web PKI. Supposedly, a malicious entity wants to impersonate an entity with NAME *.gr.edu.mmlab*. This malicious entity should persuade the brokers that manage the *.gr.edu* NAME space (i) to sign a fake public key, and (ii) to redirect NAME lookup requests to a fake broker.[5] In the current DNSSEC system there is a single such entity. On the contrary, in Web PKI every certificate authority (CA) can lawfully issue a certificate for any entity, even without the entity's consent: if the CA is considered trusted, then this certificate is successfully validated. A recent study [4] found that, when it comes to Web PKI, most end-points blindly trust 683 CAs. Each of these CA can issue a valid certificate for *any* entity.

Another advantage of the usage of the name resolution system for disseminating SP is that security breaches have local effects and it is easier to detect them: Supposedly, a malicious user succeeds in luring a broker that manages the *.gr.edu* NAME space into generating fake public keys and giving fake responses. These public keys can only be used for attacking NAMEs that use *.gr.edu* as a prefix. In contrast, in Web PKI a malfunctioning CA may affect an entity with which it has no direct relationship whatsoever. Moreover, in our system, an entity can periodically probe the name resolution system in order to proactively prevent security attacks.

Another point of consideration is the security risk introduced by name "registrars". Indeed, it is a widespread concern that with DNSSEC a malicious registrar may alter the public key of a domain. This is a valid concern, but it should be clarified that if a NAME is "locked" to a particular registrar, the NAME owner should only rely on the trustworthiness of this particular registrar (in contrast to Web PKI where a domain owner should rely on the trustworthiness of any pre-trusted CA). Moreover, it should be clarified that the NAME registrar never learns the private key(s) of an administrative domain.

5.3 Discussion

An important aspect of our scheme is the granularity of an administrative domain. The granularity of an administrative domain is determined mainly based on two factors: (i) the private key escrow problem (inherent in any (H)IBE scheme) which enables a PKG to decrypt ciphertexts and (ii) the ability of an entity to decrypt all messages encrypted with the NAME of any of its successors. Administrative domain granularity affects the depth of the NAME hierarchy (which in return affects the overhead introduced by HIBE), as well as,

---

[5] We assume that the entities that manage the root name space cannot be "lured".

the number of NAMEs that use the same SP. We can consider various levels of granularity for an administrative domain, ranging from very low (e.g., a whole multinational company) to very high (e.g., a user that maintains his own domain, therefore his own PKG). It should be noted that even when the highest level of granularity is considered, our scheme has many advantages compared to an IBE-based scheme as, even in this case, users still can digitally sign files and delegate trust without communicating with the PKG.

6   Conclusions

In this paper we designed a solution that enables NAME-based security and trust systems, using the Lewko-Waters [10] HIBE scheme. Our system achieves trust delegation and access control, enabling new applications, such as secure content delegation. Our system considers the NAME-resolution infrastructure for delivering the system parameters which offers significant security advantages. Our implementation shows that this scheme is feasible and practical, since the overhead that it introduces is acceptable. We believe that many emerging (inter)networking architectures, including Information-Centric Networking (ICN) and the Internet of Things (IoT), can benefit from the adoption of our scheme in their design. The leverage of the role of NAMEs offers content owners new possibilities and allows the construction of new forms of trust relationships. Of course, as we demonstrated through our implementation, our solution can also be applicable to existing communication systems. We envision our solution being used as an alternative to "ad-hoc" solutions that try to solve the problems of Web PKI (e.g., certificate pinning), as well as, as an alternative to existing secure communication applications (e.g., PGP).

Future work in this domain includes implementation of our scheme for various kinds of name resolution systems and its incorporation into new architectures. We will also explore the possibilities of embedding our scheme in smaller devices, in order to provide NAME-based trust for the IoT. Moreover, in this work we considered that administrative domains are isolated from each other. Of course this is not always the case: there can be administrative domains within other domains or there might be administrative domains that have some form of trust relationship. These cases are an exciting field for applying contemporary cryptographic solutions that are based on (H)IBE.

Acknowledgment. This research has been co-financed by the European Union (European Social FundESF) and Greek national funds through the Operational Program "Education and Lifelong Learning" of the National Strategic Reference Framework (NSRF)Research Funding Program: Aristeia II/I-CAN.

References

1. Akinyele, J.A., Garman, C., Miers, I., Pagano, M.W., Rushanan, M., Green, M., Rubin, A.D.: Charm: a framework for rapidly prototyping cryptosystems. J. Cryptogr. Eng. **3**(2), 111–128 (2013)

2. Arends, R., Austein, R., Larson, M., Massey, D., Rose, S.: DNS security introduction and requirement. RFC 4033, IETF (2005)
3. Boneh, D., Franklin, M.: Identity-based encryption from the weil pairing. In: Kilian, J. (ed.) CRYPTO 2001. LNCS, vol. 2139, pp. 213–229. Springer, Heidelberg (2001)
4. Durumeric, Z., Kasten, J., Bailey, M., Halderman, J.A.: Analysis of the HTTPs certificate ecosystem. In: Proceedings of the 2013 Conference on Internet Measurement Conference, IMC 2013, pp. 291–304. ACM, New York (2013)
5. Green, M., Ateniese, G.: Identity-based proxy re-encryption. In: Katz, J., Yung, M. (eds.) ACNS 2007. LNCS, vol. 4521, pp. 288–306. Springer, Heidelberg (2007)
6. Hess, F.: Efficient identity based signature schemes based on pairings. In: Nyberg, K., Heys, H. (eds.) SAC 2002. LNCS, vol. 2595, pp. 310–324. Springer, Heidelberg (2003)
7. Jacobson, V., Smetters, D.K., Thornton, J.D., Plass, M.F., Briggs, N.H., Braynard, R.L.: Networking named content. In: Proceedings of the 5th International Conference on Emerging Networking Experiments and Technologies, CoNEXT 2009, pp. 1–12. ACM, New York (2009)
8. Katsaros, K.V., Fotiou, N., Vasilakos, X., Ververidis, C.N., Tsilopoulos, C., Xylomenos, G., Polyzos, G.C.: On inter-domain name resolution for information-centric networks. In: Bestak, R., Kencl, L., Li, L.E., Widmer, J., Yin, H. (eds.) NETWORKING 2012, Part I. LNCS, vol. 7289, pp. 13–26. Springer, Heidelberg (2012)
9. Lewko, A.: Tools for simulating features of composite order bilinear groups in the prime order setting. In: Pointcheval, D., Johansson, T. (eds.) EUROCRYPT 2012. LNCS, vol. 7237, pp. 318–335. Springer, Heidelberg (2012)
10. Lewko, A., Waters, B.: Unbounded HIBE and attribute-based encryption. In: Paterson, K.G. (ed.) EUROCRYPT 2011. LNCS, vol. 6632, pp. 547–567. Springer, Heidelberg (2011)
11. Rackoff, C.: On "identities", "names", "NAMES", "ROLES" and security: a Manifesto. Technical report 2011/214, IACR Cryptology ePrint Archive (2011)
12. Smart, N.: Identity-based authenticated key agreement protocol based on weil pairing. Electr. Lett. **38**, 630–632 (2002)
13. Smetters, D.K., Durfee, G.: Domain-based administration of identity-based cryptosystems for secure email and IPSEC. In: 2011 19th IEEE International Conference on Network Protocols (ICNP) (2003)
14. Zhang, X., Chang, K., Xiong, H., Wen, Y., Shi, G., Wang, G.: Towards name-based trust and security for content-centric network. In: 2011 19th IEEE International Conference on Network Protocols (ICNP), pp. 1–6 (2011)

Trust Driven Strategies for Privacy by Design

Thibaud Antignac[✉] and Daniel Le Métayer

Inria, Université de Lyon, Lyon, France
{thibaud.antignac,daniel.le-metayer}@inria.fr

Abstract. In this paper, we describe a multi-step approach to privacy by design. The main design step is the choice of the types of trust that can be accepted by the stakeholders, which is a key driver for the construction of an acceptable architecture. Architectures can be initially defined in a purely informal way and then mapped into a formal dedicated model. A tool integrating the approach can be used by designers to build and verify architectures. We apply the approach to a case study, an electronic toll pricing system, and show how different solutions can be suggested to the designer depending on different trust assumptions.

1 Introduction

The general philosophy of privacy by design is that privacy should not be treated as an afterthought but rather as a first-class requirement in the design of IT systems. In other words, designers should have privacy in mind from the start when they define the features and architecture of a system. Privacy by design will become a legal obligation in the European Union if the current draft of the General Data Protection Regulation (GDPR) [8] eventually gets adopted. However, it is one thing to impose by law the adoption of privacy by design, quite another to define precisely what it is intended to mean and to ensure that it is put into practice. In fact, privacy by design is a particularly challenging endeavour, for plenty of reasons:

- First, privacy itself is a very general principle, but it is also a very subjective notion, which evolves over time and depends very much on the cultural and technological context. Therefore, the first task in the perspective of privacy by design is to define precisely the privacy requirements of the system.
- Privacy is often (or often seems to be) in tension with other requirements, for example functional requirements, ease of use, performances or accountability.
- A wide array of privacy enhancing technologies (PETs) have been proposed during the last decades (including zero-knowledge proofs, secure multi-party computation, homomorphic encryption, etc.) Each of them provides different guarantees based on different assumptions and therefore is suitable in different contexts. As a result, it is quite complex for a software engineer to make informed choices among all these possibilities and to find the most appropriate combination of techniques to solve his own requirements.

© IFIP International Federation for Information Processing 2015
C.D. Jensen et al. (Eds.): IFIPTM 2015, IFIP AICT 454, pp. 60–75, 2015.
DOI: 10.1007/978-3-319-18491-3_5

In this context, a major challenge for the designer is to understand all the possible options and their strengths and weaknesses. On the basis of the above, we believe that the most urgent needs in this area are:

1. The availability of strategies for the search of solutions based on the different requirements of the system and the available PETs.
2. The possibility to express these solutions in a formal framework and to reason about their properties.
3. The existence of a link between the strategies and the formal framework to capitalise on the knowledge gained in the design phase to facilitate the specification and verification phases.

The last item is of prime importance especially because designers should not be expected to be experts in formal methods (or even to be ready to be confronted with them at all). Therefore, the output of the design phase, which is conducted in a non-formal environment, should be translated automatically in the formal framework. In addition, this translation should take advantage of the knowledge conveyed by the designer during the first phase because this knowledge can be exploited to set the assumptions and prove the required properties. To this respect, a key decision which has to be made during the design phase is the choice of the trust relationships between the parties: this choice is both a driving factor in the selection of architectural options and a critical assumption for the proof of properties of the solution.

In this paper, we propose an approach for the reasoned construction of architectures and we illustrate it with one aspect of privacy which is often called data minimisation. We describe the overall approach and methodology in Sect. 2 and outline *CAPRIV*, our computer assisted privacy engineering tool in Sect. 3. In Sect. 4, we apply the approach to a case study, an electronic toll pricing system. Section 5 discusses related work and Sect. 6 outlines directions for further research.

2   Trust Driven Strategies

A wide range of PETs are now available, which can provide strong privacy guarantees in a variety of contexts [6,11,17,27]. However, the take-up of privacy by design in the industry is still rather limited. This situation is partly due to legal and economic reasons, but one must also admit that no general methodology is available to help designers choosing among existing techniques and integrating them in a consistent way to meet a set of privacy requirements. The next challenge in this area is therefore to go beyond individual cases and to establish sound foundations and methodologies for privacy by design [7,34]. We advocate the idea that privacy by design should first be addressed at the architectural level because the abstraction level provided by architectures makes it easier to express the key design choices and to explore in a more systematic way the design space. In this section, we first set the stage and define the type of system and requirements considered here (Subsect. 2.1) before defining briefly our notion of architectures (Subsect. 2.2) and describing the overall strategies and criteria used for the construction of a privacy compliant architecture (Subsect. 2.3).

2.1 Context: Data Minimisation and Integrity

Data minimisation is one of the key principles of most privacy guidelines and regulations. Data minimisation stipulates that the collection and processing of personal data should always be done with respect to a particular purpose and the amount of data strictly limited to what is really necessary to achieve the purpose[1].

In practice, however, apart from cases in which the purpose can be achieved without the collection of any personal data at all, there is usually no real notion of minimality in a mathematical sense of the term. This is the case for different reasons: first, the purpose itself cannot always be defined formally and so is subject to interpretation; for example, services can sometimes be improved through the disclosure of additional personal data[2]. In addition, different requirements (functional or non functional) usually have to be met at the same time and these requirements can be in tension or conflicting with data minimisation. One common requirement which has to be taken into account is what we call "integrity" in the sequel, to describe the fact that some stakeholders may require guarantees about the correctness of the result of a computation. In fact, the tension between data minimisation and integrity is one of the delicate issues to be solved in many systems involving personal data. For example, electronic toll pricing systems [16,26,33] have to guarantee both the correctness of the computation of the fee and the limitation of the collection of location data; smart metering systems [10,20,28] also have to ensure the correct computations of the fees and the supply-demand balance of the network while limiting the collection of consumption data, etc.

The best that can be done to cope with these requirements is therefore to be able to describe them in a uniform framework and to reason about their relationships, to select the architecture that meets them all if possible or to decide whether certain assumptions could be changed (for example by introducing a trusted third party) or whether certain requirements can be relaxed.

In this paper we illustrate our approach with the two types of requirements discussed here: on the one hand, minimisation as a requirement of the data subject and, on the other hand, integrity as a requirement of both the service provider and the data subject who need guarantees about the result of a computation involving personal data. The meaning of these requirements depends on the purpose of the data collection, which is equated to the expected functionality of the system. In the sequel, we assume that this functionality Ω is expressed as the computation of a set of equations[3] as described in Table 1.

---

[1] See for example Article 5(c) of the draft of the GDPR [8].

[2] Indeed, improving the user's experience through personalisation is a common excuse for justifying the collection of large amounts of data.

[3] Which is typically the case for systems involving integrity requirements.

Table 1. Functionality language.

$$\Omega ::= \{X = T\}$$
$$T ::= X \mid F(X_1, \ldots, X_n) \mid \odot F(X)$$

The notation $\{Z\}$ is used to define a set of elements of category Z and T defines terms over (array or simple) variables $X \in Var$. Function applications are denoted $F(X_1, \ldots, X_n)$ with $F \in Fun$ and iterative function applications are denoted by $\odot F(X)$ with F the function iteratively applied to the elements of the array X (e.g. sum of the elements of X if F is equal to $+$).

As an example, electronic toll pricing allows drivers to be charged depending on their actual behavior (mileage, time, . . .). The global fee (*fee*) due to the toll service provider (*SP*) at the end of the billing period is based on the use of the road infrastructures modeled as trajectory location parts (denoted by an array *loc* metered by the on-board unit (*OBU*) of the driver's vehicle over periods of time n). The service $fee = \sum_n (F(loc_n))$ (where F stands for a pricing function) is expressed in our language as $\Omega = \{fee = \odot + (p), p = F(loc)\}$ (with p an intermediate array variable standing for the prices corresponding to *loc*).

Privacy requirements are used to express the expected properties of an architecture in terms of confidentiality and integrity. The syntax is defined in Table 2.

Table 2. Privacy requirements language.

$$\phi ::= Has_i^{all}(X) \mid Has_i^{none}(X) \mid Has_i^{one}(X)$$
$$\mid K_i(Eq) \quad \mid B_i(Eq) \qquad \mid \phi_1 \wedge \phi_2$$

$$Eq ::= T_1 \; Rel \; T_2 \qquad\qquad Rel ::= \; = \mid < \mid > \mid \leq \mid \geq$$

The subscript i stands for a component index and Eq are equations over terms T and operators Rel. $Has_i^{all}(X)$ expresses the fact that component C_i can obtain the value of X (or all the values of X in the case of an array). $Has_i^{none}(X)$ is the confidentiality property stating that C_i cannot obtain the value of X (or any element of X in the case of an array). Finally, $Has_i^{one}(X)$ expresses the fact that component C_i can obtain the value of at most one element of the array X. It should be noted that $Has_i^{all}(X)$, $Has_i^{none}(X)$, and $Has_i^{one}(X)$ properties only inform on the fact that C_i can get values for the variables but they do not bring any guarantee about the correctness of these values. Such integrity requirements can be expressed using the $K_i(Eq)$ and $B_i(Eq)$ properties for knwoledge and belief respectively. $K_i(Eq)$ means that component C_i can establish with certainty the truthfulness of Eq while $B_i(Eq)$ expresses the fact that C_i can establish with certainty or with a limited (and reasonable) amount of uncertainty this truthfulness (C_i may detect its falsehood if he can test this truthfulness for a sample).

In the example, the provider can obtain the value of the global fee ($Has_{SP}^{all}(fee)$). Moreover, we assume that the driver does not want the provider to obtain the value of its locations (loc) or intermediate prices (p). However, the reception by the provider of a sample of these values is allowed if needed for a posteriori integrity verification ($Has_{SP}^{one}(loc)$ and $Has_{SP}^{one}(p)$). Moreover, the architecture must ensure that the provider can test the correction of the computation of the prices ($B_{SP}(p = F(loc))$) and establish the correction of the aggregation of these prices ($K_{SP}(fee = \odot + (p))$)[4].

2.2 Architectures

Many definitions of architectures have been proposed in the literature. In this paper, we adopt a definition inspired by [3][5]: *The architecture of a system is the set of structures needed to reason about the system, which comprises software and hardware elements, relations among them and properties of both.* In the context of privacy, the components are typically the PETs themselves and the purpose of the architecture is their combination to achieve the privacy requirements of the system. As suggested above, an architecture is foremost an abstraction of a system and, as argued in [3], "this abstraction is essential to taming the complexity of a system". Following this principle, a set of components C_i is associated with relations describing their capabilities. These capabilities depend on the set of available PETs. For the purpose of this paper, we consider the architecture language described in [1] as detailed in Table 3.

Table 3. Privacy architecture language.

$A ::= \{R\}$	
$R ::= Has_i(X)$	$\vert\ Receive_{i,j}(\{S\}, \{X\})$
$\vert\ Compute_i(X = T)$	$\vert\ Check_i(\{Eq\})$
$\vert\ Verif_i^{Proof}(Pro)$	$\vert\ Verif_i^{Attest}(Att)$
$\vert\ Spotcheck_{i,j}(X, \{Eq\})$	$\vert\ Trust_{i,j}$
$S ::= Pro \mid Att$	$Att ::= Attest_i(\{Eq\})$
$Pro ::= Proof(\{P\})$	$P ::= Att \mid Eq$

---

[4] Other requirements would be relevant (such as the requirements concerning OBU) but we limit our example to the concerns of SP for the sake of conciseness.

[5] This definition is a generalisation (to system architectures) of the definition of software architectures proposed in [3].

The subscript j is introduced along with i to denote a component index. $Has_i(X)$ expresses the fact that variable X is an input variable located at component C_i (e.g. sensor or meter) and $Receive_{i,j}(\{S\}, \{X\})$ specifies that component C_i can receive a set of declarations $\{S\}$ and variables $\{X\}$ from component C_j. These declarations can be proofs $(Proof(\{P\})$ with $\{P\}$ being equations or attestations) and attestations $(Attest_i(\{Eq\}))$, that is to say simple declarations by a component C_i that properties $\{Eq\}$ are true. A component can also compute a variable defined by an equation $X = T$ (denoted by $Compute_i(X = T)$), check that a set of properties $\{Eq\}$ holds (denoted by $Check_i(\{Eq\})$), verify a proof received from another component (denoted by $Verif_i^{Proof}(Pro)$), verify the origin of an attestation (denoted by $Verif_i^{Attest}(Att)$), or perform a spot-check (i.e. request by a component C_j a value taken from array X and check that this value satisfies equations $\{Eq\}$, which is denoted by $Spotcheck_{i,j}(X, \{Eq\})$ with j a component index). Last but not least, trust assumptions are expressed using $Trust_{i,j}$ (meaning that component C_i trusts attestations from component C_j)[6].

The semantics $S(A)$ of an architecture A is defined as the set of states of the components C_i of A resulting from compatible traces as described in [1]. A compatible trace contains only events that are instantiations of relations (such as $Has_i(X)$, $Receive_{i,j}(\{S\}, \{X\})$, etc.) in A. The semantics $S(\phi)$ of a privacy property ϕ is defined as the set of architectures meeting ϕ. For example, $A \in S(Has^{none}(X))$ if and only if for all states $\sigma \in \mathcal{S}(A)$, the state σ_i is such that $\sigma_i(X) = \bot$, which expresses the fact that the component C_i cannot obtain the value of the variable X (or none of them in the case of an array). A sound and complete axiomatics has been defined to derive the integrity and privacy properties from the architecture. The decidability of this axiomatics depends on the reasoning power offered to the components.

An illustration of an architecture is given in Fig. 1. It relies on the relations defined previously to fulfill the functionality Ω. The OBU measures the locations loc, computes the global fee fee, and sends this latter to SP along with an attestation of integrity. SP trusts the declaration coming from OBU and verifies its authenticity. As can be seen, architectures provide an abstract, high-level view of a system. For example, we do not express at this level the particular method used by a component to verify that another component has actually attested (e.g. signed) a declaration. The objective at this stage is to be able to express and reason about the architecture rather than diving into technical details.

2.3   Design Strategies

In order to help designers finding their way among the variety of possible options, our approach is based on a succession of interaction steps. Each step consists in a question to the designer whose answer is used to trim the design space and drive the search for a suitable solution. The two key ingredients affecting the effectiveness of the process are the criteria to be used at each step and the order

---

[6] It can be noted this language is extensible with new relations to model other PETs as needed.

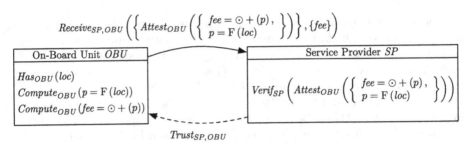

Fig. 1. Example of architecture relying on $Verif_i^{Attest}(Att)$ and $Trust_{i,j}$ primitives.

in which the questions should be asked. Based on our experience in the design of privacy preserving solutions, we propose the following strategies defined by steps 1 to 5 below. Steps 1 and 2, which have an overall effect on the possible solutions, are applied for the whole system. Then each equation of the definition of the functionality Ω is considered in turn in a bottom-up fashion[7] and Steps 3 to 5 are applied to each of them. Each choice adds a relation or a property to the architecture.

1. *Constraints:* The first question to be answered by the designer concerns the potential constraints imposed by the context or architectural choices that may have already been made by the designer. For example, the location of the input variables (e.g. sensors or meters) is often imposed by the environment and the absence of a direct communication channel between certain components may be a strong constraint. This criterion may typically have an impact on the occurrence of $Has_i(X)$, $Receive_{i,j}(\{S\},\{X\})$, or $Compute_i(X = T)$ relations for metering, communications, or computations respectively.

2. *Anonymity:* The second question is the potential anonymity requirement. When anonymity is required, it can be expressed as a relationship between components. This type of requirement has an overall effect on the possible solutions because it introduces the need to implement anonymous channels between certain components and to specify the identifying values that have to be protected.

3. *Accuracy:* The first question for each equation is the level of accuracy required for the result. If an approximate solution is acceptable, then techniques such as perturbation, rounding (on individual values), aggregation, or sampling (on sets of values) can be considered (and the functionality Ω be augmented with a new function to perform this approximation). Otherwise these techniques are ruled out.

4. *Type of Trust:* The next question for each equation is the type of trust which can be accepted by the components, which is a key driver for the construction of a solution. We distinguish three types of trust:

---

[7] Starting from input variables is more efficient because their location is usually imposed by the context and they are often personal data.

(a) *Blind trust* is the strongest form of trust: if a component C_i blindly trusts a component C_j, it assumes that C_j will always behave as expected and all its attestations $Attest_j (\{Eq\})$ will be accepted as true after verification (by $Verif_i^{Attest} (Attest_j (\{Eq\})))$. This is expressed by a relation $Trust_{i,j}$ added to the architecture. Blind trust should obviously be used parsimoniously because it leads to the weakest solutions (technically speaking), or the solutions most vulnerable to misplaced trust. However, there are very reasonable (and even unavoidable) uses of blind trust, for example on the sensors providing the input values, or on secure hardware components. As far as techniques are concerned, this type of trust only requires authentication (e.g. for C_i to check that a message has indeed been sent by C_j: because C_j is assumed to be trustworthy, the content of his message will be accepted as such). Figure 1 depicts an architecture relying on blind trust.

(b) *Verifiable trust* (a posteriori verification) also considers by default that the trusted component behaves as expected but it is not as absolute as blind trust: it provides for the possibility of a posteriori verifications that this trust is not misplaced. Two types of techniques are typically used to implement this kind of trust: commitments (for the initial, and privacy preserving, declaration of the values) and spot-checks (for the verification of sample values). In this case, the architecture includes a $Spotcheck_{i,j} (X, \{Eq\})$ relation with X the array that can be sampled and $\{Eq\}$ the equations which should be satisfied (using the sampled X). The architecture illustrated in Fig. 2 relies on verifiable trust for the computation of $p = F(loc)$.

(c) *Verified trust* (a priori verification) could be presented as a "non trust" option (or trust in the technology only) in the sense that a component C_i does not accept a statement as true if it is not able to verify it by itself (by a computation $Compute_i (X = T)$, a check $Check_i (\{Eq\})$ or the verification of a proof $Verif_i^{Proof} (Proof (\{P\})))$. Useful techniques to provide this level of guarantees include zero knowledge proofs, secure multi-party computations and homomorphic encryptions. The example in Fig. 2 relies on verified trust for the computation of $fee = \odot + (p)$ (through a homomorphic scheme relying on a hash function H).

5. *Assessment:* The last, but not least, question has to do with the preferences (e.g. in terms of performances, usability, or costs) that may lead to the rejection of certain solutions and with the detection of inconsistencies which may lead to the addition of new elements (e.g. a missing communication). For example, the limited computing power of a component, the low throughput of a communication channel, or the extra burden on the users can go against the use of certain $Receive_{i,j} (\{S\}, \{X\})$, $Compute_i (X = T)$, or $Verif_i^{Proof} (Pro)$ relations. This step is the counterpart of Step 1 (which concerns the a priori knowledge of the designer before the start of the design procedure): it leads to the filtering of the potential options resulting from the application of the previous steps of the procedure.

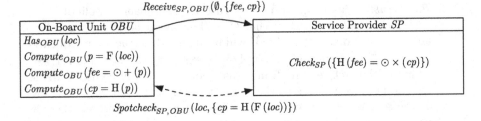

$Receive_{SP,OBU}(\emptyset, \{fee, cp\})$

On-Board Unit OBU	Service Provider SP
$Has_{OBU}(loc)$	
$Compute_{OBU}(p = \mathrm{F}(loc))$	$Check_{SP}(\{\mathrm{H}(fee) = \odot \times (cp)\})$
$Compute_{OBU}(fee = \odot + (p))$	
$Compute_{OBU}(cp = \mathrm{H}(p))$	

$Spotcheck_{SP,OBU}(loc, \{cp = \mathrm{H}(\mathrm{F}(loc))\})$

Fig. 2. Simplified *PrETP* electronic toll pricing architecture relying on verifiable trust for the computation of F and on verified trust for $\odot+$ (inspired by [2]).

These strategies guide the designer step-by-step through a succession of questions until an acceptable architecture is derived. Such architectures can be used in a purely informal way and represented as annotated graphs manipulated by designers who get an intuitive understanding of their meaning. However, this does not give strong guarantees that the obtained architectures really satisfy the privacy and integrity requirements of the system. One way to strengthen these guarantees is to rely on the formal framework detailed in [1].

This systematic design process is supported by a tool which is presented in the next section. This tool guides the designer and seamlessly builds a formal model of the architecture which can then be verified.

3   *CAPRIV* Tool

The *CAPRIV* computer aided privacy engineering tool has been developed to help non-expert designers to build architectures by following the strategies presented in this paper and to verify that the privacy requirements are met according to the formal model detailed in [1]. The interface and the back-end have been themselves developed with privacy by design in mind. For example, two components are not linked by any direct communication channel unless explicitly declared by the designer. The design of the tool makes it possible to hide the formal aspects of the model to the designer who does not want to be exposed to mathematical notations. This is mainly achieved through the use of a graphical user interface (GUI) and natural language statements. *CAPRIV* implements an iterative design procedure allowing the designer to come back to previous steps at any time. This section presents a functional description of the tool, followed by a brief overview of its implementation.

Functional Description. The GUI is divided into two parts: a Model and a View. The Model part is composed of three panes: Specify, Design, and Verify. The View part is composed of three other panes: Specification, Architecture, and Proofs. The View part shows the results of the interactions of the designer with the Model part.

Specification. The first task of the designer is to declare all the elements (components, variables, and functions) that will be used during the design process. Different properties of these elements, such as the fact that a variable is an array or a function is not invertible, can be selected throughout the process. The equations defining the functionality Ω are then declared (using these elements). Finally, the confidentiality and integrity requirements ϕ are defined based on the components and on the functionality. The current version of *CAPRIV* only supports simple equations (without function application nesting). This limitation can be circumvented by decomposing the functionality equations in simpler subequations.

Design. The next step for the designer is to build an architecture A meeting the requirements. To this aim, *CAPRIV* implements a design cycle following the strategies presented in Sect. 2.3. The designer must define the pre-existing constraints before choosing, for each equation in the functionality of the system, a location for the computation and a type of trust. Finally, the designer can add the missing communication links to make the architecture consistent. The Design panel is shown in Fig. 3.

Verification. If he chooses to do so, the designer can then verify whether the obtained architecture meets the requirements. The first verification concerns the consistency of the architecture (for example, the fact that the arguments

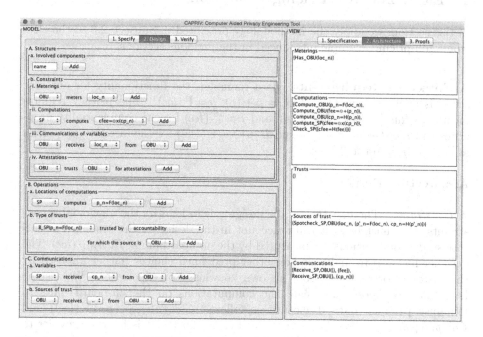

Fig. 3. Design view in *CAPRIV* at the end of the design process leading to the architecture depicted in Fig. 2.

of a computation must themselves be produced in one way or another and be available to the component performing the computation). The designer can then formally verify the satisfaction of the confidentiality and integrity requirements.

Implementation. Some of the verification features rely on external theorem provers and *CAPRIV* acts as a frontend interface for the *Why3* framework [4]. *Why3* is a platform in which theories can be expressed in an *ML*-flavored language. Standard libraries are provided to easily model structures such as rings and arrays for instance. *Why3* relies itself on external provers such as *Alt-Ergo* [5] or *Z3* [23] to prove theorems. *CAPRIV* automatically generates theories corresponding to the architecture (as axioms and conjectures to be proven), then calls *Why3*, and finally handles its answer.

When the expected property cannot be proved, an advanced designer can choose to use the *Why3* GUI offering an interactive theorem proving environment in which specific provers can be called with the possibility to apply different solving strategies. An expert designer can even exploit the detailed configuration or modify the theories — but these skills are not expected for a standard use of *CAPRIV*. This choice to rely on external tools for some parts of the verification shows that it is possible to integrate privacy by design methodologies with existing formal verification tools.

4   Electronic Toll Pricing Case Study

In this section, we apply the methodology presented in Subsect. 2.3 to the electronic toll pricing example introduced in the previous sections.

Architecture Requirements. As a reminder, the functionality for our case study is expressed by $\Omega = \{fee = \odot + (p), p = \mathrm{F}\,(loc)\}$. The privacy requirements are $Has_{SP}^{one}\,(loc)$, $Has_{SP}^{one}\,(p)$, and $Has_{SP}^{all}\,(fee)$ for the confidentiality properties and $K_{SP}\,(fee = \odot + (p))$ and $B_{SP}\,(p = \mathrm{F}\,(loc))$ for the integrity properties as defined in Subsect. 2.1.

Architecture Design

1. Constraints. The first task of the designer is to identify the unavoidable constraints that must be taken into account in the design of the system. For this case study, the locations are measured by the on-board units: $Has_{OBU}\,(loc)$. The designer has also to make explicit other predefined choices (either imposed by the customer or resulting from his own knowledge or experience). We assume here that he chooses to locate the computations on the on-board units to minimise personal data disclosure as follows: $Compute_{OBU}\,(p = \mathrm{F}\,(loc))$ and $Compute_{OBU}\,(fee = \odot + (p))$. Another obvious constraint is for the provider to get the fee: $Receive_{SP,OBU}\,(\emptyset, \{fee\})$.

2/3. Anonymity and Accuracy. No anonymity channel is required by the designer for this architecture and no approximation technique can be applied because the fee has to be computed accurately.

4. Type of Trust. The key step in the process is the choice of the types of trust accepted by the parties for each part of the functionality (the computation of individual prices and their sum). We assume that verifiable trust is acceptable for the service provider (which is consistent with the use of the privacy requirement B_{SP} defined previously). Pricing will therefore be checked a posteriori by comparing a sample of the actual locations *loc* with the corresponding commitments *cp* (using a one-way homomorphic hash function H) sent by the driver (in fact his *OBU*): $Spotcheck_{SP,OBU}(loc, \{cp = \mathrm{H}(\mathrm{F}(loc))\})$ and $Receive_{SP,OBU}(\emptyset, \{cp\})$. The homomorphism property of the function H (such that $\mathrm{H}(\Sigma_{0 \le i \le n}(T_i)) = \Pi_{0 \le i \le n}(\mathrm{H}(T_i))$ for all terms T_i) enables the provider to check the integrity property for the computation of $fee = \odot + (p)$ by verifying that the product of the committed prices is equal to the hashed fee as follows: $Check_{SP}(\{\mathrm{H}(fee) = \odot \times (cp)\})$.

5. Assessment. The last tasks for the designer are to check the consistency of the architecture and, if necessary, to add the missing elements to get a consistent architecture. In our example, it is necessary to add $Compute_{OBU}(cp = \mathrm{H}(p))$ to ensure that a component is in charge of computing the *cp* variables.

Figure 3 illustrates the design view of *CAPRIV* when the choices made previously have been input. Figure 2 pictures the architecture (which is a simplified version of [2]) obtained at the end of the design process. This latter is expressed in the formal language detailed in [1].

Architecture Verification. The designer can then formally verify that the architecture meets the requirements. This verification can be made (either automatically or interactively) using the *CAPRIV* tool sketched in Sect. 3 which implements the axiomatics presented in [1].

The solution designed here relies on heavy on-board units able to perform the billing computations. Moreover, it assumes a direct link between the on-board unit and the provider: the driver has to trust the on-board unit not to disclose too much data to the provider. This issue could be solved by adding a proxy under the control of the driver which would filter the communications between *SP* and *OBU*. This alternative can be expressed in the same framework by adding another component but space considerations prevent us from presenting it here.

5   Related Work

Several authors [12,17,19,24,30] have already pointed out the complexity of "privacy engineering" as well as the "richness of the data space" [12] calling for the development of more general and systematic methodologies for privacy by design. As far as privacy mechanisms are concerned, [17,21] points out the complexity of their implementation and the large number of options that designers have to face. To address this issue and favor the adoption of these tools, [17] proposes a number of guidelines for the design of compilers for secure computation and zero-knowledge proofs whereas [9] provides a language and a compiler to perform computations on private data by synthesising zero-knowledge protocols. In a different context (designing information systems for the cloud), [22] also proposes implementation techniques to make it easier for developers to take into account privacy and security requirements. Finally, [31] proposes a development method for security protocols allowing to derive a protocol by refinement. However, this method does not offer decision support for the designer to choose among different possibilities as we do.

The recent proposal [18] also emphasizes the importance of architectures for privacy by design. Reference [18] proposes a design methodology for privacy (inspired by [3]) based on tactics for privacy quality attributes (such as minimisation, enforcement or accountability) and privacy patterns (such as data confinement, isolation or Hippocratic management). The work described in [18] is complementary to the approach presented here: [18] does not consider formal aspects while this paper does not address the tactics for privacy by design.

Design patterns are used in [14] to define eight privacy strategies[8] called respectively: Minimise, Hide, Separate, Aggregate, Inform, Control, Enforce and Demonstrate. Other authors put forward pattern-based approaches: [13] proposes a language for privacy patterns allowing for a designer to choose relevant PETs; [29] describes a solution for online interactions; at a higher level, [25] proposes a decision support tool based on design patterns to help software engineers to take into account privacy guidelines in the early stage of development.

All the aforementioned work is very helpful and paves the way for a wider adoption of privacy by design. We believe however that there is still a gap between techniques or methods (such as design patterns or tactics) which are described informally at a very high abstraction level and formal models of privacy that usually address precise technical issues or specific requirements (such as protocols dedicated to smart metering, electronic toll pricing, or electric vehicle charging). The former are intended as guidelines for software designers and engineers but do not provide any formal guarantees; the latter provide formal guarantees but they are very specific and can hardly be used by software engineers to build a new product. Moreover, they are generic frameworks and they do not include any specific privacy by design methodology.

Filling this gap is precisely the objective of this paper. Previous work on this very topic is scarce. One exception is the framework introduced in [19] which defines the meaning of the available operations in a (trace-based) operational semantics and proposes an inference system to derive properties from architectures. Even though the goal of [19] is to deal with architectures, it remains at a lower level of abstraction than the framework sketched here and it can hardly

---

[8] Strategies are defined as follows in [14]: "A design strategy describes a fundamental approach to achieve a certain design goal. It has certain properties that allow it to be distinguished from other (fundamental) approaches that achieve the same goal".

be extended to other privacy mechanisms. In addition, it is not associated with design strategies as proposed in Sect. 2 of this paper. Complementary work by the authors are [1] which presents the formal framework (language of architectures and requirements, semantics, and axiomatics) and illustrates it with a smart metering example, and [32] which completes the formal framework with a link between architectures and actual implementations (as protocols). Any protocol consistent with an architecture would then meet the properties of the architecture as defined in this paper.

6   Conclusion

Considering that there is usually no absolute notion of personal data minimality, the only solution is to specify the requirements of the parties and try to find a solution to meet them all or to iterate otherwise. For example, in the electronic toll pricing case study discussed in Sect. 4, a solution has been found in which the only personal data disclosed to the provider is the fee to be paid by the driver (which can harldy be avoided) and occasionally (when a spot-check is initiated) the position of the vehicle. Other solutions can be found which do not involve spot-checks but rely on more expensive secure on-board units.

In addition to its interest in the design phase, the use of the methodology proposed here provides a key benefit in terms of accountability which will become an obligation with the new GDPR [8]. Accountability is defined in the Article 22 as the following obligation for data collectors: "The controller shall adopt appropriate policies and implement appropriate and demonstrable technical and organisational measures to ensure and be able to demonstrate in a transparent manner that the processing of personal data is performed in compliance with this Regulation...". A significant byproduct of the approach described in this paper is to provide to data collectors a documented and rigorous justification of the design choices, which will become a key asset for the implementation of their accountability requirements.

Another benefit of the approach presented here is that designers do not have to opt from the outset for a formal framework. Rather, they can first explore the design space based on initial inputs provided in a non formal language and analyse the suggested architectures based on their graphical representations. They can content themselves with this step or wish to go beyond and try to prove other properties of their architectures. In the latter case, depending on their level and type of expertise, they can either rely on an automatic verification mode or choose among the verification tools integrated within the design environment.

For the reasons discussed in Sect. 2, the approach described in this paper focuses on architectures. An extension of this work is the integration of other types of trust such as the trust in pairs, in particular trust conditional on the endorsement of a declaration by a minimal number (or ratio) of pairs. From an academic perspective, another avenue for further research is the use of the formal framework presented here to provide a classification of solutions presented in the literature (in the style of [15]) based on formal criteria.

Acknowledgement. This work was partially funded by the European project PRIPARE/FP7-ICT-2013-1.5, the ANR project BIOPRIV, and the Inria Project Lab CAPPRIS (Collaborative Action on the Protection of Privacy Rights in the Information Society).

References

1. Antignac, T., Le Métayer, D.: Privacy architectures: reasoning about data minimisation and integrity. In: Mauw, S., Jensen, C.D. (eds.) STM 2014. LNCS, vol. 8743, pp. 17–32. Springer, Heidelberg (2014)
2. Balasch, J., Rial, A., Troncoso, C., Geuens, C.: PrETP: privacy-preserving electronic toll pricing. In: Proceedings of the 19th USENIX Security Symposium, Washington, DC, August 2010, pp. 63–78 (2010)
3. Bass, L., Clements, P., Kazman, R.: Software Architecture in Practice. SEI series in Software Engineering, 3rd edn. Addison-Wesley, Reading (2012)
4. Bobot, F., Filliâtre, J.c., Marché, C., Paskevich, A.: Why3: shepherd your herd of provers. In: Workshop on Intermediate Veri Cation Languages (2011)
5. Conchon, S., Contejean, E.: The Alt-Ergo automatic theorem prover (2008). http://alt-ergo.lri.fr/
6. Deswarte, Y., Aguilar Melchor, C.: Current and future privacy enhancing technologies for the internet. Ann. Des Télécommun. **61**(3–4), 399–417 (2006)
7. Diaz, C., Kosta, E., Dekeyser, H., Kohlweiss, M., Girma, N.: Privacy preserving electronic petitions. Identity Inf. Soc. **1**(1), 203–209 (2009)
8. European Parliament: general data protection regulation, ordinary legislative procedure: first reading, March 2014
9. Fournet, C., Kohlweiss, M., Danezis, G., Luo, Z.: Zql: a compiler for privacy-preserving data processing. In: Proceedings of the 22Nd USENIX Conference on Security, SEC 2013, pp. 163–178. USENIX Association, Berkeley (2013)
10. Garcia, F.D., Jacobs, B.: Privacy-friendly energy-metering via homomorphic encryption. In: Cuellar, J., Lopez, J., Barthe, G., Pretschner, A. (eds.) STM 2010. LNCS, vol. 6710, pp. 226–238. Springer, Heidelberg (2011)
11. Goldberg, I.: Privacy enhancing technologies for the internet III: ten years later. In: Digital Privacy: Theory, Technologies, and Practices, pp. 3–18. Auerbach Publications (2007)
12. Gürses, S., Troncoso, C., Diaz, C.: Engineering privacy by design. In: Presented at the Computers, Privacy and Data Protection Conference (2011)
13. Hafiz, M.: Pattern language for developing privacy enhancing technologies. Softw. Pract. Exp. **43**(7), 769–787 (2010)
14. Hoepman, J.H.: Privacy design strategies. In: Cuppens-Boulahia, N., Cuppens, F., Jajodia, S., Abou El Kalam, A., Sans, T. (eds.) SEC 2014. IFIP AICT, vol. 428, pp. 446–459. Springer, Heidelberg (2014)
15. Jawurek, M., Kerschbaum, F., Danezis, G.: Privacy technologies for smart grids - a survey of options. Technical report MSR-TR-2012-119, Microsoft, November 2012
16. de Jonge, W., Jacobs, B.: Privacy-friendly electronic traffic pricing via commits. In: Degano, P., Guttman, J., Martinelli, F. (eds.) FAST 2008. LNCS, vol. 5491, pp. 143–161. Springer, Heidelberg (2009)
17. Kerschbaum, F.: Privacy-preserving computation (position paper). In: Presented at the Annual Privacy Forum Conference (2012)
18. Kung, A.: PEARs: privacy enhancing architectures. In: Preneel, B., Ikonomou, D. (eds.) APF 2014. LNCS, vol. 8450, pp. 18–29. Springer, Heidelberg (2014)

19. Le Métayer, D.: Privacy by design: a formal framework for the analysis of architectural choices. In: Proceedings of the Third ACM Conference on Data and Application Security and Privacy, CODASPY 2013, pp. 95–104. ACM, New York (2013)
20. LeMay, M., Gross, G., Gunter, C.A., Garg, S.: Unified architecture for large-scale attested metering. In: 40th annual Hawaii International Conference on System Sciences (HICSS 2007), pp. 115–124, January 2007
21. Maffei, M., Pecina, K., Reinert, M.: Security and privacy by declarative design. In: 2013 IEEE 26th Computer Security Foundations Symposium (CSF), pp. 81–96 (2013)
22. Manousakis, V., Kalloniatis, C., Kavakli, E., Gritzalis, S.: Privacy in the cloud: bridging the gap between design and implementation. In: Franch, X., Soffer, P. (eds.) CAiSE Workshops 2013. LNBIP, vol. 148, pp. 455–465. Springer, Heidelberg (2013)
23. de Moura, L., Bjørner, N.S.: Z3: an efficient SMT solver. In: Ramakrishnan, C.R., Rehof, J. (eds.) TACAS 2008. LNCS, vol. 4963, pp. 337–340. Springer, Heidelberg (2008)
24. Mulligan, D.K., King, J.: Bridging the gap between privacy and design. Univ. Pa. J. Const. Law 14(4), 989–1034 (2012)
25. Pearson, S., Benameur, A.: A decision support system for design for privacy. In: Fischer-Hübner, S., Duquenoy, P., Hansen, M., Leenes, R., Zhang, G. (eds.) Privacy and Identity Management for Life. IFIP AICT, vol. 352, pp. 283–296. Springer, Heidelberg (2011)
26. Popa, R.A., Balakrishnan, H., Blumberg, A.J.: VPriv: protecting privacy in location-based vehicular services. In: Proceedings of the 18th USENIX Security Symposium, Montreal, Canada, August 2009, pp. 335–350 (2009)
27. Rezgui, A., Bouguettaya, A., Eltoweissy, M.Y.: Privacy on the web: facts, challenges, and solutions. IEEE Secur. Priv. 1(6), 40–49 (2003)
28. Rial, A., Danezis, G.: Privacy-Preserving smart metering. Technical report MSR-TR-2010-150, Microsoft Research, November 2010
29. Romanosky, S., Acquisti, A., Hong, J., Cranor, L.F., Friedman, B.: Privacy patterns for online interactions. In: Proceedings of the 2006 Conference on Pattern Languages of Programs, PLoP 2006. pp. 12:1–12:9. ACM, New York (2006)
30. Spiekermann, S., Cranor, L.F.: Engineering privacy. IEEE Trans. Softw. Eng. 35(1), 67–82 (2009)
31. Sprenger, C., Basin, D.: Developing security protocols by refinement. In: Proceedings of the 17th ACM Conference on Computer and Communications Security, CCS 2010, pp. 361–374. ACM, New York (2010)
32. Ta, V.T., Antignac, T.: Privacy by design: on the conformance between protocols and architecture. In: Cuppens, F., Garcia-Alfaro, J., Zincir Heywood, N., Fong, P.W.L. (eds.) FPS 2014. LNCS, vol. 8930. Springer, Heidelberg (2015)
33. Troncoso, C., Danezis, G., Kosta, E., Preneel, B.: Pripayd: privacy friendly pay-as-you-drive insurance. In: Ning, P., Yu, T. (eds.) Proceedings of the 2007 ACM Workshop on Privacy in the Electronic Society, WPES 2007, pp. 99–107. ACM, New York (2007)
34. Tschantz, M.C., Wing, J.M.: Formal methods for privacy. In: Cavalcanti, A., Dams, D.R. (eds.) FM 2009. LNCS, vol. 5850, pp. 1–15. Springer, Heidelberg (2009)

Lightweight Practical Private One-Way Anonymous Messaging

Anirban Basu[1]([✉]), Juan Camilo Corena[1], Jaideep Vaidya[2], Jon Crowcroft[3], Shinsaku Kiyomoto[1], Stephen Marsh[4], Yung Shin Van Der Sype[5], and Toru Nakamura[1]

[1] KDDI R&D Laboratories, Fujimino, Japan
{basu,corena,kiyomoto,tr-nakamura}@kddilabs.jp
[2] Rutgers, The State University of New Jersey, New Brunswick, USA
jsvaidya@rutgers.edu
[3] University of Cambridge, Cambridge, UK
jon.crowcroft@cl.cam.ac.uk
[4] University of Ontario Institute of Technology, Oshawa, Canada
stephen.marsh@uoit.ca
[5] KU Leuven, Leuven, Belgium
yungshin.vandersype@law.kuleuven.be

Abstract. Opinions from people, evident in surveys and microblogging, for instance, may have bias or low user participation due to legitimate concerns about privacy and anonymity. To provide sender (the participant) anonymity, the identity of the message sender must be hidden from the message recipient (the opinion collector) and the contents of the actual message hidden from any intermediate actors (such as, routers) that may be responsible for relaying the message. We propose a novel one-way message routing scheme based on probabilistic forwarding that guarantees message privacy and sender anonymity through cryptographic means; utilising an additively homomorphic public-key cryptosystem along with a symmetric cipher. Our scheme involves intermediate relays and can work with either a centralised or a decentralised registry that helps with connecting the relays to each other. In addition to theoretical analysis, we demonstrate a real-world prototype built with HTML5 technologies and deployed on a public cloud environment. The prototype allows anonymous messaging over HTTP(S), and has been run inside HTML5 browsers on mobile application environments with no configurations at the network level. While we leave constructing the reverse path as future work, the proposal contained in this paper complete and has practical applications in anonymous surveys and microblogging.

Keywords: Privacy · Anonymity · Message · Routing · Http · Cloud

J. C. Corena—The contributions of Juan Camilo Corena to this paper represent his work during his time at KDDI R&D; and are not related in any way to his work with his current employer – Google Inc.

1   Introduction

The art of providing online anonymity has been popular with the use of proxies to avoid revealing the actual message sender to the recipient. Through the principles of Chaum mixes [1] (and other mix networks based on that), the identities of senders are delinked from the actual messages through a mixing process. Secret sharing through Dining Cryptographers networks [2] also provides sender and recipient anonymity. Onion routing [3] ensures that encrypted messages are relayed through a pre-determined path of intermediate hops such that the actual senders cannot be identified. Probabilistic forwarding (e.g., Crowds [4]) also delinks messages from their actual senders without a preset forwarding path.

The Pfitzmann and Hansen terminology [5] defines three types of anonymity in terms of unlinkability as: (a) sender anonymity, (b) recipient anonymity and (c) relationship anonymity. Sender anonymity means that a particular message is not linkable to a sender, and a particular sender cannot be linked to any message. Likewise, recipient anonymity means that a recipient and one or more messages are unlinkable. Relationship anonymity, a weaker construct, underscores that it is impossible to trace who communicates with whom. This is implied by either sender anonymity or recipient anonymity or both. The authors also define unobservability in terms of undetectability as: (a) sender unobservability, (b) recipient unobservability and (c) relationship unobservability. Unobservability means that it is impossible to detect who sends (sender unobservability) or who recieves (recipient unobservability) or that a certain set of senders and recipients are at all communicating (relationship unobservability). Unobservability is expressed in terms of undetectability, which is established through indistinguishability of messages. This means that the messages sent out or received are indiscernible from random noise. The Pfitzmann and Hansen terminology states that unobservability implies anonymity. Furthermore, similar to relationship anonymity, sender and recipient unobservability both imply relationship unobservability.

In this paper, we propose a novel one-way anonymous message routing protocol, which guarantees the privacy of the messages and the anonymity of the sender through fundamentals of public key cryptography with homomorphic properties. Our proposed scheme is usable in scenarios such as anonymous microblogging and anonymous surveys. We present a practical HTML5 cloud-deployed prototype, which piggybacks messages over HTTP(S), thus requiring no configurations at the network level and making it easy to run on mobile devices. We provide a theoretical analysis of the anonymity guarantees in our protocol as well as performance results of our prototype. The proposed protocol is pertinent to systems where the sender's identity and the message itself require protection, not only from external attackers but also from the recipient.

From a legal perspective, the one-way anonymous routing system will fall under the substantive protection of the national applicable law. As the system may typically route personal data globally, the question arises whether the strict EU legal framework might hinder the practical usability of the system for initially non-EU related processing operations. Article 25 of Directive 95/46/EC provides that the transfer of personal data outside the EU is limited to third countries with an adequate level of protection. Thus, if the routing is considered as a data transfer, EU data protection law could potentially bring an additional set of complex data protection requirements to ensure this adequate level of protection. Yet, it is pointed out that the transit or simple routing of data is not the same as the transfer of the data. Consequently the mere routing of data through the one-way anonymous routing system does not establish a data transfer under EU law[1]. Nevertheless, it is still possible that EU law is applicable in cases when, e.g., the personal data of EU citizens is processed, the controller is established in a EU Member States.

2   Related Work

Research in the last three decades has made considerable advancements in facilitating private and anonymous communication over the Internet. Anonymous communication systems can be broadly classified into two categories. (1) *High-latency systems* provide strong anonymity but are only suitable for applications that are tolerant of the rather long delays in end-to-end message delivery. (2) *Low-latency systems* offer better performance and can be used with interactive bi-directional communication, such as Web browsing. Analogous to the nature of packet transport over UDP and TCP, high-latency and low-latency systems are sometimes referred to as *message-based* and *connection-based* systems respectively. Apart from these two systems, anonymous communication have been modelled as multiparty computation such as the Dining Cryptographer Networks [2] and secret sharing schemes [6].

High-latency message-based systems: David Chaum introduced the idea of a *mix* [1] – a building block in several high-latency anonymous communication systems. The mix is characterised by the grouping of several encrypted input messages into a batch and then forwarding, after decryption, some or all messages in the batch. This necessitates that the public key of the mixing node be known by the senders. The fact that the mix node decrypts messages does not jeopardise privacy or secrecy of messages because each message could be encrypted further with the public key of its intended recipient. The original Chaum mix outputted messages in lexicographical order while more recent schemes output messages in random order [7,8]. Mix networks address the problem of a single point-of-failure of the original Chaum mix by making messages pass through an ordered sequence of mixes that constitute a path. The paths are typically either *free routes* or *mix cascades*.

Low-latency connection-based systems: Work on low-latency anonymisation dates back to traffic redirection through a centralised and trusted proxy, which hides the IP address of the actual source host from the destination. This concept is used

---

[1] UK Information Commissioner Office, "The eight data protection principle and international data transfers", 2010, http://ico.org.uk/for_organisations/guidance_index/ ~/media/documents/library/Data_Protection/Detailed_specialist_guides/internatio nal_transfers_legal_guidance_v4_290410.ashx, 1.3.2.

by the commercial Anonymizer service. Unlike mixes, a proxy forwards all incoming traffic immediately without any packet reordering. The proxy is trusted not to reveal information about original senders. Onion routing [3,9,10] utilises traffic redirection through a static set of pre-determined onion routers, each of which maintains cryptographic keys of one upstream and one downstream router. A message sent through onion routing nodes has its layers of encryption are peeled off until it is sent off to the final recipient. To cater for performance, public key cryptography is only used to establish an encrypted circuit, while faster symmetric encryption is used to transfer the actual data. Churn in onion routing nodes limits the scalability of the protocol. Onion routing has been shown [11] to be detrimental to sender or recipient anonymity if either the first or the last router is compromised. Tor [12] represents the current state-of-the-art in the evolution of onion routing. Crowds [4] and AP3 [13] make use of probabilistic forwarding through a randomly established path while the response from the recipient is relayed back to the sender using the same already established path. Denoting the total number of relay nodes by N, the number of collaborating malicious nodes by C and the forwarding probability at each node as p_f, the Crowds protocol defined a property called *probable innocence*, which means that the first collaborating malicious node's predecessor is no more likely to be the true sender of that message than not if $N \geq \frac{p_f(C+1)}{p_f-1/2}$. Tarzan [14] sends messages through a dynamically created encrypted tunnel through multiple hops in a peer-to-peer network, adding overhead costs of creating the tunnel. Similar to Tarzan, MorphMix [15] is a peer-to-peer low-latency anonymity system where any node in the network relay traffic for any other node.

3   Anonymous Message Routing

The crux of protecting the identity of any node from being traced as the sender is to ensure that an egress encrypted message is always different from an ingress encrypted message and yet both are of the same size, see Fig. 1. This implies that genuinely different messages are indistinguishable from those that look different only in the encrypted domain. Neither the sender nor any intermediate node should be able to decrypt the messages in any identifiable form. Thus, even the sender Alice, herself, is unable to identify her own message if it is forwarded back to her because there is no characteristic of the message (e.g., message signature) that remains unchanged in the multi-hop forwarding process. This *unlinkability* provides *deniability* to the sender: if Alice is to deny sending a message then there is no way to prove otherwise.

Throughout the remainder of this paper, it is assumed that all messages sent out in the network are of the same size. Messages of varying sizes should be split, padded and sequenced if necessary for re-construction. It is also assumed that nodes participating in the message relay network intermittently send out random messages containing just noise of the same size as the actual messages. The recipient will be able to filter the noise from the actual messages upon decrypting. We now briefly introduce the notion of *homomorphic encryption* before describing how we use it to devise unlinkability.

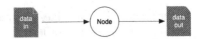

Fig. 1. The incoming and the outgoing encrypted messages to and from a node look completely different, offering no linkability.

Homomorphic encryption – a brief primer: Homomorphic encryption allows computing over encrypted data without requiring the knowledge of either the actual data or any results produced through the computation. Depending on the type of computational operations supported, homomorphic cryptosystems are classified as: (1) additive, (2) multiplicative, (3) somewhat homomorphic (e.g., allowing a number of additions and one multiplication), and (4) fully homomorphic. Denoting the encryption of a plaintext message m as $\mathcal{E}(m)$, in the generalised case of fully-homomorphic encryption, for any function f in the plaintext domain there exists a function g in the ciphertext domain, such that $\mathcal{E}(f(m_1, \ldots, m_n)) \equiv g(\mathcal{E}(m_1), \ldots, \mathcal{E}(m_n))$. Fully homomorphic schemes [16] are mathematically sound in terms of security but their computational requirements often make them unfeasible for practical applications. The Paillier public-key cryptosystem [17], and its variant, the Damgård-Jurik cryptosystem [18], have practical implementations and both exhibit only additively homomorphic properties: the encryption of the sum of two plaintext messages m_1 and m_2 is the modular product of their individual ciphertexts, i.e., $\mathcal{E}(m_1 + m_2) = \mathcal{E}(m_1) \cdot \mathcal{E}(m_2)$); and the encryption of the product of one plaintext message m_1 and another plaintext multiplicand π is the modular exponentiation of the ciphertext of m_1 with π as the exponent, i.e., $\mathcal{E}(m_1 \cdot \pi) = \mathcal{E}(m_1)^\pi$.

3.1 Unlinkable Message Forwarding

Any relay node n_i, connected to a centralised or distributed node inter-connectivity registry, can forward messages on behalf of another node. We describe how a relay node can perform unlinkable message forwarding of short messages as well as arbitrary length messages.

Note that *short* messages are those that fit within the plaintext key space of the homomorphic cryptosystem that is used while messages that do not fit are termed as *long* messages. It is possible to break long messages into multiple short messages, each fitting into the plaintext key space of the homomorphic cryptosystem. This will necessitate that multiple homomorphic operations be run over every part of the long message. To reduce the number of computationally expensive homomorphic operations, symmetric encryption can be used to encrypt longer messages.

The length of the messages plays a vital role in their indistinguishability. The implementation of our proposed protocol should use the message length for all messages, breaking down the large messages if necessary and allowing for re-construction at the recipient's end. If the implementation chooses a message length that fits within the plaintext space of the homomorphic cryptosystem then the message forwarding protocol does not need to use symmetric encryption, thus avoiding the limitation on the number of forwarding hops that we describe below.

(a) The encrypted header and actual data part of a message that is forwarded on by nodes.

(b) Inside the 2048-bits Paillier encrypted header associated with a 128-bit AES encrypted message.

Fig. 2. Homomorphic headers and parameters of the symmetric cipher

Unlinkability in Short Messages Through Homomorphic Encryption: Given a plaintext message m to be sent to a recipient with an additively homomorphic cryptosystem whose encryption function is denoted by $\mathcal{E}()$, we have an identity equation $\mathcal{E}(m)_{n_{i+1}} = \mathcal{E}(m)_{n_i} \cdot \mathcal{E}(0)$. Thus, any ingress ciphertext $\mathcal{E}(m)_{n_i}$ is transformed by the node n_i into a completely different egress ciphertext $\mathcal{E}(m)_{n_{i+1}}$ while the underlying contents of the message m remains unchanged. The final recipient can decrypt the message m from the ciphertext sent by a relay node because it possesses the equivalent private key for the public key used in the homomorphic encryption. The main limitation of this approach is that m must be contained within the plaintext domain of the additively homomorphic cryptosystem. Thus, with a 2048-bits Paillier cryptosystem, the maximum size of the message is 256 bytes. Even if it is possible to encrypt an arbitrary length message by breaking it up into small blocks (where each block fits into the plaintext domain of the cryptosystem), the encryption function of an additively homomorphic cipher is relatively slow in comparison with an equivalent strength symmetric cipher.

Unlinkability in Long Messages with Symmetric and Homomorphic Encryption: Arbitrary length messages can be encrypted by any symmetric block cipher or stream cipher. The general idea is to (re-)encrypt the ciphertext at each relay node, so that the ingress message and the egress message look different but are of the same size. Since the ingress message at any forwarding node is already encrypted, the node simply needs to encrypt it again with a random symmetric cipher key. This key and any other relevant parameters are then added to a homomorphically encrypted header, where the size of the header also remains the same. The generalised representation of the message and its headers is shown in Fig. 2(a). The size of the header, but not the actual message, is limited by the plaintext size of the homomorphic cryptosystem.

Let the size of the symmetric key be denoted as $|k|$ and that of the other relevant parameters (e.g., initialisation vector in a block cipher) as $|p|$ while $k\|p$ represents their bitwise concatenation, which is of size $|k| + |p|$. All relay nodes use same length keys and parameters. Assume that the encrypted header

---

Algorithm 1. Forwarding algorithm with homomorphic obfuscation and symmetric message encryption at relay node n_i.

Require: Additively homomorphic encryption function, $\mathcal{E}$, for the final message recipient R.

Require: Symmetric encryption function $\mathbb{E}$.

Require: Ingress encrypted message $\epsilon(m)_{n_i}$ from node n_{i-1}.

1: **if** $|\epsilon(m)_{n_i}| \leq$ the the ciphertext space of $\mathcal{E}$ **then**
2:     $\mathcal{E}(m)_{n_i} \leftarrow \epsilon(m)$.
3:     Compute ciphertext $\mathcal{E}(m)_{n_{i+1}} \leftarrow \mathcal{E}(m)_{n_i} \cdot \mathcal{E}(0)$.
4:     Egress message $\epsilon(m)_{n_{i+1}} \leftarrow \mathcal{E}(m)_{n_{i+1}}$.
5: **else**
6:     Split $\epsilon(m)_{n_i}$ into header $\mathcal{E}(h_{n_i})$ and symmetric ciphertext c_{n_i}.
7:     Generate random symmetric encryption key k_{n_i} and parameters p_{n_i}.
8:     Compute header $\mathcal{E}(h_{n_{i+1}}) \leftarrow \mathcal{E}(h_{n_i})^{2^{|k_{n_i}|+|p_{n_i}|}} \cdot \mathcal{E}(k_{n_i}||p_{n_i})$.
9:     Compute ciphertext $c_{n_{i+1}} \leftarrow \mathbb{E}(c_{n_i})$ with the key and parameters k_{n_i} and p_{n_i} respectively such that $|c_{n_{i+1}}| = |c_{n_i}|$.
10:     Egress message $\epsilon(m)_{n_{i+1}} \leftarrow \mathcal{E}(h_{n_{i+1}})||c_{n_{i+1}}$.
11: **end if**
12: With probability $p_{f_{th}}$, send $\epsilon(m)_{n_{i+1}}$ to node $n_{i+1} \in L_n$ through S.
13: With probability $1 - p_{f_{th}}$, send $\epsilon(m)_{n_{i+1}}$ to final message recipient R.

---

at the i-th relay is $\mathcal{E}(h_{n_i})$ where initially, $h_{n_1} = k_{n_1}||p_{n_1}$ (here, n_1 is the actual sender). Each relay node n_i adds the symmetric cipher information as $\mathcal{E}(h_{n_{i+1}}) = \mathcal{E}(h_{n_i})^{2^{|k|+|p|}} \cdot \mathcal{E}(k_{n_i}||p_{n_i})$. The operation in the encrypted domain is equivalent, in the plaintext domain, to a left shift of h_{n_i} by $|k| + |p|$ bits and a placement of $k_{n_i}||p_{n_i}$ in the rightmost $|k| + |p|$ bits of h_{n_i} to produce $h_{n_{i+1}}$. Since the additively homomorphic encryption guarantees semantic security, $\mathcal{E}(h_{n_{i+1}})$ and $\mathcal{E}(h_{n_i})$ are indistinguishable. Similarly, the symmetrically encrypted egress and ingress ciphertexts at any relay $c_{n_{i+1}}$ and c_{n_i} are also indistinguishable. The egress encrypted header of $\mathcal{E}(h_{n_{i+1}})$ and the egress ciphertext $c_{n_{i+1}}$ at any relay node n_i together achieve the desired unlinkability. The recipient, possessing the equivalent private key for the public key used in the homomorphic encryption, can decrypt the encrypted header, right shift by the size of $|k| + |p|$ and recover the actual message m in rounds by recovering the symmetric cipher key and other parameters for each round.

A limitation of this approach compared to the one with purely homomorphic encryption is that the forwarding operation can be continued so long as the size of $h_{n_{i+1}}$ is less than the plaintext space of the additively homomorphic cipher. However, it is not possible for any node n_i to know, in the ciphertext domain, if h_{n_i} or $h_{n_{i+1}}$ are within the maximum size of the plaintext domain of the homomorphic encryption. Once the size is exceeded, the left shift operation will lose information about symmetric keys making it impossible for the recipient to decrypt the message. The number of hops that a message goes through can be controlled by the forwarding probability. Figure 2(b) shows how the encrypted header looks like for a 2048-bit Paillier homomorphic cryptosystem and with an

---

Algorithm 2. Algorithm for dispatching a message at the sender node n_1.

Require: Additively homomorphic encryption function, $\mathcal{E}$, for the final message recipient R.

Require: Symmetric encryption function $\mathbb{E}$.

Require: Plaintext message m.

1: **if** $|m| \leq$ the plaintext space of $\mathcal{E}$ **then**
2:     Compute ciphertext $\mathcal{E}(m)_{n_1}$.
3:     Egress message $\epsilon(m)_{n_1} \leftarrow \mathcal{E}(m)_{n_1}$.
4: **else**
5:     Generate random symmetric encryption key k_{n_i} and parameters p_{n_i}.
6:     Compute header $\mathcal{E}(h_{n_1}) \leftarrow \mathcal{E}(k_{n_1}||p_{n_1})$.
7:     Compute ciphertext c_{n_1} from the symmetric encryption with the key and parameters k_{n_1} and p_{n_1}, i.e., $c_{n_1} \leftarrow \mathbb{E}(m)$.
8:     Egress message $\epsilon(m)_{n_1} \leftarrow \mathcal{E}(h_{n_1})||c_{n_1}$.
9: **end if**
10: Obtain, from the intermediary relay service S, a list L_n of nodes that the message can be forwarded to.
11: Send $\epsilon(m)_{n_1}$ to random node $n_i \in L_n$ through S.

---

instance of a 128-bit AES cipher at each hop. The tags and the initialisation vector (IV) of the AES cipher are both set to 64-bits, which are valid parameters for the CCM or the Galois/counter mode implemented by the Stanford Javascript Crypto Library.

Algorithm 1 describes the forwarding protocol at a relay node n_i. Step 3 for short messages and Steps 8 and 9 for long messages achieve the desired unlinkability of the ingress and egress messages.

3.2 Unlinkable Message Sending

The actual sender always sends the message in encrypted form to a random relay node. Since the messages sent out are of the same size, and some of the messages sent out are just random noise, it is impossible to tell by looking at an egress message that the node sending out that message is the actual sender, or simply a relay node forwarding a message from someone else. The protocol for sending out a message is similar to that for forwarding messages in terms of the cryptographic operations. Algorithm 2 describes the protocol that takes place on the sender node.

4 Adversarial Analysis

Traffic analysis [19] is regarded as the de-facto yardstick to determine resilience of anonymous communications systems against attackers. Ignoring the contents of the message, traffic analysis aims to derive information regarding senders and recipients from the traffic metadata, such as packet arrival times and message lengths. Below we discuss several of the key attacks along with the resilience of our system to these attacks.

One of the key attacks in traffic analysis is the *timing attack*. In this attack, a passive global adversary who can observe the ingress and egress connections from the anonymous relay network may be able to link the inputs and outputs based on their patterns of packet inter-arrival times. Although there are delays in message delivery in our protocol, such delays are not as large or consistent as those in high-latency systems. In our system, the order in which messages are sent can get disrupted due to the forwarding probability, thus contributing to a different order at the arrival point. Nodes can also inject noisy traffic with messages of the same length as the original messages to obfuscate the message arrival pattern at the recipient's end.

Another important attack is the *replay or tagging attack* [20] in which the adversary controls the entry and the exit points of the anonymiser network and is able to tag a message at the entry point only to be able to detect it at the exit point. The attack is able to break the Tor network[2] because of the presence of pre-established paths. In our model, the node at which the message enters or exits the anonymiser network is not fixed. Therefore our system is more robust to this attack, since (when a large number of nodes exist in the network), the attacker will have to control a large proportion of the nodes in order to ensure that most messages will enter and exit the network through a node under the control of the adversary.

In the *predecessor attack*, if the paths for message routing are observed over time, the attacker can guess with reasonable accuracy the true senders of the messages. In our protocol, the paths are not constant due to the probablistic routing. Furthermore, depending of the frequency and origins of the noisy messages, the attacker will find it hard to differentiate the senders of actual messages from senders of noise, given that the senders of actual messages may also send out noise, and vice-versa. However, our scheme is not secure against predecessor attacks by design. Given a large number of collaborating Sybil [21] nodes under control of a single attacker, the anonymity of the sender will fall back to k-anonymity whereby the attacker can be confident that the sender is one out-of-the k remaining non-malicious nodes. This can be dangerous if k is small.

In the *fingerprinting attack*, the attacker utilises the variation of the size and the rate in which the messages are sent. In the disclosure attack [22] or the refined statistical disclosure attack [23], the attacker uses set intersections over time to determine the recipient in an anonymous communication. Through our protocol, adding noisy messages in the network at certain unpredictable rates can reduce the effectiveness of such attacks. In addition, our system is not concerned with recipient anonymity.

4.1   Analysis of Anonymity

We now present a theoretical analysis of anonymity. Diaz et al. [24] formulated a measure of anonymity in terms of Shannon entropy. Our anonymous message routing protocol resembles a Crowds-style probabilistic forwarding. With the probability of any node forwarding a message set to p_f (thus, the probability of

---

[2] See: https://blog.torproject.org/blog/one-cell-enough.

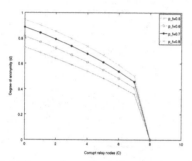 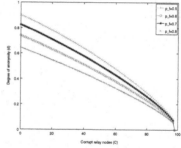

(a) The total number of nodes $N = 10$.   (b) The total number of nodes $N = 100$.

Fig. 3. The degree of anonymity d [24] with respect to the number of corrupt nodes C.

it sending to the final recipient as $1 - p_f$) and the number of forwarding nodes under the control of the attacker set to C (e.g., Sybil nodes), the entropy of the system, $H(X)$, after the attack has happened is formulated as shown as

$$H(X) = \frac{N - p_f(N - C - 1)}{N} log_2 \left[\frac{N}{N - p_f(N - C - 1)} \right] + p_f \frac{N - C - 1}{N} log_2 \left[\frac{N}{p_f} \right]$$

The maximum entropy is given as $H_M = log_2(N - C)$. The *degree of anonymity* d of the relay network is given by $d = \frac{H(X)}{H_M}$. The condition $d = 0$ applies to the special cases: (a) where there is only one user, i.e., $N = 1$; and (b) when $C = N - 1$. In all other cases, it is evident that $0 \le d \le 1$ Diaz et al. [24]. Setting $N = 10$ and $N = 100$, Fig. 3 illustrates the degree of anonymity, d, with respect to the number of corrupt nodes, C, under the control of the attacker. The higher the forwarding probability p_f, the better the degree of anonymity.

However, we have already seen that increasing the forwarding probability is not ideal for messages sent using symmetric encryption because: (a) a high forwarding probability implies a lower chance of the message reaching the final recipient; and (b) with symmetric encryption, a message passing through more than a certain number of hops is rendered undecryptable when it reaches the final recipient.

Denoting the message forwarding probability by p_f, the probability of the message reaching the k-th hop (instead of reaching the final recipient) is p_f^{k-1}. This is because the sender will never send the message directly to the recipient, so the probability of the message passing through the first hop is 1, followed by the forwarding probability at each hop. Assume that the maximum allowed value of k is some threshold k_{th} for some Paillier cryptosystem. Thus, any $k > k_{th}$ will corrupt a message. Therefore, the probability that a message is corrupted is synonymous with the probability of the message passing through the $(k_{th} + 1)$-th hop; and is given as $p_{mc} = p_f^{(k_{th}+1)-1} = p_f^{k_{th}}$.

Similarly, the average number of hops that a message passes through is given as $\bar{n} = 1 + \frac{1}{1-p_f}$ and is illustrated in Fig. 4(b). The extra unity in the equation

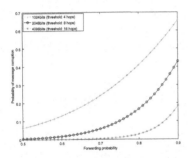
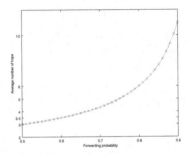

(a) The probability of message corruption versus the forwarding probability. Three Paillier plaintext sizes are shown: 1024, 2048 and 4096 bits. It is assumed that 128-bits AES ciphers are used with 64-bits initialisation vectors and 64-bits tags.

(b) The average number of hops a message passes through versus the forwarding probability.

Fig. 4. Hops and message corruption

exists because the message will pass through at least one hop, i.e., the sender will never send it directly to the recipient.

We have seen that with a 128-bits AES password, 64-bit tags and 64-bit initialisation vector, every message requires, at the time of forwarding, 256-bits of additional space in the 2048-bits Paillier plaintext space. Thus, with a 2048-bits Paillier cryptosystem, the message can go through a total of 8 hops (including the original sender) while the total number of hops is 4 and 16 for a 1024-bits Paillier cryptosystem and a 4096-bits Paillier cryptosystem respectively. Thus, $k_{th} = 4$ (1024-bits), $k_{th} = 8$ (2048-bits) and $k_{th} = 16$ (4096-bits). For the message to be corrupt, it should pass through at least a $k_{th} + 1$ relay. Figure 4(a) shows the probability of message corruption versus the forwarding probability considering 128-bits AES password, 64-bits tags and 64-bits initialisation vectors.

Diaz et al. [24] also proposed the degree of anonymity from the perspective of the sender as the probability p_H of a message passing only through honest nodes, given as $p_H = 1 - \frac{C}{N - p_f(N - C)}$. For $N = 10$ and $N = 100$, Fig. 5 illustrates the probability that a message passes through honest nodes, p_H, with respect to the number of corrupt nodes, C, under the control of the attacker. The higher the forwarding probability p_f, the worse the value of p_H.

5   A HTML5 and Google App Engine Implementation

To illustrate the practical viability of our proposal, we have implemented it as two mobile web applications and deployed on the Google App Engine for Java. One application (`WSA-CRouter`) is responsible for forwarding the messages while the other (`WSA-MB`) is a generic message recipient. The front-end of the former,

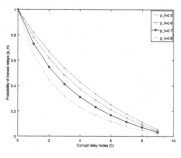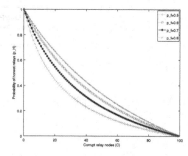

(a) The total number of nodes $N = 10$.   (b) The total number of nodes $N = 100$.

Fig. 5. The probability of a message passing through honest nodes p_H ([24]) with respect to the number of corrupt nodes C.

which is where the anonymisation algorithms run, is implemented in HTML5 technologies: Javascript and JQuery mobile. The backends of both applications are based on simple Java servlets and the no-SQL key-value datastore of the App Engine. The role of the cloud is that of an untrusted registry providing inter-connectivity between the relay nodes. We have tested our application on different HTML5 compliant browsers on various devices: multiple desktop computers, tablet computers and mobile phones. We have used two Javascript libraries from Stanford University: the JSBN (and JSBN2) and the SJCL for supporting cryptographic operations.

Due to a bug in SJCL's conversion of bit arrays to strings (base64 or hex encoded), we had to pad, on the left, the concatenation of AES parameters with 4-bits set to 1 each. Thus, with a 128-bit AES as shown in the example in Fig. 2(b), we actually had a 260-bits shift size instead of the 256-bits as illustrated. This constrains our maximum hop limit to 7 instead of 8 as one would expect from a 2048-bit plaintext space of Paillier.

5.1 Anonymous Messaging over HTTP(S)

The two applications WSA-CRouter (the message forwarding registry and front-end)[3] and WSA-MB (the public message recipient)[4] are both hosted on the Google App Engine for Java. The front-end of WSA-CRouter is run on each node in the diagram. For simplicity, the private keys corresponding to various public keys used in the messaging are stored by the WSA-MB application on the App Engine. In reality, this should not happen because a cloud insider can get hold of these keys and decrypt messages while these are being forwarded.

The application WSA-CRouter is a centralised registry service that routes messages between the different relay nodes. In essence, this type of registry can be decentralised over a structured P2P networks, such as Chord [25] or Pastry [26].

---

[3] See: https://wsa-crouter.appspot.com.
[4] See: https://wsa-mb.appspot.com.

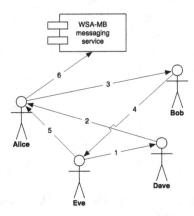

Fig. 6. The flow of a message from Eve to the final recipient.

This is especially useful if the connections to a centralised registry are blocked by a network admininstrator. In our prototype, `WSA-CRouter` implements the Google Channel API service to notify connected relay nodes of messages bound for them. In terms of functionality, the Channel API is close to the proposed Web Sockets standard (RFC 6455). The backend of `WSA-CRouter` running the cloud receives messages sent to it by a node; looks up the next hop address on that message and sends it on to the next hop if it is connected. The Algorithms 1 and 2 run entirely on the relay node client-side. The front-end of `WSA-CRouter` receives a message from another node sent through the cloud. Either it randomly forwards the message on to another connected and active relay node; or it sends the message to the final recipient. Figure 6 shows how a message, originally sent by Eve, passes through Dave, Bob and Alice to the recipient `WSA-MB` service. To the recipient, the message appears to have originated from Alice, when in reality it is from Eve.

If the message has been encrypted with a purely homomorphic obfuscation then it is impossible for the recipient to tell who the actual sender of the message is. However, if the message is encrypted with homomorphic and symmetric obfuscation and the message has not been corrupted because of passing through many hops then the recipient, upon decrypting, can tell that the number of hops the message has passed through. This will reveal that in the most likely case, the message did not originate at the node from which the final recipient received the message.

The backend of the `WSA-MB` service, upon receiving the encrypted message, looks up the public key sent with it and finds the corresponding private key. Depending on the type of obfuscation used, it decrypts either the message or its homomorphically encrypted headers and stores it in the datastore. A client Javascript application – the front-end of `WSA-MB` – can then retrieve the decrypted messages or headers, decrypting in rounds, the headers if required to retrieve the underlying plaintext messages.

5.2   Performance Evaluation

We describe the performance of our prototype in terms of the time taken for message forwarding on the client-side front-end and that of various functions on the cloud-side back-end.

Client-Side Performance: Table 1 demonstrates the performance of message forwarding on different browsers and platforms. In our set of test devices, we had:

(a) (mobile) Chrome 35.0.1916.38/iOS 7.1.1 running on a iPhone 5S;
(b) (desktop) IE 10.0.9200.16899S/Windows 8.0 running on a hardware consisting of a 3 GHz Intel Core i7 processor and 16 GB RAM;
(c) (desktop) Firefox 29.0/Ubuntu Linux 14.10 running on a hardware consisting of a 3 GHz Intel Core i7 Extreme processor and 16 GB RAM;
(d) (laptop) Chrome 35.0.1916.114/Mac OS X 10.9 running on a Macbook Air hardware consisting of a 1.8 GHz Intel Core i7 processor and 8 GB RAM.

Table 1. The mean forwarding time for different platforms using the same Javascript implementations of 2048-bits Paillier and 128-bits AES encryptions

Platform	Mean forwarding time
(mobile) Chrome/iOS	70.9s
(desktop) IE/Windows	17.2s
(laptop) Chrome/OS X	4.06s
(desktop) Firefox/Linux	1.89s

Throughout the experiment, we have used 2048-bit Paillier keys and 128-bit AES keys with 64-bit initialisation vectors and 64-bit tags. The connections to the WSA-CRouter web application have been also encrypted over HTTPS. The iPhone 5 S has the worst forwarding performance and this can be attributed to its less powerful hardware as well as the Javascript library on Chrome for iOS 7 compared to the computers. It is to be noted that Internet Explorer performs fairly badly too on reasonably high-end hardware. Use-cases such as anonymous surveys are tolerant to the relatively long delay (due to the over-a-minute delay per hop) if all the hops en-route are similar low-powered devices. However, microblogging such as a commentary of live events may not be able to tolerate large delays.

Cloud-Side Performance: Both WSA-CRouter and WSA-MB applications have been deployed on the F2 instance class (1200MHz CPU, 256MB RAM) of the Google App Engine for Java. The message forwarding delay in the Table 2(a) is negligible compared to the delays on the client-side (Table 1).

Table 2. Performances of message forwarding and cryptographic functions

(a) The performance of the WSA-CRouter (b) The performance of the WSA-MB imple-
implementation on the Google App En- mentation on the Google App Engine us-
gine.   ing 2048-bits Paillier encryption.

Function	Performance
Message forwarding	25ms

Function	Performance
Key generation	3.88s
Message receipt	0.13s
Message decryption	1.16s

Table 2(b) shows the performances of the different functions in the WSA-MB application. The functions *Message decryption* essentially has the same performance irrespective of the size of the message because it only decrypts the homomorphic header, leaving the header to be shifted and decrypted on the client-side; or it decrypts the homomorphic message. Thus, both cases involve just one 2048-bits Paillier decryption along with parsing the messaging and looking up the datastore for the private key corresponding to the public key.

6   Conclusions and Future Work

In this paper, we have proposed a private one-way anonymous messaging protocol and a real world prototype to demonstrate the applicability of our protocol in lightweight HTML5-enabled browsers on mobile devices. Our protocol is suitable for particular application scenarios where the sender's identity needs to be protected not only from external attackers but also from the recipient. Our protocol uses probabilistic forwarding through a random set of relay nodes and protects the anonymity of the sender and the privacy of the messages through principles in homomorphic cryptosystems. We are in the process of implementing a real-world anonymous survey system based on our prototype. In the future, we plan to look into the construction of the reverse path. We also plan to deal with churn that can cause message loss and intentional message loss.

References

1. Chaum, D.L.: Untraceable electronic mail, return addresses, and digital pseudonyms. Commun. ACM **24**(2), 84–90 (1981)
2. Chaum, D.: The dining cryptographers problem: unconditional sender and recipient untraceability. J. Cryptology **1**(1), 65–75 (1988)
3. Goldschlag, D.M., Reed, M.G., Syverson, P.F.: Hiding routing information. In: Anderson, R. (ed.) IH 1996. LNCS, vol. 1174, pp. 137–150. Springer, Heidelberg (1996)
4. Reiter, M.K., Rubin, A.D.: Crowds: anonymity for web transactions. ACM Trans. Inf. Syst. Secur. (TISSEC) **1**(1), 66–92 (1998)
5. Pfitzmann, A., Hansen, M.: A terminology for talking about privacy by data minimization: anonymity, unlinkability, undetectability, unobservability, pseudonymity, and identity management v0.34, August 2010
6. Kikuchi, H.: Sender and recipient anonymous communication without public key cryptography. In: CSEC (1998)

7. Danezis, G., Dingledine, R., Mathewson, N.: Mixminion: design of a type iii anonymous remailer protocol. In: IEEE Security and Privacy, pp. 2–15. IEEE (2003)
8. Moeller, U., Cottrell, L.: Mixmaster protocol version 3 (2004)
9. Syverson, P.F., Goldschlag, D.M., Reed, M.G.: Anonymous connections and onion routing. In: IEEE Symposium on Security and Privacy, pp. 44–54. IEEE (1997)
10. Reed, M.G., Syverson, P.F., Goldschlag, D.M.: Anonymous connections and onion routing. IEEE J. Sel. Areas Commun. **16**(4), 482–494 (1998)
11. Syverson, P.F., Tsudik, G., Reed, M., Landwehr, C.: Towards an analysis of onion routing security. In: Federrath, H. (ed.) Designing Privacy Enhancing Technologies. LNCS, vol. 2009, pp. 96–114. Springer, Heidelberg (2001)
12. Dingledine, R., Mathewson, N., Syverson, P.: Tor: the second-generation onion router. Technical report, DTIC Document (2004)
13. Mislove, A., Oberoi, G., Post, A., Reis, C., Druschel, P., Wallach, D.S.: Ap3: cooperative, decentralized anonymous communication. In: Proceedings of the 11th workshop on ACM SIGOPS European workshop, p. 30. ACM (2004)
14. Freedman, M.J., Morris, R.: Tarzan: a peer-to-peer anonymizing network layer. In: Proceedings of the 9th ACM Conference on Computer and Communications Security, pp. 193–206. ACM (2002)
15. Rennhard, M., Plattner, B.: Introducing morphmix: peer-to-peer based anonymous internet usage with collusion detection. In: Proceedings of the 2002 ACM Workshop on Privacy in the Electronic Society, pp. 91–102. ACM (2002)
16. Gentry, C.: Computing arbitrary functions of encrypted data. Commun. ACM **53**(3), 97–105 (2010)
17. Paillier, P.: Public-key cryptosystems based on composite degree residuosity classes. In: Stern, J. (ed.) EUROCRYPT 1999. LNCS, vol. 1592, pp. 223–238. Springer, Heidelberg (1999)
18. Damgård, I., Jurik, M.: A generalisation, a simplication and some applications of paillier's probabilistic public-key system. In: Kim, K. (ed.) PKC 2001. LNCS, vol. 1992. Springer, Heidelberg (2001)
19. Danezis, G., Clayton, R.: Introducing traffic analysis (2007)
20. Pries, R., Yu, W., Fu, X., Zhao, W.: A new replay attack against anonymous communication networks. In: IEEE International Conference on Communications, ICC 2008, pp. 1578–1582. IEEE (2008)
21. Douceur, J.R.: The Sybil attack. In: Druschel, P., Kaashoek, M.F., Rowstron, A. (eds.) IPTPS 2002. LNCS, vol. 2429, pp. 251–260. Springer, Heidelberg (2002)
22. Kedogan, D., Agrawal, D., Penz, S.: Limits of anonymity in open environments. In: Petitcolas, F.A.P. (ed.) IH 2002. LNCS, vol. 2578, pp. 53–69. Springer, Heidelberg (2003)
23. Danezis, G.: Statistical disclosure attacks. In: Gritzalis, D., Capitani di Vimercati, S., Samarati, P., Katsikas, S. (eds.) Security and Privacy in the Age of Uncertainty. IFIP, vol. 122, pp. 421–426. Springer, New York (2003)
24. Díaz, C., Seys, S., Claessens, J., Preneel, B.: Towards measuring anonymity. In: Dingledine, R., Syverson, P.F. (eds.) PET 2002. LNCS, vol. 2482, pp. 54–68. Springer, Heidelberg (2003)
25. Stoica, I., Morris, R., Karger, D., Kaashoek, M.F., Balakrishnan, H.: Chord: a scalable peer-to-peer lookup service for internet applications. ACM SIGCOMM Comput. Commun. Rev. **31**(4), 149–160 (2001)
26. Rowstron, A., Druschel, P.: Pastry: scalable, decentralized object location, and routing for large-scale peer-to-peer systems. In: Guerraoui, R. (ed.) Middleware 2001. LNCS, vol. 2218, pp. 329–350. Springer, Heidelberg (2001)

Privacy-Preserving Reputation Mechanism: A Usable Solution Handling Negative Ratings

Paul Lajoie-Mazenc[1]([⊠]), Emmanuelle Anceaume[2], Gilles Guette[1],
Thomas Sirvent[3], and Valérie Viet Triem Tong[4]

[1] Université de Rennes-1/IRISA, Rennes, France
{paul.lajoie-mazenc,gilles.guette}@irisa.fr
[2] CNRS/IRISA, Rennes, France
emmanuelle.anceaume@irisa.fr
[3] DGA Maîtrise de l'Information/IRISA, Rennes, France
thomas.sirvent@m4x.org
[4] CentraleSupélec/IRISA, Rennes, France
valerie.viettriemtong@supelec.fr

Abstract. Reputation mechanisms allow users to mutually evaluate their trust. This is achieved through the computation of a reputation score summarizing their past behaviors. Depending on these scores, users are free to accept or refuse to interact with each other. When users are virtual, volatile, or distant, an accurate evaluation of reputation scores is complex. Furthermore, users expect reputation mechanisms to preserve the privacy of their interactions and of their feedback. Existing solutions often rely on costly cryptographic tools that may lead to impractical solutions. In this article, we propose a usable privacy preserving reputation mechanism. This mechanism is distributed and handles non-monotonic ratings. Its implementation on cheap single board computers validates its adequacy to large-scale systems.

1 Introduction

Reputation mechanisms tend to be an effective tool to encourage trust and cooperation in electronic environments [1]. This is achieved by enabling users to rate services or people, based on their past experience. These ratings or feedback are aggregated to derive publicly available reputation scores. Reputation mechanisms either rely on a central authority or take advantage of the participating users to compute reputation scores. To circumvent the vulnerability of the former approach, both in terms of privacy and fault-tolerance, we present a reputation mechanism that meets security and trust requirements through distributed computations. While aggregating ratings is necessary to derive reputation scores, identifiers and ratings are personal data, whose collection and usage may fall under legislation [2]. Furthermore, as shown by recent works [3], solely relying on pseudonyms to interact is not sufficient to guarantee user privacy [4]. This has given rise to the proposition of a series of reputation mechanisms which address

This work was partially supported by the ANR French project AMORES (grant #ANR-11-INSE-010).

© IFIP International Federation for Information Processing 2015
C.D. Jensen et al. (Eds.): IFIPTM 2015, IFIP AICT 454, pp. 92–108, 2015.
DOI: 10.1007/978-3-319-18491-3_7

either the non-exposure of the history of raters [5], the non-disclosure of individual feedback [6–8], the secrecy of ratings and the k-anonymity of ratees [9], or the anonymity and unlinkability of both raters and ratees [5,10]. Regrettably, the search for privacy has led to algorithmic restrictions, in the sense that handling solely non-negative ratings seems to be the *sine qua non* condition to preserve user privacy [5,10]: existing privacy-preserving mechanisms give their users the opportunity to skip some of the received ratings to increase their privacy, which is unfortunately not compatible with negative ratings. Furthermore, Baumeister *et al.* explain that "bad feedback has stronger effects than good feedback" on our opinions [11]. Thus, it is crucial to allow clients to issue negative ratings.

In the remaining of the article, we present the design and evaluation of a non-monotonic distributed reputation mechanism preserving the privacy of both parties. This work is the continuation of our preliminary work [12]. After having presented the state of the art in Sect. 2, we present in Sect. 3 the properties that should be met by a reputation mechanism to be secure, to preserve the privacy of all parties, and to handle non-monotonic ratings. Section 4 provides a description of the main principles of our approach to build such a mechanism, and their orchestration is presented in Sect. 5. The main contribution of this paper is presented in Sect. 6. This section shows that this unprecedented mechanism is computationally efficient, and thus implementable in large-scale applications. Finally, Sect. 7 concludes.

2 State of the Art

One of the first examples of reputation mechanisms has been set up by eBay. In this mechanism, clients and service providers rate each other after each transaction: ratings are either $+1$, 0, or -1 according to the (dis)satisfaction of users. The reputation score of a user is simply the sum of the received ratings. Resnick and Zeckhauser have analyzed this mechanism and the effects of reputation on eBay [13], and have highlighted a strong bias toward positive ratings. More elaborated reputations mechanisms have been proposed, such as the Beta Reputation System [14], methods based on the Dempster-Shafer theory of belief [15], or based on distributed hash tables [16–18]. Jøsang *et al.* propose a broad survey of reputation mechanisms [19], while Marti and Garcia-Molina focus on their implementation in P2P systems [20]. Indubitably, the nature of ratings and the computation of reputation scores have been thoroughly researched. In this work, we do not make any assumptions regarding the function that computes reputation scores. Indeed, our solution handles both positive and negative ratings, and may thus use any computation function.

One of the first known reputation mechanism taking the privacy of users into account has been proposed by Pavlov *et al.* [6]. Their solution presents a series of distributed algorithms for computing the reputation score of service providers without divulging the ratings issued by clients. Their solution has been improved by Hasan *et al.* [7,18] for different adversary models, and stronger privacy guarantees. Similarly, Kerschbaum proposes a centralized mechanism computing the reputation scores of service providers without disclosing the individual ratings of the clients [8]. The secrecy of ratings contributes to the privacy of users, but is clearly insufficient: service providers can still discriminate their clients according to their identity or to additional information unrelated to the transaction. As we previously mentioned, identifiers and ratings can be considered personal data. Steinbrecher argues that reputation mechanisms must guarantee both the anonymity of their users, and the unlinkability of their transactions to be fully adopted [4]. Both properties have been lately formalized by Pfitzmann and Hansen [21]. Namely, a user is *anonymous* if this user is not identifiable within a set of users, called the *anonymity set*. The transactions of a user are *unlinkable* if the participants in two different transactions cannot be distinguished. Hence, Clauß *et al.* [9] propose a centralized mechanism guaranteeing both the secrecy of ratings and the k-anonymity of service providers. However, beyond being centralized, this mechanism does not preserve the privacy of clients. Androulaki *et al.* [10] also propose a centralized reputation mechanism guaranteeing both the anonymity and the unlinkability of both parties. However, since providers send a request to the central bank for their ratings to be taken into account, only positive ratings are handled. In addition, this mechanism is vulnerable to *ballot-stuffing* attacks [1], that is, a single client can issue many ratings on a provider to bias her reputation. Whitby *et al.* [22] propose a technique mitigating ballot-stuffing attacks, however their technique requires the ability to link the ratings concerning the same provider. Bethencourt *et al.* [5] propose to compute such a link. That is, they propose a mechanism linking all the transactions that have occurred with the same partners, while preserving their privacy. However, beyond handling only positive ratings, their reputation mechanism requires high computational power, bandwidth and storage capacity. For instance, when proving their reputation score, providers must send about 500 KiB per received rating, which is unbearable from a practical point of view.

So far, preserving the privacy of both raters and ratees and handling both positive and negative ratings has been recognized as a complex challenge. Quoting Bethencourt *et al.*, "Most importantly, how can we support non-monotonic reputation systems, which can express and enforce bad reputation as well as good? Answering this question will require innovative definitions as well as cryptographic constructions" [5]. To the best of our knowledge, no distributed reputation mechanism preserves the privacy of its users and allows clients to efficiently issue both positive and negative ratings. This is the objective of this paper.

3   Model and Properties

Terminology. In the following, we differentiate transactions from interactions. A *transaction* corresponds to the exchange of a service between a client and a service provider, while an *interaction* is the whole protocol followed by the client and the provider, during which the clients get the provider's reputation and the client issues a *rating* on the provider. Note that we make no assumption about the nature of transactions: they can be, for example, web-based community applications or e-commerce ones. Once a transaction is over, the client is expected to issue a rating representative of the provider's behavior during the transaction. Nevertheless, clients can omit to issue such a rating, deliberately or not. While dissatisfied clients almost always issue a rating, satisfied clients seldom do it. To cope with this asymmetry, we introduce the notion of *proofs of transaction*: a proof of transaction is a token delivered to providers for transactions during which the client did not issue a rating. Such proofs of transaction allow clients to distinguish between multiple providers that have the same reputation. We denote by *report* the proof of transaction associated with the client's rating, if any. These reports serve as the basis to compute reputation scores. Finally, we say that a user is *honest* if this user follows the protocol of the reputation mechanism. Otherwise, this user is *malicious*.

Model of the System. We consider an open system populated by a large number of users. A proportion of these users can be malicious (more details are given below). Before entering the system, users register to a central authority C, that gives them identifiers and certificates. Once registered, users do not need to interact with C anymore. A user can act as a client, as a service provider, or as both, and obtains credentials for both roles. We also assume that users communicate over an anonymous communication network, *e.g.* Tor [23].

Properties of our Reputation Mechanism. Our reputation mechanism aims at offering three main guarantees to users. First and foremost, the privacy of users must be preserved. Second, users must always be able to cast their report. Finally, every data needed for the computation of reputation scores must be available and unforgeable. Privacy properties are stated in Properties 1 and 2, while Properties 3 and 4 are related to the undeniability of reports. Both properties expect that providers obtain proofs of transaction, and that clients are always able to cast ratings. Property 5 deals with reports unforgeability. Finally, Properties 6 and 7 respectively stipulate that the computation of the reputation scores cannot be biased by ballot-stuffing attacks, and that reputation scores are unforgeable. Note that since clients do not know the provider they are interacting with, targeted bad-mouthing attacks cannot be launched.

Property 1. *Privacy of service providers. When a client rates an honest service provider, this service provider is anonymous among all honest service providers with an equivalent reputation.*

Property 2. *Privacy of clients. When a provider conducts a transaction with an honest client, this client is anonymous among all honest clients. Furthermore, the interactions of honest clients with different providers are unlinkable.*

Property 3. *Undeniability of ratings. At the end of a transaction between a client and a provider, the client can issue a valid rating, which will be taken into account in the reputation score of the provider.*

Property 4. *Undeniability of proofs of transaction. At the end of a transaction between a client and a provider, the provider can obtain a valid proof of transaction.*

Property 5. *Unforgeability of reports. Let r be a report involving a client and a service provider. If r is valid and either the client or the provider is honest, then r was issued at the end of an interaction between both users.*

Property 6. *Linkability of reports. Two valid reports emitted by the same client on the same service provider are publicly linkable.*

Property 7. *Unforgeability of reputation scores. A provider cannot forge a valid reputation score different from the one computed from all the reports assigned to this provider.*

4   Building Blocks

4.1   Distributed Trusted Third-Parties

As explained in Sect. 1, service providers must not manage themselves their reputation score to guarantee their reliability. To solve this issue, we propose to construct a distributed trusted authority in charge of updating and certifying reputation scores. We call *accredited signers* the entities constituting this authority. This first distributed authority has two main features. Firstly, this authority must involve fairly trusted entities or enough entities to guarantee that the malicious behavior of some of them never compromises the computation of reputation scores. Secondly, this authority must ensure that providers remain indistinguishable from each other. Moreover, to ensure the undeniability of ratings, a client must be able to issue his report, even if the service provider does not complete the interaction. However, the precautions taken for that purpose must not imply sending identifying data before the transaction. In the same way, data identifying the client must not be sent before the transaction, even to ensure the undeniability of proof of transactions. To solve all these issues, we propose a distributed trusted authority in charge of guaranteeing that reports can be built. This distributed authority must collect information before the transaction, and potentially help one of the two parties afterwards; it must thus be online. We call *share carriers* the entities constituting this authority.

Both distributed authorities could be gathered in a single one. The drawback of this approach is that this distributed trusted authority should be simultaneously online, unique, and fairly trusted or reasonably large. The uniqueness and the participation in each interaction would induce an excessive load on each entity of this distributed authority. For efficiency reasons, we thus suggest distinct authorities. Accredited signers are then a unique set of fairly trusted or numerous entities, periodically updating the reputation scores of all providers. On the other hand, share carriers are chosen dynamically during each interaction among all service providers. Accredited signers manage every reputation score, and are thus critical in our mechanism. On the other side, share carriers are responsible for the issuing of a single report. Hence, they do not need to be as trustworthy as the accredited signers.

To deal with the privacy of both clients and providers, share carriers use *verifiable secret sharing* [24]. This basically consists in disseminating shares of a secret to the share carriers, so that they cannot individually recover the secret, but allow the collaborative reconstruction of this secret.

4.2 Cryptographic Tools

Our mechanism relies on cryptographic tools to guarantee its properties. The underlying structure of those tools is a bilinear group $\Lambda = (p, \mathbb{G}_1, \mathbb{G}_2, \mathbb{G}_T, e, G_1, G_2)$ in which $\mathbb{G}_1, \mathbb{G}_2, \mathbb{G}_T$ are three groups of prime order p that we write multiplicatively. The map $e : \mathbb{G}_1 \times \mathbb{G}_2 \rightarrow \mathbb{G}_T$ is non-degenerate and bilinear. $G_1 \in \mathbb{G}_1$ (resp. $G_2 \in \mathbb{G}_2$) is a group generator of $\mathbb{G}_1$ (resp. $\mathbb{G}_2$).

First, our mechanism uses *SXDH commitments* [25]. To commit to a value in $\mathbb{G}_1$ or $\mathbb{G}_2$, one needs two random scalars. Then, our mechanism relies on the *Non-Interactive Zero-Knowledge* (NIZK) proof system proposed by Groth and Sahai [25], which allows users to prove their possession of secrets without revealing the secrets. Instead, the secrets are masked by SXDH commitments. For instance, this proof system allows users to compute *Anonymous Proxy Signatures* [26], *i.e.* to sign messages without revealing the message, the signature, or their verification key. This requires particular signature schemes, *e.g. Structure-Preserving Signatures* [27]. Finally, as previously mentioned, our mechanism relies on verifiable secret sharing. Such a scheme allows a prover to split a secret into n shares, and to reconstruct the secret from t shares (with $t \leqslant n$). More specifically, the prover sends a share to n *share carriers*, and convinces a verifier that the verifier will be able to reconstruct the prover secret. To convince the verifier, the prover uses NIZKs to prove (a) the correctness of the secret, and (b) the consistency of the shares. An optimal choice for t is $t = \lceil n/3 \rceil$, which tolerates up to $t - 1$ malicious share carriers. In this case, the verifier accepts the sharing as soon as $2t - 1$ share carriers have confirmed the reception of their share. The analysis leading to this choice is detailed in the companion paper [28].

As explained in Sect. 2, reputation mechanisms must defend themselves against ballot-stuffing attacks. Bethencourt *et al.* [5] propose such a method by computing a value that depends only on the client and the provider, but that does not allow different providers to compare their clients. We propose a similar method, yet simpler, allowing to compute such an *invariant*. Let $\mathsf{Id}_{\mathrm{SP}} \in \mathbb{G}_1$ (resp. $\mathsf{id}_{\mathrm{Cl}} \in \mathbb{Z}_p$) be the identifier of the provider (resp. client). We then define the invariant as $\mathsf{inv} = \mathsf{Id}_{\mathrm{SP}}{}^{\mathsf{id}_{\mathrm{Cl}}}$. Note that the invariant must not be computed directly: it requires the client to know the provider's identifier, and vice versa. Hence, they jointly compute the invariant in three steps, which require an additional group element $Y_1 \in \mathbb{G}_1$. First, the provider computes a *pre-invariant* with randomness $r \in \mathbb{Z}_p$: $\mathsf{pre\_inv} = (G_1{}^r, \mathsf{Id}_{\mathrm{SP}} \cdot Y_1{}^r)$. The client then randomly chooses $s \in \mathbb{Z}_p$ to compute a *masked invariant*: $\mathsf{masked\_inv} = (G_1{}^s \cdot Y_1{}^{\mathsf{id}_{\mathrm{Cl}}}, \mathsf{pre\_inv}_1{}^s \cdot \mathsf{pre\_inv}_2{}^{\mathsf{id}_{\mathrm{Cl}}})$. Finally, the provider obtains the invariant from masked_inv: $\mathsf{inv} = \mathsf{masked\_inv}_2 \cdot \mathsf{masked\_inv}_1{}^{-r} = (\mathsf{Id}_{\mathrm{SP}})^{\mathsf{id}_{\mathrm{Cl}}}$. Note that the invariant is computed *after* the transaction, otherwise the provider would know whether she has already interacted with the client or not, which might introduce a bias in the provision of the service.

5   Reputation Protocol

Throughout the reputation protocol, users need cryptographic keys and identifiers. Specifically, the central authority $\mathcal{C}$ uses a structure-preserving signature key pair $(\mathsf{vk}_{\mathcal{C}}, \mathsf{sk}_{\mathcal{C}})$ to generate certificates on users' credentials. To enter the system, users register to this authority, which may require a computational or monetary cost to mitigate Sybil attacks. Note that this authority is required only for the registration of users, and possibly for the choice of accredited signers.

Clients have a structure-preserving signature key pair, consisting of a verification key $\mathsf{vk}_{\mathrm{Cl}}$ and a signing key $\mathsf{sk}_{\mathrm{Cl}}$. When clients enter the system, they register to the central authority $\mathcal{C}$ to get a random identifier $\mathsf{id}_{\mathrm{Cl}} \in \mathbb{Z}_p$, and a certificate $\mathsf{cert}_{\mathrm{Cl}}$ on $\mathsf{id}_{\mathrm{Cl}}$ and $\mathsf{vk}_{\mathrm{Cl}}$. Similarly, service providers have a structure-preserving signature key pair $(\mathsf{vk}_{\mathrm{SP}}, \mathsf{sk}_{\mathrm{SP}})$, and register to $\mathcal{C}$ to obtain a random identifier $\mathsf{Id}_{\mathrm{SP}} \in \mathbb{G}_1$, and a certificate $\mathsf{cert}_{\mathrm{SP}}$ on $\mathsf{Id}_{\mathrm{SP}}$ and $\mathsf{vk}_{\mathrm{SP}}$.

Accredited signers have a structure-preserving signature key pair $(\mathsf{vk}_{\mathrm{AS}}, \mathsf{sk}_{\mathrm{AS}})$ and a certificate $\mathsf{cert}_{\mathrm{AS}}$ on $\mathsf{vk}_{\mathrm{AS}}$. They use these keys to sign the reputation score of service providers at regular intervals, that we call *rounds*. We denote by σ_i the signature of the i-th accredited signer on the reputation score $\mathsf{rep}_{\mathrm{SP}}$ of the provider, for current round rnd, *i.e.* a signature on $\langle \mathsf{vk}_{\mathrm{SP}}, H(\mathsf{rep}_{\mathrm{SP}}, \mathsf{rnd}) \rangle$. In the following, n_{AS} represents the number of accredited signers. We assume that a majority t_{AS} of them are honest.

Share carriers possess two key pairs, namely a classical encryption key pair $(\mathsf{ek}_{\mathrm{SC}}, \mathsf{dk}_{\mathrm{SC}})$, and a classical signature key pair $(\mathsf{sk}_{\mathrm{SC}}, \mathsf{vk}_{\mathrm{SC}})$, used to encrypt received messages and sign sent messages. They also have a certificate $\mathsf{cert}_{\mathrm{SC}}$ on $\mathsf{ek}_{\mathrm{SC}}$ and $\mathsf{vk}_{\mathrm{SC}}$, issued by the central authority $\mathcal{C}$.

Both clients and providers compute by themselves their own pseudonyms. They renew them at each interaction. Pseudonyms $\mathsf{nym}_{\mathrm{Cl}}$ and $\mathsf{nym}_{\mathrm{SP}}$ are SXDH commitments to verification keys $\mathsf{vk}_{\mathrm{Cl}}$ and $\mathsf{vk}_{\mathrm{SP}}$. Similarly, both clients and service providers compute commitments $C_{\mathsf{id}_{\mathrm{Cl}}}$ and $C_{\mathsf{Id}_{\mathrm{SP}}}$ to their identifiers $\mathsf{id}_{\mathrm{Cl}}$ and $\mathsf{Id}_{\mathrm{SP}}$. Clients compute commitments $C_{\mathsf{cert}_{\mathrm{Cl}}}$ to their certificate, and NIZK proofs of their validity $\Pi_{\mathsf{cert}_{\mathrm{Cl}}}$. Similarly, service providers compute commitments $C_{\mathsf{cert}_{\mathrm{SP}}}$ and proofs $\Pi_{\mathsf{cert}_{\mathrm{Cl}}}$. Finally, service providers compute a pre-invariant $\mathsf{pre\_inv}$ from $\mathsf{Id}_{\mathrm{SP}}$ and a randomly chosen scalar $r_{\mathsf{pre\_inv}}$.

Due to space constraints, we defer the cryptographic proofs of the security of our protocol as well as figures detailing this protocol in a companion article [28].

5.1   Proof of the Reputation Score

When a client wishes to interact with a service provider, he sends a pseudonym $\mathsf{nym}_{\mathrm{Cl}}$ and a proof of its validity $C_{\mathsf{id}_{\mathrm{Cl}}}$, $C_{\mathsf{cert}_{\mathrm{Cl}}}$, and $\Pi_{\mathsf{cert}_{\mathrm{Cl}}}$ to the provider. Once the provider has verified this proof, she chooses a nonce s_{SC} and commits to it by computing $C_{\mathrm{SC}} = H(00\|s_{\mathrm{SC}})$.[1] Then, the provider sends back her pseudonym, reputation, pre-invariant and respective proofs of validity, and committed nonce. That is, she sends $\mathsf{nym}_{\mathrm{SP}}$, $C_{\mathsf{Id}_{\mathrm{SP}}}$, $C_{\mathsf{cert}_{\mathrm{SP}}}$, $\Pi_{\mathsf{cert}_{\mathrm{SP}}}$, $\mathsf{rep}_{\mathrm{SP}}$, a proof of reputation

---

[1] This concatenation guarantees that s_{SC} and r_{SC} are chosen independently.

Π_{rep}, pre_inv, a proof $\Pi_{\text{pre_inv}}$ of its computation while masking Id_{SP} and $r_{\text{pre_inv}}$, and C_{SC}.

If the client is satisfied with the reputation of the provider, and if all the proofs are valid, the client computes the masked invariant masked_inv, chooses a nonce r_{SC}, computes a signature σ_{Cl} on $H(C_{\text{SC}}, r_{\text{SC}}, \text{nym}_{\text{SP}})$, and sends r_{SC} and σ_{Cl} to the provider. If σ_{Cl} is valid, the provider computes a signature on $H(s_{\text{SC}}, r_{\text{SC}}, \text{nym}_{\text{Cl}})$, and sends s_{SC} and σ_{SP} to the client. Note that the signatures guarantee that the client agreed to conduct a transaction with provider nym_{SP}, who uses the randomness hidden in C_{SC}, and that the provider agreed to conduct a transaction with client nym_{Cl}, who uses randomness r_{SC}. Once the client and the provider have exchanged their nonces, they choose the share carriers, using $(s_{\text{SC}} \| r_{\text{SC}} \| \text{nym}_{\text{Cl}} \| \text{nym}_{\text{SP}})$ as a seed. For that purpose, they iterate a hash function, e.g. SHA-256 [29], to randomly select n_{SC} share carriers among all service providers. In the remainder, this seed serves as an identifier of the transaction, and we note it id_{trans}.

During this step, the client sends one element in $\mathbb{Z}_p$, 86 in $\mathbb{G}_1$, and 74 in $\mathbb{G}_2$ to the provider, while the provider sends 3 element in $\mathbb{Z}_p$, $(74 t_{\text{AS}} + 92)$ in $\mathbb{G}_1$, and $(66 t_{\text{AS}} + 84)$ in $\mathbb{G}_2$. Once this step is over, besides being mutually authenticated, the provider has proven her reputation score to the client, each party is able to prove the implication of the other one in the interaction, and they finally have jointly and independently chosen the share carriers.

5.2   Sharing Ingredients of the Report

The client and the service provider now rely on the verifiable secret sharing scheme to guarantee the undeniability properties. The service provider shares her identifier Id_{SP}, that is, she chooses a polynomial Q of degree $t_{\text{SC}} - 1$, with coefficients $\text{Id}_{\text{SP}}, A_1, \ldots, A_{t_{\text{SC}}-1}$, where the A_j are randomly chosen in $\mathbb{G}_1$. The shares are the $(i, Q_i = Q(i))$ for $1 \leqslant i \leqslant n_{\text{SC}}$. To prove the sharing, the provider computes commitments C_{A_j} to the A_j, and NIZK proofs Π_{Q_i} that share Q_i was generated from Id_{SP} and from the A_j for $1 \leqslant i \leqslant n_{\text{SC}}$, while masking Id_{SP} and the A_j. Note that $\text{nym}_{\text{SP}}, C_{\text{Id}_{\text{SP}}}, C_{\text{cert}_{\text{SP}}}$ and $\Pi_{\text{cert}_{\text{SP}}}$ have already proven the correctness of the secret, that is Id_{SP}. Finally, the provider sends the (C_{A_j}) to the client, and encrypts and sends $\text{id}_{\text{trans}}, (i, Q_i), C_{\text{Id}_{\text{SP}}}, (C_{A_j})_{1 \leqslant j < t_{\text{SC}}}$, and Π_{Q_i} to the i-th share-carrier. If the received proof is valid, the share carriers send a confirmation to the client, that is $\text{id}_{\text{trans}}, i, C_{\text{Id}_{\text{SP}}}$, and (C_{A_j}), together with a signature. If these commitments are the same as the one received from the provider, the client accepts this confirmation: all the shares were generated from the same polynomial, which evaluates to the correct secret, Id_{SP}, in 0. Since the validity of the shares guarantees the undeniability properties, the client accepts the sharing once he has received $2t_{\text{SC}} - 1$ valid shares. This requires for the provider to send $(2t_{\text{SC}} - 2)$ elements in $\mathbb{G}_1$ to the client, and 4 in $\mathbb{Z}_p$, $(2t_{\text{SC}} + 3)$ in $\mathbb{G}_1$, and 4 in $\mathbb{G}_2$ to each share carrier. Each share carrier sends 2 elements in $\mathbb{Z}_p$ and $2t_{\text{SC}}$ in $\mathbb{G}_1$ to the provider.

In the meantime, the client shares his secret, that is the masked invariant masked_inv. Since masked_inv consists of two elements, he must double the sharing. That is, the client chooses two polynomial R_1, R_2 of degree $t_{SC} - 1$ with coefficients $\mathsf{masked\_inv_k}, B_{1,k}, \ldots, B_{t_{SC}-1,k}$ for $\mathsf{k} \in \{1,2\}$, and the shares are $(i, R_i = (R_1(i), R_2(i)))$ for $1 \leqslant i \leqslant n_{SC}$. To prove the sharing, the client computes commitments $C_{\mathsf{masked\_inv}}$ and $C_{B_{j,k}}$ to $\mathsf{masked\_inv}$ and to the $B_{j,k}$, and NIZK proofs Π_{R_i} that R_i was generated from $\mathsf{masked\_inv}$ and from the B_j for $1 \leqslant i \leqslant n_{SC}$, while masking $\mathsf{masked\_inv}$ and the B_j. To prove the correctness of the secret, the client also computes a proof $\Pi_{C_{\mathsf{masked\_inv}}}$ guaranteeing the computation of $\mathsf{masked\_inv}$, while masking $\mathsf{masked\_inv}$, $\mathsf{id_{Cl}}$, and the randomness used. Thus, the client sends $C_{\mathsf{masked\_inv}}$, $(C_{B_{j,k}})$, and $\Pi_{C_{\mathsf{masked\_inv}}}$ to the provider, and encrypts and sends $\mathsf{id_{trans}}$, (i, R_i), $C_{\mathsf{masked\_inv}}$, $(C_{B_{j,k}})$, and Π_{R_i} to the i-th share carrier. As previously, the i-th share carrier sends a confirmation consisting of $\mathsf{id_{trans}}$, i, $C_{\mathsf{masked\_inv}}$, $(C_{B_{j,k}})$, and a signature to the provider if the share is valid. The provider accepts such a confirmation if the commitments are identical to the ones she received, and accepts the sharing as soon as she has received $2t_{SC} - 1$ valid confirmations. Thus, the client sends one element in $\mathbb{Z}_p$, $(4t_{SC} + 14)$ in $\mathbb{G}_1$ and 16 in $\mathbb{G}_2$ to the provider, and 2 in $\mathbb{Z}_p$, $(4t_{SC} + 6)$ in $\mathbb{G}_1$ and 8 in $\mathbb{G}_2$ to each share carrier. Each share carrier sends 2 elements in $\mathbb{Z}_p$ and $4t_{SC}$ in $\mathbb{G}_1$ to the provider. Once this step is over, the client is ensured that he will be able to obtain $\mathsf{Id_{SP}}$ to issue the report. Similarly, the provider is guaranteed that she will be able to obtain a proof of transaction through the computation of $\mathsf{masked\_inv}$. Therefore, both parties can conduct their transaction.

5.3   Construction of the Reports

Once the transaction is over, the client can issue a rating and the provider can obtain a proof of transaction. Scenario A describes their interactions.

Scenario A – Nominal Case. The client chooses a rating ρ and computes a signature $\sigma_{\rho,Cl}$ on $H(\mathsf{id_{trans}}, \rho)$ to prevent any modification on ρ, and a proof $\Pi_{\mathsf{masked\_inv}}$ of the computation of $\mathsf{masked\_inv}$, while masking $\mathsf{id_{Cl}}$ and the randomness used. It is very important to note that the identity of the provider is preserved until the client issues and signs his rating, which fully preserves the objectivity of the rating. Once this is achieved, the provider can reveal her identity to the share carriers and even to the client. This allows the rating to be affected to the identity of the provider without allowing bad-mouthing attacks. Note also that by doing so, reputation scores reflect all the provider's interactions, not those conducted under a specific pseudonym. Since $\mathsf{masked\_inv}$ no longer needs to be hidden, $\Pi_{\mathsf{masked\_inv}}$ is a simpler proof than $\Pi_{C_{\mathsf{masked\_inv}}}$. The client sends message m_1 to the provider, with $m_1 = (\mathsf{id_{trans}}, \rho, \mathsf{masked\_inv}, \Pi_{\mathsf{masked\_inv}}, \sigma_{\rho,Cl})$. If both the proof and signature are valid, the provider computes the invariant inv from $\mathsf{masked\_inv}$ and $r_{\mathsf{pre\_inv}}$, and a signature $\sigma_{\rho,SP}$ on $H(\mathsf{id_{trans}}, \sigma_{\rho,Cl})$. Note that since the provider reveals her identity, this signature is a structure-preserving signature, not an anonymous proxy signature. The provider then reveals her identifier, opens commitments $\mathsf{nym_{SP}}$ and $C_{\mathsf{Id_{SP}}}$, and reveals $r_{\mathsf{pre\_inv}}$. These proofs, denoted by Π_{SP}, guarantee both the computation of $\mathsf{pre\_inv}$ and that this provider is the one hidden behind $\mathsf{nym_{SP}}$. The provider sends message m_2 to the client, with

Table 1. Components of the report in the three scenarii

	Scenario A	Scenario B	Scenario C
Provider	Id_{SP}, vk_{SP}, cert_{SP}, nym_{SP}, $C_{\mathsf{Id}_{SP}}$, Π_{SP}	Id_{SP}, vk_{SP}, cert_{SP}, nym_{SP}, $C_{\mathsf{Id}_{SP}}$, Π_{SP}	$C_{\mathsf{Id}_{SP}}$, nym_{SP}, PCert_{SP}, Id_{SP}, $(C_{A_j})_j$, $\{i_j, Q_{i_j}, \Pi_{Q_{i_j}}\}_j$
Client	$C_{\mathsf{id}_{Cl}}$, nym_{Cl}, PCert_{Cl}	$C_{\mathsf{id}_{Cl}}$, nym_{Cl}, PCert_{Cl}	$C_{\mathsf{id}_{Cl}}$, nym_{Cl}, PCert_{Cl}
Trans. id.	id_{trans}, σ_{SP}, σ_{Cl}	id_{trans}, σ_{SP}, σ_{Cl}	id_{trans}, σ_{SP}, σ_{Cl}
Invariant	$\mathsf{masked\_inv}$, inv, $r_{\mathsf{pre\_inv}}$, $\Pi_{\mathsf{masked\_inv}}$	$\mathsf{masked\_inv}$, inv, $r_{\mathsf{pre\_inv}}$, $(C_{B_{j,k}})$, $\{i_j, R_{i_j}, \Pi_{R_{i_j}}\}_j$, $C_{\mathsf{masked\_inv}}$, $\Pi_{C_{\mathsf{masked\_inv}}}$	inv, Π_{inv}
Rating	ρ, $\sigma_{\rho,Cl}$, $\sigma_{\rho,SP}$		ρ, $\{\sigma_{\rho,SC_{i_j}}\}_j$

$m_2 = (\mathsf{Id}_{SP}, \mathsf{vk}_{SP}, \mathsf{cert}_{SP}, \mathsf{inv}, \Pi_{SP}, \sigma_{\rho,SP})$. The client verifies Π_{SP} and signature $\sigma_{\rho,SP}$. Finally, both the client and the provider are able to issue the report by sending the elements given in the first column of Table 1 to the share carriers (where the first four lines represent the proof of transaction and the last one the rating together with the signatures of both parties). If all the signatures and proofs are valid, the report itself is considered valid by the share carriers. This scenario completes successfully if both parties are honest. If the client does not send message m_1 (resp. the provider does not send message m_2) then scenario B (resp. scenario C) is run. Finally, if neither the client nor the provider issue the report, then the transaction is not taken into account in the reputation score of the service provider. If this step proceeds correctly, the client sends 2 elements in $\mathbb{Z}_p$, 14 in $\mathbb{G}_1$, and 14 in $\mathbb{G}_2$ to the provider. Similarly, the provider sends 7 elements in $\mathbb{Z}_p$, 19 in $\mathbb{G}_1$, and 12 in $\mathbb{G}_2$. The report is composed of 11 elements in $\mathbb{Z}_p$, 143 in $\mathbb{G}_1$, and 116 in $\mathbb{G}_2$.

Scenario B – Dishonest Client. If the provider does not receive message m_1 from the client, she queries the share carriers for their share by sending them id_{trans}. On their turn, they query the client to get his rating and, in absence of his answer, send their shares (i, R_i) and associated proofs Π_{R_i} to the provider. The provider is then able to reconstruct the masked invariant $\mathsf{masked\_inv}$ from t_{SC} valid received shares. From that point, the provider can compute inv from $\mathsf{masked\_inv}$ and $r_{\mathsf{pre\_inv}}$ and issue the report, which only contains the proof of transaction (*i.e.*, the elements in the second column of Table 1). During this step, the provider sends one element in $\mathbb{Z}_p$ to each share carrier, while each of them sends back to her one element in $\mathbb{Z}_p$, 6 in $\mathbb{G}_1$, and 8 in $\mathbb{G}_2$. The report is made of $(t_{SC} + 10)$ elements in $\mathbb{Z}_p$, $(10t_{SC} + 132)$ in $\mathbb{G}_1$, and $(8t_{SC} + 108)$ in $\mathbb{G}_2$.

Scenario C – Dishonest Provider. If the client does not receive message m_2 from the provider, he sends the masked invariant and his rating together with their associated proofs and signatures to the share carriers. That is, the client sends id_{trans}, nym_{Cl}, $C_{\mathsf{id}_{Cl}}$, $C_{\mathsf{cert}_{Cl}}$, $\Pi_{\mathsf{cert}_{Cl}}$, nym_{SP}, $C_{\mathsf{id}_{SP}}$, $C_{\mathsf{cert}_{SP}}$, $\Pi_{\mathsf{cert}_{SP}}$, $\mathsf{pre\_inv}$, $\Pi_{\mathsf{pre\_inv}}$, $\mathsf{masked\_inv}$, $\Pi_{\mathsf{masked\_inv}}$, ρ, $\sigma_{\rho,Cl}$. If all the proofs and signatures are valid, the share carriers forward them to the provider to give her the opportunity to reveal $\mathsf{Id}_{\mathsf{SP}}$ and the invariant. In absence of any response, the share carriers send their share (i, Q_i) and associated proof Π_{Q_i} to the client. Note that they also compute a signature $\sigma_{\rho,\mathsf{SC}_j}$ on $H(\mathsf{id}_{\mathsf{trans}}, \sigma_{\rho,\mathsf{Cl}})$ to validate the fact that the client has chosen his rating before knowing the provider's identity. Once the client has received t_{SC} valid shares, he reconstructs $\mathsf{Id}_{\mathsf{SP}}$, computes inv from $\mathsf{Id}_{\mathsf{SP}}$ and $\mathsf{id}_{\mathsf{Cl}}$, and computes a proof Π_{inv} of the computation of inv while masking $\mathsf{id}_{\mathsf{Cl}}$. Finally, the client issues the report by sending the elements presented on the third column of Table 1 to the share carriers. In this step, the client sends 4 elements in $\mathbb{Z}_p$, 202 in $\mathbb{G}_1$, and 178 in $\mathbb{G}_2$ to each share carrier. Each share carrier sends back one element in $\mathbb{Z}_p$, 3 in $\mathbb{G}_1$, and 4 in $\mathbb{G}_2$. Finally, the report is made of $(t_{\mathsf{SC}} + 4)$ elements in $\mathbb{Z}_p$, $(5t_{\mathsf{SC}} + 192)$ in $\mathbb{G}_1$, and $(4t_{\mathsf{SC}} + 164)$ in $\mathbb{G}_2$.

5.4 Computation of the Reputation Scores

At the end of round rnd, each share carrier gathers all the reports received since round rnd -1, and sends them to the accredited signers. This allows the accredited signers to update the reputation scores of all the service providers concerned by valid reports. Once accredited signers have checked the validity of a report, they only keep the identifier of the provider, the identifier of the transaction, the invariant inv, and the rating of the client, if any, and sign them. Note that if two (or more) reports have the same identifier of transaction and invariant, they keep a single one to avoid duplicates. Beyond handling negative ratings, the accredited signers know the rounds during which reports have been cast. Thus, as described in Sect. 2, any reputation score function can be used, *e.g.* to lower the influence of old ratings [14] or to limit the impact of ballot-stuffing attacks [22]. In addition, the accredited signers approximate the reputation score of providers to extend their anonymity set. Once the accredited signers have computed the reputation score of a provider, they compute a signature σ_i on $\langle \mathsf{vk}_{\mathsf{SP}}, H(\mathsf{rep}_{\mathsf{SP}}, \mathsf{rnd}) \rangle$ and send it to the provider. Service providers can use these signatures to prove their reputation to their clients during round rnd $+1$.

6 Performance Evaluation

We now evaluate our privacy-preserving reputation mechanism both in theoretical and practical ways. The former evaluation is achieved through an analysis of the performance of each building block, while the latter relies on its implementation on a platform made of heterogeneous computing nodes. The number of share carriers n_{SC} and the number of accredited signers n_{AS} are respectively equal to $n_{\mathsf{SC}} = 28$ and $n_{\mathsf{AS}} = 1$. This setting is sufficient to prevent the collusions of $\lceil n_{\mathsf{SC}}/3 \rceil - 1 = 9$ share carriers with probability 2^{-20} in a system comprising 10^8 service providers, including 5×10^6 malicious ones. This analysis, based on the hypergeometric distribution, appears in a companion paper [28].

Table 2. Size of exchanged messages for $n_{SC} = 28$ and $n_{AS} = 1$, in kibibytes

Phase	Cl $\leftrightarrow$ SP	Cl $\leftrightarrow$ SC$_i$	SP $\leftrightarrow$ SC$_i$	Report
Proof of Reputation	22	0	0	—
Sharing	3.28	2.69	2.34	—
Scenario A	2.94	0	0	12.06
Scenario B	0	0	0.75	19.63
Scenario C	0	17.94	0	20.75

6.1 Theoretical Study

The correctness of our mechanism relies on the verification of NIZK proofs, which requires the computation of many pairings. To decrease the number of these operations, we adopt the technique proposed by Blazy *et al.* [30] which consists in verifying NIZKs by batches. We also ensure efficient pairing computations by relying on prime-order elliptic curves [31]. We consider elliptic curves in a subclass of the Barreto-Naehrig family. Thus, elements of $\mathbb{Z}_p$ and $\mathbb{G}_1$ (resp. $\mathbb{G}_2$) can be represented by 32 B (resp. 64 B). We use the computation costs given by Aranha *et al.* [31]. Namely, the four cores of a 3.0 GHz AMD Phenom II X4 940 processor – a top-level processor of 2010 – can compute 8 pairings in a millisecond, 16 exponentiations in $\mathbb{G}_2$, or 48 in $\mathbb{G}_1$. In the following, we study two metrics, namely (a) the size of messages exchanged between each entity, and (b) the time necessary for each entity to perform his computation. We now present and comment the main results obtained with these settings. Table 2 gives the size of messages (in KiB) exchanged between the different parties involved in the reputation mechanism, namely, between the client and the provider, the client and one share carrier, and the provider and one share carrier before the transaction takes place. Finally, it gives the size of the report sent to the accredited signer once the transaction is over.

These results are both satisfactory and reassuring. The largest messages correspond to the proof of reputation, which comprises the mutual authentication of the service provider and the client, and the proof by the provider of his reputation score. Nevertheless, this exchange requires only around 20 KiB. This is impressive compared to the mechanism proposed by Bethencourt *et al.* [5], where the proof of reputation requires 500 KiB per received rating. Table 2 also shows that share carriers only need 3 KiB when a transaction goes well, and less than 10 KiB in the worst case situation. This clearly shows that the design of a distributed trusted third party requires very little resources. The same comment applies for the accredited signers. The size of the report, that comprises all the proofs, requires no more than 20 KiB in the worst case. It is important to note that the only message that scales (linearly) as a function of the number of the accredited signers is the proof of reputation. Thus, even for larger sets of accredited signers, which typically do not grow to more than 20 entities, the communication cost remains acceptable. These results are very reassuring because they show that,

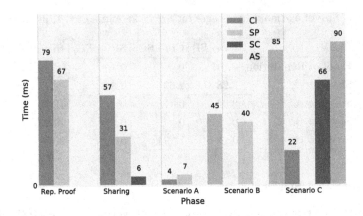

Fig. 1. Theoretical computation times (ms)

from a theoretical point of view, privacy-preserving reputation mechanisms are entirely viable. The next section will show that this holds in practice!

Figure 1 details the computation cost (in ms) of each phase of the reputation mechanism for each of the involved entities. Several remarks are in order. The main one is that computation times are very low. Indeed, each user needs no more than 200 ms for all their computations. In particular, each share carrier needs no more than 6 ms when both the client and the provider are honest. Even in the worst case, they need only 75 ms to perform their computations. Finally, the verification of a report requires between 45 ms and 90 ms. This clearly shows that participating to one of the two distributed trusted third parties computing entities costs little. Actually, the largest costs are due to scenarii B or C. We can minimize those costs by penalizing malicious users, *e.g.* by preventing them from interacting for a given period of time.

6.2   Implementing the Reputation Mechanism

We have implemented our reputation mechanism in Python 2.7 with the Charm framework [32]. This framework facilitates the implementation of complex cryptographic primitives, such as Groth-Sahai's NIZK proof system [25], and the combination of multiple primitives, *e.g.*, to build anonymous proxy signatures [26]. Furthermore, Charm provides the means to benchmark applications, both by giving their running time and by counting each elementary cryptographic operation. We also use Twisted, an event-driven networking engine, to handle communications between the different parties. Experiments have been conducted on heterogeneous entities, namely, a virtual machine running on a Dell Latitude E6430 laptop with a 2.60 GHz Core i7-3720 QM processor, and cheap Raspberry Pi model B machines with the Raspbian operating system.

Figure 2 presents the results of the conducted experiments. It shows the mean and standard deviation of the computation times of each user for every step of the interaction, namely, the proof of reputation, the sharing, and the issuing

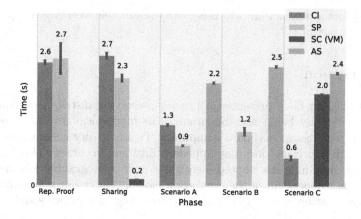

Fig. 2. Practical computation times (s)

of the report in every scenario. Note that the "SC" columns correspond to the computation times of one share carrier running on the virtual machine, and that the "AS" columns relate to the verification of one report by an accredited signer.

Clearly, the computation times are higher than the one obtained in theory, which can easily be explained. First, Aranha *et al.* carefully select a Barreto-Naehrig curve, and optimize the computation of pairings using Assembly and C code on this specific curve [31]. In our case, we rely on the MNT-159 curve proposed by Charm, which is a Python framework wrapping around Lynn's pbc library.[2] Furthermore, the theoretical number of operations per second assumes that they are all ran in parallel, which is not the case in our experiments. Finally, all the users except one share carrier were run on a single virtual machine. This does not slow down the phases where users run computations sequentially, *e.g.* the proof of reputation or the construction of the report in Scenario A, but it does slow down the concurrent ones, *e.g.* the sharing of the secrets.

Even with those limitations, we observe that our mechanism allows clients to interact with providers, and to run all the preparation in no more than 5 s. Issuing the report may take longer, but the most important point is that clients can rapidly verify the reputation of a provider and get involved in the transaction. Similarly, the pre-transaction and the post-transaction phases respectively require no more than 5 s and 1 s which clearly allows the provider to interact with many clients simultaneously. Note that share carriers can even be run on cheap Raspberry Pi machines. In that case, sharing the secrets requires no more than 4.7 s, while issuing the rating in presence of malicious clients needs no more than 59 s. Such cheap machines increase the waiting time of both clients and providers, but this delay remains acceptable (less than 15 s), compared for example to the time required to buy items on any e-commerce web sites. Finally, running clients on Raspberry Pi requires about 75 s for conducting the reputation proof and 115 s for the sharing. That is, clients need about 3 min before being

---

[2] http://crypto.stanford.edu/pbc/.

able to conduct a transaction, which is clearly reasonable to engage in (possibly) financial transactions.

7 Conclusion

In this article, we have presented a privacy-preserving distributed reputation mechanism. Beyond being non-monotonic, this mechanism reveals to be fully usable even with cheap on-board computers. This is a very encouraging result as it shows that privacy does not impede utility and accuracy. This has been achieved by combining distributed algorithms and cryptographic schemes. Our mechanism is independent of the reputation model, that is, our system can integrate any reputation model [14], preferably one using both positive and negative ratings.

As future works, we plan to study more deeply an off-line version of the secret sharing, which requires the share carriers only in Scenarii B and C, and to improve the report verification when the service provider does not want to collaborate.

References

1. Dellarocas, C.: Immunizing online reputation reporting systems against unfair ratings and discriminatory behavior. In: ACM Conference on Electronic Commerce (EC), USA (2000)
2. European Parliament and Council of the European Union: Directive 95/46/EC. Official Journal of the European Communities (1995)
3. Narayanan, A., Shmatikov, V.: Robust de-anonymization of large sparse datasets. In: IEEE Symposium on Security and Privacy, Oakland, USA (2008)
4. Steinbrecher, S.: Enhancing multilateral security in and by reputation systems. In: Matyáš, V., Fischer-Hübner, S., Cvrček, D., Švenda, P. (eds.) The Future of Identity. IFIP AICT, vol. 298, pp. 135–150. Springer, Heidelberg (2009)
5. Bethencourt, J., Shi, E., Song, D.: Signatures of reputation. In: Sion, R. (ed.) FC 2010. LNCS, vol. 6052, pp. 400–407. Springer, Heidelberg (2010)
6. Pavlov, E., Rosenschein, J.S., Topol, Z.: Supporting privacy in decentralized additive reputation systems. In: Jensen, C., Poslad, S., Dimitrakos, T. (eds.) iTrust 2004. LNCS, vol. 2995, pp. 108–119. Springer, Heidelberg (2004)
7. Hasan, O., Brunie, L., Bertino, E.: Preserving privacy of feedback providers in decentralized reputation systems. Comput. Secur. **13**, 816–826 (2012)
8. Kerschbaum, F.: A verifiable, centralized, coercion-free reputation system. In: Workshop on Privacy in the Electronic Society (WPES), Chicago, USA (2009)
9. Clauß, S., Schiffner, S., Kerschbaum, F.: k-anonymous reputation. In: Symposium on Information, Computer and Communications Security (ASIACCS) (2013)
10. Androulaki, E., Choi, S.G., Bellovin, S.M., Malkin, T.: Reputation systems for anonymous networks. In: Borisov, N., Goldberg, I. (eds.) PETS 2008. LNCS, vol. 5134, pp. 202–218. Springer, Heidelberg (2008)
11. Baumeister, R.F., Bratslavsky, E., Finkenauer, C., Vohs, K.D.: Bad is stronger than good. Rev. Gen. Psychol. **5**, 323–370 (2001)

12. Anceaume, E., Guette, G., Lajoie-Mazenc, P., Sirvent, T., Viet Triem Tong, V.: Extending signatures of reputation. In: Hansen, M., Hoepman, J.-H., Leenes, R., Whitehouse, D. (eds.) Privacy and Identity 2013. IFIP AICT, vol. 421, pp. 165–176. Springer, Heidelberg (2014)
13. Resnick, P., Zeckhauser, R.: Trust among strangers in Internet transactions: Empirical analysis of eBay's reputation system. Econ. Internet E-Commerce 11, 127–157 (2002)
14. Jøsang, A., Ismail, R.: The beta reputation system. In: Bled Electronic Commerce Conference, Bled, Slovenia (2002)
15. Yu, B., Singh, M.P.: Distributed reputation management for electronic commerce. Comput. Intell. 18, 535–549 (2002)
16. Kamvar, S.D., Schlosser, M.T., Garcia-Molina, H.: The EigenTrust algorithm for reputation management in P2P networks. In: International World Wide Web Conference (WWW) (2003)
17. Anceaume, E., Ravoaja, A.: Incentive-Based robust reputation mechanism for P2P services. In: Shvartsman, M.M.A.A. (ed.) OPODIS 2006. LNCS, vol. 4305, pp. 305–319. Springer, Heidelberg (2006)
18. Hasan, O., Brunie, L., Bertino, E., Shang, N.: A decentralized privacy preserving reputation protocol for the malicious adversarial model. IEEE Trans. Inf. Forensics Secur. 8(6), 949–962 (2013)
19. Jøsang, A., Ismail, R., Boyd, C.: A survey of trust and reputation systems for online service provision. Decis. Support Syst. 43(2), 618–644 (2007)
20. Marti, S., Garcia-Molina, H.: Taxonomy of trust: Categorizing P2P reputation systems. Comput. Netw 50, 472–484 (2006)
21. Pfitzmann, A., Hansen, M.: A terminology for talking about privacy by data minimization: Anonymity, unlinkability, undetectability, unobservability, pseudonymity, and identity management (2010). http://dud.inf.tu-dresden.de/literatur/Anon_Terminology_v0.34.pdf
22. Whitby, A., Jøsang, A., Indulska, J.: Filtering out unfair ratings in bayesian reputation systems. In: International Workshop on Trust in Agent Societies (2004)
23. Dingledine, R., Mathewson, N., Syverson, P.: Tor: The second-generation onion router. In: USENIX Security Symposium (2004)
24. Feldman, P.: A practical scheme for non-interactive verifiable secret sharing. In: Foundations of Computer Science (FOCS), USA (1987)
25. Groth, J., Sahai, A.: Efficient non-interactive proof systems for bilinear groups. In: Smart, N.P. (ed.) EUROCRYPT 2008. LNCS, vol. 4965, pp. 415–432. Springer, Heidelberg (2008)
26. Fuchsbauer, G., Pointcheval, D.: Anonymous proxy signatures. In: Ostrovsky, R., De Prisco, R., Visconti, I. (eds.) SCN 2008. LNCS, vol. 5229, pp. 201–217. Springer, Heidelberg (2008)
27. Abe, M., Fuchsbauer, G., Groth, J., Haralambiev, K., Ohkubo, M.: Structure-preserving signatures and commitments to group elements. In: Rabin, T. (ed.) CRYPTO 2010. LNCS, vol. 6223, pp. 209–236. Springer, Heidelberg (2010)
28. Lajoie-Mazenc, P., Anceaume, E., Guette, G., Sirvent, T., Viet Triem Tong, V.: Efficient distributed privacy-preserving reputation mechanism handling non-monotonic ratings. Technical report (2015). https://hal.archives-ouvertes.fr/hal-01104837
29. National Institute of Standards and Technology: Secure hash standard (2012)
30. Blazy, O., Fuchsbauer, G., Izabachène, M., Jambert, A., Sibert, H., Vergnaud, D.: Batch groth-sahai. In: Zhou, J., Yung, M. (eds.) ACNS 2010. LNCS, vol. 6123, pp. 218–235. Springer, Heidelberg (2010)

31. Aranha, D.F., Karabina, K., Longa, P., Gebotys, C.H., López, J.: Faster explicit formulas for computing pairings over ordinary curves. In: Paterson, K.G. (ed.) EUROCRYPT 2011. LNCS, vol. 6632, pp. 48–68. Springer, Heidelberg (2011)
32. Akinyele, J.A., Garman, C., Miers, I., Pagano, M.W., Rushanan, M., Green, M., Rubin, A.D.: Charm: a framework for rapidly prototyping cryptosystems. J. Cryptographic Eng. **3**, 111–128 (2013)

Obscuring Provenance Confidential Information via Graph Transformation

Jamal Hussein[1,2]([✉]), Luc Moreau[1], and Vladimiro Sassone[1]

[1] Electronics and Computer Science, University of Southampton, Southampton, UK
[2] Department of Computer Science, University of Sulaimani, Sulaimani,
Iraqi Kurdistan
{jah1g12,vs,l.moreau}@ecs.soton.ac.uk

Abstract. Provenance is a record that describes the people, institutions, entities, and activities involved in producing, influencing, or delivering a piece of data or a thing. In particular, the provenance of information is crucial in deciding whether information is to be trusted. PROV is a recent W3C specification for sharing provenance over the Web. However, provenance records may expose confidential information, such as identity of agents or specific attributes of entities or activities. It is therefore essential for confidential information to be obscured before sharing provenance. This paper describes PROV-GTS, a provenance graph transformation system, whose principled definition is based on PROV properties, and which seeks to avoid false independencies and false dependencies. PROV-GTS is shown to preserve graph integrity, to be terminating and to be confluent.

Keywords: Provenance · PROV model · Privacy · Anonymization · Graph transformation

1 Introduction

Provenance is a record that describes the people, institutions, entities, and activities involved in producing, influencing, or delivering a piece of data or a thing [1]. Provenance is crucial to validate the quality of data and to enable the reusability of data. It has been used in a variety of domains, including scientific workflow [2], healthcare [3], sensor networks [4], and access control [5]. For example, full provenance of medical decisions enriches medical history captured in health records and enables scientists to find the cause of diseases and care providers to improve health services [3]. Overall the provenance of information is essential to decide whether information is to be trusted [1].

However, provenance may include confidential information, such as agents identities, time information, specific attributes of, and relations between, entities, activities and agents. Such a confidential information must be obscured before exposing provenance, but this presents challenges given the graphical nature of provenance and associated graph inference [6]. Indeed, deleting a node or an edge containing confidential information may affect what can be inferred from a

© IFIP International Federation for Information Processing 2015
C.D. Jensen et al. (Eds.): IFIPTM 2015, IFIP AICT 454, pp. 109–125, 2015.
DOI: 10.1007/978-3-319-18491-3_8

graph. For instance, if $a \rightarrow b$ and $b \rightarrow c$ for some transitive relation, confidential information in b, and subsequent deletion of b, will prevent us from inferring $a \rightarrow c$. Such a problem is being referred to as *false independency* [7] since the transformed graph may lead us to believe that a and c are unrelated (in the sense that one has no influence over the other [1]). Likewise, one needs to ensure that a transformed provenance graph does not enable the inference of nodes or edges that cannot be inferred from the original graph, a problem referred to as *false dependency* [8]. The problems of false dependency and independency have not been considered together by previous work on provenance privacy protection [5,9], but should critically be addressed in order to maintain the usefulness of provenance in establishing trust of data.

The model of provenance we adopt is the recently standardized PROV, aimed at sharing provenance information over the Web [6,10]. The richness of PROV requires a principled approach to defining a graph transformation and formalising its properties. To address the problem of false (in)dependency, we have established that, when a node needs to be deleted, we need to consider not only the edges incident to that node, but also the edges between its adjacent nodes. To do so, graph transformation rules need to be equipped with a variety of graph rewriting capabilities, such as negative application conditions (NAC) [11] and nested constraints [12].

The aim of this paper is to propose PROV-GTS, a provenance graph transformation system that prevents false dependencies by creating nodes and edges according to the semantics of PROV. Concretely, the contributions of the paper are threefold: (*i*) A principled definition of transformation rules that is based on the properties of PROV such as its inference rules. (*ii*) An approach to avoiding false independencies and false dependencies in the transformed graph. (*iii*) The system termination and confluence shows that the rules are parallel-independent (no inconsistency and all critical pairs are safe).

In Sect. 2, the most relevant approaches found in the literature are presented. The intuition of our approach to deleting nodes in PROV model is described in Sect. 3. In Sect. 4 the formal definition of graph transformation used in PROV-GTS is presented followed by the construction of the transformation rules in Sect. 5. The issue of inconsistency is resolved in Sect. 6. Nested graph predicate and the properties of PROV-GTS are presented in Sects. 7 and 8, respectively. Finally, we provide the conclusion and future work in Sect. 9.

2   Previous Work

Provenance graph transformations have been mainly used in two broad domains: provenance access control and scientific workflow run provenance. A provenance access control language has been proposed in [5] based on integrity criteria which reduces the original query entered by a user and deletes the paths that are in the original query but not in the reduced query. In [9], data, module, and structural privacy in scientific workflow have been examined. A module clustering approach has been proposed by creating new composite modules from the old ones preventing the visibility of private information while preserving completeness. However, clustering may require adding new dependencies which are not part of the original graph thus breaching the validity of the provenance information by adding false dependencies.

The issue of false dependencies has been solved in the following research works. However, the proposed approaches, by deleting extra information other than the sensitive nodes, have not been able to avoid false independency. A redaction-based graph grammar [13] for rewriting provenance graph replaces two or more nodes and the edges connecting them with a new node and applies node relabelling as necessary to hide sensitive information. The paper [14] shows how a variety of user requests such as abstracting, anonymizing, or hiding nodes may lead to provenance policy violations such as false dependencies, false independencies, or cyclic graphs. The paper suggests inventing new non-functional nodes when it is necessary and maintaining the essential relationships.

The approach proposed in [7,15] performs abstractions on provenance graphs by replacing a graph chunk by one node while avoiding adding false dependencies to the graph. In [16] an abstraction model has been proposed using node grouping. It replaces a set of sensitive nodes by a single node. The approach avoids cycles and invalid relations otherwise a set of nodes will be extended such that sink nodes in the set are of the same type, entity or activity. Finally the system replaces the set by a new node of the same type as the sink node.

3   Deleting Nodes in the PROV Model

PROV [10] defines a notion of graph, formed of nodes and edges, each equipped with an identifier and optionally decorated by attributes. Figure 1 illustrates the nodes and edges of the core PROV data model; they include three node types - entity, activity, and agent - and seven edge types which are wasDerivedFrom (der), wasGeneratedBy (gen), used (use), wasInformedBy (info), wasAttributedTo (attr), wasAssociatedWith (asso), and actedOnBehalfOf (del). We use the abbreviated labels of these edges throughout this paper to refer to them.

In the proposed system, the sensitive parts of the provenance graph are specified by a set of *restricted* nodes. Confidentiality levels will be used to represent *plain* □, *restricted* ▦ , and *anonymous* ▧ nodes. The full description of these notations will be provided in Sect. 4.

The goal of our proposed approach is to obscure the confidential information by removing the restricted nodes. If a node cannot be deleted then it will be

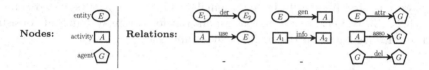

Fig. 1. Core PROV data model

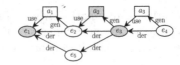

Fig. 2. A provenance graph

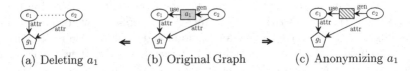

(a) Deleting a_1 (b) Original Graph   (c) Anonymizing a_1

Fig. 3. Node anonymization

replaced by a less sensitive anonymous node. There are two reasons why we prefer removing nodes over anonymization. First, the topology of the graph can be used by an attacker, who has prior knowledge on the content of the graph, to infer the hidden identity and attributes of the nodes [17]. Second, if we only anonymise, then it is possible to have a graph redundant and useless nodes, which could have been removed.

However, deleting restricted nodes may result in omitting non-relevant information. For example, the implicit *info* edge between activities a_3 and a_2, in Fig. 2, disappears as a consequence of deleting e_3. Since this relation can be inferred, we need to ensure that we create the edge *info* between a_3 and a_2 before deleting e_3.

If the relations cannot be inferred then the node will be anonymized. In Fig. 3(b), no relation between e_1 to e_2 can be inferred; therefore, deleting the restricted activity a_1 will cut the path between e_1 and e_2 as shown in Fig. 3(a). Instead, a_1 will be anonymized as illustrated in Fig. 3(c). Node anonymization is carried out by obscuring the node's *id* and deleting all its attributes [18].

4   PROV Graph Transformation System (PROV-GTS)

Algebraic graph transformation approaches rely either on two gluing diagrams, referred to as double-pushout approach (DPO) [19], or one gluing diagram, referred to as single-pushout approach (SPO). SPO is capable of removing nodes and their incident edges from the graph, including dangling edges [20]. Algebraic approaches can be extended by additional application conditions, such as existence and non-existence of certain nodes and edges [21], as well as conditions that are repeated frequently in the original graph and known as nested conditions [22]. PROV-GTS is an algebraic graph transformation system that consists of a set of rules based on the single-pushout approach.

4.1   PROV Graph

Provenance graphs are typed, which means we need to define a type for each of the nodes, edges, and confidentiality levels. Let ν, ε, and ρ represent the node types, the edge types, and the confidentiality levels, respectively, where $\nu = [entity, activity, agent]$, $\varepsilon = [use, gen, der, info, asso, attr, del]$, and $\rho = [plain, restricted, anonymous]$. By default, all graph nodes are *plain*, except those that have been annotated by the user as *restricted*. PROV-GTS either deletes the *restricted* nodes or makes them *anonymous*, according to the intuition of Sect. 3.

To avoid having too many rules and conditions to achieve a particular goal, we define *abstract* nodes and edges based on the core PROV data model [23]. For example, to say that a node has incoming edges, we use an abstract node and edge to construct a single condition, instead of defining multiple conditions for each type of incoming edges. These abstract nodes and edges, as shown in the hierarchies of Fig. 4, have been used to construct PROV-GTS rules, where *node* (the *triangle* in Fig. 4(a)) represents all node types, and *artifact* (the *diamond* in Fig. 4(a)) represents *entity* and *agent*. The top-level edge *link* shown in Fig. 4(c) represents all core PROV edges and *rel* represents each of *der, attr, use, asso*, and *del*. Regarding the confidentiality levels shown in Fig. 4(b), *any* represents the top-level ancestor of *plain, anonymous* and *restricted*. Three new sets $\bar{\nu}$, $\bar{\varepsilon}$, $\bar{\rho}$ are defined, where $\bar{\nu} = \nu \cup [node, artifact]$, $\bar{\varepsilon} = \varepsilon \cup [link, rel]$, and $\bar{\rho} = \rho \cup [any]$.

Definition 1 (Extended PROV Graph). *An extended PROV graph is a typed graph $G = (N_G, E_G, s_G, d_G, p_G, c_G, h_G)$ where N_G is the set of nodes, E_G is the set of edges, $s_G, d_G \colon E_G \to N_G$ are functions which assign respectively a source and a target node to each edge, the function $p_G : N_G \to \bar{\rho}$ assigns confidentiality level to the nodes, and the functions $c_G : N_G \to \bar{\nu}$ and $h_G : E_G \to \bar{\varepsilon}$ map nodes and edges to their types, respectively.*

Given the type hierarchies of Fig. 4, we extend the definition of graph morphisms [24] with binary relations $\leq_N$, $\leq_E$, and $\leq_P$ which are implicitly defined in Fig. 4 by the subtype arrows. These relations are used in mapping nodes, edges, and confidentiality levels in PROV-GTS rules to their corresponding nodes, edges, and confidentiality levels in PROV graphs, respectively.

Definition 2 (Extended Graph-Morphism). *Let G and H be graphs. A morphism $f : G \to H$ is the mappings $f_N : N_G \to N_H$, $f_P : N_G \to N_H$ and $f_E : E_G \to E_H$, such that the diagrams below commute.*

A partial graph morphism $f : G \to H$ is a total graph morphism from some sub-graph K of G to H, where $N_K \subseteq N_G$ and $E_K \subseteq E_G$.

$$f_N \circ s_G = s_H \circ f_E \qquad c_G \leq_N c_H \circ f_N \qquad p_G \leq_P p_H \circ f_P \qquad h_G \leq_E h_H \circ f_E$$
$$f_N \circ d_G = d_H \circ f_E$$

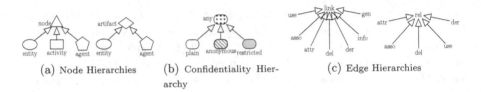

(a) Node Hierarchies   (b) Confidentiality Hierarchy   (c) Edge Hierarchies

Fig. 4. Type hierarchies for PROV-GTS rules

Definition 3 (Extended Graph Category). *Let $Graph_p$ be the category of extended PROV graphs and extended partial graph-morphisms between them. We use Graph to denote the category of extended PROV graph and their extended (total) morphism.*

4.2 PROV Rules

The graph transformation modifies a graph G according to a rule of the form $r : L \to R$ by replacing an instance of L in G by R [24].

Definition 4 (PROV Rule). *A PROV graph transformation rule $r : L \to R$ is a partial morphism r in $Graph_p$; L and R are called the left-hand side (LHS) and the right-hand (RHS) side of the rule, respectively.*

The match of the rule r is given by a total morphism $m : L \to G$. The rule is applied by using the derivation $G \overset{r,m}{\Rightarrow} H$, which is given by the pushout of r and m using a single-pushout approach [20].

The rule r can be extended to have negative application conditions which forbid the existence of certain graph patterns before applying the rule [21].

Definition 5 (Negative Application Condition). *A negative application condition (NAC) for the rule r is a total morphism $n : L \to N$ in Graph; n is satisfied by a graph morphism $m : L \to G$ if there exists no total morphism $p : N \to G$ such that $p \circ n = m$.*

Definition 6 (PROV Graph Transformation System). *A PROV graph transformation system PROV-GTS consists of a set of graph transformation rules set_R (possibly with NACs).*

5   Construction of PROV-GTS Rules

We use PROV properties prov1–5 (see Table 1) to construct the provenance graph transformation rules in a principled manner. All the inferences related to core PROV [6] are used to define PROV-GTS, except for [6, Inference 11] which is related to the time information of generation and usage relations and is outside the scope of this paper. While formally there is no explicit inference relevant to prov4, the narrative of PROV makes it clear that the existence of an activity can be inferred from the derivation relation. Table 1 provides a graphical representation of PROV properties, which we comment below.

Table 1. PROV model properties

Property	Graph Patterns ($C_i \rightarrow E_i$)		Property	Graph Patterns ($C_i \rightarrow E_i$)	
prov1	$A_1 \xleftarrow{\text{info}} A_2$	$\Rightarrow$ $A_1 \xleftarrow{\text{gen}} E \xrightarrow{\text{use}}$ $A_1 \xleftarrow{\text{info}} A_2$	prov2	$A_1 \xleftarrow{\text{gen}} E \xleftarrow{\text{use}} A_2$	$\Rightarrow$ $A_1 \xleftarrow{\text{gen}} E \xleftarrow{\text{use}} A_2$ with info
prov3	E	$\Rightarrow$ $A \xleftarrow{\text{gen}} E$	prov4	$E_1 \xleftarrow{\text{der}} E_2$	$\Rightarrow$ $E_1 \xleftarrow{\text{use}} A \xrightarrow{\text{gen}} \xleftarrow{\text{der}} E_2$
prov5	$G \xleftarrow{\text{attr}} E$	$\Rightarrow$ $G \xleftarrow{\text{asso}} A \xrightarrow{\text{gen}} \xleftarrow{\text{attr}} E$			

- prov1: The existence of an entity generated by an activity and used by another can be implied from their communication (*info*) relation ([6, Inference 5]).
- prov2: The communication between two activities can be inferred if there exists an entity generated by one of the activities and used by the other ([6, Inference 6]).
- prov3: The existence of an entity implies the existence of the activity that generated it ([6, Inference 7]).
- prov4: The derivation (*der*) edge implies the existence of an activity which connects the generated and used entities [1].
- prov5: The attribution relation (*attr*) between an entity and an agent implies that there is an activity that generated the entity and is associated with the agent ([6, Inference 13]).

Definition 7 (PROV Property). *A PROV property* prov*i is* $p : C_i \rightarrow E_i$ *in Graph for* $i = 1..5$ *where Ci and Ei are respectively premise and conclusion of inference rules, and p is the obvious inclusion morphism.*

These properties are used for two purposes. First, to define conditions necessary to construct the *deletion rules*. Second, to create the inferred nodes and edges that are not explicitly in the PROV graph and required to trigger the deletion rules by defining a set of *creation rules*. For example, prov1 can be used not only to delete an entity if it is part of a communication relation, but also to infer the existence of the entity if its identity is unknown. Any restricted nodes that are not part of the patterns that are represented by those properties and cannot be inferred from them will be used to construct *anonymization rules*.

The following sections respectively introduce deletion, creation, and anonymization rules, consisting of LHS, RHS, and/or NACs based on the aforementioned properties. The rules are presented progressively, starting with the functionality, and continuing with the more involved versions, in Sect. 6 to deal with inconsistency, and in Sect. 7 with nested conditions.

5.1   Deletion Rules

Based on prov1, a restricted entity can be deleted when the *info* edge between the generating and using activities exists. Additionally, the prov3, 4, 5 are used

Table 2. Deletion rules

rule	L	R	NAC	Rationale
rule 1 delete-entity				prov1
rule 2 delete-activity-in-out				prov4–5
rule 3 delete-activity-no-out				prov3

to form two activity deletion rules. By using the shapes and the colour patterns defined in Fig. 4, Table 2 illustrates the deletion rules and specifies the properties used in their construction in the 'Rationale' column. Note that the (labelled) nodes in L are fixed for the entire rule. The negative application condition for *rule 3* indicates that the rule is applicable if the restricted activity has no outgoing edges.

Definition 8 (Deletion Rule). *A deletion rule is a rule* $r : L \rightarrow R$ *in* $Graph_p$ *constructed from PROV property* provi, *where* $L = E_i$, $R = C_i$ *and the nodes in* $N_{E_i} \backslash N_{C_i}$ *are restricted.*

5.2   Creation Rules

The *info* relation can be inferred with prov2. In addition, generating and using activity can be inferred by prov4–5. Furthermore, generating activities can be inferred with prov3, if the restricted entity has no outgoing edges. Using prov1, we can add an entity to *info* edges to enable the *delete-activity-no-out* rule. The creation rules are shown in Table 3.

Definition 9 (Creation Rule). *A creation rule is a rule* $r : L \rightarrow R$ *in* $Graph_p$ *constructed from PROV property* provi *where* $L = C_i$, $R = E_i$, *and one of the nodes in* N_{C_i} *is restricted.*

5.3   Anonymization Rules

The restricted nodes are not always part of the patterns used to construct the deletion rules, or the patterns that can be completed using the creation rules. If this is the case, the restricted nodes will be anonymized. Examples of the restricted nodes that cannot be removed include an entity with no incoming edges, an activity that generated an entity and used another without derivation edges. Since there are no properties that help eliminate agents, they are always anonymized. The patterns that have been used to construct the anonymization rules are shown in Table 4. The rules *create-entity-in-info* (Table 3) and *anonym-activity-in-info* (Table 4) share the same LHS and NAC but conflict in their RHS which will be addressed in Sect. 6.

Table 3. Creation rules

rule	L	R	NAC	Rationale
rule 4 *create-entity-in-info*				prov1
rule 5 *create-info-use-gen*				prov2
rule 6 *create-activity-in-der*				prov4
rule 7 *create-activity-out-der*				prov4
rule 8 *create-activity-attr*				prov5
rule 9 *create-activity-no-gen*				prov3

Table 4. Anonymization patterns

rule	L	R	NAC	Rationale
rule 10 *anonym-entity-no-in*				entity with no incoming edge
rule 11 *anonym-activity-no-in*				activity with no incoming edge
rule 12 *anonym-agent*				agent
rule 13 *anonym-activity-out-info*				outgoing info with no entity
rule 14 *anonym-activity-in-info*				incoming info with no entity
rule 15 *anonym-activity-no-rel*				gen and use with no der gen and asso with no attr

Definition 10 (Anonymization Rule). *The anonymization rules are rules* $r : L \to R$ *in* $Graph_p$ *constructed from a pattern and a NAC as listed in Table 4. They only match if the none of the deletion and creation rules do.*

Observe that the matching condition is beyond the expressive power of classical transformation systems. We will address this in Sect. 7 by formulating our system in terms of the more expressive nested rules.

6 Inconsistency in PROV-GTS

In order to avoid non-determinism in GTS, we must ensure that rules are independent of each other, and that the output of a transformation is not dependent

Table 5. Extra negative conditions to ensure consistency

rule	conflicting rules	added NAC
rule 1 delete-entity	**rule 2-3** delete-activity-*	(diagram)
rule 14 anonym-activity-in-info	**rule 4** create-entity-in-info	(diagram)

Table 6. Extended LHS-RHS to ensure consistency

rule	conflicting rules	extended L	extended R
rule 10 anonym-entity-no-in	**rule 7** create-activity-out-der	(diagram)	(diagram)
	rule 8 create-activity-attr	(diagram)	(diagram)
	rule 9 create-activity-no-gen	(diagram)	(diagram)
rule 2 delete-activity-in-out	**rule 14** anonym-activity-in-info	(diagram)	(diagram)

on the order in which rules are applied. With the rules as presented so far, these properties do not hold. For instance, restricted activities with incoming *info* edge but no outgoing edges can be anonymized by the rule *anonym-activity-in-info* but it also deleted by the rule *delete-activity-no-out*. In addition, the activities with incoming *info* and outgoing edges must be anonymized by the rule *anonym-activity-in-info*, however, it could be preceded by creating an unnecessary entity by the rule *create-entity-in-info*. The key to ensure the determinism of PROV-GTS is embedding appropriate positive or negative conditions in the transformation rules. Furthermore, deleting activities before entities when matchings of the *delete-entity* rule and the *activity-deletion-* rules overlap, may required more transformation steps. For example, in Fig. 2, deleting the activity a_2 before the entity e_3, requires an extra transformation step by adding an anonymous activity in place of a_2. To resolve this issue we prevent deleting activities until all linked restricted entities are processed by adding two NACs to the *activity-deletion-* rules. Some PROV-GTS rules are provided with extended LHS and RHS (see Table 5), or NACs (see Table 6), which must be added to the conflicting rules, to ensure consistency. There are other overlapped matchings between some of the anonymization rules resulting in critical pairs, but fortunately all these pairs are safe as shown in Sect. 8.3.

7   Nested Graph Predicate

The simple rule consisting of *LHS*, *RHS*, and *NAC*s is not always enough to define transformation rules. For example, in Fig. 2 the entity e_3 has been used in derivation of the two entities e_2 and e_5. The *entity-deletion* rule deletes e_3 based on one of the outgoing edges, ignoring the other relation. To delete these nodes, we have to check conditions that repeat frequently in the host graph and have a universal nature which can only be represented using nested graph predicates [25]. In our system, we adopt the approach defined in [25,26] limited to graph predicates of depth three and one rule application. Each nested rule consists of two parts: the nested graph predicate for rule matching, represented by a root (LHS) and a set of universal-existential pairs (u_i, e_i), and an *RHS* for rule application.

Definition 11 (Nested Graph Predicate). *A nested graph predicate is the tree-shaped diagram in the category Graph consisting of three nested levels:*

1. **The Root** L_p: *each nested predicate has only one root which must be satisfied existentially (that is, in the usual way). The root L_p plays the same role as LHS in simple rules.*
2. **Universal Extensions**: *each root L_p has at least one universal extension which must be satisfied universally (that is, each possible match is considered, one at the time). It consists of a finite set $U(L_p)$ which represents the universal extensions of the root L_p, where $U(L_p) \neq \emptyset$ and $u_i \in U(L_p)$ is ith universal extension.*
3. **Existential Extensions**: *each universal extension may have an associated existential extension, to be satisfied existentially for each match of the universal extension. We denote by e_i the existential extension of u_i.*

Definition 12 (Nested Predicate Satisfaction). *Let p be a nested graph predicate and G be a provenance graph, p satisfied by the graph G if*

- *The predicate p existentially satisfied by $f : L_p \to G$, and*
- *For each universal extension $u_i \in U(L_p)$, p universally satisfied by all $g : u_i \to G$ and $k : L_p \to u_i$ such that $f = g \circ k$, and*
- *For each existential extension e_i, p existentially satisfied by at least one $h : e_i \to G$ and $l : u_i \to e_i$ such that $g = h \circ l$.*

If e_i is non-empty, then u_i must be satisfied universally. If e_i is empty, then u_i is de facto a negative application condition NAC, in that no match for it can exist in the graph for p to be satisfied. The nested graph predicates of the deletion rules of PROV-GTS and the properties used in their construction are shown in Fig. 5.

The unlabelled nodes are fixed between u_i and e_i while the labelled nodes are fixed for the entire rule. The provided graph patterns for u_i and e_i represent only the required conditions. The full graphical representation can be obtained by $L \cup u_i$ (and $L \cup e_i$) such that N_L and $N_{u_i} \setminus [X]$ (also N_L and $N_{e_i} \setminus [X]$) are two disjoint sets where $X \in L$ is a restricted node. The completeness of these graph predicates is proven in Sect. 8.1 via Lemma 1.

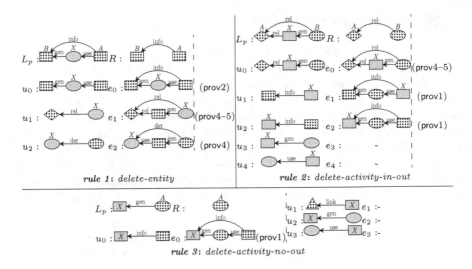

Fig. 5. Graph predicates for deletion rules

8   Properties of PROV-GTS

In PROV-GTS, provenance graphs are transformed by applying the rules again and again until no rule applies any more. In the following sections, the proofs of graph integrity, termination, and confluence are provided.

8.1   Graph Integrity

To trust the provenance information, it is important to show that the transformed graph is semantically correct. This can be done by proving that the rules do not create false-dependencies and do not result in false-independencies.

Theorem 1 (No False Dependency). *Suppose G is the original graph and G_T is the graph transformed by the PROV-GTS rules. Then $N_{G_T} \backslash N_G$ and $E_{G_T} \backslash E_G$ can be inferred from the graph G, i.e. there are no false dependencies.*

Proof (No False Dependency). Because of the way the creation rules are constructed (see Definition 9), the transformation rules add to the transformed graph G_T only what can be inferred from the original graph G. In addition, the modified rules in Table 5 do not affect this property, as they add the same positive condition to each of LHS and RHS of the conflicting rules, i.e. always $N_R \backslash N_L = N_{E_i} \backslash N_{C_i}$ and $E_R \backslash E_L = E_{E_i} \backslash E_{C_i}$ for all the creation rules $(r : L \rightarrow R)$ constructed from the PROV properties $(p : C_i \rightarrow E_i)$.

Lemma 1 (Completeness of Nested Graph Predicates). *Suppose G is the original graph and G_T is the graph transformed by the PROV-GTS rules. Deleting the restricted nodes in G_T, by the deletion rules shown in Fig. 5, will not affect what can be inferred from G.*

Proof (Completeness of Nested Graph Predicates). For the graph predicate to be complete, it must check that all possible relations between the nodes adjacent to the restricted nodes have been preserved. To this end, the nested graph predicates consist of universal-existential pairs that represent all PROV properties relevant to the type of the restricted node. For instance, in the *delete-entity* rule shown in Fig. 5, the PROV properties prov2, prov4–5, and prov4 have been used to construct the universal-existential pairs (u_0, e_0), (u_1, e_1), and (u_2, e_2), respectively. Therefore, the edges that are not incident to the restricted nodes, including the inferred ones, will not be affected by the node deletion.

Theorem 2 (No False Independency). *Suppose G is the original graph and G_T is the graph transformed by the PROV-GTS rules, $N_H = N_{G_T} \backslash N_G$ and $E_H = E_{G_T} \backslash E_G$. No false independency will be created as a consequence of deleting the restricted nodes.*

Proof (No False Independency). To prove that there is no false independency, it is sufficient to prove that all nodes in N_H are restricted nodes and the source or target of each edge in E_H is a restricted node in N_H.

All nodes in N_H are restricted because the deletion rules of PROV-GTS, according to Definition 8, removes only restricted nodes. In addition, the proof of completeness of the nested graph predicates in Lemma 1 shows that only the edges incident to the restricted nodes will be deleted.

8.2   Termination

To ensure that the graph transformation in PROG-GTS always terminates, we use a termination count which is computed by counting the number of occurrences of the graph patterns shown in Table 7. Each pattern has a positive part R and may have a negative part N. The pattern P_1 is used to compute the number of *restricted* nodes, whereas patterns $P_2 \ldots P_7$ are used to count the number of creation rule applications for each *restricted* entity. Suppose $m(G)$ is the termination count for graph G and m_1 and m_8 are the number of occurrences of P_1 and P_8 respectively, while $m_j^{e_i}$ is the number of occurrences of P_j for the

Table 7. Termination measurement patterns

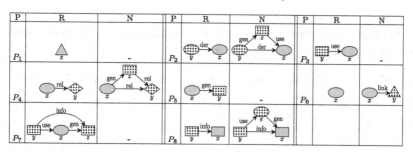

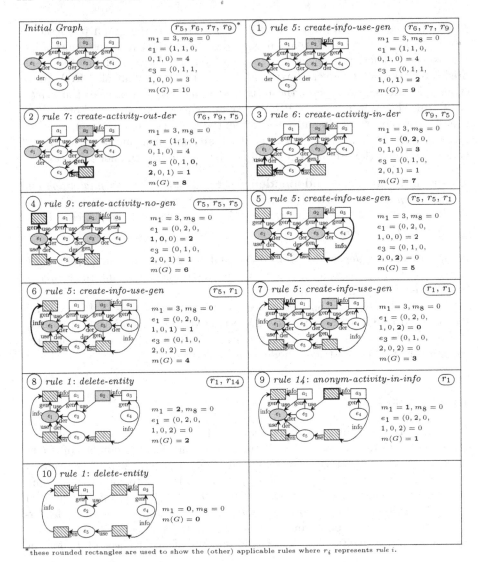

Fig. 6. Step-by-step rule application with the termination count

restricted entity e_i where $j = 2..7$. The total number of pattern matchings can then be computed using the following equations:

$$m(G) = m_1 + \sum_{i=1}^{n} E_i + m_8 \text{ where } n \text{ is the number of restricted entities,}$$
$$E_i = m_2^{e_i} + m_4^{e_i} + m_6^{e_i} + f_i - m_7^{e_i} \text{ and}$$
$$f_i = (m_2^{e_i} + m_3^{e_i}) * (m_4^{e_i} + m_5^{e_i} + m_6^{e_i})$$

The example in Fig. 6 shows step-by-step PROV-GTS rules application with the termination count at each step. For conciseness, we use a vector notation $(m_2, \ldots, m_7)$ for e_i. In each step, one of the applicable rules are (randomly) chosen and applied on the graph.

8.3 Confluence

Confirming the termination of the graph transformation process is not enough. It is essential to guarantee that the graph rewriting always terminates with the same resulting graph despite the order in which the rules have been applied, i.e. confluent.

Definition 13 (Confluence). *A graph transformation system is called confluent if for all derivations $G \overset{*}{\Rightarrow} H_1$ and $G \overset{*}{\Rightarrow} H_2$ there is a graph X and the derivations $H_1 \overset{*}{\Rightarrow} X$ and $H_2 \overset{*}{\Rightarrow} X$.*

To prove the local confluence, it is enough to prove that all critical pairs in PROV-GTS are strictly confluent [24].

In PROV-GTS, any of the rules *anonym-activity-out-info*, *anonym-activity-in-info*, and *anonym-activity-no-rel*, when applies on the same activity, makes the other two inapplicable. The same conflict happens when the matchings of the rules *anonym-activity-no-in* and *anonym-activity-out-info* overlap. Since the above rules are anonimyzing activities, the resulting graph is the same for all rule applications. This proves that the system is confluent.

9 Conclusion

In this paper, PROV model properties have been used to construct a set of rewriting rules, which form the PROV graph transformation system (PROV-GTS). The relations are preserved by creating nodes and edges that lead to the deletion of restricted nodes. If this preservation is not possible or does not lead to node deletion, the restricted nodes will be anonymized. The integrity of provenance graph has been proven by showing that no false dependencies or independencies are generated by PROV-GTS, thereby the transformed graph can be trusted. The termination has been proven by defining a count that indicates the progress of graph transformation. We show that the system is confluent using termination proof and confluence of critical pairs.

The proposed system should be expanded to cover concepts that have not been included in this paper. First, new transformation rules must be defined to process the extended terms of the PROV model. In addition, it is important to preserve other concepts, such as the time sequence in which different operations in the provenance graph occur. Finally, the system must be integrated into provenance-based applications and then its functionality, in terms of obscurity and graph utility, must be evaluated by defining proper measurements.

References

1. Moreau, L., Missier, P.: PROV-DM: the PROV data model. Technical report, W3C Recommendation, W3C (2013). http://www.w3.org/TR/prov-dm/
2. Davidson, S.B., Freire, J.: Provenance and scientific workflows: challenges and opportunities. In: Proceedings of the 2008 ACM SIGMOD International Conference on Management of Data, pp. 1345–1350. ACM (2008)
3. Kifor, T., Varga, L., Vazquez-Salceda, J., Alvarez, S., Willmott, S., Miles, S., Moreau, L.: Provenance in agent-mediated healthcare systems. IEEE Intell. Syst. **21**(6), 38–46 (2006)
4. Lim, H.S., Moon, Y.S., Bertino, E.: Provenance-based trustworthiness assessment in sensor networks. In: Proceedings of the Seventh International Workshop on Data Management for Sensor Networks, pp. 2–7. ACM (2010)
5. Cadenhead, T., Khadilkar, V., Kantarcioglu, M., Thuraisingham, B.: A language for provenance access control. In: Proceedings of the First ACM Conference on Data and Application Security and Privacy, pp. 133–144. ACM (2011)
6. Cheney, J., Missier, P., Moreau, L., DeNies, T.: Constraints of the PROV data model. Technical report, W3C Recommendation, W3C (2013). http://www.w3.org/TR/prov-constraints/
7. Missier, P.: Preserving Privacy in Shared Provenance Data. Computing Science. Newcastle University, Newcastle upon Tyne (2013)
8. Dey, S.C., Zinn, D., Ludäscher, B.: PROPUB: towards a declarative approach for publishing customized, policy-aware provenance. In: Bayard Cushing, J., French, J., Bowers, S. (eds.) SSDBM 2011. LNCS, vol. 6809, pp. 225–243. Springer, Berlin Heidelberg (2011)
9. Davidson, S.B., Khanna, S., Roy, S., Stoyanovich, J., Tannen, V., Chen, Y.: On provenance and privacy. In: Proceedings of the 14th International Conference on Database Theory, pp. 3–10. ACM (2011)
10. Moreau, L., Missier, P., Cheney, J., Soiland-Reyes, S.: PROV-N: the provenance notation. Technical report, W3C Recommendation, W3C (2013). http://www.w3.org/TR/prov-n/
11. König, B., Stückrath, J.: Well-structured graph transformation systems with negative application conditions. In: Ehrig, H., Engels, G., Kreowski, H.-J., Rozenberg, G. (eds.) ICGT 2012. LNCS, vol. 7562, pp. 81–95. Springer, Heidelberg (2012)
12. Ehrig, H., Golas, U., Habel, A., Lambers, L., Orejas, F.: M-adhesive transformation systems with nested application conditions. Part 1: Parallelism, concurrency and amalgamation. Math. Struct. Comput. Sci. 93–102 (2012)
13. Cadenhead, T., Khadilkar, V., Kantarcioglu, M., Thuraisingham, B.: Transforming provenance using redaction. In: Proceedings of the 16th ACM Symposium on Access Control Models and Technologies, pp. 93–102. ACM (2011)
14. Dey, S., Ludascher, B.: A declarative approach to customize workflow provenance. In: Proceedings of the Joint EDBT/ICDT 2013 Workshops, EDBT 2013, pp. 9–16. ACM, New York (2013)
15. Missier, P., Bryans, J., Gamble, C., Curcin, V., Danger, R.: PRovenance Graph Abstraction by Node Grouping. Computing Science. Newcastle University, Newcastle upon Tyne (2013)
16. Missier, P., Bryans, J., Gamble, C., Curcin, V., Danger, R.: ProvAbs: model, policy, and tooling for abstracting PROV graphs. In: Ludaescher, B., Plale, B. (eds.) IPAW 2014. LNCS, vol. 8628, pp. 3–15. Springer, Heidelberg (2015)

17. Blaustein, B., Chapman, A., Seligman, L., Allen, M.D., Rosenthal, A.: Surrogate parenthood: protected and informative graphs. Proc. VLDB Endowment 4(8), 518–525 (2011)
18. Backstrom, L., Dwork, C., Kleinberg, J.: Wherefore art thou r3579x?: anonymized social networks, hidden patterns, and structural steganography. In: Proceedings of the 16th International Conference on World Wide Web, pp. 181–190. ACM (2007)
19. Corradini, A., Montanari, U., Rossi, F., Ehrig, H., Heckel, R., Löwe, M.: Algebraic approaches to graph transformation-part i: basic concepts and double pushout approach. In: Handbook of Graph Grammars, pp. 163–246 (1997)
20. Ehrig, H., Heckel, R., Korff, M., Löwe, M., Ribeiro, L., Wagner, A., Corradini, A.: Algebraic approaches to graph transformation-part ii: single pushout approach and comparison with double pushout approach. In: Handbook of Graph Grammars, pp. 247–312. Citeseer (1997)
21. Habel, A., Heckel, R., Taentzer, G.: Graph grammars with negative application conditions. Fundamenta Informaticae 26(3), 287–313 (1996)
22. Habel, A., Pennemann, K.-H.: Nested constraints and application conditions for high-level structures. In: Kreowski, H.-J., Montanari, U., Orejas, F., Rozenberg, G., Taentzer, G. (eds.) Formal Methods. LNCS, vol. 3393, pp. 293–308. Springer, Heidelberg (2005)
23. Moreau, L., Groth, P.: Provenance: an introduction to prov. Synth. Lect. Semant. Web Theor. Technol. 3(4), 1–129 (2013)
24. Ehrig, H., Ehrig, K., Prange, U., Taentzer, G.: Fundamentals of Algebraic Graph Transformation, vol. 373. Springer, Heidelberg (2006)
25. Rensink, A., Kuperus, J.H.: Repotting the geraniums: on nested graph transformation rules. Electron. Commun. EASST 18, 1–15 (2009)
26. Rensink, A.: Nested quantification in graph transformation rules. In: Corradini, A., Ehrig, H., Montanari, U., Ribeiro, L., Rozenberg, G. (eds.) ICGT 2006. LNCS, vol. 4178, pp. 1–13. Springer, Heidelberg (2006)

Social Network Culture Needs the Lens of Critical Trust Research

Natasha Dwyer[1(✉)] and Stephen Marsh[2]

[1] Victoria University, Melbourne, Australia
natasha.dwyer@vu.edu.au
[2] University of Ontario Institute of Technology, Oshawa, Canada
stephen.marsh@uoit.ca

Abstract. Trust is essential to the success of the social networks that are aggregating and applying masses of information about us. In this position paper, we argue that a critical approach to exploring trust and social networks is required; this entails genuinely working in the interests of users and acknowledging the power relations and wider social context of this form of technology that is impacting more and more of our everyday life. Without a critical approach, digital environments may become monopolised by corporate interests.

1 Introduction

The digital traces left by individuals can now easily be collected, crosschecked and stored as part of a phenomenon known as social networking and what is loosely described as 'big data'. Because this complex set of information can be used as a form of social control, social science researchers argue that we need to handle social network data and culture critically; to question the ways the data is gathered and used and to produce alternative means to understand and participate in the phenomenon [1]. But what does this mean for trust researchers? In this position paper, we contend that critical approaches to trust and social networks require researchers to work *genuinely* in the interests of users and to respond to the power relations connected with social networks. We suggest that trust researchers should follow the lead provided by privacy researchers, in acknowledging that the interests of an individual can clash with those of governments and corporations. Before we outlay our argument, we describe what social network data is and explain the central role trust plays in the success of the social networks that produce the data. As a final point, we discuss how social network data can be of use to trust researchers.

2 Social Network Data

Social network data is generally considered to be information generated at networks designed for exchange between users, for example, messages exchanged at websites such as Twitter and Facebook. Social network content has existed in some form for some time. More recently, content collected from disparate locations can be united, compared and stored at a magnitude not previously possible. The digital data provided by individuals can be analysed and applied in a variety of ways. For instance, social network users, such as subscribers to Facebook, now receive advertisements for products their friends have bought: the underlying idea behind the strategy is that individuals trust the recommendations of their friends so the technique is an effective way to convince users to buy a product or accept a message. Social network analysis, used by industry and the academy, explores the links between individuals, behavior and artifacts (for instance, messages) to find patterns, such as the flows of information and influence.

A social network occurs when a computer connects individuals or organizations, according to Garton [2], so the data could include material as diverse as logs indicating which individuals share a printer to transcripts of credit card transactions. Self-tracking systems, applications that gather data about individuals' health performance also now need to be considered as a type of social network content. Systems are now available that enable individuals to track and compare their personal health indicators such as eating habits, sleep, blood pressure etc. There is the option to share this information with others via broadcasts on social networks. Daly [3] outlines how although these systems were once the domain of a few 'enthusiasts', interested in the response of their bodies of the course of a day, the information is now in the hands of multinationals who are beyond the reach of local laws describing how personal information should be protected. Another ramification of self-tracking technology is that now, according to Lupton [4], individuals are not trusting their own insights about their bodies and health because it's easier to trust the 'numbers over physical sensations'. Self-tracking systems teach us to adhere to expected societal norms regarding sleeping, eating, and drinking, which are reinforced through the act of sharing data. One aim of these systems is to use personal data as a form of motivation to improve one's health through self-reflection, guilt and peer pressure [4]. Soon employers may demand access to their employees' health information and decide on who is trustworthy on the basis of these results [5].

3   Social Networks and Trust

Trust plays a central role in the continuing flow of social network content to adapt Fukuyama's famous line [6], trust greases the wheels of the networks. If a user does not trust the information received from a network, it will not be passed on [7]. The business model of the social network sites depends on users creating, sharing and consuming content. IBM's CEO, Ginni Rometty in 2014 described the opportunity for the sale of individual private data as the goldmine for the 21st century [8]. So social network sites are designed to provoke high levels of disclosure from users. For instance, participation can be set up in a popularity contest framework where users strive to receive more attention in the form of 'likes' and 'shares' etc. [9]. The website 'Dark Patterns' (www.darkpatterns.org) is a collection of instances where the designer has applied a solid understanding of human nature in order to coerce the user into doing something that is not in the user's individual interest, for instance, disclosing personal information. An example provided by Dark Patterns is Yahoo's Hotjob site. In order to interact, the user is required to answer a series of personal information, even though the information required by a potential hirer is already provided in the job application. As the user is required to complete the information fields in order to progress an application, there is pressure to comply.

The uneven power relations propagated by social networks means that individuals can be manipulated and controlled, whether by marketing companies, governments, or any other entity that has access to the data and the means to analyse it. This is known as 'information injustice'. Individuals are often unaware of the data traces they are leaving and the value of the information they leave behind [10], as demonstrated by the disturbing effect of the viral website 'Take This Lollipop' (www.takethislollipop.com). Upon entry to this site, the user is asked to provide permission for an app to access the user's personal Facebook account. This is a common request from many websites, so users are accustomed to agreeing without much consideration. Once permission is granted, there is a film sequence of a grimy house with a menacing looking man typing on computer. The camera moves closer and we see what he is looking at. Integrated into the film image is the personal Facebook profile view of the user that contains information that the user has not yet set to public display. This includes information that the user may not have given directly to Facebook, such as birth date, that Facebook has collected from one of its partner organisations. The intention of 'Take This Lollipop' is to shock. Even if an individual is alert to the circulation of personal data via a social network, it is difficult for an individual to retract a data trace once it is distributed [10]. The exploitation of users is built into the design of technology, as price for use. When someone uses technology to conduct some sort of activity, such as a searching, buying products, or catching up with friends, the user enters into an arrangement where personal data is collected as a condition of use of the technology [11].

As trust plays a central role in the creation of successful social networks, it is easy to see how the work of trust researchers is attractive to owners of digital environments such as corporations and governments. Trust research can be used to exploit users and to create environments that are commercially successful by giving the appearance of trustworthiness. If trust researchers take their work seriously and believe it has an impact on the direction of both the research field and industry, then an implication is that the work could be used to improve the profits and control of a private company. For instance, [12] study trust interactions on social network sites from a user's perspective, in particular, how a user can improve social capital in these environments. They recommend that as well as having many 'loose ties' users should stay visible in these spaces and remain attentive to their contacts. Social networks such as Twitter and Facebook could use this advice to encourage users to keep engaging with their systems. Similarly, Lui et al. [13], working with the notion that different users in a social network seek a range of trust evidence, seek a means to calculate tailored trust ratings, which they refer to as Quality of Trust. However, a social network developer could use this research to persuade users to buy the products they endorse. There may be researchers who may be comfortable with their work servicing the support of the status quo. However, for those researchers are not, we argue that a critical approach is required. Of course, as Gupta [14] points out, it is possible that any idea and critique can be subsumed by the mainstream to maintain the current state of affairs, but this does not mean that resistance is useless.

There are other roles that trust research can play and one importance stance is to work in the interests of users first, not commerce. To argue for a critical approach to technology is not to declare the technology as dystopic. Rather it is to understand technology as a 'double-edged sword' reliant on 'the context and comportment' of a particular scenario including the actions of and interplay between digital environment owners, developers, designers, and users [15].

4   A Critical Approach to Trust and Social Networks

So what does a critical approach to studying and designing trust consist of? A critical perspective entails two key actions by researchers that are reviewed in this section. Firstly, an acknowledgement is required of the power relations inherent in the domain of social network data, trust and research. Acknowledgement entails questioning whose biases and expectations are served by the production of digital systems and the research that surrounds digital technology [16]. Acknowledgement can lead to research and design that deciphers technology as a social construct that enables a range of social relations not just those that suit governments and corporations [17]. (Alternatively, acknowledgement of the power relations can lead to the researcher identifying that there is limited possibility for research with a critical perspective, a discussion beyond the scope of this paper).

However, according to Stolterman [18], scientists and engineers are not well-suited to undertake a consideration of the socio-political framework their work exists in. They are unaccustomed to such a practice as their training involves focusing on one problem and isolating it away from context much as possible. Zelenko and Felton [16] add that designers are also not well suited to consideration of the wider milieu that their work exists in as they are trained to acquiesce to the instructions of the client. But education and practice is changing. The trust research field, including practitioners from a range of disciplines, now conceptualise trust as a social phenomenon. The next step is to move beyond conceptualising trust as a scenario between individuals or groups and consider the wider social and political structures impacting on individual interactions. An example of research that includes a consideration of social context is the work of Pearson and Tsiavos [19] who explore 'smart notices'; a means for individuals to control their information and to set the expectations for the products and services they seek. Although they are working in a corporate environment (HP Bristol), these authors place their research in a socio-technical context, the Creative Commons movement, and design around the inherent power relations that occur between an individual and a network.

Secondly, researchers need to commit to working *genuinely* in users' interests; addressing information imbalances, making users aware of their trust interactions, enabling users to negotiate trust on their own terms and learning from users. Trust researchers can learn from privacy researchers who have a natural inclination to study a scenario from the perspective of users' welfare. As Krontiris [20] review, privacy research has a long history of conceptualisation as tussle between an individual and others who might gain advantage from private knowledge about that individual. Some protection for individuals is legislated and there is also a long history of privacy advocacy that provides a framework that researchers' work can fit into. Some privacy researchers explore the risks that users are exposing themselves to by interacting with social networks. For instance, Nurse et al. [21] investigate the hazards from the occurrence of incidental individual interactions online. Some actions are as innocuous as printing from a device. A mass of data is left behind that can be used to infer about that individual's 'real world social relationships', without the individual having any knowledge of the disclosure. Those inferences could be used in a myriad of ways depending on who had access to the data. Netter et al. [22] add that there is often a mismatch between a user's perception of privacy controls in a social network and what is really occurring. To solve this problem, they have developed identity management software to assist a user to handle disclosures made online. Basu et al. [23] suggest a system that could work without the disclosures and privacy trade-offs users are accustomed to offering in order to participate. Games are becoming a location for mass amounts of social network data, as players reveal physiological and psychological data (for instance, response time, prioritisation of strategies and attention rate) and Martinovic et al. [24] argue that this is an area that needs attention from privacy researchers.

Readdressing information imbalance is to strive so that individuals have as much access and control to the data generated by networks as do powerful bodies such as governments and private corporations. Mann [25] is a proponent of this technique. His response to surveillance is 'sousveillance', that he defines as 'the recording of an activity by a participant in the activity' to 'reverse the otherwise one-sided panoptic gaze'. In this vision, individual users adopt the recording technologies in the spaces they inhabit and combine their resources to form lobby groups. We see these types of community groups already happening in the form of police observation groups such as *Copwatch* in Canada and *FITwatch7* in the United Kingdom [26]. The result is a challenge to traditional sources of power, where trust is qualified rather than just given. Individuals are enabled to form trust decisions using their own data rather than information mediated by news sources. Of course, there are shortcomings to Mann's vision. For instance, there would need to be a change in the governance framework of a society so that individuals can access information that is currently closed, and also resourcing so that individuals can obtain the required technology. However, these limitations should not mean that the idea is dismissed. As Goldsmith [26] points out, the potential for individuals to perform some level of sousveillance increases with every improvement in camera technology.

Another example of practice that works genuinely in users' interests is the creation of digital environments that make users *aware* of the implications of their social network interactions. This alternative is a shift away from the majority of trust research that as far as possible claims that trust should be managed in the background and automatically handled by the digital system. The underlying objective is that trust in a digital environment should be a fluid state that it is not explicitly addressed by the user. This type of design can allow participants to attend to activities, whether that is shopping, finding a date or exploring a medical issue [27]. In contrast, we, the authors (as outlined in [27]), wish to create designs that make users mindful of their inter-actions so users become contributors to the wisdom of the digital ecosystems they inhabit (in other words, the users are 'strong links'). In particular, we wish to design a device that combines several factors (such as time, nearby devices and previous user preferences) in order to communicate an overall 'comfort level' to the user for the user to interpret. What the user does with this guidance is ultimately up to the user. The idea is to provide an opportunity for the user to have a 'second thought'. Awareness can be created by 'obstructive interfaces', which could be as simple as a message to the user, "Are you sure that you really want to do this?" Storey et al. [28] have prepared a range of interface elements such as persistent, oversized, and insistent stop buttons and messages that require a deliberate hand action to dismiss. Different user's require tailor made obstructions, add [29]. Nuanced communication styles for obstruction are a subject of further exploration. In previous research by the authors, [30] investigate Twitter messages coded as 'trust' by users as a means to understand how trust is conceptualised by users in social media networks.

Practitioners and researchers wishing to learn from users or to create systems that draw attention to the trust implications of interactions can learn from the research field of critical interactive design (see [31] for an overview), which is a subset of the larger practice known as Human Computer Interaction (HCI). Critical interactive design is working on similar notions of bringing in the user as an active participant and aims to create a space whereby a "user" can make a reflective choice about interaction. Within critical interaction design, there is the practice of 'seamful design' that aims to present to the user the 'seams' of a design; its constituent parts, and how it integrates with other systems [31]. The practice is a response to the automation culture we discussed earlier in this paper, the mission of mainstream technology designed to create interconnected, distributed systems that deliver ease and convenience seamlessly that are not noticed by the use. Within a seamful design, the biases, contradictions and problems of technology are exposed, rather than smoothed over by a design and a spirit of critique is engendered [31]. The role of researchers and designers is to identify which seams, out of all the possible data, will be important to the user and how best to present the seams.

As a final note, we add that as well as the trust community having something valuable to contribute to social network culture, social network data can be of use to trust researchers. Although social network data can be difficult to interrogate and reproduce scientifically (due to the control retained by the owners of social network sites), the data contains users discussing issues of importance to them within a 'real world' context. Trust researchers recognise how difficult it is to gather data from participants about trust either in laboratories, isolated from the impact of demands of everyday life or in the context of 'real' situations. In contrast, within social networks there are users around the world providing their view on trust in the form of publically accessible conversations in text format. Rather than a top-down view of trust, an abstract understanding developed by a researcher, social network data offers a 'bottom-up' view of trust from the perspectives of individuals. Sardana and Cohen [32] use social network data for this purpose and insert material from users to substantiate their trust models.

5   Conclusion

In conclusion, a critical approach to social media data use is necessary if social networks are not to become monopolised by commercial interests telling us who to trust and what trust means. A critical approach needs to: acknowledge and respond to the wider power relations that social networks generate and work genuinely in users' interests.

Trust researchers can learn from the orientation of privacy researchers, to put the individual user first. Some trust researchers are already exploring from a user's perspective, investigating how to readdress information imbalances, to make users more attentive to the implications from interacting with social networks, and to enable users to form trust choices about their trust negotiations within social networks on their own terms.

References

1. Dalton, C., Thatcher, J.: What does a critical data studies look like, and why do we care? Seven points for a critical approach to "Big Data". Soc. Space Open Site (2014)
2. Garton, L., Haythornthwaite, C., Wellman, B.: Studying online social networks (2010)
3. Daly, A.: The law and ethics of 'self quantified' health information: an australian perspective. In: International Data Privacy Law (2015, forthcoming)
4. Lupton, D.: Beyond techno-utopia: critical approaches to digital health technologies. Societies 4(4), 706–711 (2014)
5. Walston, S.L., Bennett, C.J., Al-Harbi, A.: Understanding the factors affecting employees' perceived benefits of healthcare information technology. Int. J. Healthc. Manag. 7(1), 35–44 (2014)
6. Fukuyama, F.: Trust: The Social Virtues and the Creation of Prosperity. Free Press, New York (1995)
7. Kim, Y., Ahmad, M.A.: Trust, distrust and lack of confidence of users in online social media-sharing communities. Knowl.-Based Syst. 37, 438–450 (2013)
8. Sathi, A.: Engaging Customers Using Big Data: How Marketing Analytics Are Transforming Business. Palgrave Macmillan, New York (2014)
9. Yu, B., Chen, M., Kwok, L.: Toward predicting popularity of social marketing messages. In: Salerno, J., Yang, S.J., Nau, D., Chai, S.-K. (eds.) SBP 2011. LNCS, vol. 6589, pp. 317–324. Springer, Heidelberg (2011)
10. Johnson, J.: From open data to information justice. In: Midwest Political Science Association Annual Conference (2013)
11. Langlois, G.: Meaning in the Age of Social Media. Palgrave Macmillan, New York (2014)
12. Ellison, N.B., Vitak, J., Gray, R., Lampe, C.: Cultivating social resources on social network sites: facebook relationship maintenance behaviors and their role in social capital processes. J. Comput.-Mediated Commun. 19(4), 855–870 (2014)
13. Liu, G., Wang, Y., Orgun, M.A.: Quality of trust for social trust path selection in complex social networks. In: Proceedings of the 9th International Conference on Autonomous Agents and Multiagent Systems, vol. 1, pp. 1575–1576. International Foundation for Autonomous Agents and Multiagent Systems (2010)
14. Gupta, R.: Has neoliberalism knocked feminism sideways? Centrestage (2012)
15. Marx, G.T.: "Your papers please": personal and professional encounters with surveillance. In: Kevin, D., Lyon, D. (eds.) Routledge Handbook of Surveillance Studies. Routledge, London (2012)
16. Zelenko, O., Felton, E.: Framing perspectives on design and ethics. In: Felton, E., Zelenko, O., Vaughan, S. (eds.) Design and Ethics: Reflections on Practice, pp. 3–9. Taylor & Francis, Routledge (2012)
17. Verbeek, P.-P.: Moralizing technology: Understanding and designing the morality of things. University of Chicago Press, Chicago (2011)

18. Stolterman, E.: The nature of design practice and implications for interaction design research. Int. J. Des. 2(1), 55–65 (2008)
19. Pearson, S., Tsiavos, P.: Taking the creative commons beyond copyright: developing smart notices as user centric consent management systems for the cloud. Int. J. Cloud Comput. 3 (1), 94–124 (2014)
20. Krontiris, I., Langheinrich, M., Shilton, K.: Trust and privacy in mobile experience sharing: future challenges and avenues for research. IEEE Commun. Mag. 52(8), 50–55 (2014)
21. Nurse, J.R., Pumphrey, J., Gibson-Robinson, T., Goldsmith, M., Creese, S.: Inferring social relationships from technology-level device connections. In: Twelfth Annual International Conference on Privacy, Security and Trust (PST), pp. 40–47. IEEE (2014)
22. Netter, M., Riesner, M., Weber, M., Pernul, G.: Privacy settings in online social networks–preferences, perception, and reality. In: 46th Hawaii International Conference on System Sciences (HICSS), pp. 3219–3228. IEEE (2013)
23. Basu, A., Vaidya, J., Kikuchi, H., Dimitrakos, T.: Privacy-preserving collaborative filtering for the cloud. In: 2011 IEEE Third International Conference on Cloud Computing Technology and Science (CloudCom), pp. 223–230. IEEE (2011)
24. Martinovic, D., Ralevich, V., McDougall, J., Perklin, M.: "You are what you play": breaching privacy and identifying users in online gaming. In: 2014 Twelfth Annual International Conference on Privacy, Security and Trust (PST), pp. 31–39. IEEE (2014)
25. Mann, S., Fung, J., Lo, R.: Cyborglogging with camera phones: steps toward equiveillance. In: Proceedings of the 14th Annual ACM International Conference on Multimedia, pp. 177–180. ACM (2006)
26. Goldsmith, A.J.: Policing's new visibility. Br. J. Criminol. 50(5), 914–934 (2010)
27. Marsh, S., Wang, Y., Noël, S., Robart, L., Stewart, J.: Device comfort for mobile health information accessibility. In: Eleventh Annual International Conference on Privacy, Security and Trust (PST), pp. 377–380. IEEE (2013)
28. Storer, T., Marsh, S., Noël, S., Esfandiari, B., El-Khatib, K., Briggs, P., Renaud, K., Bicakci, M.V.: Encouraging second thoughts: obstructive user interfaces for raising security awareness. In: Eleventh Annual International Conference on Privacy, Security and Trust (PST), pp. 366–368. IEEE (2013)
29. Murayama, Y., Hikage, N., Fujihara, Y., Hauser, C.: The structure of the sense of security, anshin. In: Lopez, J., Hämmerli, B.M. (eds.) CRITIS 2007. LNCS, vol. 5141, pp. 83–93. Springer, Heidelberg (2008)
30. Dwyer, N., Marsh, S.: What can the hashtag# trust tell us about how users conceptualise trust? In: Twelfth Annual International Conference on Privacy, Security and Trust (PST), pp. 398–402. IEEE (2014)
31. Boehner, K.A.: Interfaces with the Ineffable. Cornell University, London (2006)
32. Sardana, N., Cohen, R.: Validating trust models against realworld data sets. In: Twelfth Annual International Conference on Privacy, Security and Trust (PST), pp. 355–362. IEEE (2014)

Predicting Quality of Crowdsourced Annotations Using Graph Kernels

Archana Nottamkandath[1]([⊠]), Jasper Oosterman[2], Davide Ceolin[1],
Gerben Klaas Dirk de Vries[3], and Wan Fokkink[1]

[1] VU University Amsterdam, Amsterdam, The Netherlands
{a.nottamkandath,d.ceolin,w.j.fokkink}@vu.nl
[2] Delft University of Technology, Delft, The Netherlands
j.e.g.oosterman@tudelft.nl
[3] University of Amsterdam, Amsterdam, The Netherlands
g.k.d.devries@uva.nl

Abstract. Annotations obtained by Cultural Heritage institutions from the crowd need to be automatically assessed for their quality. Machine learning using graph kernels is an effective technique to use structural information in datasets to make predictions. We employ the Weisfeiler-Lehman graph kernel for RDF to make predictions about the quality of crowdsourced annotations in Steve.museum dataset, which is modelled and enriched as RDF. Our results indicate that we could predict quality of crowdsourced annotations with an accuracy of 75 %. We also employ the kernel to understand which features from the RDF graph are relevant to make predictions about different categories of quality.

Keywords: Trust · Machine learning · Crowdsourcing · RDF graph kernels

1 Introduction

Cultural Heritage institutions are digitizing their collections. This process involves manually making digital copies of the artifacts in their collection and registering relevant information about the metadata of the artifacts into their systems. Professionals are employed by the institutions to provide this information according to their high quality standards.

In most cases, providing such information for large collections is an exhaustive task in terms of human resources and requires expertise knowledge from many domains. Hiring more professionals with domain expertise in order to speed up the tasks is not feasible, so these institutions are looking into crowdsourcing this artwork description (annotation). The crowd provides diversified information about artifacts, hence issues dealing with the quality of annotations arise. Consider, for instance, the artwork collection item (a sculpture) from Steve.museum depicted in Fig. 1; the figure includes the annotations produced by crowd annotators in a real-world annotation campaign. The annotations in green indicate the ones which were considered useful by the professionals at institution while

© IFIP International Federation for Information Processing 2015
C.D. Jensen et al. (Eds.): IFIPTM 2015, IFIP AICT 454, pp. 134–148, 2015.
DOI: 10.1007/978-3-319-18491-3_10

the red ones indicate the ones which were not considered useful to be added to their collection. Employing human reviewers to assess the quality of annotations is as expensive as hiring professional annotators and thus there is a need for automated processes to assess the quality of these annotations or, in other words, to develop methods to estimate the trust in them.

19th century
Asian
Black
Clearly female
Contrast
Detailed face
Gold / Gold
Man-bird
Metal
Wings
Yellow

Fig. 1. The artwork titled *Kinarra* from the Steve.museum dataset and associated crowd annotations. Green = useful, red = non-useful (Color figure online).

Properties of the annotations such as annotator, annotated artifact, time stamp etc. and properties of the artifact and of the annotators themselves can all be modeled using the Resource Description Framework (RDF), i.e. as a labeled graph. Apart from representing the entities and the relations between them, such an RDF graph also captures the structural information of the information. In an earlier work [3], we modelled the annotations and employed some annotation properties such as semantic similarity and reputation of the users to predict the quality of annotations. Machine learning techniques such as Support Vector Machines (SVMs) can be used to make predictions about features in the dataset. Recently, machine learning using graph kernels has arisen as an efficient method for learning from RDF graphs [6,13], that can effectively exploit the structural properties of the graph using SVMs. To show the potential of such a graph kernel we apply it on the Steve.Museum dataset. First we transform the annotations and contextual information from the dataset to a semantic model and enrich the model with external vocabularies and knowledge sources. We then leverage this model to make predictions about the annotation quality by applying the Weisfeiler-Lehman RDF graph kernel.

Our contributions are threefold; (1) We propose a workflow to transform and enrich Cultural Heritage datasets into semantic (RDF) data; (2) We show how a specialized kernel for RDF can be applied on a semantic Cultural Heritage annotation dataset to predict annotation quality and relevant features; and (3) We provide insights into the benefit of RDF kernel for Cultural Heritage datasets.

The paper is structured as follows. In Sect. 2 we describe related work. In Sect. 3 we describe the overall workflow and explain in detail about the enriched semantic model and RDF kernel. Section 4 describes the Steve.Museum dataset and the metrics used, followed by the results and their analysis in Sect. 5. We provide discussion and future work in Sect. 6.

2   Related Work

Utilizing knowledge from the crowds to perform tasks is widely used on the Web [7]. Open Mind Common Sense [23] is a knowledge acquisition system designed to acquire commonsense knowledge from the general public over the Web. Several Cultural Heritage institutions have been looking towards users on the Web to provide information about their artifacts such as depicted visuals, meta data, sentiments etc. These institutions define tasks for gathering annotations from the users either as a game as in ESP game [25] or through online systems as shown in examples from "Your Paintings Tagger" by BBC[1] Accurator for Rijksmuseum Amsterdam[2], and others such as Brooklyn Museum, New York Library and others [17].

We consider the estimation of quality of crowdsourced annotations as a task equivalent to the estimation of the trustworthiness of the annotations, and indirectly of the trustworthiness of the annotator. We refer the reader to the works of Artz and Gil [1] for an extensive survey of trust models in the Semantic Web, Golbeck [9] for trust models on the Web, Sabater and Sierra [18] for trust models in computer science and Prasad et al. [15] for Bayesian computational trust models.

Studies have been done to understand the quality of information provided by the crowd as shown by Snow et al. [24]. Inel et al. [11] have been studying the annotations obtained from the crowdsourcing platforms such as Crowdflower to make quality assessments. There have also been many methods developed to determine the quality of these crowdsourced information, where majority voting has been widely used. For example, in ESP game, a label is added to the picture if at least two randomly picked users suggest the same label. This research extends two previous works of ours. We extend a Semantic Web representation of cultural heritage annotations that we previously introduced [3], and we explore how to make machine learning-based quality assessments from such a model. These machine learning-based assessments implicitly introduce a measure of similarity between Semantic Web data. The use of semantic similarity measures to semi-automatically predict the quality of crowdsourced cultural heritage annotations has been explored in another previous work of ours [2]. However, in that work semantic similarity is computed only between the annotations, while here it extends to the metadata.

In this paper we utilize RDF graph kernels to utilize structural properties of graphs to make predictions about annotation quality. Although features about the user and of the annotations were used to make predictions of quality with SVMs in a previous work of ours [14], we did not employ RDF graph kernels

---

[1] http://tagger.thepcf.org.uk/.
[2] http://rma-accurator.appspot.com.

for the predictions. This paper aims to provide a new method employing RDF graph kernels for automatically predicting quality of crowdsourced annotations in the cultural heritage domain.

3   Approach

In this section we describe the workflow that we propose to assess the quality of crowdsourced annotations. We begin with an overview of the workflow and then we describe each component in detail.

3.1   Workflow Overview

The workflow that we adopt to estimate the quality of the user-provided annotations is depicted in Fig. 2 and consists of three steps:

1. Representing Annotations in RDF
2. Annotations Enrichment
3. Machine learning with graph kernels for RDF

Whenever an annotation is introduced in the system, it is modeled in RDF, along with its related metadata (e.g., its author). The resulting RDF graph is then enriched by linking it with information provided by authoritative and trusted Linked data sources. In this manner, we expand the knowledge graph describing the annotation. Lastly, we use Support Vector Machines and the Weisfeiler-Lehman graph kernel to estimate the quality of the annotation, exploiting the information provided in the enriched graph and using a set of previously evaluated (and enriched) annotations. The following sections describe these steps in detail.

3.2   Representing Annotations in RDF

Annotations describing artworks provided by the users from the Web are represented using the Open Annotation Model [19] which helps to link annotations to the user who created them and the artifact for which an annotation was created. A subset of annotations are reviewed by the experts at the cultural heritage institutions and their reviews are represented as an annotation of an annotation. The review indicates an expert opinion about the annotation that the user provided according to standards of the institution. Apart from information about annotations, we would like to extend our information about the user who provided the annotation. For users who registered in the system and provided profile information, we model their information using the FOAF ontology [5], while anonymous users do not have any additional information in their profile. Also the artifact has some meta data such as the creator of the artifact, a title, and material properties. We use the Eurpeana Data Model (EDM) [10] to represent these properties. Figure 3 shows our generic semantic model for the annotations contributed to the cultural heritage domain.

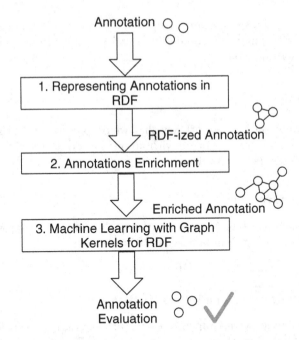

Fig. 2. Annotation evaluation workflow. First, the annotation is represented in RDF. Then it is enriched. Lastly, we use the RDF-based machine learning to predict its quality.

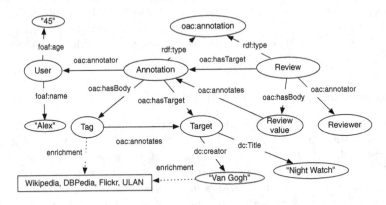

Fig. 3. Semantic model of cultural heritage annotations

3.3 Annotations Enrichment

Enrichment of the annotations is done since RDF graph kernels can easily use additional information since all additional information is part of RDF graph to make predictions. The properties related to the artwork, the creator of the artwork and the annotation itself are relevant to be enriched. Unfortunately, to the best of our knowledge, there were no publicly accessible knowledge repositories related to artworks. We extend the creator data using the Union List of Artist Names (ULAN) and DBPedia, and annotation data with DBPedia, Flickr and Wikipedia.

The ULAN is a structured vocabulary maintained by professionals of the Getty Research Institute and contains information such as date of birth and nationality of 202.720 past and current artists (in 2011[3]). Wikipedia[4] is a mostly unstructured knowledge base maintained by tens of thousands of volunteers worldwide and contains information on a very broad spectrum of topics. The information is intended for human consumption. DBpedia[5] is a semantic reposi- tory of information that is extracted from Wikipedia. Most pages on the English Wikipedia have a corresponding entry in DBPedia. Information in DBPedia is structured in RDF and is machine processable. Flickr is a website where people upload and share their images. Most images are tagged with descriptive labels.

Institutions store creator information either as structured, semi-structured or unstructured text. For linking purposes we assume creator text is unstructured. We map ULAN resources using the `getty:labelPreferred` (e.g. Rembrandt van Rijn) and `getty:labelNonPreferred`(e.g. Rembrandt Hermanszoon van Rijn) properties. We also map DBPedia resources of type `dbpedia-owl:Artist` using the `foaf:name` property.

The textual annotations are compared to DBPedia resources based on the `rdfs:label` property to check whether the annotation corresponds to existing words. The popularity of each annotation is calculated using Flickr by counting the number of images that have been uploaded in 2014 and were labeled with that annotation.

3.4 Machine Learning with Graph Kernels for RDF

In a typical machine learning classification task, one tries to predict a class for a set of instances. Each instance is represented by a feature vector: a list of properties of that instance. This approach fits well to the scenario where the dataset is a table in a database, and each instance is a row. But it does not easily translate to RDF graphs. For example, consider the simple RDF graph given in Fig. 4A. Suppose we want to predict a property of things (i.e. people) that are Persons, then our instances are the two nodes: person1 and person2. It is not immediately obvious what the features of person1 and person2 are.

Machine learning for RDF data using graph kernels was introduced in [13] as a way to deal with this issue by using structural patterns of the RDF graph as input for kernel based learning algorithms [20, 21]. For each instance we consider the subgraph around that instance (up to a certain depth) as its 'features', see Fig. 4B. For these subgraphs structural properties are computed as something that is called a 'kernel', which is essentially a similarity function between objects,

---

[3] http://www.getty.edu/research/tools/vocabularies/ulan/faq.html.
[4] http://en.wikipedia.org/wiki/Wikipedia:About.
[5] http://wiki.dbpedia.org/About.

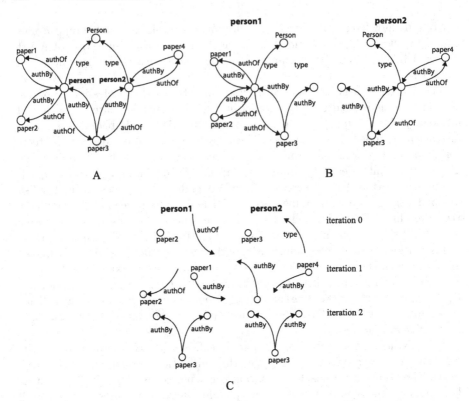

Fig. 4. Example RDF graph (A), with two subgraphs of depth 2 (B) and examples of extracted features (C).

for instance, between subgraphs of an RDF graph. This kernel is used as the input data for a learning algorithm. The main advantage of using graph kernels for learning from RDF, compared to other techniques, is that it is a generically applicable and flexible approach [16]. Little knowledge of the dataset is required to use these methods and it allows for easy integration of additional knowledge into the learning process, by simply adding triples to the RDF graph.

In this paper we will use the Weisfeiler-Lehman [22] graph kernel for RDF (WLRDF), introduced in [6]. This is a state of the art graph kernel for learning from RDF data in terms of prediction accuracy, with very good computational performance. For each instance, the WLRDF kernel efficiently computes subtree patterns as features, in a number of iterations, where each iteration computes more complex patterns. These patterns are illustrated in Fig. 4C. Typically, the features that are considered by a kernel are computed implicitly. However, subtree features of the WLRDF kernel are computed explicitly and we can therefore inspect which subtree patterns are important in the learning process.

As our learning algorithm, we use the well-known Support Vector Machine (SVM). SVMs are very efficient and robust classification algorithms that try to separate classes by finding a maximally separating hyperplane. For more see for example the books [20,21].

In the machine learning step in our workflow, the instances that we use are annotations, i.e. nodes that are of type Annotation. For each annotation a subgraph is extracted up to a specified depth. From Fig. 3 we can see that larger depths leads to the inclusion of more levels of information in the graph. The WLRDF kernel is computed using these subgraphs and then used to train a SVM on labelled (in terms of quality) annotations. This SVM is then used to predict the annotation quality of unseen annotations.

4   Experimental Setup

We apply our approach on the Steve.museum dataset, which is described in Sect. 4.1. The details of the enrichment step is discussed in 4.2 followed by the experimental parameters set to run the experiment in Sect. 4.3.

4.1   Steve.museum Dataset

The Steve.museum [12] project was started together with United States art museums with the aim to explore the role that user-contributed descriptions can play in improving on-line access to works of art. Annotations were gathered for $1,784$ artworks and the usefulness of each annotation was evaluated by professional museum staff. The reviewers distinguished 12 categories of usefulness. The category usefulness-useful and usefulness-not_useful indicated positive and negative usefulness. Other categories described why the annotation was not useful (e.g. problematic-misspelling, judgement-positive). The annotations including their evaluations and annotator information were published as a SQL dataset.

The dataset contains $49,767$ artifacts annotations in total, along with the related metadata, created by 730 anonymous[6] and 488 registered users, where anonymous users created 24.016 annotations (43 % of the total). Registered users could enter additional profile information. Table 1 lists those properties and the percentage of registered users who provided a value for a property.

There are some differences in the behaviour of anonymous and registered users: the first contributed on average 15 annotations per session, the latter 33. Moreover, we see a clear pattern in the week day distribution: registered users contribute annotations mostly between Tuesday and Thursday and the anonymous users during the other days of the week. Also, registered users contributed most of their annotations in the morning and in the evening, although the pattern here is less definite.

Out of the $49,767$ annotations, $48,789$ (98 %) have been evaluated, of which 87 % as usefulness-useful. Table 3 shows the average performance per session of the registered and anonymous users. The annotations contributed by the

---

[6] Anonymous users were identified using a disambiguation process based on their web session identifier since multiple annotations may have been created by the same user at different times. However, we do not know if two sessions were created by the same anonymous user, but for registered users we see that this happens quite rarely: the average number of sessions per registered user is 1.03.

registered users are of slightly higher quality than those contributed by anonymous users.

4.2 Dataset Transformation

We transformed the data into Linked Data using the model illustrated in Fig. 3.
Most properties of the users and the annotation could be mapped one-to-one.
However, some annotations were reviewed multiple times. For the purpose of
prediction we required each annotation to have exactly one review; therefore, we
applied the following strategy: if any of the reviews stated the usefulness of an
annotation as usefulness-useful, we selected that review, giving more weight
to a potentially useful annotation. If not, we selected the usefulness value with
the single highest frequency. When there were multiple reviews with the highest
frequency, we removed the annotation as this happened in very few cases. This
resulted in the deletion of $1,246$ annotations leaving $47,543$ annotations. Also
we removed the reviewer information from the graph since that information
would not be present for future (un-reviewed) annotations which we want to
automatically assess.

The Steve.museum dataset contains $1,082$ unstructured creator names. Our
goal was to identify creators pointing to individual persons. Therefore we fil-
tered the creator names containing the string *unknown*, locations (countries and
places), time periods, and hashed strings to anonymize the details of certain
artefacts. This resulted in 742 creator strings (of which some could still point
to the same person) which we considered candidate artists. When possible we
put the name in $< firstname > < lastname >$ order. We used the preprocessed
name to match to DBPedia and ULAN.

For each name that could not be matched we performed a Wikipedia search
on that name where we automatically retrieved the top 5 results and checked if
the corresponding DBPedia resources were of the type dbpedia-owl:Artist. We
automatically made the mapping if there was only one Artist in the results and
decided manually when there were multiple Artists. In total 579 candidate artists
were mapped onto 479 distinct DBPedia resources. For the ULAN mapping we
used both the preprocessed name and the spelling variations on DBPedia if there
was a match. In total 470 candidate artists were mapped to 422 distinct ULAN
resources. The mapping process resulted in 605 mapped candidates of which 442
mapped by both ULAN and DBPedia, 138 only mapped to DBPedia and 27
only mapped to ULAN.

To enrich the annotation as described in Sect. 3 we tokenized the annotation
and removed stopwords, special characters such as "" and ">", and words of
length 1. We added a custom:wikipediaMatchCount property to each annotation with the number of matched words from the preprocessed annotation.
For Flickr we used the flickr.photos.search API function searching for all
photos containing all annotation words as label and which were uploaded in
2014. We added a custom:flickrMatchCount property to each annotation with
the amount of photos returned by the API. Finally, to match with the Wikipedia
description of the creators we tokenized and stemmed the description, stemmed

Table 1. Annotator properties and the percentage of registered annotators who filled in the property.

Community	Experience	Education	Age	Gender	Household income
431 (88%)	483 (99%)	483 (99%)	480 (98%)	447 (92%)	344 (70%)
Works in a museum	Involvement level	Tagging experience	Internet connection	Internet usage	
428 (88%)	411 (84%)	425 (87%)	406 (83%)	432 (89%)	

Table 2. Summary of the transformed and enriched Steve.museum dataset.

Total number of triples	473,986
Annotators/registered annotators	1,218/488 (40%)
Annotated artworks	1,784
Annotations/unique annotations	45,733/13,949 (31%)
Candidate creators/mapped creators	1,082/605 (56%)
Annotations in Flickr (> 0 images retrieved)	25,591 (56%)
Annotations in DBpedia (> 0 words matched)	25,163 (55%)

Table 3. Comparison of the average performance per session between registered and anonymous users.

Evaluation category	Average frequency per session (Registered users)	Average frequency per session (Anonymous users)
Usefulness-useful	75.57%	74.46%
Usefulness-not_useful	11.19%	11.96%
Problematic-personal	0.53%	0.61%
Problematic-no_consensus	0.69%	0.63%
Problematic-foreign	0.99%	1.13%
Problematic-huh	0.36%	0.55%
Problematic-misperception	2.65%	2.76%
Problematic-misspelling	0.88%	0.89%
Judgement-positive	0.70%	0.48%
Judgement-negative	0.75%	0.95%
Comments	2.15%	1.72%
Not evaluated	3.54%	3.86%

the preprocessed annotation words and added a `custom:hasCreatorMatchCount` property indicating the amount of matched words.

Table 2 provides a summary of the complete dataset. The transformed dataset and the enrichments are available as RDF/XML files online.[7]

4.3   Experimental Parameters

As can be seen in Table 3 the distribution of the usefulness categories is very skewed and many categories are very small. For our experiments we therefore kept the larger usefulness-useful and usefulness-not_useful categories, grouped together both problematic and judgement subcategories and removed both the comments category and annotations which were not evaluated.

Our experiments have been implemented in Java using the 'mustard' library[8], which implements different graph kernels, such as the WL RDF kernel, for RDF data and wraps the Java versions of the LibSVM [4] and LibLINEAR[9] [8] SVM libraries.

The experiments were run on depth 1 (including annotation properties), depth 2 (additionally including annotator and artwork properties) and depth 3 (additionally including properties from the linked datasets). On each depth we created 10 subsets of the graph and performed a 5-fold cross-validation, optimizing the C-parameter of the SVM in each fold, using again 5-fold cross-validation. The number of iterations parameter h for the WLRDF kernel was fixed to the depth $\times 2$. This parameter can also be optimized, however this has relatively little impact, since the higher iterations include the lower iterations. Subsets were created by taking a random sample of annotations in the usefulness-useful category of size equal to the other categories combined and took all annotations from those categories. Each subset contained approximately 9000 annotations. For each depth and subset we calculated the accuracy, precision, recall and F1 score for the categories combined and individually.

5   Results and Analysis

In this section we present our experimental results. First we give our quantitative results and then we qualitatively analyse important features for predicting the different categories.

5.1   Comparison of Accuracy, Precision and Recall for Predictions at Different Depths

We compare the accuracy, F1-measure, precision and recall for predicting four different categories (usefulness-useful, usefulness-not_useful, judgment, problematic) at three different depths of the graph and present the results in

---

[7] The dataset can be downloaded at https://www.dropbox.com/s/0l8zo023hhsrsjt/all_data.zip?dl=0.

[8] Our code can be found in the org.data2semantics.mustard.experiments.IFIPTM package of the library at https://github.com/Data2Semantics/mustard.

[9] http://liblinear.bwaldvogel.de/.

Table 4. The features for the graph which were included at different depths are described in Sect. 4.3. We repeated the experiment for predicting two types of review categories (usefulness-useful and usefulness-not_useful) and found that the results are comparable to the ones mentioned in Table 4, while the overall F1-measure was higher, with 0.76 for every depth. This is to be expected since the two classes which were hard to predict were not included. The best overall results were achieved under the depth 2 setting. The judgement class is very hard to predict, as we can see from the very low precision, recall and f1 scores.

5.2   Comparison of Relevant Graph Features at Different Depths

The multi-class SVM implementation in LibLINEAR computes a SVM for each class, which can be used to identify the important graph features for each class. Thus, we trained a SVM for the first of our 10 four-class subsets. A manual analysis of these important features (those with the highest weight) for the different classes at different depths shows some interesting results. We will not mention the results for the judgement class, since it was predicted very poorly.

At depth 1, the useful class has a large number of specific date strings, e.g. "2007-07-18T00:22:04", as important features. However, the not-useful class is recognized by features pointing to the artwork that is annotated, such as oac:hasTarget->http://purl.org/artwork/1043. The problematic class has important features similar to the useful class.

Table 4. Comparison of results from predictions using the WLRDF kernel at different depths

Depth	Prediction class	Avg. Accuracy	Precision	Recall	F1 measure
1	Usefulness-useful		0.75	0.78	0.76
	Usefulness-not_useful		0.74	0.74	0.74
	Judgement		0.00	0.00	0.00
	Problematic		0.68	0.25	0.37
	All classes	0.75	0.54	0.44	0.47
2	Usefulness-useful		0.77	0.77	0.77
	Usefulness-not_useful		0.74	0.75	0.75
	Judgement		0.30	0.04	0.07
	Problematic		0.64	0.34	0.45
	All classes	0.75	0.61	0.48	0.51
3	Usefulness-useful		0.77	0.76	0.77
	Usefulness-not_useful		0.74	0.76	0.75
	Judgement		0.05	0.01	0.01
	Problematic		0.64	0.32	0.42
	All classes	0.75	0.55	0.46	0.49

Graph features containing `edm:object_type` and `oac:hasBody` are almost exclusively the most important features for identifying **useful** annotations at depth 2 and 3. In contrast, the type of features that are used in classifying `not-useful` annotations is more diverse. They include graph features with the material used in the artwork or information about the annotators. For example a set of important features has the graph pattern that includes the information that the annotator has "Intermediate" experience. The `problematic` class at depth 2 and 3 is recognized with very specific features, like date strings, that are not as general as for the other two classes.

6   Discussion and Future Work

In this paper we presented a workflow to convert datasets in the Cultural Heritage domain to RDF and to enrich the datasets to be used for predictions of annotation quality using RDF graph kernels. We have provided both a qualitative and quantitative analysis of the results and have shown that RDF kernels are quite beneficial in making predictions about quality.

From our experiments it can be seen that employing RDF graph kernels helps in predicting classes of annotations with a overall best accuracy of 75 %, which is a good rate of acceptance. The single class measures of accuracy, precision, recall and f1-measure for the classes of `judgement` and `problematic` are not useful since the percentage of their classes were too small to perform a good training and thus they were predicted badly.

We also identified which features are relevant at different depths to make the predictions per category and provided an analysis. The features which are relevant to predict a certain class of quality are useful to design annotation tasks in the future. If a particular creator is selected as a relevant feature and if the majority of annotations by different users to an artwork belonging to that creator tend to be evaluated mostly as `usefulness-not_useful`, then it might indicate that the annotation task is difficult for that particular artwork. Similarly for different datasets such in-depth analysis helps to re-design the annotation tasks to obtain better quality from the crowds.

The approach of using graph kernels for RDF is very flexible as additional information can easily be added to the learning process by extending the RDF graph. However in Steve.museum dataset, some node labels provide very specific information, which is not beneficial for generalization. For example, the annotations are timestamped with exact times in seconds, whereas the day of the week might be more informative. Some (light) graph pre-processing can help to alleviate these issues, without hindering the flexibility and extensibility of the approach. We will investigate this in future work.

The automatic prediction of quality of annotations based on their metadata helps Cultural Heritage institutions alleviate the task of reviewing large number of annotations and helps to add the most useful annotations directly to their system for better search and retrieval through their collection. As part of future work, we would like to perform our experiments on different datasets from the

Cultural Heritage domain to understand how and which features are most relevant in predicting quality from these datasets.

Acknowledgement. This publication is supported by the Dutch national program COMMIT.

References

1. Artz, D., Gil, Y.: A survey of trust in computer science and the semantic web. J. Semant. Web **5**(2), 58–71 (2007)
2. Ceolin, D., Nottamkandath, A., Fokkink, W.: Automated evaluation of annotators for museum collections using subjective logic. In: Dimitrakos, T., Moona, R., Patel, D., McKnight, D.H. (eds.) IFIPTM 2012. IFIP AICT, vol. 374, pp. 232–239. Springer, Heidelberg (2012)
3. Ceolin, D., Nottamkandath, A., Fokkink, W.: Efficient semi-automated assessment of annotation trustworthiness. J. Trust Manag. **1**, 1–31 (2014)
4. Chang, C.-C., Lin, C.-J.: LIBSVM: a library for support vector machines. ACM Trans. Intell. Syst. Technol. **2**, 27:1–27:27 (2011). http://www.csie.ntu.edu.tw/cjlin/libsvm
5. Dan Brickley, L. M.: FOAF, January 2014. http://xmlns.com/foaf/spec/
6. de Vries, G.K.D.: A fast approximation of the weisfeiler-lehman graph kernel for RDF data. In: Blockeel, H., Kersting, K., Nijssen, S., Železný, F. (eds.) ECML PKDD 2013, Part I. LNCS, vol. 8188, pp. 606–621. Springer, Heidelberg (2013)
7. Doan, A., Ramakrishnan, R., Halevy, A.Y.: Crowdsourcing systems on the world-wide web. Commun. ACM **54**(4), 86–96 (2011)
8. Fan, R.-E., Chang, K.-W., Hsieh, C.-J., Wang, X.-R., Lin, C.-J.: LIBLINEAR: a library for large linear classification. J. Mach. Learn. Res. **9**, 1871–1874 (2008)
9. Golbeck, J.: Trust on the world wide web: a survey. Found. Trends Web Sci. **1**(2), 131–197 (2006)
10. Hennicke, S., Olensky, M., de Boer, V., Isaac, A., Wielemaker, J.: A data model for cross-domain data representation. The "Europeana Data Model" in the Case of Archival and Museum Data (2011)
11. Inel, O., Khamkham, K., Cristea, T., Dumitrache, A., Rutjes, A., van der Ploeg, J., Romaszko, L., Aroyo, L., Sips, R.-J.: CrowdTruth: machine-human computation framework for harnessing disagreement in gathering annotated data. In: Mika, P., Tudorache, T., Bernstein, A., Welty, C., Knoblock, C., Vrandečić, D., Groth, P., Noy, N., Janowicz, K., Goble, C. (eds.) ISWC 2014, Part II. LNCS, vol. 8797, pp. 486–504. Springer, Heidelberg (2014)
12. U. institute of Museum and L. Services. Steve Social Tagging Project, January 2012
13. Lösch, U., Bloehdorn, S., Rettinger, A.: Graph kernels for RDF data. In: Simperl, E., Cimiano, P., Polleres, A., Corcho, O., Presutti, V. (eds.) ESWC 2012. LNCS, vol. 7295, pp. 134–148. Springer, Heidelberg (2012)
14. Nottamkandath, A., Oosterman, J., Ceolin, D., Fokkink, W.: Automated evaluation of crowdsourced annotations in the cultural heritage domain. In: URSW. CEUR Workshop Proceedings, vol. 1259, pp. 25–36. CEUR-WS.org (2014)
15. Prasad, T.K., Anantharam, P., Henson, C.A., Sheth, A.P.: Comparative trust management with applications: bayesian approaches emphasis. Future Gener. Comput. Syst. **31**, 182–199 (2014)

16. Rettinger, A., Lösch, U., Tresp, V., d'Amato, C., Fanizzi, N.: Mining the semantic web–statistical learning for next generation knowledge bases. Data Min. Knowl. Discov. **24**(3), 613–662 (2012)
17. Ridge, M.: Introduction. In: Ridge, M. (ed.) Crowdsourcing Our Cultural Heritage. Digital Research in the Arts and Humanities. Ashgate, Farnham (2014)
18. Sabater, J., Sierra, C.: Review on computational trust and reputation models. Artif. Intell. Rev. **24**, 33–60 (2005)
19. Sanderson, R., Ciccarese, P., de Sompel, H.V., Clark, T., Cole, T., Hunter, J., Fraistat, N.: Open annotation core data model. Technical report, W3C Community, 9 May 2012
20. Schölkopf, B., Smola, A.J.: Learning with Kernels: Support Vector Machines, Regularization, Optimization, and Beyond. MIT Press, Cambridge (2001)
21. Shawe-Taylor, J., Cristianini, N.: Kernel Methods for Pattern Analysis. Cambridge University Press, Cambridge (2004)
22. Shervashidze, N., Schweitzer, P., van Leeuwen, E.J., Mehlhorn, K., Borgwardt, K.M.: Weisfeiler-lehman graph kernels. J. Mach. Learn. Res. **12**, 2539–2561 (2011)
23. Singh, P., Lin, T., Mueller, E.T., Lim, G., Perkins, T., Zhu, W.L.: Open mind common sense: knowledge acquisition from the general public. In: Meersman, Robert, Tari, Z. (eds.) CoopIS/DOA/ODBASE 2002. LNCS, vol. 2519, pp. 1223–1237. Springer, Heidelberg (2002)
24. Snow, R., O'Connor, B., Jurafsky, D., Ng, A.Y.: Cheap and fast–but is it good?: Evaluating non-expert annotations for natural language tasks. In: Proceedings of the Conference on Empirical Methods in Natural Language Processing, EMNLP 2008, pp. 254–263. Association for Computational Linguistics (2008)
25. von Ahn, L., Dabbish, L.: Labeling images with a computer game. In: Proceedings of the SIGCHI Conference on Human Factors in Computing Systems, CHI 2004, pp. 319–326. ACM (2004)

An Architecture for Trustworthy Open Data Services

Andrew Wong[⊠], Vicky Liu, William Caelli, and Tony Sahama

Science and Engineering Faculty, Queensland University of Technology,
Brisbane, Australia
{jianwye.wong,v.liu,w.caelli,t.sahama}@qut.edu.au

Abstract. This paper addresses the development of trust in the use of Open Data through incorporation of appropriate authentication and integrity parameters for use by end user Open Data application developers in an architecture for trustworthy Open Data Services. The advantages of this architecture scheme is that it is far more scalable, not another certificate-based hierarchy that has problems with certificate revocation management. With the use of a Public File, if the key is compromised; it is a simple matter of the single responsible entity replacing the key pair with a new one and re-performing the data file signing process. Under this proposed architecture, the Open Data environment does not interfere with the internal security schemes that might be employed by the entity. However, this architecture incorporates, when needed, parameters from the entity, e.g. person who authorized publishing as Open Data, at the time that datasets are created/added.

Keywords: Open data · Integrity · REST · Security · Public file

1 Introduction

During the course of his doctoral study, Roy Fielding generalized the architectural principles that drove the Web conceived of by Tim Berners-Lee in the early 1990s and presented these principles as an architectural style which was underpinned by a framework of constraints. This framework was named Representational State Transfer (REST) [1] and systems which adhere to this framework are called "RESTful" systems or services. Because of the REST framework's ease of use and deployment, it has since been used in a variety of other development methodologies, including web services and application programming interface (API) development, and has since become a serious rival to the use of the earlier Simple Object Access Protocol (SOAP) [2] which is a successor to the Remote Procedure Call (RPC) programming style. These SOAP and REST based APIs have been used to communicate data and information in many fields, most recently, Open Data.

Open Data is data that can be freely used, shared and built-on by anyone, anywhere for any purpose [3]. The recent global trends towards Open Data have organizations and governments relying on these APIs to communicate Open Data in a greater extent than before.

© IFIP International Federation for Information Processing 2015
C.D. Jensen et al. (Eds.): IFIPTM 2015, IFIP AICT 454, pp. 149–162, 2015.
DOI: 10.1007/978-3-319-18491-3_11

One of the key advantages of Open Data is that it increases the availability of data for consumers in decision making as well as providing potential for massive cost reduction through implicit outsourcing of information system development. At regional governmental level, a combination of Open Data with appropriate interrogation programs could possibly replace physical publication of such documents as guidebooks, listings, etc. The active interest and support by various national and international non-governmental organization as well as state and federal government sponsored 'hack-athons' such as GovHack [4] and HealthHack [5] aiming to develop new applications that use Open Data also could lead to a strong upsurge in the use of Open Data in various fields.

As the capacity for acquiring and storing data increasing from year to year and with data analytics exerting greater influence on decision making than in years past, trust has to be placed in not just the processes and algorithms used to analyse data, but in the authenticity and integrity of data as well. There is now a fast developing trend for enterprises; both public and private, to incorporate Open Data with proprietary and private data collections in order to provide better decision making and other reports. However, how can users trust conclusions or decisions made on the basis of results obtained from largely, untrusted data?

An adversary, wishing to use any means necessary to cause disruption, may wish to misuse the Open Data movement to achieve this disruption within the society by:

1. Diverting Open Data requests to a fraudulent site containing fraudulent datasets.
2. Insertion of a fraudulent dataset into a legitimate site.
3. Deliberate modification of a legitimate dataset.
4. Denial of Service should Open Data become an integral and essential part of a community service.

Therefore, it becomes of vital significance to ensure the authenticity and integrity of Open Data in order to placing trust in decision making based on that same Open Data, for users, businesses, industry and government alike.

2 Paper Scope

Because of the nature of Open Data, methods such as encryption which is aimed at the confidentiality aspect of data may not be completely relevant in the broad philosophy of Open Data, but may be briefly discussed.

This paper addresses development of trust in the usage or adaptation of Open Data through the incorporation of appropriate authentication and integrity parameters for data included in end-user Open Data applications by developers. The principle here is that the average person would not normally access raw Open Data collections but would view them through the lens of an appropriate application. The user would therefore need to be able to trust both the authenticity and integrity of data supplied by the application.

The proposed architecture makes use of the Domain Name System Security Extensions (DNSSEC) for host/server verification. However, the full description of DNSSEC functionality lies outside the scope of this paper, and will only be briefly discussed in relation to how it fits into the proposed architecture as a whole. It should be noted that DNSSEC does not use digital certificates but rather a public key hierarchical registry.

The paper will also discuss the proposed architecture's use of a public key hierarchical registry and digital signatures instead of the traditional certificate authority for the authentication of data publishers and integrity of datasets.

3 Related Work

3.1 Trustworthy Open Data

Open Data, which at its core, is the idea that certain types of data should be freely accessible to the public has its roots in the concept of open access to scientific data in the 1950s [6]. In more recent years, researchers have indicated the potential benefits of using Open Data analytics for positive effect in various fields [7–11] and coupled with the rise of Open Government [12–14], the Open Data movement stands to make even greater impact in the near future. However there are certain challenges that Open Data faces, not the least of which is ensuring data quality and fostering trust in Open Data [15]. Strong [16] and later Mazon [17] recognize "fitness for use" as being the definition of data quality and an important criterion for data analytics and business intelligence, and security plays an important role in ensuring both data quality and trust.

A database search returned few works relating to on methods for Open Data security. Telikicherla and Chopella [18] propose a library for secure web application development as a means of preventing "frame busting" and other attacks in HTML5 based Open Data mashups. Eckert et al. [19] present a workflow model which preserves provenance for Linked Data and can be applied to Open Data. These approaches have their merits in the area of browser security and preserving provenance for data, however, as Open Data depends on the ability to transmit data that can be verified as both coming from an authenticated source while retaining integrity through the transmission process and therefore is trustworthy to the user, this issue still needs to be addressed.

3.2 Security for REST

The United States, United Kingdom, Japan, and Australia among others, use a software called the Comprehensive Knowledge Archive Network (CKAN), an open source data management platform to manage and publish their Open Data [20]. CKAN's Action API is based on the RPC programming style. Another well-known Open Data Management Suite is Socrata. The Socrata Open Data API (SODA) provides an open, standards-based REST API [21]. In the case of the United States, the wide variety of government services and organizations has led to the use of both CKAN [22] and SODA [23] at the state and federal government levels.

As APIs for Open Data is mostly disseminated through the platform of the World Wide Web (WWW), and the WWW is based on REST principles as coded by Fielding [1], in order for Open Data to be secure, REST also needs to be secure. In Fielding's thesis, REST was designed to provide simplicity of implementation and scalability but has no pre-defined security protection mechanisms [24] when compared to SOAP, which uses the WS-Security [25] standard. In response to this, several authors have recently suggested mechanisms by which to provide security for REST:

Forsberg [26] proposed an approach where content protection was based on keys being delivered to clients via secure session. Forsberg's approach eliminates the need for repeated SSL/TLS encryption of cached content. Forsberg further notes that their solution is adjusted to match better with caching for data that requires confidentiality protection. An approach which used extended HTTP headers to effect extended username tokens was proposed by Dunlu et al. [27] for user authentication. A secondary password for the username token was required in order to avoid leakage of user password. The approach proposed by Serme et al. [28] had some similarities to Dunlu et al. where they used extended HTTP headers, except that Serme's approach uses the HTTP headers to convey digital certificate and encryption information.

Lee and Mehta [29], investigating some of the security threats to REST-based Web Services concluded that although message encryption by HTTPS was a costly protection method, HTTPS-based data transfer was the best method to ensure data confidentiality. Backere et al. [30] states that the best solution to the RESTful security problem, or the one most conforming to RESTful principles, is to differentiate between messages that need to be encrypted and those that do not, that a message is not-modifiable, and that replayed messages be avoided. They propose a login and REST resource access mechanism that leveraged these concepts.

There is a common consensus that it is necessary for appropriate security mechanisms to be employed in REST Web Services, however the means of accomplishing this as well as the security properties to be protected vary from approach to approach. Most of the solutions presented by these authors however, focus on authenticating the user or protecting the confidentiality of information held in RESTful systems while using certificate-based Secure Sockets Layer/Transport Layer Security (SSL/TLS). This however, begs the question: Is it necessary to protect the confidentiality of *publicly available* Open Data, or even to authenticate users of Open Data?

The answer to this question is: Open Data by its very nature is public data, therefore it should be viewable by the public and not restricted by confidentiality mechanisms. With this, authentication of the end user for read-only access to Open Data is not strictly necessary. Having said this, restricting access to the methods that can be used to alter Open Data resources to authenticated entities, such as the original publisher of the data, or other authorized parties is still required. An important quality that was brought up by Backere et al. [30] which relates to Open Data is that messages and content should be unmodifiable, which basically refers to the integrity of Open Data resources and collections even as they are transferred and cached over the Web.

3.3   Public Key Infrastructures

There are two aspects to Open Data; (1) the management of Open Data collections, one of which involves actions by an authoritative source like adding, modifying or deleting datasets, and, (2) the usage or modification of datasets post-addition. Both of these aspects require authentication that: (1) The host of the data is genuine, and, (2) the data has been published by an authentic source, and, (3) the data being transmitted itself is genuine and remains unchanged through the communication process. This authentication can be accomplished through the use of message digests and digital signatures.

Diffie and Hellman [31] proposed a "public file" which could be used as a central authority for the binding of a specific identity to a particular public key for authentication purposes, thereby establishing a hierarchy of trust. Because of the technological limitations of the time, this approach has proven unfeasible when compared with the public key certificate concept proposed by Kohnfelder [32]. The public key certificate authentication scheme based on Kohnfelder's thesis is now ubiquitous, however, despite the technological barrier for the use of the "public file" no longer being applicable and issues with public key certificate management that have been highlighted by Clarke [33], most notably complexity and the problems with certificate revocation mechanisms.

Rivest attempts to address the issue of certificate revocation by proposing that proper certificate infrastructure organization can allow a signer to present a collection of certificates as evidence of authenticity [34]. Another paper authored a few years later by McDaniels and Rubin [35] state that addressing PKI requirements in large, loosely coupled environments using certificate revocation lists is difficult and a web environment based on REST, as envisioned by Fielding, is designed to be a large, loosely coupled environment.

There have been recent attempts to address the problems with public key certificate based authentication and trust through initiatives that leverage the abilities of multiple certificate notaries, such as the Perspectives Project, [36] and Convergence [37]. The Perspectives Project and Convergence provide trust agility in which the user is given the ability to decide which party they wish to trust for authentication of certificates. In general, these initiatives provide trust that the certificate is genuine by leveraging multiple certificate notaries to provide additional trust perspectives on the Certificate in question.

However, in this emerging landscape of Open Data, a distributed trust model may not be the answer as usage of Open Data depends on whether or not a user trusts the owner or original creator of the Open Data. If that owner or creator is not a reputable source, or if the identity of said owner cannot be verified, then any data coming from that source is untrustworthy. In other words, an instance of a public key must be verified as belonging to a genuine entity, taking into account the threat of the addition of false identities and/or public keys, in order for data gleaned from that source to be considered trustworthy and/or having authenticity and integrity.

4 Proposed Solution

This paper proposes a Trustworthy Architecture for Open Data Systems (Fig. 1) which would serve as a precaution against tampering, enabling users to know when a particular resource is genuine or has been tampered with, thus augmenting the REST framework. As mentioned in a previous section, the SSL/TLS level encryption of request-response messages represents an expenditure of processing resource which is not critical for communicating Open Data. However, measures to protect message integrity and authenticity to ensure trustworthiness are still required.

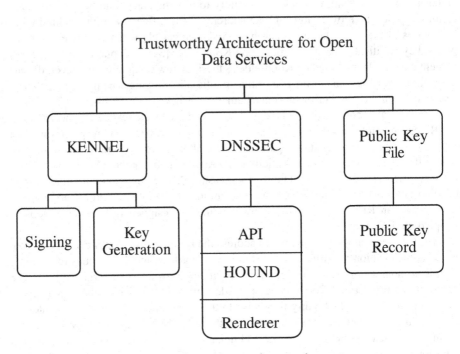

Fig. 1. Trustworthy architecture for open data systems

4.1 Key Components

The architecture proposed hinges on several key components, a Key Generation component, a Public Key File, DNSSEC and a Verifier Module which interfaces with regular REST framework activity as needed.

Certification Authority vs Public Key Registry. Effective key management is essential for the smooth operation of cryptographic systems. In regular circumstances, a trusted Certification Authority is responsible for issuing digital certificates and maintaining certificate revocation lists, and is also responsible for the generation of cryptographic key pairs and digital signatures. If a certificate model is to be used then this would be the normal procedure, however, given that Open Data is of its own essence, "open", proposing a complex certificate architecture including certificate revocation should be unnecessary. Moreover, access to confidentiality/privacy services and mechanisms is not required. It would seem reasonable, then, that each Open Data publishing entity could maintain its own public key, relevant to verification of data integrity alone, in an appropriately managed and controlled public key registry (PKR) file similar to the Diffie-Hellman concept of the "public file", in line with the design philosophy of DNSSEC.

Public Key File. The Public Key File is a central location where public keys associated with recognized identities may be retrieved. It is proposed that any entity wishing to publish Open Data generates a cryptographic key pair and submit the public key to the Open Data Public Key File maintained by this Registry (using the Key Generation and Signing Module). Users of Open Data will then be able to retrieve the appropriate public key to verify a signature from this central location.

Key Generation and Signing Module (KENNEL). For ease of explanation the Key Generation and Signing module will be referred to as KENNEL. To become an Open Data Publisher, owners of Open Data first need to use KENNEL to generate a cryptographic key pair. This local generation of the key pair eliminates the need to securely transmit the private key over network channels and just exposes the public key, which is what the public key is designed for. The module then submits the generated Public Key to the Registry along with sufficient proof of identity over a secure channel (Fig. 2). This information will be the basis of a record in the Public Key File (Fig. 3).

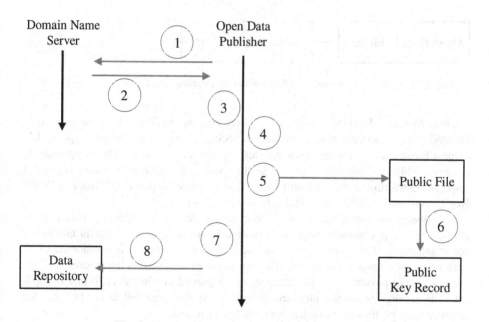

Fig. 2. Open data publisher process using KENNEL

The Open Data Publisher is responsible for maintaining the secrecy of its Private Key, and uses this key in conjunction with a cryptographic one-way hashing function to generate a Digital Signature Table 1.

Table 1. Process of Fig. 2. Open Data Publisher Process using KENNEL

Steps	Description
1	DNS resolution request
2	DNS resolution response
3	DNSSEC verification using zone signing key
4	KENNEL computes cryptographic key pair, retains private key
5	Public key sent with identification documents securely
6	Public key bound with identity and stored securely
7	KENNEL signs Open Data using private key
8	Signed Open Data stored

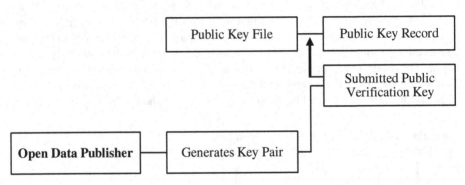

Fig. 3. Role of the open data certificate authority in relation to the open data publisher

Verifier Module (HOUND). For ease of reference, the Verifier will be referred to as HOUND. After address resolution with DNSSEC implemented is accomplished, a request for resources reaches the server and the server responds with the appropriate resource which is digitally signed. At the client-side, HOUND reads the server response, extracting signer's identity, retrieves the matching public key from its Public Key Record and verifies the digital signature.

A message digest is recovered by decrypting the digital signature with a valid public key and is compared to a message digest computed at the recipient end of the communication. If both digests are identical, then the response is considered to be authentic and retains its integrity. The operation of the verifier terminates and the content is then passed to the Renderer and is displayed in whichever format is applicable. If the digests are not identical, then the recipient is alerted to the fact that the resource may be fraudulent or has been altered in transit.

DNSSEC. The Internet Engineering Task Force has developed RFC3833 [38] the Domain Name System Security Extension specification to resolve various threats to the DNS using public-key cryptography to establish a chain of trust, which in practice each zone has a public key which is deposited in the parent domain for authentication purposes. Therefore, DNSSEC does not make use of digital certificates but rather a public key hierarchical registry.

In order for DNSSEC to be incorporated, the domain host first needs to have DNSSEC enabled on the server-side and the client needs to install a DNSSEC validator which can read verification information from the server.

4.2 Use Case Scenario

Communication without the Proposed Architecture. A request for data to a server follows a standard request-response paradigm. This is an example of a standard HTTP request for a resource without the use of the proposed architecture:

Address Resolution is performed after the initial request is made by the Domain Name System. DNS uses Root or Authoritative Name Servers which are heavily supplemented by DNS caches as a workaround to reduce DNS traffic and increase efficiency. Caching DNS request-response records reduces load on individual servers but is vulnerable to DNS cache poisoning and other interception attacks.

After the 200 OK response, there is no further communication from hosting server and there is no provision for integrity verification. Content is then displayed. It is difficult to place confidence in the data because, as mentioned previously, without any

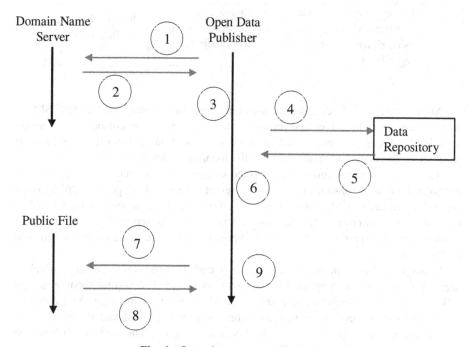

Fig. 4. Open data user case illustration

security or integrity-checking mechanism in place, the file is still vulnerable to accidental corruption and interception attacks.

Communication using the Proposed Architecture. The following example illustrates use of the proposed architecture from the perspective of the end user:

In communication with the end-user, the proposed architecture does not change the request-response format of HTTP communication, but rather augments it with the previously mentioned security components Table 2.

Table 2. Process of Fig. 4. Open Data User Case

Steps	Description	Process
1	DNS Resolution Request	DNSSEC enabled Address Resolution
2	DNS Resolver Response	
3	Verified using zone public key	
4	Open Data request	Open Data Resource Lookup
5	Digitally signed Open Data response	
6	Signature Verifier begins operations	
7	Request for Public Key	HOUND Integrity Verification Process
8	Public file responds with signer's public key	
9	Verifier extracts message digest from signature using signer's public key and verifies integrity of Open Data file	

At this stage, as before, address resolution is performed, incorporating DNSSEC to authenticate the DNS Server and provide defence against cache poisoning or man-in-the-middle attacks. As mentioned in a previous section, a DNSSEC validator is installed on the client-side and validates the incoming content.

After the address resolution is performed successfully, communications proceed as per normal and a response from the hosting server is received. As per RFC2616 [39], a successful request should contain a 2xx or a 3xx status code depending on the HTTP method used. If an error on the client-side is perceived, the server should return a 4xx status code but if an error occurs on the server-side a 5xx status code should be returned to the client.

In this case, the response contains a status code and the actual message which is digitally signed and accompanied by a digital certificate. The verifier module is then called to verify the integrity and authenticity of the received message. At the end of verifier module process, the message or content should be displayed if both the certificate and signature pass verification. The following is pseudocode describing the functioning of the verifier module:

```
#VERIFIER-PSEUDOCODE
GET DownloadedContent
READ Digital_Sign from DownloadedContent
EXTRACT KeyFileNumber from Digital_Sign

GET PublicKeyFile matching KeyFileNumber
RETRIEVE PublicKey from PublicKeyFile
CALL   Decrypt_Sign with PublicKey and Digital_Sign
       RETURNING decrypt_result
STORE decrypt_result in hash1

CALL   hash_compute with DownloadedContent
       RETURNING hash_result
STORE hash_result in hash2

IF hash1 = hash2 THEN
   SHOW message: integrity and authenticity verified
   DISPLAY DownloadedContent
ELSE
   SHOW message: failed integrity check
   TERMINATE
END IF
END
```

This procedure assumes DNSSEC is enabled. However, should DNSSEC not be available, HOUND should use HTTPS as a minimum for integrity to retrieve the appropriate public key from the Public Key File at the Registry for signature verification.

REST URI Interface with Proposed Architecture. Each dataset may contain one or more resource files, which is linked to a particular digital signature file and is associated with the identity and public key of the dataset owner/creator at the Registry.

When a GET request is called for a dataset, e.g. GET /datasets/sampledataset, the server returns a listing of resource files and their URIs. From the information in that list, a GET request may then be sent for an individual resource, e.g. GET /datasets/sampledataset/resource1, which should retrieve both the resource file and the associated digital signature. All the information is then used in the signature value with the algorithm described in Sect. 4.2.

4.3   Conclusion and Future Work

This paper proposes an architecture that uses digital signatures in conjunction with an associated public key file with the main goal to protect the integrity of Open Data communicated over the Web. This is a simplification of current public key certificate structures which use large revocation lists for certificate currency and have demonstrated problems in scalability and "certificate authority" trust.

Table 3. URI interface

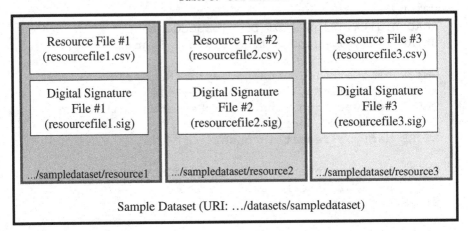

The key element of this architecture is that it is based on DNSSEC, which is more appropriate to the new world of IPv6. The advantages of this architecture scheme is that it is far more scalable, not another certificate authority hierarchy with massive dispersion of key certificates which has of late become too widespread and unmanageable. With the use of a Public Key File, if the key is compromised; it is a simple matter of the single responsible entity replacing the key pair with a new one and re-performing the data file signing process.

Responsibility for authenticating Open Data is separated from any other certificate authority that might be used by the publishing entity. Under this proposed architecture, the Open Data environment does not interfere with the internal security schemes that might be employed by the entity. However, this architecture incorporates, when needed, parameters from the entity, e.g. person who authorized publishing as Open Data, at the time that datasets are created/added.

Future work will include the building of a proof-of-concept system using the architecture in this paper and performing benchmarking against regular systems in conjunction with penetration testing. An interesting philosophical question which may be studied in further papers is: what responsibility does an entity, whether private or public, take on when it makes Open Data available? Further study on the issue of Open Data and governance requirements must be done.

References

1. Fielding, R. T.: Architectural styles and the design of network-based software architectures Doctoral dissertation, University of California, Irvine (2000)
2. Box, D., Kavivaya, G., Layman, A., Thatte, S., Winer, D.: SOAP: Simple Object Access Protocol, Internet Draft draft-box-http-soap-01, November 1999

3. Defining Open Data, Open Knowledge Foundation Blog (2013). http://blog.okfn.org/2013/10/03/defining-open-data/
4. GovHack. http://www.govhack.org/
5. HealthHack. http://www.healthhack.com.au/
6. The Open Definition. http://opendefinition.org/
7. Arzberger, P.W., Schroeder, P., Beaulieu, A., Bowker, G.C., Casey, K., Laaksonen, L., Wouters, P.: Promoting access to public research data for scientific, economic, and social development. Data Sci. J. **3**(29), 135–152 (2004)
8. Davies, T.: Open data, democracy and public sector reform: A look at open government data use from data.gov.uk (2010)
9. Molloy, J.C.: The open knowledge foundation: open data means better science. PLoS Biol. **9** (12), e1001195 (2011)
10. Samwald, M., Jentzsch, A., Bouton, C., Stie Kallesøe, C., Willighagen, E., et al.: Linked open drug data for pharmaceutical research and development. J. Cheminform. **3**, 19 (2011). doi:10.1186/1758-2946-3-19
11. Zuiderwijk, A.M.G., Jeffery, K.G., Janssen, M.F.W.H.A.: The potential of metadata for linked open data and its value for users and publishers. JeDEM-e J. e-Democracy Open Gov. **4**(2), 222–244 (2012)
12. Janssen, M., Charalabidis, Y., Zuiderwijk, A.: Benefits, adoption barriers and myths of open data and open government. Inf. Syst. Manage. **29**(4), 258–268 (2012)
13. Kassen, M.: A promising phenomenon of open data: a case study of the Chicago open data project. Gov. Inf. Q. **30**(4), 508–513 (2013)
14. Zuiderwijk, A., Janssen, M.: Open data policies, their implementation and impact: a framework for comparison. Gov. Inf. Q. **31**(1), 17–29 (2014)
15. Jaakkola, H., Makinen, T., Etelaaho, A.: Open data: opportunities and challenges. Paper presented at the Proceedings of the 15th International Conference on Computer Systems and Technologies, Ruse, Bulgaria (2014)
16. Strong, D.M., Lee, Y.W., Wang, R.Y.: 10 potholes in the road to information quality. IEEE Comput. **30**(8), 38–46 (1997)
17. Mazon, J.N., Zubcoff, J.J., Garrig, I., Espinosa, R., Rodríguez, R.: Open business intelligence: on the importance of data quality awareness in user-friendly data mining. Paper presented at the Proceedings of the 2012 Joint EDBT/ICDT Workshops, Berlin, Germany (2012)
18. Telikicherla, K.C., Choppella, V.: Enabling the development of safer mashups for open data. Paper presented at the Proceedings of the 1st International Workshop on Inclusive Web Programming - Programming on the Web with Open Data for Societal Applications, Hyderabad, India (2014)
19. Eckert, K., Ritze, D., Baierer, K., Bizer, C.: RESTful open workflows for data provenance and reuse. Paper presented at the Proceedings of the Companion Publication of the 23rd International Conference on World Wide Web Companion, Seoul, Korea (2014)
20. CKAN instances around the world. http://ckan.org/instances/
21. Socrata Open Data Portal. https://opendata.socrata.com/
22. CKAN Multisite Draft Proposal. https://usopendata.org/2014/12/08/ckan-multisite/
23. Socrata Open Data API. http://www.socrata.com/industries/open-data-state-local-government/
24. Comerford, C., Soderling, P.: Why REST security doesn't exist? http://www.computerworld.com/s/article/9161699/Why_REST_security_doesn_t_exist
25. OASIS, Web Services Security: SOAP Message Security 1.1 (2006)
26. Forsberg, D.: RESTful security. In: Web 2.0 Security & Privacy 2009 in conjunction with 2009 IEEE Symposium on Security and Privacy (2009)

27. Peng, D., Li, C., Huo, H.: An extended username token-based approach for REST-style web service security authentication. In: 2nd IEEE International Conference on Computer Science and Information Technology, ICCSIT 2009, pp.582–586, 8–11 August 2009. doi:10.1109/ICCSIT.2009.5234805

28. Serme, G., de Oliveira, A.S., Massiera, J., Roudier, Y.: Enabling message security for RESTful services. In: 2012 IEEE 19th International Conference on Web Services (ICWS), pp. 114–121, 24–29 June 2012. doi:10.1109/ICWS.2012.94

29. Lee, H., Mehta, M.R.: Defense against REST-based web service attacks for enterprise systems. Commun. IIMA 13(1), 57–68 (2013). http://search.proquest.com/docview/1518604854?accountid=13380

30. De Backere, F., Hanssens, B., Heynssens, R., Houthooft, R., Zuliani, A., Verstichel, S., Dhoedt, B., De Turck, F.: Design of a security mechanism for RESTful web service communication through mobile clients. In: 2014 IEEE Network Operations and Management Symposium (NOMS), pp. 1–6, 5–9 May 2014. doi:10.1109/NOMS.2014.6838308

31. Diffie, W., Hellman, M.E.: New directions in cryptography. IEEE Trans. Info. Theory **IT-22**, 644–654 (1976)

32. Kohnfelder, L.M.: Towards a practical public-key cryptosystem. Ph.D. Diss., Massachusetts Institute of Technology (1978)

33. Clarke, R: Conventional public key infrastructure: An artefact ill-fitted to the needs of the information society. In: Proceedings of the 9th European Conference on Information Systems (2001)

34. Rivest, R.L.: Can we eliminate certificate revocation lists? In: Hirschfeld, R. (ed.) FC 1998. LNCS, vol. 1465, pp. 178–183. Springer, Heidelberg (1998)

35. McDaniel, P., Rubin, A.D.: A response to can we eliminate certificate revocation lists? In: Frankel, Y. (ed.) FC 2000. LNCS, vol. 1962, pp. 245–258. Springer, Heidelberg (2001)

36. Wendlandt, D., Andersen, D. G., Perrig, A.: Perspectives: improving SSH-style host authentication with multi-path probing. In: Proceedings of the USENIX 2008 Annual Technical Conference (2008)

37. Marlinspike, M.: SSL and the Future of Authenticity. BlackHat USA (2011)

38. RFC3833. https://tools.ietf.org/html/rfc3383

39. RFC2616. https://www.ietf.org/rfc/rfc2616.txt

Short Papers

1,2, Pause: Lets Start by Meaningfully Navigating the Current Online Authentication Solutions Space

Ijlal Loutfi$^{(\boxtimes)}$ and Audun Jøsang

University of Oslo, Oslo, Norway
ijlall@uio.no, josang@ifi.uio.no

Abstract. Consuming services online is an exponentially growing trend within different industries. A robust online authentication solution to these services is a critical requirement for establishing trust between end users and service providers. Currently, the shortcomings of password based authentication solutions are well recognized. Hence, many alternative strong authentication solutions are being adopted. However, the latter create a siloed model where each service provider dictates a different method (OTP, SMS...) to end users. To resolve these challenges, considerable efforts are being deployed by both academia and industry. However, assessing these efforts is not a trivial task. This paper provides a framework of a well-motivated set of attributes, for categorizing and assessing online authentication solutions. Based on this framework, two main approaches for online authentication are identified and exemplified: LUCIDMAN and FIDO. The results of this research are anticipated to make the navigation of the online authentication solutions space more systematic, and facilitate knowledge transfer between all stakeholders.

Keywords: Authentication · FIDO · LUCIDMAN · Framework

1 Introduction and Background

A growing number of service providers from different industries are moving their businesses online. In online environments, Trusted interactions between users and their chosen service provider depends on robust mutual authentication. Given the exponential growth in the number of interconnected online entities, the challenge of ensuring robust authentication between all these identities is daunting [2]. Currently, password based authentication methods are the most prevalent solution. However, their shortcomings are very well documented and recognized [6]. Indeed, the average end user is unable to handle the growing number of online accounts they own. Hence, end users compromise their own security by resorting to using weak passwords. In order to resolve this issue, the adoption of different alternative strong authentication solutions is quickly growing. By definition, strong authentication mechanisms are cryptographically based and

© IFIP International Federation for Information Processing 2015
C.D. Jensen et al. (Eds.): IFIPTM 2015, IFIP AICT 454, pp. 165–176, 2015.
DOI: 10.1007/978-3-319-18491-3_12

have the properties of not being trivially susceptible to common attack techniques, such as credential theft and replay (i.e., phishing), and credential forgery (e.g., password guessing). Strong authentication mechanisms can be implemented in various fashions. They involve at least protocol support and may leverage physical authenticators implemented as platform hardware features, or discrete security tokens, for example: Trusted Platform Module (TPM), biometric sensors, One-Time-Password (OTP) generators, etc. [3]. While strong authentication may seem at first glance to be a perfect solution, the way it has been adopted and implemented presents many challenges. While strong authentication increases the strength of a solutions, it often decreases its usability. Furthermore, It is creating an ever more siloed authentication scene, where each service provider (hereafter abbreviated as SP) governs a separate silo domain with its own name space of user identities, and dictates a different solution to its end users. This silo model is the result of online Identity management being still studied in its traditional way. It dictates that managing user identities should be focused on processes located on the server side, where solutions are optimized for simple management from the service provider point of view [1]. One of the main most recent approaches to identity management which is identity federation. Identity federation comes in many variations but is typically based on the SAML1 standard which is implemented in applications such as Shibboleth, and FacebookConnect. However, Identity federation does not fundamentally solve the problem of identity overload. There will always be different federation domains, because not all SPs will merge their respective user identity domains into a single federated domain.

Having recognized the shortcomings of both password based authentication solutions and the currently implemented strong authentication solutions, further efforts are being deployed by both academia and industry. Currently, the solutions space of online authentication is cluttered, with little resources available to interested stakeholders to assess and analyze the different proposed solutions.

Hence, the aim of this paper is to present a framework/taxonomy of a well-motivated set of attributes, for categorizing and assessing online authentication solutions. Based on this framework, two main approaches for online authentication are identified and exemplified: LUCIDMAN and FIDO. The goal of this research is that the framework would make the categorization and assessment of online authentication solutions more systematic. It will also focus discussions around two oimportant proposed solutions: LUCIDMAN and FIDO. The framework is not meant to present a detailed analysis of each online authentication solution, but rather a basis of comparison and assessment between a set of solutions.

2   Navigating the Current Solutions Space: Proposed Framework

The solutions space of online authentication is a complex one. Different proposed schemes are making claims about the superiority of their solution. Having a systematic way to categorize and assess these solutions, would allow us to form a well-rounded judgment about each one, and transfer knowledge between teams. For our proposed framework to be as holistic as possible, we identified the below aspects as a point of reference, around which the framework properties are defined:

- **Strength of the solution.**
- **Usability for end users and service providers.**
- **Privacy.**
- **Readiness of adoption by the market**.

Before presenting the framework properties, we would like to formally introduce the definitions of the below concepts.

2.1 Basics First

Digital Identities. A digital entity is a set of digitally expressed attributes of an entity, where one of the attributes typically is a name or identifier for uniquely selecting the entity within a name-space domain. Each entity can have multiple identities simultaneously or at different points in time [2] (Fig. 1).

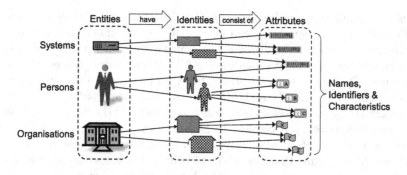

Fig. 1. Relationships between entities, identities and attributes

Entity Authentication. In the context of this research, it is crucial to make a clear distinction between a system entity (client or server) and a legal/cognitive entity (person or organization). This brings into play multiple entities on each side in the client-server model. This is because a requirement for trusted interaction in this scenario is to have mutual authentication between pairs of interacting entities whenever relevant, leading to 4 possible types of mutual entity authentication described in Tables 1 and 2.

For online service access the entity authentication classes [U → S] (user authentication) and [S → U] (cognitive server authentication, defined below) are the most relevant. The importance of these authentication classes emerges from the need for end-to-end security. End-to-end communication between the human user (U) and the server system (S) takes place during online service access. It is

Table 1. Authentication classes for user-side entities

Class	Authentication of user-side entities
[U → P]	User (U) authentication by the service provider (P)
[U → S]	User (U) authentication by the server system (S) (commonly called *user authentication*)
[C → P]	Client (C) authentication by the service provider (P)
[C → S]	Client (C) authentication by the server system (S)

Table 2. Authentication classes for SP-side entities

Class	Authentication of SP-side entities
[P → U]	Service provider (P) authentication by the human user (U)
[P → C]	Service provider (P) authentication by the user client (C)
[S → U]	Server (S) authentication by the human user (U) (here called *cognitive server authentication*)
[S → C]	Server (S) authentication by the user client (C)

therefore pragmatic to require mutual authentication between those two entities. Traditional user authentication can provide [U → S] authentication. It is often incorrectly assumed that traditional server authentication with Browser PKIX[1] server certificates and TLS[2] provides [S → U] authentication, however in reality it does not. This might seem surprising but is in fact easy to understand [9].

According to the X.800 standard, entity authentication is *"the corroboration that a peer entity in an association is the one claimed"* [7]. So in case a phishing victim user intends to connect to https://www.paypal.com, but is tricked into connecting to a phishing website called https://www.peypal.com, then the server certificate claims that the server identity is www.peypal.com which then is correctly authenticated according to X.800. However, something is clearly wrong here, and this indicates that the above definition of entity authentication is inadequate. What is needed is a richer modality of authentication. In the next section, we define three authentication modalities [12].

2.2   Authentication Modalities:

The above definition of entity authentication, and the distinction made between a system and end user, as well as the server provider and the system service provider, gives rise to three main authentication types, which will be called modalities:

– **Syntactic Entity Authentication:** *The verification by the relying entity that the unique name of the remote entity in an interaction is as claimed.* This

---

[1] PKIX: Public-Key Infrastructure based in X.509 certificates [8].

[2] TLS: Transport Layer Security.

basic form of entity authentication is equivalent to peer-entity authentication as in X.800. Alone, it does not provide any meaningful security and can e.g. not prevent phishing attacks since the relying party is indifferent to the identity of the authenticated entity.

- **Semantic Entity Authentication:** *The verification by the relying entity that the unique name of the remote entity in an interaction is as claimed, and in addition the verification by the relying entity that semantic characteristics of the remote entity are compliant with a specific security policy.* It can be enforced by an automated system e.g. with a white list of authorized identities.

- **Cognitive Entity Authentication:** *The verification by the cognitive relying party that the unique name of the remote entity in an interaction is as claimed, the verification by the relying party that semantic characteristics of the remote entity are compliant with a specific security policy, where the latter is supported by presenting in a user-friendly way identity attributes that enable the cognitive relying party to recognize relevant aspects of the remote entity and to judge policy compliance.* It requires the relying party to have cognitive reasoning power, such as in humans, animals or advanced AI systems. This authentication modality effectively prevents phishing attacks because users recognize the identity of a server and decide whether it is the intended one.

2.3 Frameworks Properties

In this section, we will formally define the attributes upon which our proposed framework is base.

Entity Authentication. User identity management is frequently discussed in the identity management literature, whereas SP identity management is mostly discussed in the network security literature. One added value of our proposed framework is that it consolidates types, because users must manage their own identities as well as those of SPs, in order to be authenticated by server systems on a semantic level, and to authenticate the server systems on a cognitive level. Our proposed framework is aimed at providing adequate security assurance and usability for the management of both user identities and server identities, with the goal of enabling trusted interaction between online entities.

Server Authentication and User Authentication. For mutual authentication, user authentication is implemented on the application layer while server authentication on the transport layer. Since mutual authentication goes between the user and the server, we require server authentication by the user as $[S \rightarrow U]$ which most often is not satisfied in current implementations, and user authentication by the server as $[U \rightarrow S]$ which currently is satisfied in most implementations.

Our proposed framework mandates that server authentication as well as user authentication should be classified as following one of the below 3 modalities:

- *Syntactic.*
- *Semantic.*
- *Cognitive.*

Threat Immunity. A paradox in today's Internet computing environment is that we continue to build vulnerable client platforms while still expecting them to support trusted online interactions. According to PandaLabs' estimates, approximately one third (31.63 %) of the world's PCs are infected with some sort of malware (Q2 2012) of which most (78.92 %) are Trojans [11]. It must therefore be assumed that sooner or later a client platform will be infected by malware, which means that it can never be trusted.

Our proposed framework mandates that the above assumption of having an infected client platform is a reasonable one to hold, and that the solution being studied should be evaluated against it.

Data Authentication. According to the X.800 standard, data origin authentication is *"the corroboration that the source of data received is as claimed"* [7]. This is different from entity authentication because knowing the identity of a remote entity in a session is different from knowing whether the data received through a session with a specific remote entity genuinely originates from that entity. This difference might seem subtle at first glance but it is in fact fundamental for security, as explained below.

Malware infection on client platforms opens up for attacks against data authentication that entity authentication can not prevent. A typical example is the situation of online banking transactions with mutual entity authentication. Even with strong 2-factor user authentication, and users' correct interpretation of server certificates, there is the possibility that malware on the client platform can modify data communicated between client and server platforms. Current attacks against online banking are typically mounted in this way. Such attacks lead to breach of data integrity, but not a breach of entity authentication. The separation between the human/legal entity and the system entity on each side of a client-server session makes it necessary to specify which entity in particular is the assumed origin of data. Our proposed framework mandates that data authentication, just like entity authentication, should be classified as following one of the 3 modalities defined below:

- *Syntactic.*
- *Semantic.*
- *Cognitive.*

User Experience. The success of any online authentication solution requires that many stakeholders come together: end users, service providers, policy makers, device manufacturers and integrators. These stakeholders are what we refer to, in the context of this framework, when we talk about the concept of the ecosystem.

The framework mandates to measure how the identified stakeholders relate to the solution in the present time as well as in the future.

Privacy. By definition, online authentication deals with sensitive and private users data. The strength or the usability of the solution, should not overshadow the way the solution deals with the privacy of users data.

The framework requires the evaluation of the privacy level of the solution. The below list identifies a minimum set of requirements that a solution should be compared against before forming a proper judgment about its privacy level. The items outlined in the table below are defined by the FIDO alliance [4].

- Require explicit, informed user consent for any operation using personal data.
- Limit collection of personal data to the solution-related purposes Only.
- Use personal data only for the solution authentication operations.
- Prevent identification of a user outside of solution operations.
- If biometric data is used, it must never leave the users' personal computing environment.
- Protect user-related data from unauthorized access or disclosure.

3 Two Main Trends

3.1 Overview

Based on this proposed framework, a hypothetically ideal online authentication solution would try to implement the above defined properties up to their highest level. Assuming that we have two solutions A and B, which implement the properties identified in the framework up to the same level, one still would not be able to conclusively state that the two solutions are equally appropriate or not. Indeed, at this point of the analysis, one needs to answer one more question: at which end are these properties implemented (end user system, service provider system, end user device, network etc...)? The research work leading up to this paper, made us involved in evaluating a great number of solutions. By using an earlier, less elaborate version of the proposed framework, we identified two major emerging current trends. They can be contrasted to traditional online authentication solutions where the solutions implementations were focused on the service provider side.

- **Local Centric/Top-Down:** It can be described as a puritarian local-centric approach, where the solution requirements are locked into the implementation. Most often, this approach is implemented with a special hardware which the end user leverages to perform the online authentication ceremonies. In this case, the solution would mandates to the device manufacturers the specific requirements they need to adhere to, as well as how the properties described in the above framework should be implemented. In this approach, the communication protocol used between end users and their service providers remains unchanged.

- **Network Centric/Bottom-Up:** In this approach, the core properties are implemented in the network protocol layer. Any changes to the solution would be invisible to the communicating end user/service provider pair. In this approach end users and service providers need to have dedicated software that would allow them to communicate with the newly implemented protocol.

We will focus in the subsequent section on real life example for each one the two approaches.

3.2   Top Down Approach: LUCIDMAN Basics

LUCIDMAN, which stands for local user-centric identity management, is a principle for identity management. It aims to distinguish between its identity management model and other models that are often called user-centric in the literature. More specifically, LUCIDMAN not only provides robust security and adequate security usability, it is also based on placing technology and computing processes for identity management locally on the user side in the client-server architecture. LUCIDMAN as a solution belongs to the user centric Top/down approach, as it defines a specific set of requirements for its implementation, that are achieved through a user device named OffPAD. The OffPAD represents technology for improving the user experience and for strengthening security, which already makes it user centric. Since the OffPAD is, in addition, located on the user side, it is physically local to the user, and thereby represents technology for local user-centric identity management. The OffPAD can be used for a number of different security services [12], but this article only focuses on how it enables trusted interaction through mutual entity (user and server) authentication as well as data origin authentication. The OffPAD can also support incremental authentication modalities, i.e. syntactic, semantic or cognitive authentication, as shown in Figure [12]. The OffPAD (Offline Personal Authentication Device) described by Klevjer et al. [10] and Varmedal et al. [12] is an enhanced version of the PAD, where an essential characteristic is to be offline, i.e. not connected to the Internet. Keeping the OffPAD offline strengthens its security by eliminating exposure to Internet threats. The OffPAD supports authentication of both user and SP identities (i.e. mutual authentication) and can in addition support data authentication. A possible OffPAD design is illustrated in Fig. 2.

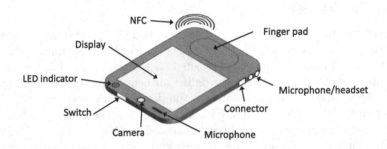

Fig. 2. OffPAD design ideas

The OffPAD enables mutual user-server entity authentication as well as data authentication. Each authentication type is illustrated with a ceremony [2] which is simply a protocol where relevant actions by users and the context environment are included. The 3 ceremonies can be chained and seen as one general ceremony that provides all 3 types of authentication, starting with server authentication, followed by user authentication and finally data authentication. The novelty of this solutions is that it supports trusted interaction even in the presence of malware infected client platforms [12].

3.3   Bottom Up: FIDO Basics

The FIDO (Fast IDentity Online) Alliance is a 501(c)6 non-profit organization nominally formed in July 2012 to address the lack of interoperability among strong authentication devices as well as the problems users face with creating and remembering multiple usernames and passwords. its FIDO is to break with the server centric online authentication solutions, and bring devices to end users which would allow them to have a strong, yet a usable authentication experience. While the analysis of FIDO can be a lengthy one, for the purposes of this paper, we will focus on presenting its approach, and then evaluating its claims using our proposed framework (Fig. 3).

Being an example of a network centric solution, at FIDO's core lies the FIDO client. The FIDO client implements the client side of the FIDO protocols, and interfaces with the FIDO Authenticator abstraction layer via the FIDO Authenticator API. While the FIDO client software implementation will be platform-specific, the FIDO specifications will define the interactions and APIs between the protocol-handling code provided by any FIDO- specific browser extensions, the devices that handle the user authentication and provide the authenticators,

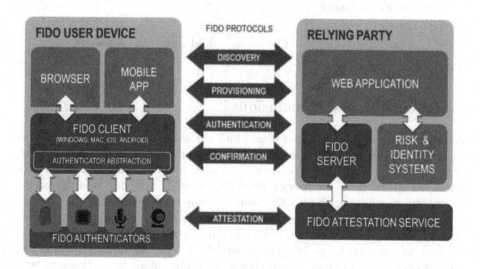

Fig. 3. Overview of FIDO Architecture

and what the user experience should be, in order to ensure as consistent an experience as possible from platform to platform [3]. To better illustrate the concept of FIDO the below figure shall be used.

FIDO Authenticator. A FIDO authenticator is a secure entity, attached to or housed within FIDO user devices, that is remotely provisional with key material by relying parties, and is then capable of participating in cryptographic strong authentication protocols. For example, the FIDO authenticator will be capable of providing a cryptographic challenge response based on the key material thus authenticating itself [3,4].

In order to meet the goal of simplification of authentication capability integration, a FIDO authenticator will be able to attest to its particular type (e.g., biometric) and capabilities (e.g., supported crypto algorithms), as well as to its provenance [3,5].

3.4   FIDO and LUCIDMAN Under the Proposed Framework

The framework presented in this research paper provided us with a structured and systematic way to categorize and compare LUCIDMAN and FIDO. Table 3 below summarizes the results of our analysis.

Table 3. Summary of LUCIDMAN and FIDO analysis

Properties	LUCIDMAN	FIDO
User Authentication	Cognitive	Syntactic
Server Authentication	Cognitive	Syntactic
Data Authentication	Cognitive	Syntactic
Threat Immunity	Yes	No
Privacy	Yes	No
User Experience	End Users	End users, SP, Integrators

4   Discussion and Conclusions

While there are numerous angles from which the above comparison table can be analyzed, the two most notable differences between FIDO and LUCIDMAN are threat immunity and user experience. The network centric approach of FIDO allows for great gains for service providers as well as device manufacturers. Indeed, by just having the FIDO module on the server side once, the service provider can change and allow for different user experiences (fingerprint, voice, ping etc.) without incurring extra costs. Further, device manufacturers also benefit from this approach, as they have a good balance between implementing the user authentication method of their choice, while not having to worry about how to communicate with the service provider. They can hence communicate with any incremental number of service providers with no extra costs. All of these great benefits for service providers, device manufacturers as well as end users, were achieved because of the top down approach. Since all the properties of the solution are network centric, service providers and device manufacturers have to satisfy a reasonable set of requirements in order to be FIDO compliant. However, as stated in the FIDO security reference, preventing malicious applications from arriving to the FIDO user device are outside the scope of the solution [5]. Given the extent to which user platforms are infected with malware, this raises more than one question. On the other hand, LUCIDMAN through its OffPAD implementation, makes the requirement of protecting the user dwevice, from outside threats as well as platform ones, its main priority. This, unsurprisingly, came at the price of flexibility. Given the specific requirements a LUCIDMAN device needs to adhere to, device manufacturers lose the flexibility to bring their own expertise to the table. At the same time, many service providers might judge the security requirements to be too good for them, and that the cost of obliging end user to acquire a specific type of device in order to consume their services, outweighs the security benefits the OffPAD night brings. Given that having a healthy ecosystem of service providers, device manufacturers and end users is a crucial success factor for the success of any new online authentication solution, the lack of flexibility fo LUCIDMAN might become an inhibiting feature. Interestingly enough, the two approaches put forward different types of strengths and weaknesses. Having used the framework proposed in this paper for their assessment, has allowed us to strategically spot and analyze them in meaningful ways. We argue that LUCIDMAN and FIDO can be integrated or at least take some learnings from each other in order to enhance their current specifications. One way to achieve this would be to for the OffPAD team to work on making their device FIDO ready. This will give the OffPAD a very strong ecosystem and a real chance to gain scale within the market. On the other hand, FIDO would have a device that satisfies strong immunity requirements, and which can be used for service providers that are working in industries that are highly regulated and which require high assurance levels. The Online authentication problem has long been a very challenging one. While different stakeholders are coming up with great innovative ideas to resolve it, all implementation have, so far, failed to cover all aspects of the problem. Breaking the siloed state of online authentication is no easy task. However, we believe that as a security community, academia and industry alike, we should start by breaking our own working silos, and have more knowledge transfer between our solutions. The framework proposed in this paper as well as the two approaches exemplify, have helped us meaningfully evaluate and cross compare two seemingly different solutions, to only arrive at the conclusion that there is much each can learn from the other. If we are to dissolve the silos of online authentication, we are first to dissolve our own learning silos.

Acknowledgments. This work has been partially supported by eurostars project E!8324 OffPAD.

References

1. Jøsang, A., et al.: Assurance requirements for mutual user and service provider authentication. Journal of Trust Management 2(1) (2014)
2. Jøsang, A., et al.: Local user-centric identity management. Journal of Trust Management 2(1) (2015)
3. Alliance, F.: Draft reference architecture (2014). http://fidoalliance.org
4. Alliance, F.: Fido Alliance Whitepaper: Privacy Principles (2014). http://fidoalliance.org
5. Alliance, F.: Fido Security Reference (2014). http://fidoalliance.org
6. Florencio, D., Herley, C.: A large-scale study of web password habits. In: Proceedings of the 16th International Conference on the World Wide Web, pp. 657–666. Association for Computing Machinery, Inc., May 2007. http://research.microsoft.com/apps/pubs/default.aspx?id=74164
7. ITU: Recommendation X.800, Security Architecture for Open Systems Interconnection for CCITT Applications. International Telecommunications Union (formerly known as the International Telegraph and Telephone Consultantive Committee), Geneva (1991). (X.800 is a re-edition of IS7498-2)
8. ITU: Recommendation X.509 v3, The Directory: Authentication Framework (also known as ISO/IEC 9594-8). International Telecommunications Union, Telecommunication Standardization Sector(ITU-T), Geneva, June 1997
9. Jøsang, A.: Trust extortion on the internet. In: Meadows, C., Fernandez-Gago, C. (eds.) STM 2011. LNCS, vol. 7170, pp. 6–21. Springer, Heidelberg (2012)
10. Klevjer, H., Varmedal, K.A., Jøsang, A.: Extended HTTP digest access authentication. In: Fischer-Hübner, S., de Leeuw, E., Mitchell, C. (eds.) IDMAN 2013. IFIP AICT, vol. 396, pp. 83–96. Springer, Heidelberg (2013)
11. PandaLabs: PandaLabs Quarterly Report, Q2, June 2012. http://press.pandasecurity.com/wp-content/uploads/2012/08/Quarterly-Report-PandaLabs-April-June-2012.pdf
12. Varmedal, K.A., Klevjer, H., Hovlandsvåg, J., Jøsang, A., Vincent, J., Miralabé, L.: The OffPAD: Requirements and Usage. In: Lopez, J., Huang, X., Sandhu, R. (eds.) NSS 2013. LNCS, vol. 7873, pp. 80–93. Springer, Heidelberg (2013)

Data Confidentiality in Cloud Storage Protocol Based on Secret Sharing Scheme: A Brute Force Attack Evaluation

Alexandru Butoi[✉], Mircea Moca, and Nicolae Tomai

Business Information Systems Department,
Babeş-Bolyai University of Cluj-Napoca, Cluj-Napoca, Romania
{alex.butoi,mircea.moca,nicolae.tomai}@econ.ubbcluj.ro

Abstract. Outsourcing a company's data storage and management system increases data security risk and generates a mistrust among adopters, that their data will remain secure and undisclosed. Due to limitations of the SLAs in this direction, the challenge is to build mechanisms that provides *data security by design* and assures data nondisclosure protection implicitly. In this paper we present an evaluation of the Data Confidentiality in Cloud Storage using a brute-force setup with the aim of studying its effectiveness. Through experimentation on the CloudSim environment we found that the probability of unauthorized data reconstruction can be exponentially decreased by using a sufficiently large number of chunks. Also, increasing the number of used storage volumes leads to a linear decrease of unauthorized data reconstruction.

Keywords: Cloud data · Security · Confidentiality · Secret sharing scheme · Brute force evaluation

1 Introduction

Certain studies like [1] show that data security still remains the main barrier for cloud service adoption in business. While it is true that nowadays public clouds represent affordable data storage alternatives, outsourcing a company's storage increases data security risk and emphasizes the problem of unauthorized data disclosures performed by malicious insiders. This indirectly leads to mistrust among possible adopters, as complex or unclear SLAs fail to reduce the risks of information disclosure after moving it into the cloud. The need of built-in interaction mechanisms for achieving *security by design* is mandatory while it can build trust between the two involved parties [2]. The challenge is to build mechanisms for public cloud infrastructures such that the confidentiality attribute is guaranteed through their own definition.

This work was co financed from the European Social Fund through Sectoral Operational Programme Human Resources Development 2007–2013, project number POSDRU/159/1.5/S/134197 "Performance and excellence in doctoral and postdoctoral research in Romanian economics science domain".

C.D. Jensen et al. (Eds.): IFIPTM 2015, IFIP AICT 454, pp. 177–184, 2015.
DOI: 10.1007/978-3-319-18491-3_13

This paper is a continuation of the work conducted on Data Confidentiality in Cloud Storage Protocol (DCCSP) [3]. In this paper we evaluate the security strength of DCCSP using a brute force attack setup as a proxy. The implementation of DCCSP in a real system would help cloud adopters to assure a protection against unauthorized disclosure of sensitive data by malicious insiders or other attackers.

The remainder of this paper is structured as follows: Sect. 2 describes the addressed problem, Sect. 3 overviews the DCCSP protocol, Sect. 4 presents the conducted experiments and findings, while Sect. 5 gives an overview of related or similar approaches. Section 6 concludes our work.

2   Background

In this section we give a short description of the main concepts used in our discussion. We consider two interacting parties: the **cloud consumer** and the **cloud provider**. The cloud consumer can be any user which contracts and use cloud storage resources to store her data. The cloud provider is an organization that owns, fully administers and rents cloud resources to the cloud consumer. Resources delivery to the cloud consumer is made according to a previously agreed SLA (cost, availability, security policies, usage etc.).

In our context the cloud consumer is willing to move data to a public storage cloud service. Due to cloud-specific resource elasticity achievable mainly through virtualization, the storage resources are managed and delivered in form of storage volumes. These may also be virtualized or not. We assume that the cloud consumer has access to *multiple storage volumes* from the cloud provider in order to save her data, according to the agreed SLA. The public cloud provider is a storage service provider which grants access for a cloud consumer to n distinct storage volumes $(V_1, V_2, ..., V_n)$. Each such volume has a certain amount of storage space that the cloud consumer uses for storing data.

In our setup the cloud consumer holds and fully controls a private cloud infrastructure (like own managed servers and storage). On the other side, the cloud consumer has only limited control over the public cloud resources regarding data administration. This aspect may be considered a source of security risk and mistrust [4].

3   DCCSP Definition Overview

In this section we give a brief description of the algorithms underlying the DCCSP protocol, detailed in [3]. This protocol insures that prior to the data storing into the public cloud, it will be secured by computing the secret sharing scheme on the user's private cloud. The secret is the file that holds sensitive information and the sharers are public cloud storage volumes. By this, only the cloud consumer knows the distribution pattern of the data into the public cloud. The protocol is transparent to any cloud infrastructure that fulfills the above

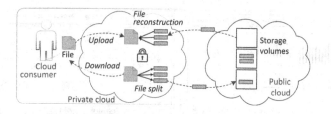

Fig. 1. Protocol overview

assumption of instantiating multiple storage volumes, being implemented on the private cloud side as an interaction layer with the public cloud storage services.

Figure 1 depicts an overview of the protocol, which defines two main phases: the file send and file retrieve.

The File Send Phase of the protocol takes place when the user wants to store or update a sensitive file in the public cloud storage. Before the upload of the file, the protocol splits the file into several smaller data chunks, denoted by $C_1, C_2, ..., C_m$. These chunks are stored into available storage volumes in public cloud in a way that the probability of reconstructing the initial file by a malicious insider or by an attacker is minimized. The protocol uses two algorithms to fulfill its purpose:

I. A secret splitting algorithm [3, p. 993] that implements the strategy of computing each chunk with the optimum size from the information security point of view. It uses the Shanon entropy and Kullbach-Leibler information for discrete distributions as metrics for minimizing the useful information content carried by each chunk relative to the whole information in the original file. The total amount of information in the file is quantified by the Shanon entropy which computes the average information contained in a sequence of data [5, pp. 367–368], while the Kullbach-Leibler measures "the distance" between informational content of a new chunk ($I(c_i)$) and the entire file informational content ($I(f)$) [5,6]:

$$I(f) = -\sum_{i=1}^{s} P(x_i) ln P(x_i); I(f, c_i) = \sum_{i=1}^{s} P(x_i) ln\left(\frac{P(x_i)}{Q(x_i)}\right); \qquad (1)$$

$P(x_i)$ = probability of byte x_i occurrence in file f, $P(x_i) = \frac{k_{x_i}}{s}$ where k_{x_i} equals with the number of x_i occurrences in file f, and s is the file size in number of bytes; ln is the natural logarithm function; $Q(x_i)$ = probability of byte x_i occurrence in chunk c_i when x_i is selected from the original file; $Q(x_i) = \frac{kc_{x_i}}{s}$, kc_{x_i} = number of occurrences for byte x_i in chunk c_i;

As plot (a) in Fig. 2 shows, each chunk size is selected with regards of having it's calculated K-L metric as higher as possible compared with the original file entropy $I(f)$: $I(f, c_i) >> I(f)$ [3].

II. A chunk distribution algorithm [3, p. 995] which implements the distribution of computed file chunks in the public cloud storage. These are

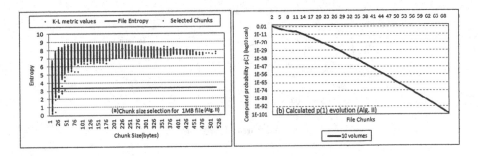

Fig. 2. Chunk optimal size computation [3]

distributed among available storage in a way that the probability of unauthorized reconstruction of the file is constantly minimized (Eq. 2):

$$p(1) = \frac{t!}{(t-1)!} P(1-P)^{t-1} = t \cdot P(1-P)^{t-1} \tag{2}$$

$p(1)$ is the probability of 1 successful reverse engineering modeled as Bernoulli trials; t is the number of trials; P is the event probability of choosing the right chunk in a trial calculated as a product of the two event probabilities: the probability of reconstructing the volume set used to store the file and the probability of reconstructing the right sequence of chunks in the original file, $P = \frac{1}{C_{n_v}^{k_v}} \cdot \frac{1}{A_{n_c}^{k_c}}$ [3, pp. 994–995].

The above strategy stores the file chunks in a manner that probability $p(1)$ of obtaining 1 success of file reconstruction to be as small as possible regardless the number of trials t. The plot (b) in Fig. 2 depicts the evolution of calculated $p(1)$ in the process as more chunks are being stored among 10 storage volumes. The $p(1)$ values have an exponential decrease and are represented on a log10 scale chart for easier reading purposes.

A Chunk Distribution Dictionary (CDD) is used for each data chunk upload operation to be recorded into it. Each record in this dictionary has three key fields: (1) The **index of the chunk in the original file**. This provides the exact position of the chunk within its belonging file; (2) The **virtual volume(s)** where the chunk is stored. (3) The **hash sum of the chunk** for integrity check purposes. The file splitting process takes place on the private cloud side, the resulting chunks being sent to the public cloud in a random order and associated CDD is stored on the private cloud infrastructure too. By this, only the cloud consumer which is the owner of data is aware of the distribution scheme.

The File Retrieve Phase takes place when a file is accessed or downloaded from the public cloud infrastructure. The operation can be triggered only through the private cloud which stores the corresponding dictionary. The CDD is used here to identify every data chunk of the file together with its associated storage volume. Similar to the send strategy, the chunks are randomly selected for retrieval. Finally, based on the chunk index, the original file is reconstructed.

4   Experiments and Results

In this section we present a set of experiments performed to evaluate the effectiveness of our DCCSP protocol. We used the CloudSim [7] environment running the experiments. As experimental data we used files exported from an e-learning platform, containing records with sensitive user account details.

4.1   Experimental Setup

The strategy of storing chunks into the public cloud storage is based on constantly minimizing the probability of successful reconstruction of the original file, mainly by a malicious insider. In order to evaluate the security strength of our protocol we have implemented a brute force attack simulation model which tries to reverse engineer the process of reconstructing the original file without prior knowledge of the chunk distribution dictionary. The simulation is based on a brute force search strategy which searches the storage volumes for data chunks files while trying to reconstruct the original file. As an output for bench-marking, it counts the number of trials needed for a complete retrieval of the original file.

The main issue in mistrusting the data protection in public cloud system is mainly related to the problem of malicious insiders, super-users or administrators which can easily gain unauthorized access to already stored data.

Assumptions:

(a) the attacker is a malicious insider which knows the exact total set of volumes used in storing the target file;
(b) the attacker does not have knowledge about how chunks are distributed;
(c) the attacker does not have knowledge of the right chunk order in the file;
(d) the storage volumes are storing only the chunks of the targeted file.

The approach is an optimistic one which can be differentiated from a real world scenario by certain aspects like: the attacker does not have knowledge of the distribution records for chunk trial validation purpose after each chunk selection, the volumes may contain other data than targeted chunk files or it is likely for the attacker to not be able to know the exact volume set used in storing the targeted file. All the above are hardening the process of reverse engineering in a real world scenario.

Every file can be considered as a data chunk arrangement. The brute force strategy searches for a valid arrangement of data chunks. When the candidate arrangement is identical with the chunk arrangement of the original file, the search stops:

1. *while unconsidered storage volumes exists, randomly select one;*
2. *on selected volume, search for the next valid chunk: a selected chunk is considered valid if it's position in the candidate arrangement built so far, is the same as in the original file arrangement;*

We used two setups for a 1 MB target file:

(I) we varied the number of used volumes, keeping the number of file chunks constant at 4361;

(II) we varied the number of chunks from 100 to 100000 keeping the used volumes number constant at 50.

The output of these simulations were the number of *Volume trials* and number of *Chunk trials*. The number of *Volume trials* represents the total number of volume selections made in the brute force reverse engineering strategy. The number of *Chunk trials* is the total number of chunk selections made in the brute force search process.

4.2   Brute Force Trials

I. For the first setup, results are depicted in Fig. 3. We can see that volume trials have a linear evolution rapidly ascending from 44000 trials to 650000 trials as used volumes increase from 10 to 150. As for the chunk trials we can see that the figures are maintained at a high level, even when 10 volumes are used. Both charts indicate a low probability of unauthorized reconstruction of the file while the number of unsuccessful trials increase.

II. In the second simulation setup, when the number of chunks is increased, Fig. 4 shows that both output indicators follow the same pattern of an exponential growth. Furthermore, we observe that when the number of chunks is above 10000, the number of trials rapidly increases towards infinity and rapidly lowering the probability of reverse engineering of the original file.

Splitting a file in a higher number of chunks seems to be a better strategy because if we increase the chunks number, we can exponentially decrease the chances of breaking the protocol, while increasing the used volumes number, we decrease the chances of a security breach only linearly.

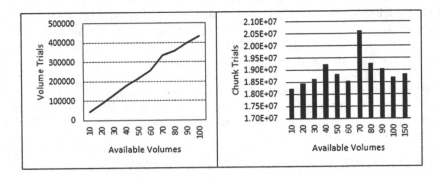

Fig. 3. Volume and chunk trials for 1 MB[4361 chunks] file when varying the number of used storage volumes

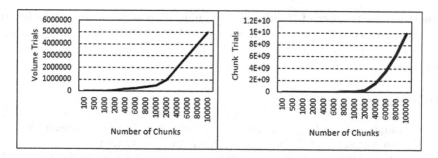

Fig. 4. Volume trials when varying the number of chunks

5 Related Work

The existing data protection oriented cloud systems like Depsky [8] and Belisarius [9] may be vulnerable to malicious insiders. These approaches use classic
security concepts to protect data, like encryption which can be efficient but when
comes to data processing, the access to data can be difficult. In contrast, DCCSP
aims to minimize the issue of malicious insiders and protect data from unauthorized disclosure even against cloud administrators, without using a mandatory
encryption step.

Other secret shared scheme approaches to data protection in cloud [10,11]
make use of multiple cloud providers, while DCCSP uses multiple virtual storage
from one single provider.

Similar to our brute force attack evaluation strategy, Galbally et al. [12]
employ brute force attack schemes to evaluate the strength of a HMM-based
dynamic signature verification system. Also, in [13] the authors propose a hybrid
RSA+Difie-Hellman symmetric encryption strategy which is mathematically
evaluated against brute force attacks. Reference [14] evaluates the encryption
efficiency to digital images against brute force attacks, statistical and differen-
tial attacks while [15] evaluates simple block ciphers using different strategies
for brute force search like genetic algorithms or particle swarm optimisation.

6 Conclusions

This paper presents a continuation of work presented in [3] introducing DCCSP
protocol for assuring a lower as possible probability of unauthorized data disclosure in public cloud storage services. The current work addressed the problem
of evaluating the strength of DCCSP using a brute force search strategy. We
found that the probability of unauthorized data reconstruction can be exponentially decreased by using a sufficiently large number of chunks. Also, we observed
that increasing the number of used storage volumes leads to a linear decrease
of unauthorized data reconstruction. This leads to the idea that DCCSP can be
cost efficient by using a constant number of storage volumes (fixed cost) and

leveraging the number of chunks for obtaining high security levels. As future work we aim to development of a new flavor of the splitting algorithm operating at the word level for text files. Also, we plan to experiment with this protocol into a real cloud infrastructure.

References

1. Subashini, S., Kavitha, V.: A survey on security issues in service delivery models of cloud computing. J. Netw. Comput. Appl. **34**(1), 1–11 (2011)
2. Abbadi, I., Alawneh, M.: A framework for establishing trust in the cloud. Comput. Electr. Eng. **38**, 1073–1087 (2012)
3. Butoi, A., Tomai, N.: Secret sharing scheme for data confidentiality preserving in a public-private hybrid cloud storage approach. In: IEEE/ACM 7th International Conference on Utility and Cloud Computing (UCC), 2014, pp. 992–997 (2014)
4. Rocha, F., Abreu, S., Correia, M.: The final frontier: confidentiality and privacy in the cloud. Computer **44**(9), 44–50 (2011)
5. Hsu, H.P.: Probability, Random Variables, and Random Processes. McGraw-Hill, New York (1997)
6. Burnham, K.P., Anderson, D.R. (eds.): Model Selection and Multimodel Inference: a Practical Information-Theoretic Approach. Springer, New York (2002)
7. Calheiros, R.N., Ranjan, R., Beloglazov, A., De Rose, C.A., Buyya, R.: Cloudsim: a toolkit for modeling and simulation of cloud computing environments and evaluation of resource provisioning algorithms. Softw. Pract. Exp. **41**(1), 23–50 (2011)
8. Bessani, A., Correia, M., Quaresma, B., André, F., Sousa, P.: Depsky: dependable and secure storage in a cloud-of-clouds. In: Proceedings of the Sixth Conference on Computer Systems, pp. 31–46. ACM (2011)
9. Padilha, R., Pedone, F.: Belisarius: BFT storage with confidentiality. In: 2011 10th IEEE International Symposium on Network Computing and Applications (NCA), pp. 9–16. IEEE (2011)
10. Fahl, S., Harbach, M., Muders, T., Smith, M.: Confidentiality as a service-usable security for the cloud. In: 2012 IEEE 11th International Conference on Trust, Security and Privacy in Computing and Communications (TrustCom), pp.153–162. IEEE (2012)
11. Kajiura, Y., Kanai, A., Tanimoto, S., Sato, H.: A file-distribution approach to achieve high availability and confidentiality for data storage on multi-cloud. In: 2013 IEEE 37th Annual Computer Software and Applications Conference Workshops (COMPSACW), pp. 212–217. IEEE (2013)
12. Galbally, J., Fierrez, J., Martinez-Diaz, M., Ortega-Garcia, J.: Evaluation of brute-force attack to dynamic signature verification using synthetic samples. In: 2009 10th International Conference on Document Analysis and Recognition, ICDAR 2009, pp. 131–135 (2009)
13. Mandal, B., Bhattacharyya, D., Bandyopadhyay, S.: Designing and performance analysis of a proposed symmetric cryptography algorithm. In: 2013 International Conference on Communication Systems and Network Technologies (CSNT), pp. 453–461 (2013)
14. Ahmed, H., Kalash, H., Allah, O.: Encryption efficiency analysis and security evaluation of RC6 block cipher for digital images. In: 2007 International Conference on Electrical Engineering, ICEE 2007, pp. 1–7 (2007)
15. Nalini, N., Rao, G.R.: Attacks of simple block ciphers via efficient heuristics. Inf. Sci. **177**(12), 2553–2569 (2007)

The Detail of Trusted Messages: Retweets in a Context of Health and Fitness

Natasha Dwyer[1](✉) and Stephen Marsh[2]

[1] Victoria University, Melbourne, Australia
natasha.dwyer@vu.edu.au
[2] University of Ontario Institute of Technology, Oshawa, Canada
stephen.marsh@uoit.ca

Abstract. Our aim is to know more about the content of a message that is trusted in order to create template messages that users can configure within a system we are designing. To this end, we examine messages that have been forwarded within the social network Twitter in the context of health and fitness. Using content analysis we divide the messages into 3 categories of trust evidence: continuity, competence and motivation. Motivational messages were the most common.

1 Introduction

What evidence do users seek in order to trust another in social network? In this paper, we investigate trust from a user's perspective and using data provided by users theorise about evidence they seek. To explore our question, we start with and build on Metaxas et al's claim [1] that a message that is forwarded on is likely to be a trusted message. From the social network site Twitter, we collected forwarded messages (otherwise known as 'retweets'). Twitter conversations revolving around the Nike Training Club, a fitness programme originated by the company Nike is used as a case study. The messages have been categorised into three sets using Cofta's [2] dimensions of trust; continuity, competence and motivation.

Our focus is the context of health, in particular, group fitness apps that integrate with social networks. The purpose of this research is to inform the development of health-orientated digital systems (apps and accompanying social media environments) that negotiate trust in the user's interest. Our impetus is to use social network analysis as a form of user study. By studying the messages users create and circulate using Twitter, coined by [3] as the 'language of the wire', we wish to explore how users conceptualise trust and consider trust on their own terms. We intend to build our own trust-enabling system for health messages. It is likely that our users will wish to configure the messages we offer. To create a base template, which users can work with, knowledge is required of the type of content and delivery style users find relevant to trust.

This research is important, as more and more people will turn to digital tools as a way to support their exercise. In the times of a recession, gymnasium memberships are one of the first items to be removed from a weekly budget [4]. Digital environments

© IFIP International Federation for Information Processing 2015
C.D. Jensen et al. (Eds.): IFIPTM 2015, IFIP AICT 454, pp. 185–194, 2015.
DOI: 10.1007/978-3-319-18491-3_14

could deliver health and fitness communications much better than what is currently available, deconstructing how users function in existing environments can point to fruitful directions [5].

2 Background Research

Like other industries, those in the health and fitness domain have adopted social media networks, such as Twitter, Facebook and Instagram as a means to communicate, develop knowledge, and research. It can be a way to research how best to develop a new digital product, which is what we are using the system for, to understand how to create a mobile application interface (an app). There is now a strong connection between apps and social networks. Users can discuss their apps on social networks via their laptops and work computers and also digital environments are technically inter-connected, users can participate in social networks from within an app.

In the context of health informatics and digital environments, understanding trust is crucial. Trust can mean that the listener to a health message not only hears a health message but acts upon it [6]. Currently, users and stakeholders have limited ways to gauge trust and health advice in the digital environment [7]. The result has an impact on health care resources; Kim and Kim [8] itemise inappropriate health service adoption, increased time inefficiency and patients incorrectly concerned about symptoms. There is a complex pattern of influence that occurs in social networks that has changed the nature of health communications [9]. Rather than communicating with their audiences via broadcasts, such as television advertisements, health communicators need to listen and develop understanding, the traditional actions associated with building trust.

The majority of the work studying social networks in the trust research area is from a quantitative perspective, analysing patterns of behaviour and developing algorithms. For instance, Golbeck [10] models how users evaluate the trustworthiness of another user whilst Tavakolifard et al. [11] study who are the most influential message creators. Suh et al. [12] study the contextual elements associated with a trusted social network message, such as the amount of follows, the length of time a social network account as existed and how active a message sender is (in contrast, to our work that studies the content of messages). This early work, developing quantifiable measures of trust in social networks, has led to research by several researchers [1,11] that ascertain a link between a forwarded message and trust.

A retweeted message is likely to be a trusted message, according to recent research by Metaxas et al. [1] who studied retweeted messages and then surveyed those who sent the messages. Retweeting is the practice of broadcasting a message from another user, on the social network Twitter (on which we base our own study). The convention is for a user to copy the original message that the user wishes to broadcast and precede the words with the text RT. The retweet can also contain the name of the originating author preceded with the '@' symbol. An example is 'RT @NTC: I've been training for 2 years'. Retweeting is the main way information is distributed on Twitter [12]. Certainly, as Metaxas et al. [1] acknowledge, there are a complex set of reasons why users may send on a message, such as the desire to be the first in a network to distribute news; but trust is a common denominator underlying a range of intentions. Metaxas et al. study the act of retweeting in general. Their claim linking retweeting and trust has been used by [13], who uses the notion to analyse the Gamegate phenomenon (a particular episode where female video game professionals where subjected to misogynistic abuse). In the domain of journalism, [14] use Metataxas et al's claim to build a system designed for journalists that verifies Twitter messages which may be relevant to a news report. The research we describe in this paper applies Metaxas et al's claim to the domain of health and fitness. We seek detail regarding the type of content in messages that are deemed as trustworthy in order to understand the trust evidence that users value.

According to Cofta [2], there is general agreement between researchers that trust evidence falls into three dimensions: continuity, competence and motivation. Those considering whether to trust or not, trustors, look for evidence across these three categories. The evidence may lie in elements such as the past actions or reputation of the party they are considering whether to trust, the trustee. Continuity evidence is connected with social embededness, how connected is a trustee to relevant communities? Considerations such as reputation and the length of time a trustee has been connected with a community are pertinent. The evidence dimension of competence refers to whether the trustee has the ability and skill to fulfill the requirements of the interaction. Finally, the dimension of motivation has to do with shared interest: Does the trustee have an interest in working towards the welfare of the trustor? Castelfranchi and Falcone [15] use the label 'belief of unharmfulness' to describe when the trustor feels positive about the trustee's intention. According to Kranz [16], motivation can be expressed by providing personalised feedback to users of a digital health service.

In order to use these dimensions of evidence as a lens to understand social network messages, a structure is required. Health communication and trust researchers, McNeill and Briggs [17] provide a structure that allows a conceptualization of trust (such as Cofta's) to understand the micro-detail of trust evidence, in social network messages. McNeill and Briggs [17] provide a precedent for understanding how the evidence in social network messages can build a picture of trust or distrust. All messages are framed in terms of a metamessage, a predominant message that influence the receiver's worldview. For instance, a 'motivational' frame evokes support and encouragement to the recipient of a message. An example of a 'continuity' frame is when a message conveys a sense that the message sender is connected to a community. A 'competence' frame could suggest a level of skill or experience.

3 Methodology

The methodology involved a process of collecting messages from Twitter, in particular coding and categorizing the messages using content analysis. To develop a system to code the material, we used Cofta's dimensions of trust evidence. The social network, Twitter, was used for this research because there is a large amount of public data available, making it popular with a range of authors (see Bruns for an overview). It needs to be mentioned that the use of Twitter is controversial, the business model behind Twitter means that it is not possible to query the nature of the sample Twitter offers to researchers, meaning that it is difficult to develop scientific claims.

For this reason, Twitter data collection is likened to stepping in the river; it's a different experience every time. However, this does not mean that the data is useless or should not be considered. Rather, we argue, the data has a limitation that must be acknowledged; the ability to make generalisations is constrained. As the aim of this paper is to develop insights into how users conceptualise trust evidence for a design context, the limitations of Twitter do not problematise our research. In order to download our sample from Twitter, we used the Twitter Archiving Google Spreadsheet (TAGS) system developed by Martin Hawksey. TAGS uses Twitter's REST API to access the data. Our sample was 539 messages collected over a 12-day period in late 2014. We collected data until we had in excess of 500 messages.

The collected messages were all associated with the *Nike Training Club* (NTC). Run by the clothing company Nike, the NTC programme is an app and a social media presence where users can undertake custom exercise workouts on their own or with others and share their reflections. In particular, we collected retweeted messages marked by users with the hashtag #NTC. As mentioned in the literature review, a retweet is a message written by one user and forwarded by another. It is marked by the text 'RT', usually at the start of the message. (The text 'via' is sometimes used but is not common). A hashtag, denoted by the symbol '#' preceding a term, is a convention on Twitter that users implement when they want their message to be part of a public conversation (in our example the hashtag text looked like this: #NTC). When a user includes a hashtag in a Twitter message, it is likely that the user is aware that this means that others can search for that certain hashtag and view their message alongside other messages labeled with that hashtag.

Messages around #NTC were selected as the focus of our research to find users discussing fitness in a community environment. As the inclusion of the word 'club' in the name suggests, #NTC aims to develop a community around fitness, so there is a lot of data with users discussing exercise together and motivating each other; displaying trustworthiness. Other fitness programmes tend to have users lodging their accomplishments with minimal interaction or conversation with others. The wide exposure of Nike brand means there is a large volume of data to be tapped into. There was a stark difference between the quantities of messages collected across different days. The difference is due to whether the Nike department controlling #NTC issued a message that resonated in the NTC community and forwarded by members. Within our message collection, there are also messages originally generated by community members not part of the NTC official team, but these messages are small in comparison with the coverage that the Nike itself can generate.

There are precedents for academic researchers studying #NTC. #NTC is one of only three digital systems that currently meet medical researcher, Padmasekara [18] recommendations for what a fitness digital systems should be; free, and not requiring any special equipment (which are qualities we plan with our app). Researchers Yoganathan and Duwaraka [19] have also used digital systems produced by Nike as a focus of their study. Less corporate orientated programmes were also reviewed for possible inclusion in our research, such as #ZombieRun, but interestingly, we found that within these conversations, users tended to discuss a range of issues beside fitness that were difficult to code in a meaningful fashion.

To analyse our data, content analysis (CA) was used, to filter and categorise the messages. Trust researchers across several domains use CA as a systematic way to form valid elucidations from a body of text data, whether the data is a television news transcript or a body of social network communiqué [20]. For example, business researchers, [21] use the technique to understand the link between informal social network recommendations and purchases. In the domain of Public Relations, [22] investigates how not-for-profit organisations use Twitter. Health communication researchers Sillence et al. [23] use CA to explore the content of websites to understand user's trust perceptions. The method can give a sense of how users 'really' feel about an issue in the context of their daily lives [20].

To adopt meaningful categories to allocate the messages and guide the basis by which a message was allocated to a particular category, we were informed by the work of Cofta [2] to divide trust evidence into three categories, as discussed in the literature review of this paper. Depending on the emphasis of the message, the twitter messages in our corpus were allocated into one of the three categories: continuity, competence and motivation. The two researchers crosschecked coding decisions.

The problems that affect all content analysis and qualitative coding techniques were also encountered during this project. There is no means within a small-scale research design with limited resourcing to validate the category choices made by researchers. Sometimes the nature of a message means that it is difficult to easily categorise the content. Alternatively, sometimes a message could be placed into more than one category, and it is a judgment call on the part of the researcher to allocate the message. However, as qualitative coding can gather detail informing a research question that other methods cannot access, we adopted the method to inform our research.

4 Findings and Discussion

During the process of categorising retweeted twitter messages, we observed users displaying and considering trust. In this section we discuss how the three categories of trust evidence, continuity, competence and motivation were expressed in the messages. The most significant category in our data set was motivational messages (total of 329 messages), followed by continuity messages (total of 119 messages) and finally the category of competence was represented by 89 messages. However, an exploration of the data from a quantitative perspective will be the focus of another paper. Some of these messages may have been distributed by Nike's marketing department rather than by individual users. However, the origin of the message is not important to us, it is the validation of messages expressed through the act of retweeting a message. Nike's marketing department may know how to design messages that are trusted by their target audience and our research taps into their findings.

To examine the data from a qualitative perspective, we build on the claim of McNeill and Briggs [17], mentioned in the literature review, that there is an essence to a message that can be categorised. We combine this work with that of Verbeek [24], a technology philosopher who presents a design methodology that focuses on the values within the messages produced by technology design. In Verbeek's view, technology and design is a mediator. Users shape their own communications using technology and technology design changes in response to user needs. Verbeek's work is useful because it is a means to link analysis of technology and design with a wider socio-political context. In particular, Verbeek identifies 'user logic', which underlies how users interpret and value messages they exchange, and this notion underlies our following analysis of our data.

In the context of fitness digital communities, the **continuity** dimension of trust was expressed in messages demonstrating that the writer has social connections and is part of a community. For example:

> RT Got my best friends in the #NikeZoom campaign with me!!!

> RT Together soon! RT @liztrinnear: @EvaRedpath you yelling "don't give up, push harder girls" in my head, gets me through my #NTC app workouts

> RT @SuperNoodleRach: Thanks kailoha for my Waanngg yoga mat _Ù÷ ! This morn's @nikewomen #ntc session - post Christmas http://t.co/saHcG1dTC5

Some writers hint at their contribution to a community as well as their connection:

> RT @geniebouchard: So amazing to inspire young girls to be active! Had so much fun working out & dancing! @nikewomen @mariepurvis #NTC

Several messages use a sense of community as a way to promote an event. For instance:

> RT @NikeSF: The city is our playground. Step up to 2015 with Nike Training Club. Tonight at 6:30pm. #NTC

The dimension of **competence** is demonstrated in messages that communicate the message writer's level of skill to those in the network. The design of the Twitter technology allows users to broadcast and share their fitness exploits. An example message is:

> RT @surayafaye: I just smashed 45 minutes with Nike+ Training Club http://t.co/0zEnHSVGns #NTC #TrainLikeAMachine #ChristmasWorkOut

Some display their competence by providing expert advice to others. For instance:

> RT Trainer tip from @evaredpath: Strengthen your
> core and hamstrings with The Roll Up

Nike, who design the #NTC campaign, has capitalised on the popularity of new media formats to display competence and provide tools for users to capture and distribute their achievements, as these messages indicate:

> RT @SkyDigg4: Check out my Zoom in 5 #NTC
> workout with @NikeWomen!!

> RT @nikewomen: Earn your selfie. Share minutes,
> milestones and your personal bests in the new #NTC
> app.

Finally, the **motivation** category of trust evidence in the context of our research was expressed in the messages as encouragement to and support for others to improve their skill and commitment levels. For example, the message might be to inspire others to tackle a particular fitness goal. A message illustrating this point is:

> RT @nikewomen: Challenge the weather one rep at a
> time with @evaredpath on #Vine

The intention conveyed in these messages resonates with Hardin's [25] claim that those who are trusted demonstrate an intention of concern for others and to work in their interests; in other words, 'encapsulated interest'. Some examples from our data, of messages written to inspire others, include:

> RT Get ready to relax and recharge with my
> @NikeWomen ab workout!! Coming soon to the #NT

> RT @nikewomen: @imagin_IT_ive Congrats on your
> #NTC milestone. Keep getting after it.

> RT @vshuguet: A big shout out for the #Nutanix french
> team. Thanks for being awesome guys!

Sometimes the message is written in the format of a question, which is a way to draw in the reader. For example:

> RT @nikewomen: @thefaradaykage No better time to
> break them in. Which #NTC session did you smash?

Trust researchers such as [25] and [26] outline how difficult it is for individuals to establish encapsulated interested in the 'real', offline world as individuals may need to demonstrate binding commitment to each other and expose themselves to an element of risk. However, we see on Twitter, that it is easy to express motivation to assist another with their goals. What we may be seeing here is the development of familiarisation. Building on authors such as Luhmann and Möllering, Frederiksen (2014) [26] argues that familiarization is part of the process of demonstrating encapsulated interest, the development of 'from one of being strangers to then acquaintances and finally friends involves the transition from risk to trust. Perhaps the writers of the Twitter messages are establishing the basis of trust by broadcasting gestures of support. If this is correct, it explains why Twitter has the potential to be a powerful marketing tool.

So how can we use the insights from our analysis of the Twitter messages? Commercial researchers would suggest that these insights inform the type of messages a product-owner can send out in order to increase the appearance of trustworthiness. However, the aim of our project is to design systems that enable users to negotiate trust on their own terms. The emphasis is on how users communicate with each other in a system. Users may need to decide who to socialise and train with in a system, or whose training advice to accept. Using the insights we have gathered, we will design base messages, guided by what users consider important in the formation of trust (which will form the basis of another paper) and what they expect or prefer from others. In terms of Verbeek's [24] design methodology, this is 'script logic' (as distinct from 'user logic') the design of norms into technology as a base for users to appropriate. Verbeek describes the design process as modest, not an autocratic steering of user behaviour but rather an activity that creates tools for others to adapt during use.

5 Conclusion

In conclusion, using content analysis, we explored the trust evidence users prefer as represented by 'retweeted' social network messages. Some messages demonstrated trust by expressing continuity and connections with community. Others indicated competence and a level of skill. The most popular type of trusted communications contained motivational messages, for instance, encouraging others to commit to their fitness training. These insights will be used to design template messages for a digital system we are creating that aims to enable users to negotiate trust on their own terms.

References

1. Metaxas, P.T., Mustafaraj, E., Wong, K., Zeng, L., O'Keefe, M., Finn, S.: Do Retweets Indicate Interest, Trust, Agreement? arXiv preprint arXiv:14113555 (2014)
2. Cofta, P.: Distrust. In: Proceedings of the 8th International Conference on Electronic Commerce: The New e-commerce: Innovations for Conquering Current Barriers, Obstacles and Limitations to Conducting Successful Business on the Internet, pp 250–258. ACM (2006)

3. Marres, N., Weltevrede, E.: Scraping the social? Issues in live social research. J. Cult. Econ. **6**(3), 313–335 (2013)
4. Kelley, M.C.: The Impact of Fitness Technology on Health Outcomes (2014)
5. Conroy, D.E., Yang, C.-H., Maher, J.P.: Behavior change techniques in top-ranked mobile apps for physical activity. Am. J. Prev. Med. **46**(6), 649–652 (2014)
6. Clayman, M.L., Manganello, J.A., Viswanath, K., Hesse, B.W., Arora, N.K.: Providing health messages to Hispanics/Latinos: understanding the importance of language, trust in health information sources, and media use. J. Health Commun. **15**(sup3), 252–263 (2010)
7. Albrecht, U.-V.: Transparency of health-apps for trust and decision making. J. Med. Internet Res. **15**(12), e277 (2012)
8. Kim, J., Kim, S.: Physicians' perception of the effects of internet health information on the doctor-patient relationship. Inform. Health. Soc. Care **34**(3), 136–148 (2009)
9. Lalli, P., Trust, Inequalities and Health Literacy: The Tangle Meeting with Dr Google (2014) (SSRN)
10. Golbeck, J.: Generating predictive movie recommendations from trust in social networks. In: Stølen, K., Winsborough, W.H., Martinelli, F., Massacci, F. (eds.) iTrust 2006. LNCS, vol. 3986, pp. 93–104. Springer, Heidelberg (2006)
11. Tavakolifard, M., Almeroth, K.C.: The Hidden Trust Network Underlying Twitter. On Some Challenges for Online Trust and Reputation Systems: 79 (2012)
12. Suh, B., Hong, L., Pirolli, P.: Chi EH Want to be retweeted? Large scale analytics on factors impacting retweet in twitter network. In: Proceedings of the 2010 IEEE Second International Conference on Social Computing (SocialCom), pp 177–184. IEEE (2010)
13. Csefalvay, C Gamergate series 2: Retweets (2014). http://chrisvoncsefalvay.com/2014/12/16/Gamergate-2-retweets.html
14. Finn, S., Metaxas, P., Mustafaraj, E., O'Keefe, M., Tang, L., Tang, S., Zeng, L.: TRAILS: a system for monitoring the propagation of rumors on twitter. In: Computation and Journalism Symposium, NYC, NY (2014)
15. Castelfranchi, C.: Falcone R Trust Theory: A Socio-Cognitive and Computational Model, vol. 18. Wiley, New York (2010)
16. Kranz, M., Möller, A., Hammerla, N., Diewald, S., Plötz, T., Olivier, P., Roalter, L.: The mobile fitness coach: towards individualized skill assessment using personalized mobile devices. Pervasive Mob. Comput. **9**(2), 203–215 (2013)
17. McNeill, A.R., Briggs, P.: Understanding twitter influence in the health domain: a social-psychological contribution. In: Proceedings of the Companion Publication of the 23rd International Conference on World Wide Web Companion, pp. 673–678. International World Wide Web Conferences Steering Committee (2014)
18. Padmasekara, G.: Fitness apps, a valid alternative to the gym: a pilot study. J. Mob. Technol. Med. **3**(1), 37–45 (2014)
19. Yoganathan, D., Kajanan, S.: Persuasive Technology for Smartphone Fitness Apps (2013)
20. Riff, D., Lacy, S., Fico, F.: Analyzing Media Messages: Using Quantitative Content Analysis in Research. Routledge, London (2014)
21. See-To, E.W., Ho, K.K.: Value co-creation and purchase intention in social network sites: The role of electronic Word-of-Mouth and trust–A theoretical analysis. Comput. Hum. Behav. **31**, 182–189 (2014)
22. Waters, R.D., Jamal, J.Y.: Tweet, tweet, tweet: a content analysis of nonprofit organizations' Twitter updates. Pub. Relat. Rev. **37**(3), 321–324 (2011)
23. Sillence, E., Briggs, P., Fishwick, L., Harris, P.: Trust and mistrust of online health sites. In: Proceedings of the SIGCHI Conference on Human Factors in Computing Systems, pp. 663–670. ACM (2004)

24. Verbeek, P.-P.: Moralizing Technology: Understanding and Designing the Morality of Things. University of Chicago Press, Chicago (2011)
25. Hardin, R.: Trust and Trustworthiness. Russell Sage Foundation, New York (2002)
26. Frederiksen, M.: Trust in the face of uncertainty: a qualitative study of intersubjective trust and risk. Int. Rev. Sociol. 24(1), 130–144 (2014)

Reusable Defense Components for Online Reputation Systems

Johannes Sänger[✉], Christian Richthammer, Artur Rösch,
and Günther Pernul

Department of Information Systems, University of Regensburg,
Regensburg, Germany
{johannes.sanger,christian.richthammer,artur.roesch,
gunther.pernul}@wiwi.uni-regensburg.de
http://www.ifs.uni-regensburg.de

Abstract. Attacks on trust and reputation systems (TRS) as well as defense strategies against certain attacks are the subject of many research papers. Although proposing valuable ideas, they all exhibit at least one of the following major shortcomings. Firstly, many researchers design defense mechanisms from scratch and without reusing approved ideas. Secondly, most proposals are limited to naming and theoretically describing the defense mechanisms. Another issue is the inconsistent denomination of attacks with similar characteristics among different researchers. To address these shortcomings, we propose a novel taxonomy of attacks on TRS focusing on their general characteristics and symptomatology. We use this taxonomy to assign reusable, clearly described and practically implemented components to different classes of attacks. With this work, we aim to provide a basis for TRS designers to experiment with numerous defense mechanisms and to build more robust systems in the end.

Keywords: Trust · Online reputation · Reputation systems · Attacks · Taxonomy · Components · Reusability

1 Introduction

Electronic marketplaces like eBay and Amazon have greatly facilitated transaction processes between entities on the Internet. This provides many benefits but at the same time also poses significant challenges. One of the fundamental problems in electronic marketplaces is that, unlike in traditional face-to-face transactions, buyers do neither get a complete picture of a product's actual quality nor do they know about the trustworthiness of the particular seller. To address this, trust and reputation systems (TRS) have become important elements for the decision making process in this mostly anonymous environment. According to a recent study carried out by Diekmann et al. [2], sellers with better reputation are able to obtain higher prices and an increased number of sales. On the one hand, this can encourage good behavior because users seek good reputation to benefit from it. But on the other hand, TRS are likely to face an increasing amount of

© IFIP International Federation for Information Processing 2015
C.D. Jensen et al. (Eds.): IFIPTM 2015, IFIP AICT 454, pp. 195–202, 2015.
DOI: 10.1007/978-3-319-18491-3_15

attacks by malicious users who try to gain unfair advantages by manipulating the reputation system through specific behavior [6]. Therefore, it is fundamental for the providers to use TRS that are robust against all kinds of attacks that could lead to deceptive reputation scores and trust.

In order to be able to cover every possible attack scenario, we firstly develop a taxonomy of attacks in electronic marketplaces. On the highest level, we distinguish between attacks performed as a seller (*seller attacks*) and attacks carried out in the role of the buyer (*advisor attacks*). Then, we identify defense mechanisms for different types of attacks by assigning reusable TRS components that can be employed to extend the functionality of the computation engine. These components are provided in the form of both a conceptual description and fully implemented reusable web-services in the component repository[1] introduced by Sänger and Pernul [10]. The additional attack view on TRS components constitutes an important extension to the yet largely functional view. We argue that the assignment of TRS components to attack types not only supports the development of more reliable and robust TRS with already existing components but also helps to identify weaknesses that have not been addressed so far.

The remainder of the paper is organized as follows. Firstly, we give an overview of the general problem context of our work in Sect. 2. Thereby we delineate the research gap we discovered and define the objectives of our proposal. In Sect. 3, we introduce our novel taxonomy of attack types on TRS. We use this taxonomy in Sect. 4 to assign TRS components to the different classes of attacks. At the same time, we point out how the outcomes of this allocation are described in clearly structured attack profiles and integrated in the knowledge repository. In Sect. 5, we discuss our findings before we conclude in Sect. 6.

2   Problem Context and Related Work

As opposed to traditional face-to-face interactions, the "universe of strangers" [1] found in electronic marketplaces makes it hard to determine the trustworthiness of an actor. This is due to insufficient information as entities commonly never have transacted with each other before. The problems resulting from the lack of information can be mitigated through TRS, which have become a widely adapted element for the decision making process in online environments. To establish a common understanding, we firstly point out related work on attacks on TRS. After that, we briefly describe the reusable TRS repository whose components we map against our attack classes. This leads us to the research gap we address in this paper.

2.1   Attacks on Trust and Reputation Systems

TRS can be subject to attacks by their participating entities in various ways. Attacks may be dependent on the specific application scenario, influenced by the social environment underlying the reputation system, and performed by one

---

[1] http://trust.bayforsec.de/.

single entity or by several colluding entities. Because of the increasing attention paid to attacks against TRS, several security analyses were carried out in recent years [3,4,6,13]. The resulting proposals of attack taxonomies and formulations of challenges for robust TRS in turn motivated studies on defense strategies (for related surveys see [5,8]). As the various trust models are specifically designed to cope with certain attacks, they are not completely robust against various attacks in different settings. Therefore, security and robustness still remain the key challenges in the design and development of TRS.

2.2 Reusable Component Repository

Since most of the TRS described in literature use computation methods that are entirely built from scratch [12], well-established approaches are rarely considered. To foster reusability, Sänger and Pernul [10] proposed a hierarchical component taxonomy of computation engines along with a repository containing design knowledge both on a conceptual and an implementation level. On the conceptual level, they described each building block as a design pattern-like solution. On the implementation level, they provided fully implemented reusable components by means of web-services. The classes of the component repository were the result of the analysis of their generic process of reputation systems as well as various computation methods described in different surveys [7,9,11–13].

2.3 Research Gap

Apart from the component repository described before, further important steps toward reusability were made by Hoffman et al. [5] and Koutrouli and Tsalgatidou [8]. They conducted surveys on attacks and defense mechanisms and thus helped to collect the ideas for the research community. The main shortcoming of these surveys is that they are limited to naming and theoretically describing the defense mechanisms.

In this paper, we want to go one step further and employ the reusable computation components described by Sänger and Pernul [10] as defense mechanisms for attacks on TRS. The uniform format of their design pattern-like artifacts helps to establish clear guidelines for developing new defense mechanisms. Moreover, their fully implemented components by means of web-services allow researchers to experiment.

In a preparatory step, we aim to extend their repository by an attack view in which we systematically describe attack types with certain characteristics instead of basing the discussions on particular examples of attacks. While this helps to avoid the yet inconsistent denominations of some attacks (e.g. re-entry vs. whitewashing), it also makes our remarks more generic and extendable. Most importantly, we are then able to assign reusable computation components to entire classes of attacks instead of matching the same defense methods against numerous examples of attacks.

3 Taxonomy of Attacks on Trust and Reputation Systems

In this section, we introduce a novel attack taxonomy for electronic marketplaces in order to organize possible kinds of attacks. On the highest level, we distinguish between seller attacks and advisor attacks. In these major classes, we classify every attack type along two dimensions: attackers and behavior.

3.1 Seller Attacks vs. Advisor Attacks

In a common electronic marketplace, we have two parties: the buyer and the seller. In terms of TRS, both can take the role of the ratee (the one being rated, usually the seller) and the advisor (the one who provides a referral, usually the buyer).

To decide which seller to transact with, buyers rely on ratings of other buyers to evaluate the reputation of sellers. A seller that delivers an item as specified in the contract is referred to as an honest seller, whereas a seller that does not deliver an item as specified in the contract is called a dishonest or malicious seller. Note that the term "item" includes both physical and non-physical products as well as services. Seller attacks denote manipulations of the reputation system that one or more entities of an electronic marketplace perform in the role of the seller. The intention behind these manipulations is to be able to act as a malicious seller while maintaining a reputation profile that buyers would assess as honest. Even though cheating behavior from dishonest sellers (e.g. not delivering an item at all) can be sentenced by law, TRS should aim to prevent these actions from the first.

Advisor attacks, in contrast, are implemented by the rating parties. Since buyers can usually rate a seller's performance in a particular transaction, they are able to shape his reputation profile and thus act as advisors for other buyers. According to Jøsang and Golbeck [6], advisor attacks can be summarized under the term "unfair rating attacks" because they are based on one or several digital identities providing unfair ratings to other digital identities. These unfair ratings are used to manipulate the reputation profile of sellers – either boosting or vilifying it to an unjustified extent. As opposed to seller attacks, advisor attacks can generally not be sentenced by law.

3.2 Dimensions: Attackers and Behavior

Within the classes of seller and advisor attacks, our taxonomy systematizes attack types along the two dimensions: attackers and behavior.

Attackers. The attackers dimension refers to the number and characteristics of the digital identities participating in an attack. Although seller attacks are typically performed by one single digital identity, some of them may also be performed by a colluding group of attackers. Depending on the trust model and identity management concept used by the reputation system, attackers may also create additional digital identities on their own in order to boost their leverage.

– One identity: An attacker performs all actions on his own, independently and without the help of other entities. Furthermore, he does not create any additional accounts but conducts the attack with one single digital identity.
– Multiple identities: In online environments, which are mostly anonymous, pseudonyms can generally be created with minimal costs. Hence, a malicious entity may easily acquire multiple digital identities with which he is able to create pseudo-referrals and boost his reputation in the system.
– Multiple entities: A group of attackers agrees to perform a joint attack. Typically, the damage caused by multiple colluding entities is considerably higher than by entities independently performing malicious actions.

Behavior. The behavior dimension characterizes the actions of an attacker. Here, we differentiate attackers acting maliciously all the time from attackers alternating between malicious and honest actions.

– Consistent: Attackers act maliciously all the time and do not perform any honest actions.
– Inconsistent: Attackers perform both honest and dishonest actions. Thus, the dishonest actions can be used to gain higher profits, for instance, while the honest actions ensure that the reputation value is kept at a level that makes other users assess the attacker as honest.

4 Introducing an Attack View on the Component Repository

In this section, we show how we implemented the novel "attack view" on the component repository. Thereto, we firstly accomplish the assignment of attack classes and defense components. Secondly, we delineate how the taxonomy of attacks was integrated as part of the knowledge repository and linked to the computation components.

4.1 Assignment of Defense Components

Most research papers on defense mechanisms against attacks in TRS propose a variety of possible solutions in form of "unstructured" textual recommendations. In this work, in contrast, we assign reusable components. These components are not only implemented in a web-service but also clearly described in well-structured design pattern-like artifacts. In this way, a developer can directly make use of both the ideas and the web-services that can be integrated in existing reputation systems to extend their capabilities.

To accomplish the assignment, we analyzed the single classes of our taxonomy of attacks on TRS in electronic marketplaces introduced in the former section with regard to their general characteristics. Table 1 shows an excerpt of the results. The terms listed on the right side of the table reflect the unique component terms as used in the component repository. These components provide a range of different defense approaches that can be applied either alone or in combination.

Table 1. Excerpt of assignment table

Primary class	Secondary class	Tertiary class	Component
Seller	One identity	Consistent	Summation, Bayesian Probability, Average, Share (positive)
		Inconsistent	Asymetric rating, Absolute time discounting, Relative time discounting, Age-based filter, Context similarity, Criteria similarity
...	...	...	...
Advisor	Multiple identities	Consistent	Clustering filter, Subjective reliability
		Inconsistent	Absolute time discounting, Beta-statistic filter, Clustering filter, Propagation discount, Relative time discounting, Subjective reliability

Table 2. Example profile of one attack class, shortened

Attack Classes	Advisor attack: consistent (One identity)
Description	In a consistent advisor attack carried out by one identity, a single advisor consistently assigns deceptive ratings to transactions. This means consistently providing unfairly low ratings to honest sellers and/or consistently providing unfairly high ratings to dishonest sellers
Examples	− Consistent ballot stuffing: The attacker provides unfairly high ratings toward other actors to increase their reputation − Consistent bad mouthing: The attacker provides unfairly low ratings toward other actors to discourage their reputation. [...]
Solution	There are several ways to filter out unfair ratings made by single attackers. Detection/filtering mechanisms can broadly be divided into two groups: endogenous filtering/discounting and exogenous filtering/discounting. Endogenous discounting methods try to detect unfair ratings on the basis of their statistical properties. [...]
Pattern/ web-service	− Beta-statistic filter − Clustering filter − Objective reliability (reputation) [...]
Literature	− Tavakolifard, M.,Almeroth, K. A Taxonomy to Express Open Challenges in Trust and Reputation Systems. Journal of Communications, North America, 7, 7. 2012. [...]

4.2 Implementation as Part of the Knowledge Repository

In the second step, we implemented the taxonomy of attacks as part of the knowledge repository[2].

To give a more detailed view on the single classes as well as the possible defense strategies, we described each block in a clearly structured "profile". Each profile contains a general description for that block, a number of example attacks, a solution (defense strategy) to that problem, hyperlinks to design patterns/ web-services that can be used to implement the solution, and a list of relevant literature. All these profiles can be found online as part of the knowledge repository. Table 2 depicts an example profile for a *consistent* advisor attack based on *one identity*.

5 Discussion

Reviewing the assignment of our taxonomy of attacks and defense mechanisms, we made some interesting findings. In contrast to most surveys on attacks and defense mechanisms for TRS, we did not introduce a range of different attacks in this work but rather focused on the general characteristics and symptomatology of attacks such as the continuity and the number of attackers. We thereby found that many attacks that have been described as distinct challenges in literature are actually different manifestations of the same symptomatology. Consequently, defense mechanisms against specific characteristics of attacks may help to cover a variety of challenges.

Overall, the assignment of attack classes and computation components brings some valuable benefits:

- Developers not only gain solutions to challenges stemming from weaknesses against attacks in form of a short recommendation but find a clearly structured design pattern-like description of the exact problem, a solution to that problem, a generic code example and further literature. Moreover, they can directly make use of a web-service implementing that logic.
- Having a range of already implemented services, developers can experiment with different combinations of components to find the best solution for their specific problem, TRS and use case.
- Researchers are encouraged to use this clearly defined structure when developing new ideas and defense mechanisms, and make them available in form of both design patterns and web-services in the component repository.

6 Conclusion

Lots of research on attacks and defense strategies on TRS has been done in the past. In this paper we developed a novel taxonomy which, to the best of our knowledge, is the first taxonomy that can be used to describe all attacks that focus on the manipulation or exploitation of the reputation computation in

---

[2] http://trust.bayforsec.de/ngot/index.php?section=knowledge_repository.

e-commerce settings. We then identified defense mechanisms for different types of attacks by mapping reusable TRS components against classes of attacks. In this way, we not only support reputation system designers in the development of more reliable and robust TRS with already existing components but also help to identity weaknesses that have not been addressed so far. Furthermore, our taxonomy is valuable for future research in that it provides a basis to describe attacks by their characteristics and symptomatology and contributes to a common understanding of attacks on TRS.

Acknowledgements. The research leading to these results was supported by the "Bavarian State Ministry of Education, Science and the Arts" as part of the FORSEC research association.

References

1. Dellarocas, C.: Reputation mechanisms. In: Hendershott, T. (ed.) Handbook on Economics and Information Systems, pp. 629–660. Elsevier Publishing, Amsterdam (2006)
2. Diekmann, A., Jann, B., Przepiorka, W., Wehrli, S.: Reputation formation and the evolution of cooperation in anonymous online markets. Am. Sociol. Rev. **79**(1), 65–85 (2014)
3. European Network and Information Security Agency: Reputation-based Systems: A Security Analysis. European Network and Information Security Agency (2007)
4. Fraga, D., Bankovic, Z., Moya, J.M.: A taxonomy of trust and reputation system attacks. In: Proceedings of the 11th International Conference on Trust, Security and Privacy in Computing and Communications (TrustCom), pp. 41–50 (2012)
5. Hoffman, K., Zage, D., Nita-Rotaru, C.: A survey of attack and defense techniques for reputation systems. ACM Comput. Surv. **42**(1), 1–31 (2009)
6. Jøsang, A., Golbeck, J.: Challenges for robust trust and reputation systems. In: Proceedings of the 5th International Workshop on Security and Trust Management (STM) (2009)
7. Jøsang, A., Ismail, R., Boyd, C.: A survey of trust and reputation systems for online service provision. Decis. Support Syst. **43**(2), 618–644 (2007)
8. Koutrouli, E., Tsalgatidou, A.: Taxonomy of attacks and defense mechanisms in P2P reputation systems - lessons for reputation system designers. Comput. Sci. Rev. **6**(2–3), 47–70 (2012)
9. Noorian, Z., Ulieru, M.: The state of the art in trust and reputation systems: a framework for comparison. J. Theor. Appl. Electron. Commer. Res. **5**(2), 97–117 (2010)
10. Sänger, J., Pernul, G.: Reusability for trust and reputation systems. In: Zhou, J., Gal-Oz, N., Zhang, J., Gudes, E. (eds.) IFIPTM 2014. IFIP AICT, vol. 430, pp. 28–43. Springer, Heidelberg (2014)
11. Sherchan, W., Nepal, S., Paris, C.: A survey of trust in social networks. ACM Comput. Surv. **45**(4), 1–33 (2013)
12. Tavakolifard, M., Almeroth, K.C.: A taxonomy to express open challenges in trust and reputation systems. J. Commun. **7**(7), 538–551 (2012)
13. Yao, Y., Ruohomaa, S., Xu, F.: Addressing common vulnerabilities of reputation systems for electronic commerce. J. Theor. Appl. Electron. Commer. Res. **7**(1), 3–4 (2012)

Continuous Context-Aware Device Comfort Evaluation Method

Jingjing Guo[1]($\boxtimes$), Christian Damsgaard Jensen[2], and Jianfeng Ma[1]

[1] School of Computer, Xidian University, Xi'an 710071, China
xdgjj@foxmail.com
[2] Department of Applied Mathematics and Computer Science,
Technical University of Denmark,
2800 Kongens Lyngby, Denmark

Abstract. Mobile devices have become more powerful and are increasingly integrated in the everyday life of people; from playing games, taking pictures and interacting with social media to replacing credit cards in payment solutions. The security of a mobile device is therefore increasingly linked to its context, such as its location, surroundings (e.g. objects and people in the immediate environment) and so on, because some actions may only be appropriate in some situations; this is not captured by traditional security models. In this paper, we examine the notion of *Device Comfort* and propose a way to calculate the sensitivity of a specific action to the context. We present two different methods for a mobile device to dynamically evaluate its security status when an action is requested, either by the user or by another device. The first method uses the predefined ideal context as a standard to assess the comfort level of a device in the current context. The second method is based on the familiarity of the device with doing the particular action in the current context. These two methods suit different situations of the device owner's ability to deal with system security. The assessment result can activate responding action of the device to protect its resource.

Keywords: Context-aware · Mobile device · Device comfort

1 Introduction

Mobile devices, such as smartphones, tablets and laptops are growing in both popularity and capability. A large amount of sensing capabilities has been embedded into these mobile devices [3], which enables them to establish their context, such as where a device is, what is it used for, etc. Although there are lots of methods [4] proposed to secure mobile devices, e.g. using technologies such as machine learning [1] or probabilistic approaches [12]), most of them consider the security status of a mobile device from the user's perspective, that is to say, they consider the owner-device relationship. The concept of *device comfort* proposed by Marsh et al. [6] draws a grand blueprint that a mobile device can be smart enough to perceive its current context and synthesize the cognized cues, then

© IFIP International Federation for Information Processing 2015
C.D. Jensen et al. (Eds.): IFIPTM 2015, IFIP AICT 454, pp. 203–211, 2015.
DOI: 10.1007/978-3-319-18491-3_16

use the internal models to reason about its security status under the cognized context (including its user).

We use device comfort to measure the feeling of a mobile device in terms of the security status of an operation in the perceived context, such as "a user is checking the photos in the private album on a bus at 10 a.m."or "a medical professional is accessing the healthcare data in a pub using an unknown wireless network" [8]. If the device feels uncomfortable about performing an action in a specific context, it can express its concerns, but the final decision to proceed is up to the user [7]. Storer et al. have examined user interface designs to express these concerns [11]. Because of the uncertainty of the environment, the result of security policy enforcement maybe wrong, while it is also not a wise option to make a decision without considering it. Morisset et al. presented a formal model for soft enforcement [9]. Soft enforcement means the agent in charge of enforcing a security policy can influence the agent in charge of making the decision rather than force the decision maker to adopt a certain action or leave them make a decision. The optimal influencing policy they proposed took both the control of the influencer and the environment uncertainty into account.

Marsh divides device comfort into three levels: basic comfort level, general comfort level and situational comfort level, with the accuracy of the considered context varying from low to high. The general comfort level is calculated based on the basic comfort level. Situational comfort level is calculated based on both of the two other comfort levels, which should consider the user, physical and virtual environment and the concrete behaviour of other entities. The literature on device comfort defines the general ideas of this concept, but there are few concrete examples of how to measure the comfort level of a mobile device and enforce suitable behaviour in the real world.

In this paper, we propose two methods for evaluating the situational comfort level of a mobile device. The aim of these methods is to reason about whether an action is suitable to be done in the current sensed context even if the action has passed the verification of the traditional access control method (identity ID and password and so on). We propose this computational method to assess the sensitivity of a specific action running on the mobile device in the current context and provide an approach to measure the difference between two contexts in an action's perspective. The first proposed method uses the predefined ideal context as a standard to assess the comfort level of a device in the current context. The second evaluation methods can monitor the status of the mobile device continuously rather than enforcing a static security policy used in traditional access control methods, which allows better reasoning about the risk of running an action in a certain context.

The rest of this paper is organized in the following way. Section 2 explores the notion of device comfort and describes how to represent contextual factors and their influence on the situational comfort level. We present the first method for calculating device comfort in Sect. 3. The second method (familiarity based method) is given in Sect. 4. Finally, we present conclusions and outline a few directions for future work in Sect. 5.

2 Mathematic Expression of Contextual Factors

As mentioned earlier, security of mobile applications has become increasingly dependent on the context [2,10]. We define a specific context in which the device is currently involved as a tuple $C = \langle c_1, c_2, \cdots, c_n \rangle$, where each element (c_i) represents the value of a certain context factor, such as the device's physical location, the current time of day, the name of the network to which the device is connected, the surrounding devices, etc. Depending on the action, the different context factors that may influence the device's feeling about the security implications of performing that particular action may carry different weight. For example, the feeling of a mobile device about doing a type of action A (such as checking the mailbox) depends only on its physical location, so the current time and the network to which the device is connected are not important, but another type of action B (such as accessing a confidential file on the company's server) may depend on both its physical location and the network to which it is connected. We therefore say that different types of actions are sensitive to different context factors. We use another tuple $S^A = \langle s_1^A, s_2^A, \cdots, s_n^A \rangle$ to indicate the feature of an action A where s_i^A indicates the sensitivity of the device's comfort level about doing A to context factor c_i and we have $0 \leq s_i^A \leq 1 (1 \leq i \leq n)$, $\sum_{i=1}^{n} s_i^A = 1$. The intention behind this normalization is to measure the importance of each context factor using uniform criteria. If action A is more sensitive to context factor c_i than to c_j, s_i^A should be bigger than s_j^A. We define the sum of all elements is equal to 1 to meet the range of the computation result of the comfort level shown below.

3 Predefined-Standard Based Method for Situational Comfort Level Assessment

This method suits situations where the owner of a device wants to ensure that a certain type of action is only allowed in a specific predefined context. In this case, the ideal context should be defined and stored in the device beforehand as the standard to reason about the device's feeling. Taking the location as an example, like Marsh said in [5], there are some places where the device should be less comfortable in sharing its data with other devices than other places, so a device in a Comfort Zone can enhance its comfort, while in a Discomfort Zone, the comfort will be decreased. If the sensed context is different from the owner's assumption, the device will feel uncomfortable. The more difference there is between them, the lower the device's comfort level will be.

We assume that the predefined context for a certain type of action A given by device's owner is $P = \langle p_1, p_2, \cdots, p_n \rangle$. We then use the following equation to measure the difference between the perceived context $C = \langle c_1, c_2, \cdots, c_n \rangle$ and the predefined context $P = \langle p_1, p_2, \cdots, p_n \rangle$ when doing action A. We use a function D to compute the difference between two contexts to a certain action A and it is defined as: $D : C_1 \times C_2 \to D_{C_1 C_2}$, where $D_{C_1 C_2}$ is the variable to indicate the result of the function $D(C_1, C_2)$. Equation (1) is the function to compute the difference between context C and P to action A.

$$D_{CP} = D(C, P) = \overline{\left(\begin{array}{c} c_1 \\ c_2 \\ \vdots \\ c_n \end{array}\right) - \left(\begin{array}{c} p_1 \\ p_2 \\ \vdots \\ p_n \end{array}\right)} \cdot \left(\begin{array}{c} s_1^A \\ s_2^A \\ \vdots \\ s_n^A \end{array}\right) \tag{1}$$

The "$-$" in Eq. (1) is the operator used to measure the difference between two values of the same context factor. Its meaning depends on the concrete meaning of each context factor. For example, if the factor is physical location, "$-$" could be a method to compute the distance between two locations; if the factor is the network to which the device is connected, "$-$" will become a compare operator to judge whether the two networks are the same; and so on. It is obvious that the difference between each c_i and p_i ($i \in [1, n]$) should be normalized, so that the metric of each $c_i - p_i$ which is used to compute D_{CP} is the same. The operator "$\overline{x}$" in Eq. (1) is the function which maps $c_i - p_i$ to a certain difference level which is a real number between 0 and 1 (0 means exactly the same and 1 is exactly the opposite), so we know $D_{CP} \in [0, 1]$. As with the "$-$" operator, the mapping rule of "$\overline{x}$" in terms of each context factor depends on the concrete meaning of the factor and the device owner's preference.

If context C matches with context P, D_{CP} will be zero. The more difference between them, the bigger D_{CP} will be, and consequently the device will feel more uncomfortable. Here the meaning of "match" is not completely equal to the word "same". For example, if the value of an element in C (c_i) is different from the value of the corresponding element in P (p_i), while s_i^A is zero, then this difference won't impact the comfort level of the device in terms of action A, because action A is not sensitive to the ith context factor. In this case, we also say context C matches with context P, even if they are not, strictly speaking, the same.

We use $1 - D_{CP}$ to measure the comfort level of a device about doing an action in a certain context. We define a comfort threshold T_c and a discomfort threshold T_{dc} to map $1 - D_{CP}$ to three comfort levels. If $1 - D_{CP} \geq T_c$, the device feels the security status is safe and it feels comfortable; if $T_{dc} \leq 1 - D_{CP} < T_c$, the device feels the security status is fair and its comfort level falls between comfortable and uncomfortable; if $1 - D_{CP} < T_{dc}$, the device senses it may be compromised and feels uncomfortable.

4   Familiarity Based Situational Comfort Level Evaluation Method

Sometimes, the owner of the device cannot give a clear concept of a desirable context for an action. In this case, the device will consider the familiarity of doing the action in a certain context to measure its comfort level. If an action has already been done in a context many times without problems, the device will feel more familiar with the context for that action. The more familiar the device is with the current context of doing the action, the more comfortable the device feels, and vice versa. We use Eq. (1) to measure the difference between two contexts. Because of the limited precision of most sensed information (such as GPS coordinates), we consider two contexts the same if the difference between them is sufficiently small. In order to verify whether two contexts encountered by action A can be seen as the same, we define an equivalence relationship "$\sim$" for two contexts, so that all the contexts of A which have equivalence relationship "$\sim$" can be seen as the same and should be classified to one equivalence class. More contexts within an equivalence class means that the device will feel more comfortable to do the action in the context which belongs to the equivalence class.

The definition of "$\sim$" is: Assume P and P' are two contexts within the context set of action A, which means that action A has been done in both contexts P and P'. We say $P \sim P'$, if $D_{PP'} \leq \sigma$, where σ is the boundary condition used to distinguish two contexts defined by the owner.

When the device senses a new context C_{new}, when A is being performed, it must determine which equivalence class of A to use. If the new context is close enough to an existing equivalence class, C_{new} should be added to that class. When an equivalence class already has many contexts in it, how do we then measure the distance between the new context and the equivalence class? We can learn from the physics method of computing the distance from one point to an object in the space. In physics, a point is computed to represent the center of the object and the distance between the tested point and the center point can be seen as the distance between the tested point and the object.

Here we also define a core for an equivalence class to represent the feature of the contexts within this equivalence class. Assume an equivalence class of A is $X = \{C^1, C^2, \cdots, C^n\}$, ($C^i$ is the contexts belonging to X), the core of it is $X_{core} = avg(X) = \{c'_1, c'_2, \cdots, c'_n\}$, c'_i is the average value of the ith context factor in all the contexts (C^i) within class X, while how to compute the average value depends on the concrete meaning of the factor. If C_{new} and the core of an available equivalence class have the equivalence relationship, this means C_{new} is close enough to the contexts within this class and C_{new} should be added to it. If there is no available equivalence class whose core has equivalence relationship with C_{new}, a new equivalence class should be established where C_{new} is both the only context in it and the core of it. If there is a new member adding to an available equivalence class, the core of this class must be updated accordingly.

Adding a new context to an existing equivalence class requires the identification of the equivalence class of A that closest to C_{new}. One situation that may happen is that C_{new} is equally close to more than one existing equivalence classes of A, so we should decide to which class C_{new} should be added. Because the differences between C_{new} and each of these classes are the same, we should use other metrics to decide C_{new}'s destination. In this paper, we adopt the class which has the maximum cardinal number among all the candidate equivalence classes. For example, if the new context C_{new} shows that the device may be either in the owner's home or in the neighbour's home, this could happen when the owner is using it in his or her garden, we add C_{new} to the owner's home because the owner rarely uses the device in his or her neighbour's home compared to using this device in his or her own home, i.e. probability that the device's owner is in his or her own home is greater than at the neighbours. Finally, we use the ratio of the cardinal number of the selected class to the maximum scale of the action's equivalence class A as the device's comfort level. When the device obtains the value of $comfort\_level$, then it can map it into the corresponding comfort status using the same method mentioned in predefined-standard based method.

The strategy of adopting the maximum scale class as the new context's final destination may not suit all cases, so other metrics can also be adopted, such as take the minimum scale class or just select a class among the candidate classes randomly. If we use the maximum strategy, the scale of the selected class will become larger and larger, while if the minimum strategy is adopted, the scale of these candidate classes will finally tend to the same, moreover, the random strategy cannot explicitly influence the scale evolution of those candidate classes. It is obvious that these different scale evolution situations will lead to different result of the $comfort\_level$, so different mapping rules should be used to map the different values of $comfort\_level$ to a certain comfort level of the device. Here, we used the ratio of the scale of the current context's equivalence class to the maximum scale of the action's equivalence class as the result of the $comfort\_level$, while in different scenario or with different preference of the mapping rule, other methods can also be adopted to get the desired result.

In the following, we present the algorithm for measuring the comfort level of a device to do an action A in a new perceived context C_{new}. We assume there are m existing equivalence classes of action A noted $\{X^1, X^2, \cdots, X^m\}$ and use $[C]_\sim$ to represent the equivalence class to which context C belongs. σ is the boundary to determine whether two contexts have the equivalence relationship mentioned above.

5   Discussion and Future Works

In this paper, we presented two methods for evaluating the feeling of a mobile device in terms of security when an action is requested in a certain context. The different evaluation results can activate corresponding measures to protect the resource on the device. Although a thorough discussion of implementation issues and technical solutions goes beyond the scope of this introductory work, some of the issues are worth being mentioned and briefly discussed.

With respect to the sensitivity of a kind of action A, we use a tuple (tuple S^A mentioned in Sect. 2) to represent its sensitivity to different contextual factors. From Eq. (1) we can see that applying different sensitivity tuples to an action, we will obtain different comfort levels for performing this action given the same context. So properly assigning the weigh of each contextual factor is crucial to get a satisfactory evaluation result. There are already some consensuses on the

---

Algorithm 1. familiarity based comfort level evaluation method

---

Require: new perceived context $"C_{new}"$, σ, all existing context equivalence class $\{X^i, i \in [1, m]\}$ of action A stored in the device

Ensure: the comfort level of doing A in context C_{new}

    for each equivalence class X^i **do**

        $m = \min\{D_{X^i_{core}C_{new}}, i \in [1, m]\};$ // $D_{X^i_{core}C_{new}}$ is the difference between X^i_{core}

                                      //and C_{new} calculated by Eq. 1

    end for

    if $m > \sigma$ **then**

        create a new equivalence class X^{m+1};

        put C_{new} into X^{m+1};

        $X^{m+1}_{core} = C_{new}$;

    else

        create an empty set E;

        for each X^i **do**

            if $D_{X^i_{core}C_{new}} == m$ **then**

                put X^i into E;

            end if

        end for

        put C_{new} into class X^f ($|X^f| = \max\{|X^i|, X^i \in E\}$);

        update X^f_{core};

    end if

    $comfort\_level = \frac{|[C_{new}]_{\sim}|}{\max\{|X^i|\}}$;

---

sensitivity of some actions, e.g. we should check our bank account in a privacy space rather than a public place, and so on. There are, however, also situations where the situational factors are more complex, so more works need to be done in the future on how to properly assign the weight of each factor.

Similar to the assignment of weights to the situational factors, it is possible to use different metrics for measuring the distance between two, or more, contexts. We currently propose to use the distance between the center of a context equivalence class and a perceived context as the distance between the equivalence class and the perceived context, rather than compute the shortest distance between the perceived context and any context within the equivalence class. We can consider the context space of a mobile device as an $N-$ dimension space, each contextual factor is an axis, so a concrete context is a point in this space and an equivalence class is a mass within this space. The more contexts within an equivalence class gathers at a point, the greater the density of this point will be. So we should measure the center of the equivalence class just as find the center of gravity of a non-uniform density distribution object in physics. If we select any context within the class to compute the distance, the range of the context within the equivalence class will be expanded indefinitely, because a point (perceived context) may be close to the edge of an object (the equivalence class) but far away from its center of gravity (the center of the equivalence class). In this case, the context equivalence class will lost the meaning of equivalence and it can not represent a type of context anymore. Because the assignment of the sensitivity vector will influence the distance between two given contexts, different values assigned to the situational vector will lead to different evolution of a context equivalence class given the same perceived contexts sequence. It is possible that all the contexts can be included into the same equivalence class, and it is also possible that each perceived context falls into different equivalence class. To get a desired evaluation result, the relationship between the assignment of the situational vector and the evolution of the context equivalence class of an action should be further studied.

A drawback of the familiarity based method is that the accuracy of the evaluation result depends on the scale of the obtained context data. A device needs a lot of context data to obtain the usage pattern of each action. So the evaluation result will be more accuracy with the increasing use of the device. If we want to get a satisfactory effect, maybe some tests should be done before the first formal use of the method in a mobile device to get enough usage data.

Now we are exploring a security policy language to represent our methods, so that we can further implement them in the future. We will continue to improve the methods to better evaluate the security relevant feeling of the mobile devices in a certain context to enhance its security. Concretely speaking, we will study the method which is able to self-adjustment according to its performance feedback from the user, so how to get these feedbacks from user will also be considered in our future work.

Acknowledgements. This work was partly supported by the China Scholarship Council, the Program for Changjiang Scholars and Innovative Research Team in University (China) under Grant No. IRT1078, the Key Program of NSFC-Guangdong Union Foundation (China) under Grant No. U1135002 and the Major National S&T Program (China) under Grant No. 2011ZX03005-002.

References

1. Bose, A., Shin, K.G.: Proactive security for mobile messaging networks. In: Proceedings of the 5th ACM Workshop on Wireless Security, WiSe 2006, pp. 95–104. ACM, New York (2006). http://doi.acm.org/10.1145/1161289.1161307
2. Chen, G., Kotz, D., et al.: A survey of context-aware mobile computing research. Technical report, Technical Report TR2000-381, Department of Computer Science, Dartmouth College (2000)
3. Khan, W., Xiang, Y., Aalsalem, M., Arshad, Q.: Mobile phone sensing systems: a survey. IEEE Commun. Surv. Tutorials **15**(1), 402–427 (2013)
4. La Polla, M., Martinelli, F., Sgandurra, D.: A survey on security for mobile devices. IEEE Commun. Surv. Tutorials **15**(1), 446–471 (2013)
5. Marsh, S.: Comfort zones: location dependent trust and regret management for mobile devices. In: Proceedings of LocationTrust (2010)
6. Marsh, S., Briggs, P., El-Khatib, K., Esfandiari, B., Stewart, J.A.: Defining and investigating device comfort. J. Inf. Process. **19**, 231–252 (2011)

7. Marsh, S., Noël, S., Storer, T., Wang, Y., Briggs, P., Robart, L., Stewart, J., Esfandiari, B., El-Khatib, K., Vefa Bicakci, M., Cuong Dao, M., Cohen, M., Da Silva, D.: Non-standards for trust: foreground trust and second thoughts for mobile security. In: Meadows, C., Fernandez-Gago, C. (eds.) STM 2011. LNCS, vol. 7170, pp. 28–39. Springer, Heidelberg (2012)
8. Marsh, S., Wang, Y., Noël, S., Robart, L., Stewart, J.: Device comfort for mobile health information accessibility. In: 2013 Eleventh Annual International Conference on Privacy, Security and Trust (PST), pp. 377–380. IEEE (2013)
9. Morisset, C., Yevseyeva, I., Groß, T., van Moorsel, A.: A formal model for soft enforcement: influencing the decision-maker. In: Mauw, S., Jensen, C.D. (eds.) STM 2014. LNCS, vol. 8743, pp. 113–128. Springer, Heidelberg (2014)
10. Perera, C., Zaslavsky, A., Christen, P., Georgakopoulos, D.: Context aware computing for the internet of things: a survey. IEEE Commun. Surv. Tutorials 16(1), 414–454 (2014)
11. Storer, T., Marsh, S., Noël, S., Esfandiari, B., El-Khatib, K., Briggs, P., Renaud, K., Bicakci, M.V.: Encouraging second thoughts: obstructive user interfaces for raising security awareness. In: 2013 Eleventh Annual International Conference on Privacy, Security and Trust (PST), pp. 366–368. IEEE (2013)
12. Xie, L., Zhang, X., Seifert, J.P., Zhu, S.: pBMDS: a behavior-based malware detection system for cellphone devices. In: Proceedings of the Third ACM Conference on Wireless Network Security, pp. 37–48. ACM (2010)

Special Session: Toward Trusted Cloud Ecosystems

Foreword: Towards Trusted Cloud Ecosystems

Businesses are using Cloud, hosting and managed services to facilitate growth, not just cut costs. For business critical applications to move to the Cloud, however, significant challenges to widespread adoption still remain, mostly concerning security, assurance and compliance, notably data protection, control, availability and resilience. The UK government, for example, also created the G-Cloud Digital Market Place (previously CloudStore) that includes products and services that have been assessed and classified against standardized level of assurance and other sector specific requirements such as Public Services Network (PSN) connectivity. As cloud services mature, European providers such as Atos, BT and Telecom Italia start to differentiate their Cloud and IT services by specializing them to specific vertical market sectors. Trust, transparency and governance remain both significant challenges and opportunities for Cloud services. Those who manage to produce high-assurance Cloud services that allow businesses and consumers to have transparency and governance of their assets in the Cloud are more likely to attract Cloud-enabled business in the future. For Cloud business to flourish this has to be combined with vertical market sector specialization and policy harmonization, as is noted in the report "Trusted Cloud Europe: Have your Say" by the European Cloud Partnership (ECP) on Trusted Cloud. Harmonizing levels of service quality and assurance, compliance requirements, supply chain relationships and streamlining procurement and contract management underpins sector specific clouds that emerge in Government with Health and Finance following.

Another significant characteristic of the market evolution towards the Cloud-enabled business of the future is the explosion of personal data and personal information in the Cloud. The amount of such data that is generated and collected on a daily basis is rapidly growing due to the increasing number of activities performed online especially following the commoditization of smart phones and tablets. The availability of such big data represents a novel opportunity for organizations and individuals to benefit from business intelligence and innovative services relating to an emerging "market of data". As is also recognized by EIT ICT Labs who have established a High Impact Initiative on Trusted Cloud, the enablement of an eco-system of trusted services and application that allows individuals to gain visibility and control of the exploitation of their data in the Cloud is another important to address.

The papers presented in this invited session of the IFIP Trust Management Conference present innovations that enable the realization of Trusted Cloud ecosystems for data, platforms, applications and services in vertical market sectors such as Government, Health, Finance, Retail and Consumer Services.

In the first paper, Ana Juan Ferrer examines the role of Service Level Agreements (SLAs) in building a Trusted Cloud for Europe by providing the mechanisms that allow both users and providers to establish a common understanding of the services to be provided and enforce guarantees around performance, transparency, conformance and data protection. It proposes a taxonomy of terms to support more tight and detailed SLA definitions that help improving reliability and transparency in the Cloud.

In the second paper, the STRATEGIC consortium present progress towards the vision of a Cloud store or a marketplace of Trusted Cloud applications, services and

© IFIP International Federation for Information Processing 2015
C.D. Jensen et al. (Eds.): IFIPTM 2015, IFIP AICT 454, pp. 215–216, 2015.
DOI: 10.1007/978-3-319-18491-3_17

infrastructure that offer sufficient assurance for use in the public sector. The paper focuses on the "STRATEGIC Cloud Orchestrator" – a key innovation that underpins the automation behind such market place of governmental services – and explains how such innovations have been enabling local governments in Europe to use a Trusted Cloud in order to offer services to their citizens.

In the third paper, Joshua Daniel and Fadi El-Moussa focus on innovations that enable organizations to enforce homogeneous security, patching and application management policies across multiple Cloud environments and to analyze and remediate threats of cyber-attacks or data loss. Such innovations increase the confidence of organizations of all sizes in using the Cloud while enabling them to keep visibility and control of their assets and to limit their reliance on the Cloud providers offering such assurance guarantees in proprietary ways that cannot be easily inspected, validated or harmonized and controlled by the Cloud user. Embedding such innovations in platforms for Cloud application assembly, deployment and life-cycle management can potentially create a Trusted Cloud platform upon which future eco-systems of Trusted Cloud applications and services are built.

In the fourth paper, Pramod Pawar and Ali Sajjad explain how a federation of the European Future Internet experimental facilities has been used for validating, proving and analyzing Cloud-based security services at a large scale and over heterogeneous environments. Such experimentation results guide the evolution of Cloud-based services aiming at the protection of data and applications in the Cloud.

In the fifth paper, Michele Vescovi et al. focus on the complementary challenge of managing the exploitation of personal data and information in the Cloud. It examines the emerging market of personal data and presents innovations leading towards the development of an ecosystem of trusted applications, which offer individuals transparency and control on the exploitation of their data in the Cloud.

All these papers share a common vision of a Cloud-enabled market over a Trusted Cloud ecosystem. Freedom of choice prevails, stakeholders compete on differentiation on service delivery, businesses can use Cloud services to fulfil "concept-to-market" processes without compromising assurance and compliance and while maintaining visibility and control of their applications, processes and data. In this vision, enterprises of all sizes can create high-assurance application and business services efficiently at lower costs and can manage complex supply networks from heterogeneous providers. Individuals benefit from the higher assurance and better transparency and control of how their data is exploited in the Cloud.

We hope you will enjoy the proceedings of IFIPTM 2015 and that you will find this invited session informative and useful for your ongoing and future research.

May 2015

Theo Dimitrakos
Special Session Chair

A Cloud Orchestrator for Deploying Public Services on the Cloud – The Case of STRATEGIC Project

Panagiotis Gouvas[1(✉)], Konstantinos Kalaboukas[1], Giannis Ledakis[1],
Theo Dimitrakos[2], Joshua Daniel[2], Géry Ducatel[2],
and Nuria Rodriguez Dominguez[3]

[1] SingularLogic, Al. Panagouli and Siniosoglou, 14234 Nea Ionia,
Athens, Greece
{pgouvas,g.ledakis}@gmail.com,
kkalaboukas@singularlogic.eu
[2] BT Research and Innovation, Adastral Park, Ipswich IP5 3RE, UK
{theo.dimitrakos,joshua.daniel,gery.ducatel}@bt.com
[3] ATOS Spain, C/Albarracín 25, 28037 Madrid, Spain
nuria.rodriguez@atos.net

Abstract. In recent times, public bodies are adopting IaaS solutions for deploying online governmental services. A sufficient number are adopting private cloud solutions while others hybrid or public offerings, making the necessity of a Cloud Orchestrator highly imperative. In this paper, the STRATEGIC Cloud Orchestrator is presented which targets deployment services in multi-cloud providers. The Cloud Orchestrator architecture and design have been developed using a purely top-down approach, driven by user requirements coming from the three different European Municipalities (London Borough of Camden-UK, Genoa-IT and Stari Grad-SR) that will adopt the STRATEGIC solution. Also, the summary of the user requirements, the technical approach and value proposition are being described.

1 Introduction

Cloud computing services (including public cloud services) hold the promise to deliver a host of benefits to both public sector organizations and enterprises, including reduced Capital Expenditure (CAPEX), improved performance and scalability, and enhanced reliability, as well as a reduced overall Total Cost of Ownership (TCO) for their ICT infrastructures and services. According to the European Union Agency for Network and Information Security (ENISA), public bodies can also benefit from the improvement of citizen interactions with government in respect of reducing information processing time, lowering the cost of government services and enhancing citizen data security [1]. These benefits are particularly important for public bodies, especially for governmental agencies, municipalities and regions; the adoption of public cloud services as part of their numerous e-government interactions is expected to have a significant economic and social impact.

© IFIP International Federation for Information Processing 2015
C.D. Jensen et al. (Eds.): IFIPTM 2015, IFIP AICT 454, pp. 217–225, 2015.
DOI: 10.1007/978-3-319-18491-3_18

The main objective of STRATEGIC is to boost the adoption of public cloud services by the creation of a STRATEGIC Cloud Orchestrator. The STRATEGIC Cloud Orchestrator builds upon leading edge R&D results (Optimis Toolkit [2], STORK [3] and Semiramis [4] projects), to provide tools and techniques for the interoperable migration and replication of public cloud services across different EU countries and their regions. It has the following principal features:

Cloud Enablement: Cloud enablement is the migration/porting of existing on-line distributed services to the Cloud.

Replication: Replication and re-use of existing services, which have been already successfully deployed across EU countries and regions. This will result in localization and adaptation of the services to different legal, ethical and governance requirements.

Composition of New Value-Added Services: The ability to compose and integrate novel public cloud services based on other existing/legacy services could allow public administrations to streamline their processes thereby reducing overheads, alleviating bureaucracy and overall improve citizens' benefits and satisfaction [6].

The primary incentive for an organization/public body to adopt a Cloud Orchestrator is to increase automation. The need to orchestrate really becomes clear as when using cloud environments as the automation of storage, network, performance and provisioning are in most cases handled by miscellaneous solutions that have been added incrementally over time. Even for organizations that take a transformational approach, jumping to an advanced cloud to optimize their data centers, the management of heterogeneous environments with disparate systems can be a challenge not simply addressed by automation alone [5].

In this paper, a summary of the identified user requirements for a Cloud Orchestrator are provided, STRATEGIC Cloud Orchestrator is presented in terms of technical approach and value proposition offered. Furthermore, the pilot scenarios of the three different European Municipalities (London Borough of Camden-UK, Genoa-IT and Stari Grad-SR) that will evaluate the STRATEGIC Cloud Orchestrator are depicted.

2 STRATEGIC Cloud Orchestrator

2.1 Requirements Identification

The methodology for requirements identification comprised two main axes: a questionnaire supported by selected interviews to get input from a diverse set of stakeholders, including both cloud users and providers and analysis of pilot Municipalities applications' requirements. The requirements of the target communities were identified after analyzing a diverse set of public and private sector organizations. Public sector bodies covered included central government agencies, and municipalities and other regional or local governments, while the private sector bodies covered included cloud application developers, cloud solution providers, cloud services providers, cloud solution integrators, Independent Software Vendors (ISVs) and more. A total of 117 questionnaire responses were received and analysed [7].

Regarding users who want to adopt cloud services, the most important requirements that were considered as functional, identified from the questionnaire analyses are:

Security and privacy.
High Availability.
Interoperability, portability.

In the same time the requirements of lowering costs and having good performance have been identified, but were considered non-functional.

In addition, specific technical requirements were raised after analyzing 11 applications that are operated by the three large European Municipalities within the STRATEGIC project. These will now be described.

Common Application Packaging Format: This will be expressive enough to cover many aspects of the application lifecycle. The challenges here are many, since the notion of cloud enabling an application entails many difficulties. Applications may be monolithic, or multi-tier with several interdependencies between them. Furthermore, applications may have external dependencies at the service-level, at the OS-level or even at hardware-level. In addition, a proper application-packaging should take under consideration interoperability and "docking points" between packages. Beyond dependency-management, a packaging format should take under consideration the notion of application and configuration and application scalability.

Configuration Management: This deals with post-installation configuration management and covers many issues such as the setup of encryption channels, the configuration of logging handlers, the installation and configuration of security management services etc. in a multi-cloud context.

Interoperability at the Hypervisor Level: A critical requirement is the avoidance of vendor lock-in at the hypervisor level. Many mature hypervisors (KVM, ESXI etc.) are already able to process VMs that comply to specific formats. However these hypervisors expose their functionality with different API; therefore any Orchestrator should be able to use an abstraction layer on-top of these diverse APIs.

Interoperability on Monitoring: Additionally, a de facto need of any orchestrator is for interoperability with monitoring platforms. Indeed, most of the core entities that are deployed in a Cloud Environment can be "patched" in order to expose performance measurements on many levels (application-level, VM-level). This exposed information can be used for anomaly detection, deployment optimization or even SLA enforcement.

2.2   STRATEGIC Cloud Orchestrator Architecture

Taking under consideration the requirements identified for the creation of the Cloud Orchestrator, a modular high-level architecture has been defined (Fig. 1).

The Packaged-Applications Repository contains all applications that can be instantiated in an Infrastructure as a Service (IaaS) environment. The critical aspect regarding the repository is the formulation of an expressive enough application-packaging schema. This repository can be used as the basis of a STRATEGIC marketplace. A separate OS Virtual Machines (VM) Template Repository contains the available Operating Systems that can be instantiated by various IaaS environments.

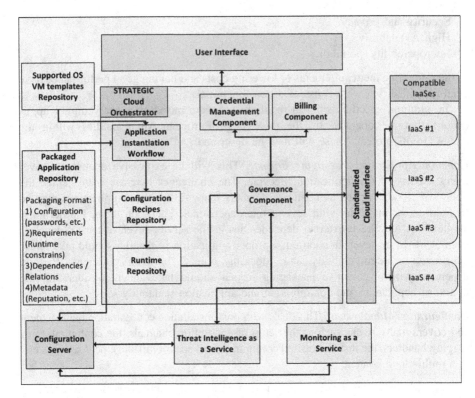

Fig. 1. STRATEGIC cloud orchestrator high level architecture components

The Credential Management Component is responsible for persistently storing the credentials of an end-user for each IaaS provider. The Application Instantiation Workflow coordinates the deployment of an Application to an IaaS provider. This implies the selection of the proper host-OS (based on the application packaging information), the target-IaaS and the initialization of the configuration-logic that is dependent to the application. The instantiation process combines user-oriented and system-imposed information that is required in order for a successful deployment to be performed.

One of the most crucial components is the Configuration Recipes Repository that contains the available configuration templates that can be applied after an Application instantiation. A configuration template is valuable only in the context of the adoption of a Configuration Management Framework. Therefore, although a Configuration Server is not an organic part of the Orchestrator, it constitutes a critical point since it assures that running instances maintain during runtime of a proper configuration. Beyond that, the Configuration Framework acts as a single point of reference for any functionality that has to be horizontally integrated. Indicative functionalities that are subjected to horizontal integration are Monitoring and Security.

Finally, the Governance Component is responsible for interacting with several underlying IaaS providers to start, stop, pause or delete workloads. This has to rely on an abstraction layer between the Orchestrator and the various Hypervisors. Since the risk of vendor-lock-in is high, the exploitation of Open Cloud Computing Interface (OCCI) interfaces is imperative [8]. OCCI is a set of specifications delivered through the Open Grid Forum for cloud computing service providers that provides is a boundary API that acts as a service front-end to an IaaS provider's internal infrastructure management framework [9].

2.3   STRATEGIC Workload Metadata Model

Workloads are a key concept and capability in the STRATEGIC Cloud Orchestrator, and are designed to make it possible to manage not just simple (single server) apps, but also much more complex multi-tier applications, as found in the enterprise or distributed applications consisting of many distinct server elements.

The STRATEGIC Workload Metadata Model has been created in order to capture the semantics of any possible workload. The metadata model has several sections. The first section covers basic details about the <Name>, <Version>, <License> and <Category> of the application. These elements of the schema are indexable - instances of the model will be aggregated in a central repository in order for a customer (public body) to be able to search and deploy them.

The next section is a group of <Informational> elements. These elements are used for guiding the end-user through installation and support actions. Moreover, the <SupportedOS> element is intended to capture the compatible OS that can be used for installation. Additionally, the <DeployMethod> element is used to identify the target Cloud of the installation.

One of the most crucial parts is the <ConfigurationParameters> section where the entire configuration layer of the application is exposed and initialized. In parallel, the <DeploymentDescriptor> is used to capture the Installation scripts that are required in order to perform the systemic installation.

Finally, the <ServerConfiguration> element is used to model the post-installation part. The Puppet Framework has been used in order to automate the DevOps tasks. Puppet uses <Recipes> as the basic notion of orchestration-bundle. The Workload Metadata Model contains placeholders for Recipes [10].

The XSD schema is provided in Fig. (2).

3   STRATEGIC Pilot Scenarios Overview

STRATEGIC as a project has the vision to deliver the necessary cloud-enabled infrastructure, associated tools and services to governmental bodies that will let them migrate existing public services to the cloud and easily extend their portfolio of services offered to the public. To achieve this vision, three large European Municipalities (London Borough of Camden, City of Genoa and Municipality of Stari Grad) are contributing several services, and also providing realistic use cases for validation of STRATEGIC Cloud Orchestrator.

Table 1 provides a summary of the application and the expected usage of the STRATEGIC cloud orchestrator for each scenario.

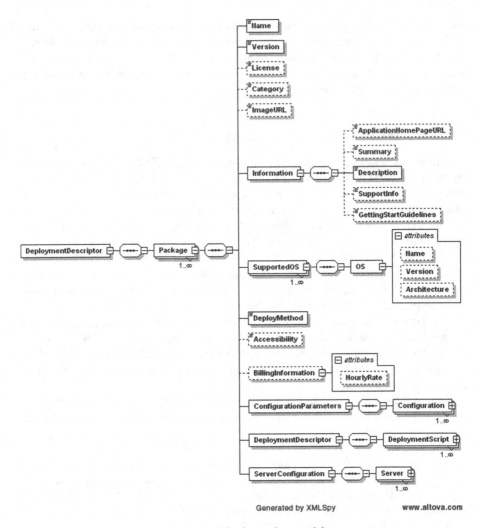

Fig. 2. Workload metadata model

4   STRATEGIC Cloud Orchestrator Value Proposition

The primary incentive for an organization/public body to adopt the STRATEGIC Cloud Orchestrator is to increase automation. The need to orchestrate really becomes clear when various aspects of cloud management are brought together. The value of adopting an orchestrator derives from the convergence of multiple hypervisors, the need for efficient resource usage, availability, scalability, performance and more. Through the STRATEGIC Marketplace, the pieces are woven together and can be managed more effectively to ensure smooth and rapid service delivery - and delivered in a user-friendly catalogue of services accessible through a single pane. In essence, STRATEGIC orchestration implies simultaneous speed of automation, ease of integration and clear adoption of best practices.

Table 1. Usage of STRATEGIC cloud orchestrator from the applications of pilot use cases.

Application description	Usage of STRATEGIC cloud orchestrator	Involved pilot
Application for managing OpenData based on SharePoint	Migration of existing SharePoint to Cloud with usage of STRATEGIC Cloud Orchestrator, publish on STRATEGIC Marketplace for reselling and deploy to selected IaaS	London Borough of Camden
Application for managing Citizen Blue-Badge information	Cloud Enable Application with usage of STRATEGIC Cloud Orchestrator, publish on STRATEGIC Marketplace for reselling and deploy to selected IaaS	London Borough of Camden
Application for managing user identity and their associated attributes in Camden	Cloud Enable Application with usage of STRATEGIC Cloud Orchestrator and deploy to selected IaaS	London Borough of Camden
Service for business activities	Cloud Enable Application with usage of STRATEGIC Cloud Orchestrator and deploy to selected IaaS	City of Genoa
Cross-border authentication service for business activities, based on Stork project	Integrate Cross-Border features offered by STRATEGIC and deploy to selected IaaS	City of Genoa
Semiramis-based, cross-border authentication service for Cross-border issuance of resident certificate	Integrate Cross-Border features offered by STRATEGIC and deploy to selected IaaS	City of Genoa
Application for managing OpenData	Cloud Enable Application with usage of STRATEGIC Cloud Orchestrator, publish on STRATEGIC Marketplace for reselling and deploy to selected IaaS	City of Genoa
Certificate issuance service	Cloud Enable Application with usage of STRATEGIC Cloud Orchestrator, publish on STRATEGIC Marketplace for reselling and deploy to selected IaaS	Municipality of Stari Grad
Semiramis-based, cross-border certificate issuance service	Integrate Cross-Border features offered by STRATEGIC, publish on STRATEGIC Marketplace for reselling and deploy to selected IaaS	Municipality of Stari Grad
Mail server for Municipality of Stari Grad	Cloud Enable Application with usage of STRATEGIC Cloud Orchestrator, publish on STRATEGIC Marketplace for reselling and deploy to selected IaaS	Municipality of Stari Grad
Application for managing OpenData	Configure an application that is already published in STRATEGIC Marketplace and deploy to selected IaaS	Municipality of Stari Grad

In addition to rapid service delivery, adoption of STRATEGIC Cloud Orchestrator and Marketplace can deliver significant cost savings by eliminating manual intervention and management of varied IT resources or services. Specific benefits include:

Integration of cloud capabilities across heterogeneous environments and infrastructures to simplify, automate and optimize service deployment.

Self-service portal for selection of cloud services, including storage and networking, from a predefined menu of offerings.

Reduced need for intervention to allow lower ratio of administrators to physical and virtual servers.

Automated high-scale provisioning and de-provisioning of resources with policy-based tools to manage virtual machine sprawl by reclaiming resources automatically.

Ability to integrate workflows and approval chains across technology silos to improve collaboration and reduce delays.

Real-time monitoring of physical and virtual cloud resources, as well as usage and accounting chargeback capabilities to track and optimize system usage.

Pre-packaged automation templates and workflows for most common resource types to ease adoption of best practices and minimize transition time.

Ability to create cross-Authentication applications and share them in a re-usable manner through an app-store.

In short, many of the capabilities that we associate with cloud computing are in essence elements of orchestration. Using the STRATEGIC cloud orchestrator, public bodies can manage their cloud workloads through a single interface, providing greater efficiency, control and scalability. As cloud environments become more complex and organizations seek greater benefit from their computing resources, the need for sophisticated management solutions that can orchestrate across the entire environment will become ever clearer.

5   Conclusion

The rationale of this paper is to provide an overview of STATEGIC Cloud Orchestrator. For this reason a brief description of STRATEGIC project main goals and the identified requirements and desirable features of a Cloud Orchestrator are provided. For the conception of STRATEGIC Cloud Orchestrator, the high level architecture and component overview has been briefly described, along with the proposed Workload Metadata Model. Finally the pilot use cases overview and the value proposition of the STRATEGIC Cloud Orchestrator are provided.

Acknowledgments. The work performed in this paper is funded by the Strategic CIP-PSP Project (http://www.strategic-project.eu).

References

1. Good Practice Guide for securely deploying Governmental Clouds (2013). www.enisa. europa.eu
2. Optimis Project Consortium: Optimis Project Website. www.optimis-project.eu. Accessed January 2015
3. Stork Project Consortium: Stork Project Website. https://www.eid-stork.eu/. Accessed January 2015
4. Semiramis Project Consortium: Semiramis Project Website. http://www.semiramis-cip.eu/ index.html. Accessed January 2015
5. IBM: IBM Cloud Orchestrator. http://www-03.ibm.com/software/products/en/ibm-cloud-orchestrator. Accessed January 2015
6. STRATEGIC Project Consortium: Description of Work of "STRATEGIC: Service disTRibution network And Tools for intEroperable proGrammable, and UnIfied public Cloud services" (2014)
7. STRATEGIC Project Consortium: D2.1 Report on Stakeholders Requirements (2014)
8. STRATEGIC Project Consortium: D2.3 Strategic Framework Architecture Technical Specifications (2014)
9. OCCI Community: The Open Cloud Computing Interface Website. http://occi-wg.org/. Accessed January 2015
10. STRATEGIC Project Consortium: D3.1 Specification of Cloud-Enablement and Migration Solutions and Services (2014)

Integrating Security Services in Cloud Service Stores

Joshua Daniel[1]([⊠]), Fadi El-Moussa[1], Géry Ducatel[1], Pramod Pawar[2],
Ali Sajjad[2], Robert Rowlingson[1], and Theo Dimitrakos[1,2]

[1] BT Research and Innovation, Ipswich, UK
{joshua.daniel, fadiali.el-moussa, gery.ducatel,
robert.rowlingson, theo.dimitrakos}@bt.com
[2] School of Computing, University of Kent, Canterbury, UK
{pramod.pawar, ali.sajjad}@bt.com

Abstract. Protecting systems, applications and data hosted on a Cloud environment against cyber-threats, and accounting for security incidents across the Cloud estate are prerequisites to Cloud adoption by business, and a fundamental element of both national and corporate cyber-security and Cloud strategies. Yet, Cloud IaaS and PaaS providers typically hold Cloud consumers accountable for protecting their applications, while Cloud users often find that protecting their proprietary system, application and data stacks on public or hybrid Cloud environments can be complex, expensive and time-consuming. In this paper we describe a novel Cloud-based security management solution that empowers Cloud consumers to protect their systems, applications and data in the Cloud, whilst also improving the control and visibility of their Cloud security operations. This is achieved by enhancing the security policy management of commercial technologies, and via their integration with multiple Cloud-based hosts and applications. The result of this integration is then offered as a re-usable service across multiple Cloud platforms through a Cloud service store.

Keywords: Security as a service · Cloud security · Cloud services provisioning and management · Service stores

1 Introduction

In the last decade there has been an expanding body of work in academia and industry about protecting data and applications on large-scale virtualized IT and network platforms, and Cloud infrastructures. Publications range from surveys, such as [1, 2], to security landscaping, such as [3, 4], to analyses of security risks [5] and security control recommendations [6]. Yet, the security mechanisms offered by Cloud infrastructure and platform providers in practice typically consider application protection to be beyond the provider's concerns and thus they fail to protect comprehensively against attacks exploiting application vulnerabilities. Cloud users often find it complicated and expensive to deploy integrity and protection mechanisms on 3rd party public, or on hybrid Cloud environments, and lack the required security expertise or the security

© IFIP International Federation for Information Processing 2015
C.D. Jensen et al. (Eds.): IFIPTM 2015, IFIP AICT 454, pp. 226–239, 2015.
DOI: 10.1007/978-3-319-18491-3_19

operations capability that can scale accordingly to the Cloud use. The constant change in security perimeter due to the elastic boundaries in Cloud services further complicates the security management problems. Cloud adoption will always be limited until these gaps are filled. Lack of transparency, loss of confidentiality, as well as legal and regulatory context is widely recognized as a barrier to Cloud adoption by public authorities, companies and individuals [7]. Recent studies have provided further evidence to ground these concerns: for example the "Cloud Adoption & Risk Report" [8] evidences that "only 9 % of Cloud services used by enterprise customers in Europe today offer enterprise-grade security" and "beyond that, only 1 % of Cloud services in use in Europe offer both enterprise-grade security and meet the EU data protection requirements".

The Cloud-based security services market will be worth $2.1 billion in 2013, rising to $3.1 billion in 2015 [27], and the top three most sought-after Cloud services moving forward will remain email security, web security services and identity and access management (IAM), according to a report from Gartner. In 2013 and 2014, the most growth is forecast to occur in Cloud-based encryption, security information and event management (SIEM), vulnerability assessment and web application firewalls. For Cloud adoption for enterprise use to materialize at a scale, there is a growing demand for innovations that enable businesses to maintain high levels of visibility and governance of their ICT assets, data and business applications in the Cloud and to enforce the controls required for operating high-assurance applications in the Cloud.

This paper presents BT Intelligent Protection [12, 13] - a Cloud-based security service prototype (currently in beta testing) designed in collaboration with security and service management technology vendors, to address these problems. The core technology behind Intelligent Protection is based on available commercial technologies but extends them by further automating their governance, their security policy management, and their integration with multiple Cloud-based hosts and applications. The result of this integration is offered as a re-usable Cloud based service across multiple Cloud platforms from different Cloud providers.

Section 2 reviews the background work in this area particularly in the context of Cloud security and Cloud marketplaces (or Cloud service stores). In Sect. 3 we describe the rationale and approach to the design of Intelligent Protection. We also examine the challenges associated with the introduction of common capabilities for security into Cloud service stores. In Sect. 4 we present the high-level architecture of the Cloud-based security service (Intelligent Protection) and the fundamental concepts underpinning security integration with a Cloud Service Store. Section 5 describes two examples of the use of Intelligent Protection in representative scenarios. Firstly in the case of the security administration and user experience of assembling, deploying and managing a protected Cloud application. And secondly, in the novel case of establishing a managed Cloud re-seller service, in effect allowing a reseller to access and manage the necessary tools to run a Cloud service in which they can customize security to the needs of their customers.

2   Background and Related Work

Protecting hosts and applications in the Cloud has been the focus of recent academic research, such as [14–17, 28] and some emerging commercial products, such as [29–31]. However research and industry alike still lack a fully managed and comprehensive solution to the problem, and especially one that can scale to protecting complex distributed applications on multi-cloud environments.

If Cloud providers have paid less attention to supporting the security of customer applications they have paid much more attention to providing software marketplaces, or what we might call Cloud Service Stores. Cloud providers such as Amazon WS have launched their own service stores while innovative solution providers such as Appcara AppStack [18], Jamcracker Service Delivery Network [19], Canopy [20], Parallels Automation [21], SixSQ SlipStream [22], Cloudsoft AMP [23], and the open-source projects Brooklyn [24] and Juju [25] are developing solutions that integrate with the programmatic interfaces of several Cloud platforms in order to automatically assemble complex applications, deploy them on one or multiple 3rd party Cloud infrastructure chosen by the user and in some cases manage their life-cycle. Any advanced security for cloud based applications will need to integrate with such cloud service stores [38].

With respect to security one approach, recently taken by the UK government CloudStore Service [26], is to focus on compliance and accreditation to assure the quality of available solutions and enable them to be used both in the public and private sector without repeated compliance measures. The European Commission too has been highly active in describing accreditation and compliance regimes for cloud users. Currently however compliance is a relatively static and manual process. It is not a good fit to the dynamic nature of cloud deployments where loss of visibility and control is a significant risk. The constant change in security perimeter due to the elastic boundaries in Cloud usage also necessitates a more dynamic security approach.

Examples of commercial Cloud-based security solutions that can enable a cloud-based security service include, among others, Trend Micro Deep Security [29], McAfee [30] and Symantec [31], for application and host protection, Trend Micro Secure Cloud [32], Vormetric [33] and SafeNet Protect V [34] for Cloud data volume encryption as a service, Z-Scaler [35] for web threat protection, CA CloudMinder [36] and SailPoint [37] for corporate identity as a service. Beyond their proprietary and function specific technological advancements, the common novelty of these services is mainly about offering security & protection of hosted systems, application and data as a value-added service (multi-tenant security SaaS), while enforcement is delivered via the Cloud infrastructure, with minimal integration overhead. This approach enhances Cloud user experience by offering more secure, flexible, automated security management for applications deployed or on-boarded to Cloud Infrastructures (IaaS).

3   Approach

In this paper we present an example of a Cloud-based security service that has been integrated into a Cloud Service Store as a "horizontal" service, i.e. a reusable common capability offered via a subscription-based service delivery model. This involves using conceptually similar security service design and service management automation patterns in order to enhance the same service store with capabilities for data protection, secure communications and identity management. For example, the data protection capability offers encryption as a service for volume (block storage), data-base and object-storage protection while keeping critical information such as encryption keys and algorithms under the Cloud consumers control and out of the Cloud provider's reach. The main goals in offering "horizontal" security services in PaaS are:

1. To offer Cloud consumers a choice of which security capabilities to use for a system and on what Cloud environment.
2. To offer corporate security operations teams - to extend their corporate policy to the Cloud and offer comparable- if not better- levels of assurance for Cloud-hosted applications as for any other enterprise application.
3. To create a new scalable and cost-efficient channel to market for managed security service providers and re-sellers by automating the purchasing and integration of the managed service into PaaS.

A common issue in providing such security capability as Cloud services and platforms is that service assemblies are simple, mission specific, and generally do not cater for combining Cloud platforms and applications with security services in a muti-tenant environment. Through our experimentation and trials with customers and partners we identified the following as common characteristics of the security operations experience that corporations deploying and managing their applications in the Cloud aspire to:

- A choice of which security functions to apply on any application stack they deploy into the Cloud.
- Security controls automatically integrated into the system and application stack they deploy in a Cloud environment with minimal intervention.
- A security management dashboard that allows the security operation teams to interact with

  Tools for defining application or data specific security policy once and automatically applying this homogeneously across multiple Cloud environments that may host instances of the same application stack.

  Tools for automatically detecting the vulnerabilities of their applications and automatically deploying security patches to fix them in the Cloud.

  Tools for detecting and preventing intrusion attempts in any Cloud environment their IT assets reside in.

  Tools for analyzing security risks for their applications in terms of criticality and define how to manage these risks.

  Tools to help analyze security events associated with their IT assets across their whole (multi-)Cloud estate.

The overall environment needs to be truly multi-tenant, isolating security policies, security events, security controls, security control communications between tenants (i.e. corporations using the capability) and restricting access and visibility only to the Cloud environments parts and to the systems and applications that correspond to the tenant.

Intelligent Protection addresses the problems described above by enabling the protection of systems, applications and data processing on a mix of public and private Cloud environments through a collection of security functions that can be offered as managed or self-service Cloud-based integrity and security services. Controls to enforce the integrity and security functions can also be integrated in a Cloud Application and Service store as "horizontal" common capabilities at the Cloud service management automation layer thereby enabling the application and data protection functions to become selectable properties of any application stack that the user chooses to assemble on any Cloud platform or infrastructure. Cloud users can therefore maintain the visibility and control of their applications in the Cloud. With a few clicks, users can deploy protected applications in several Cloud infrastructures or Cloud platforms and to manage their security and integrity through a single unifying multi-Cloud security operations management layer. Through this integration, we offer a new customer experience to seamlessly manage security in the Cloud, focusing on the following traits:

1. Fusion: security management becomes an integral part of Cloud application assembly.
2. Uniformity and Customization: the integrity and security functions become management parameters of any application in the service store, while the form and coverage of the functions automatically adjust to user selection.
3. Automation: "click-to-buy" security services and "click-to-build" secure applications with a few mouse clicks.
4. Versatility: automatic generation of security policy based on vulnerability analysis of the application stack, Cloud characteristics, user preferences and desired business impact levels.
5. Universality: one Cloud-based service securing applications and data on multiple private and public Cloud infrastructures and platforms.
6. Visibility: a customizable security dashboard is automatically created for each customer offering a unifying view of the security state of user's applications on any Cloud platform.
7. Control: enables enforcing a common security policy to all instances of an application on multiple Cloud environments.

4   Architectural Overview

4.1   General Architecture: Cloud-Based Security Capability

An architectural overview of the Cloud-based Intelligent Protection solution offered to each tenant can be divided in three dimensions as depicted in Fig. 1:

- *Policy enforcement:* this is the mechanism used to manage the protection of a system; it can be an agent installed on a Virtual Machine (typically on an external Cloud) or a physical server or a virtual appliance that together with a hypervisor plugin installed on the physical nodes of an internal Cloud.

- *Policy administration:* this is the management mechanisms at the Intelligent Protection server used for defining security policies based on a library of rules that include virtual patches for a very large number of systems and applications, firewall and protocol rules, etc., and for updating the configuration and enforcement rules of the agents or hypervisor-level virtual appliances.
- *Threat intelligence:* this is the mechanism for enhancing the data-base of primitive rules, attacks or virus signatures, vulnerabilities, etc., via a network that includes a large number of security and application vendors, as well as contributions from BT's security ecosystem.

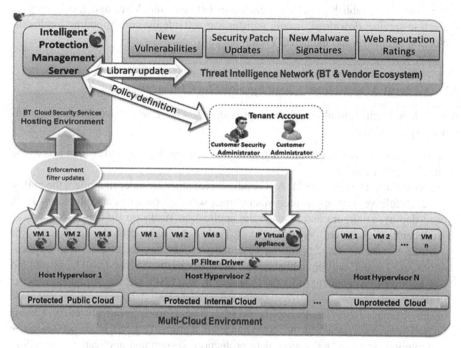

Fig. 1. Overview of the Intelligent Protection Capability High Level Architecture

Using an agent-based on-boarding model, Virtual Machines (VMs) running on any 3rd party Clouds or physical servers can be connected to the Intelligent Protection service and enable their administrators to remotely monitor and manage the protection of their environment.

In addition to the Cloud Service Store integration, there are three further ways of making a VM manageable by Intelligent Protection, depending on the level of integration of the corresponding Cloud environment with the Intelligent Protection service:

- The user specifies their VM architecture and operating system, and downloads from the service a light-weight agent installer. The installer will then automatically contact the BT Intelligent Protection service and automatically download, register and activate the appropriate agent software. The same process also works for any physical server that is connected to the internet.

- The Cloud provider offers a template with a pre-installed agent installer that is then activated by the user by providing their Intelligent Protection service credentials for verification.
- The Cloud provider includes the Intelligent Protection agent and appropriate configuration in a VM template or a contextualized image [43, 45] creation process.

The Intelligent Protection service has a plug-in for the management APIs of the corresponding Cloud provider. The users simply use their Intelligent Protection service account and their Cloud account credentials in order to execute an installation script on the targeted VMs that will automatically obtain all the VM architecture and operating system details, establish a secure connection between the VMs and the Intelligent Protection service, download, install, register and activate the corresponding Intelligent Protection agents on the managed VMs.

4.2   General Architecture: Cloud Service Store Integration

A high-level architectural overview is provided in Fig. 2 where we identify the following types of actors:

- Cloud Service Provider (CSP): A Cloud provider and service host, which acts as the IaaS or PaaS provider.
- Service Store Provider (SSP): A (Cloud) service store provider that offers the ability to assemble vertical application stacks from software components offered by ISVs and deploy, configure and manage the application stacks on different CSPs.
- Independent Software Vendor (ISV): Their role is to provide applications or software elements (e.g. operating systems, web servers, data-bases, web applications, etc.) which will be published in catalogues by the SSP and will be assembled by application owners in order to be hosted by the CSPs that the application owner selects.
- (Self-)Managed Service Providers (MSPs): These are offering hosted or Cloud-based services that allow the governance of features (e.g. network performance, encryption, security, federation, data protection, system and application protection, etc.) that are integrated into the SSP and via the SSP on the CSPs.
- Application Owner: Finally, we refer to the entity that exploits or consumes compound services as the application owner. These application owners need to create complex services and integrate cross services features that fulfil their regulatory and compliance requirements (e.g. security policies, data retention, etc.).

CSPs may use an SSP in order to offer access to application catalogues that are specific to a range of vertical sectors and have been populated by themselves or ISVs. This can include application elements ranging from operating systems, database servers, ERP application and web servers to web store front-ends.

The application owner selects a pre-defined application assembly from application catalogues. The application assembly defines basic configurations and policy templates for vertical application stacks that cover the Cloud life-cycle of the whole stack from network connectivity to an operating system, to core components such as databases and

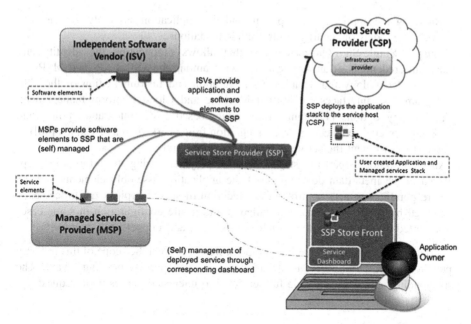

Fig. 2. Overview of the architectural pattern of Intelligent Protection Pattern with a Cloud Service Store

web servers to business applications and processes. System intelligence encoded in policies, dependencies and constraints guide the selection of a consistent assembly. The resulting application may be single or multi-tiered and be contained in a single server or distributed over a group of networked nodes, and even across Cloud regions.

The integration architecture of MSP services such as Intelligent Protection into a Cloud-based SSP is based on:

- Using clear meta-data models in order to describe dependences, configuration, installation and service management requirements for each application element in the service store catalogues.
- Using clear meta-data models in order to describe how the elements of an application stack (e.g. operating system, server, data-base, application, etc.) are assembled, how their dependences are managed and associate installation and post-installation configuration scripts that ensure the proper set-up and operation of all application stack elements.
- Using clear meta-data models in order to describe the dependences, configuration, installation and service management requirements of the security control implementations; these are typically software elements that are jointly installed and integrated with a virtual machine, server, operating system or application element during the deployment of an application and connect to the Cloud-based security management service via a secure channel establishing a continual "heart-beat" though which security policy updates propagate.

- Extending the application component and the application assembly models with matching models of security control implementations.
- Using a Single-Sign-On mechanism that allows propagating the identity and account credentials of an Application Owner among the SSP, CSPs and MSPs.
- Using a technology that enables the integration and instrumentation of the CSP programmatic interfaces for Virtual Machine and Cloud Platform management. Technology options [12] range from policy-based XML integration point (e.g. [38]), proprietary connectors or an integration framework such as J-Clouds [40]) in order to instrument the set-up of virtual machines and
- An orchestrator to perform staged Cloud deployment using the information captured in the meta-data descriptions of the application assembly elements and the corresponding security controls. The execution of staged deployment processes is assisted by scripts automating installation and in-life configuration in some cases supported by automation tools such as Chef [41] and Puppet [42].

A detailed description of the integration design is beyond the scope of this industry experience paper and subject to awarded patents and patents pending award. The corresponding author can provide further detail to interested parties upon request.

5   User Experience

In this section we present the experience of using Intelligent Protection in two scenarios:

1. Deploying and managing applications via a Cloud Service Store such as AppStack [43] - the user experience described is based on live system trials on BT's Beta environment but application scenario and corporate user details have been abstracted and generalized as appropriate.
2. Cloud Infrastructure Integration via a managed Cloud re-seller service, in effect allowing any client to access and manage the necessary tools to run a Cloud service which they can customize to the needs of their customers.

5.1   User a Cloud Service Store

Let Omega be a user that wishes to deploy an Apache web server application deployed into a Cloud environment with Intelligent Protection enabled. In order to do this Omega first registers with the Service Store which allows deployment applications ranging from operating systems, database servers, ERP application and web servers to web store front-ends, etc. The customer is then able to assemble and deploy simple or multi-tier applications. BT Compute Service Store offers pre-defined workloads for multi-tier applications that can be instantiated within five clicks and also allows Omega to define new assemblies that fit better with their specific business needs.

Having been exposed as a horizontal service via the BT Compute Service Store, in order to be able to use the security capability, Omega will have to subscribe to BT Intelligent Protection (Fig. 3) and either create a new security management account or provide the details of an already existing account. Omega notices that the overall the Service Store application assembly portal adapts their offering with a selection of options about the selected qualities and corresponding types of protection. Configurable options about these qualities will automatically be made available for all compatible application security elements and assembly workloads in all catalogues available to Omega.

Omega is then able to select a pre-defined application assembly from the catalogue that includes the required Apache web server. The resulting application may be a single or multi-tier and be contained in a single server or distributed over a group of networked nodes, and even across Cloud regions.

Intelligent Protection is able to enforce the policies on the targeted Cloud environment that Omega may choose. This is achieved via the service quality and policy enforcement controls and the advanced service management mechanisms. This allows the user to enforce a different set of security policy based on the application assembly and Cloud infrastructure. Upon deployment the user is then able to monitor and manage the status of all their deployments from a common Intelligent Protection dashboard as shown in Fig. 4.

5.2   Cloud Infrastructure Integration

BT Cloud Compute is an IaaS service with a wide range of availability zones including public and private service offerings across different geographical locations. The forthcoming generation of BT Cloud Compute (currently in Beta testing) also extends

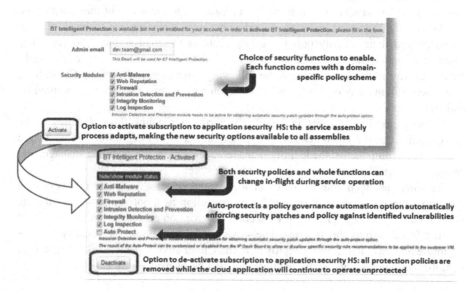

Fig. 3. Subscription to BT Intelligent Protection – Omega can select among a mixture of functions, each function coming with its own policy scheme

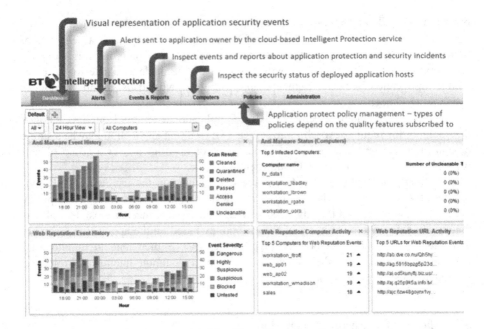

Fig. 4. Example of Intelligent Protection Dashboard

IaaS and provides on top a PaaS service store with a range of security services for customer applications. Upon this forthcoming extension BT is building a managed Cloud re-seller service, in effect allowing any client to access and manage the necessary tools to run a Cloud service which they can customize to the needs of their customers.

As already discussed, offering Cloud consumers visibility and control of their resources and their security policy are key enablers to cloud service adoption. The philosophy underpinning the Cloud re-seller model for the virtual server and application security in this case includes the following aspects: security of the Cloud host, protection and integrity of re-sellers' information and security compliance required by end customers.

Creating security features in re-seller's portfolio requires those features to be contextualized at the customer level. This requires a tight integration of four Cloud management components: the identity management solution, the customer management service, the virtualization layer, and the service store.

Re-sellers are then able to build catalogues and select appropriate products with appropriate levels of security on intelligent protection as a horizontal service for the vertical markets. On the Intelligent Protection subscription page users are able to select security features from check boxes. The service enforces the selected security features on future and past applications deployed in the Cloud environment. Depending on the compliance requirements, some features can also be overridden by end users.

6 Conclusion and Further Work

In this paper we have shared experiences for integrating a Cloud-based security service for host and application protection with a Cloud Service Store and described how this can give rise to the first instance of a new kind of security capability for PaaS, IaaS and Cloud-hosted Applications. This approach provides users with similar, or even enhanced, security management experience over diverse, dynamic and elastic cloud environments, compared with a traditional static IT infrastructure.

In relation to Intelligent Protection, our current and future work involves validating the usability and capability in vertical market sectors through further trials and experimentation with a range of partners in collaborative projects. We are also working towards integrating more security capabilities with the service store and the forthcoming Cloud Services Management layer of BT Compute including Cloud-based services for data protection ("encryption as a service"), security analytics, identity and federation services, information assurance reporting and content cleansing (e.g. email filtering) among others.

Protecting IT assets on a Cloud environment against cyber-threats and accounting for security incidents are prerequisites to Cloud adoption by business across the globe and a fundamental element of UK and Europe's cyber-security and Cloud strategies [7, 10, 11]. An underlying cause for many successful cyber-attacks on Cloud services is the lack of a suitable security, resilience and protection mechanism for applications that run on 3rd party or hybrid Cloud environments. The work presented here directly addresses these concerns.

Finally we believe that the concepts presented in this paper can provide the basis for more fundamental research on concepts as "Horizontal Security Services" while also extending the scope to a wider class of Cloud-based services beyond security, integrity and assurance. A future paper will explore this further.

References

1. Subashini, S., Kavitha, V.: A survey on security issues in service delivery models of cloud computing. J. Netw. Comput. Appl. **34**(1), 1–11 (2011)
2. Yu, H., Powell, N., Stembridge, D., Yuan, X.: Cloud computing and security challenges. In: ACM-SE 2012 Proceedings of the 50th Annual Southeast Regional Conference, pp 298–302 (2012)
3. Cloud Security Alliance. Top Ten Big Data Security and Privacy Challenges, November 2012
4. Cloud Security Alliance. Cloud Computing Vulnerability Incidents: A Statistical Overview, May 2013
5. Catteddu, D., Hogben, G.: Cloud Computing Risk Assessment. European Network and Information Security Agency (ENISA) (2009)
6. Cloud Security Alliance. Cloud Controls Matrix v3.0.1, July 2014
7. European Commission Communication on "Unleashing the Potential of Cloud Computing in Europe". http://eurlex.europa.eu
8. Skyhigh, Cloud Adoption & Risk Report. http://www.skyhighnetworks.com/

238   J. Daniel et al.

9. Lachal L.: "Public Clouds are becoming vertical market-centric" Ovum. http://ovum.com/
10. UK Government CloudStore. http://govstore.service.gov.uk/Cloudstore/
11. ECP Trusted Cloud Europe: Have your Say. http://europa.eu/
12. El-Moussa F., Dimitrakos, T.: Protecting systems and applications on virtual data centres and in the Cloud: challenges, emerging solutions and lessons learnt. https://Cloudsecurityalliance.org/events/secureCloud-2012/#_downloads
13. Dimitrakos, T.: Cloud Security Challenges and Guidelines. EIT ICT Labs Symposium on Trusted Cloud and Future Enterprises, Oulu, Finland, August 2014. http://www.eitictlabs.eu/news-events/events/article/eit-ict-labs-symposium-on-trusted-Cloud-and-future-enterprises/
14. Modi, C., Patel, D., Borisaniya, B., Patel, H., Patel, A., Rajarajan, M.: A survey of intrusion detection techniques in Cloud. J. Netw. Comput. Appl. 36(1), 42–57 (2013)
15. Patel, A., Taghavi, M., Bakhtiyari, K., Júnior, J.C.: An intrusion detection and prevention system in cloud computing: a systematic review. J. Netw. Comput. Appl. 36(1), 25–41 (2013)
16. Alsafi, H.M., Abdullah, W.M., Pathan, A.-S.K.: IDPS: an integrated intrusion handling model for cloud computing environment. Int. J. Comput. Inf. Technol. 4(1), 1–16 (2012)
17. Dastjerdi, A.V., Bakar, K.A., Tabatabaei, S.: Distributed intrusion detection in clouds using mobile agents. In: Third International Conference on Advanced Engineering Computing and Applications in Sciences, pp. 175–180 (2009)
18. AppStack by Appcara. http://www.appcara.com/products/appstack-r3
19. Jamcracker Services Delivery Network (JSDN). http://www.jamcracker.com/jamcracker-servicesdelivery-network-jsdn
20. Canopy by Atos, EMC, VMWare. http://www.canopy-Cloud.com/enterprise-application-store
21. Parallels Automation. http://www.parallels.com/uk/products/automation/
22. SixSQ Slipstream. http://sixsq.com/products/slipstream.html
23. CloudSoft AMP. http://www.Cloudsoftcorp.com/product/
24. Brooklyn project. http://brooklyncentral.github.io/
25. Ubuntu Juju. https://juju.ubuntu.com/
26. G-Cloud Cloudstore. http://govstore.service.gov.uk/Cloudstore/
27. Gartner: Market Trends: Cloud-Based Security
28. Hashizume, K., Rosado, D.G., Fernández-Medina, E., Fernandez, E.B.: An analysis of security issues for Cloud computing. J. Internet Serv. Appl. 4(1), 1–13 (2013)
29. Trend Micro Deep Security. http://www.trendmicro.com/us/enterprise/Cloud-solutions/deep-security/
30. McAfee Cloud Security. http://www.mcafee.com/uk/solutions/Cloud-security/Cloud-security.aspx
31. Symantec Cloud Security suite. http://www.symantec.com/en/uk/productssolutions/solutions/detail.jsp?parent=Cloud&child=extend_Cloud
32. Trend Micro Secure Cloud. http://www.trendmicro.co.uk/products/secureCloud/
33. Vormetric. http://www.vormetric.com/
34. SafeNet: ProtectV. http://www.safenet-inc.com/data-protection/virtualization-Cloud-security/protectv-Clouddata-protection/
35. Z-Scaler. http://www.zscaler.com/
36. CA CloudMinder. http://www.ca.com/gb/Cloud-identity.aspx
37. SailPoint IDaaS. http://www.sailpoint.com/solutions/customer-solutions/iam-for-todays-Cloudenvironments
38. Nair S.K., Dimitrakos, T.: On the security of data stored in the cloud secure. In: SecureCloud 2012. https://Cloudsecurityalliance.org/events/secureCloud-2012/

39. CA Layer 7. The Value of Application Service Governance for Cloud Computing. Cloud Computing White Paper. http://www.layer7tech.com/resources/files/white_papers/Value%20of%20SOA%20Governance%20for%20Cloud%20Computing.pdf
40. Apache J-Clouds: Java Multi-Cloud Toolkit. https://jClouds.apache.org/
41. Chef IT Automation. http://www.getchef.com/chef/
42. Puppet Enterprise. http://puppetlabs.com/solutions
43. Appcara. Cloud Management versus Cloud App Management. http://www.appcara.com/wp-content/uploads/2014/07/Cloud-Management-versus-Cloud-App-Management-v2.0.pdf
44. Armstrong, D., Djemame, K., Nair, S., Tordsson, J., Ziegler, W.: Towards a contextualization solution for cloud platform services. In: Proceedings - 2011 3rd IEEE International Conference on Cloud Computing Technology and Science, CloudCom 2011, pp. 328–331 (2011)
45. Armstrong, D., Espling, D., Tordsson, J., Djemame, K., Elmroth, E.: Runtime virtual machine recontextualization for clouds. In: Caragiannis, I., et al. (eds.) Euro-Par 2012 Workshops. LNCS, vol. 7640, pp. 567–576. Springer, Heidelberg (2013)

Building an Eco-System of Trusted Services via User Control and Transparency on Personal Data

Michele Vescovi[1(✉)], Corrado Moiso[2], Mattia Pasolli[1],
Lorenzo Cordin[1,2], and Fabrizio Antonelli[1]

[1] Semantic and Knowledge Innovation Lab (SKIL), Telecom Italia,
via Sommarive 18, 38123 Trento, Italy
{michele.vescovi,mattia.pasolli,lorenzo.cordin,
fabrizio.antonelli}@telecomitalia.it
[2] Future Center, Telecom Italia, via Reiss Romoli 274, 10148 Turin, Italy
{corrado.moiso}@telecomitalia.it

Abstract. The amount of personal information that is generated and collected on a daily basis is rapidly growing due to the increasing number of activities performed online and, in particular, in mobility. The availability of such a huge amount of data represents an invaluable opportunity for organizations and individuals, respectively to enable precise business intelligence and innovative services. Nevertheless, it represents the commodity of a flourishing "market of data", mostly fostered by the biggest ICT companies, from whereof benefits users are almost excluded, significantly increasing the public concern on data privacy. In this scenario we developed a framework, based on a personal data store, enabling the development of an eco-system of trusted application, which allow users to full transparency and control on the exploitation of their data.

1 Introduction

The increasing adoption of smartphones and their capability of collecting personal and contextual information have generated a tremendous increment in the production of Personal Data (PD). The amount of PD that is available and generated on a daily basis is rapidly growing also due to the increasing number of activities performed online and, in particular, in mobility. Nowadays, a constantly increasing number of users access the internet mostly (or exclusively) by means of their smartphones/tablets; they use an innumerable variety of online/Web services, often through specifically designed mobile applications (shortly apps). Very often these apps, which possibly connect to external devices/sensors, are their self-generated source of novel types of PD that are transmitted and collected server-side.

The availability of such a huge amount of data (ranging from locations or interactions record, to the content produced by users, e.g. describing choices, preferences, etc.) represents an invaluable opportunity for organizations and individuals to enable

© IFIP International Federation for Information Processing 2015
C.D. Jensen et al. (Eds.): IFIPTM 2015, IFIP AICT 454, pp. 240–250, 2015.
DOI: 10.1007/978-3-319-18491-3_20

new application scenarios and to benefit from innovative services. Nevertheless, they represent the commodity of a flourishing market mostly fostered by the biggest ICT companies. The collected data are exploited for internal business analytics or sold to drive third party business intelligence or advertisement.

However, it has also significantly increased the public concern on data privacy. In fact users have, in general, very scarce opportunities to control how their data are accessed and collected and to use them for their purposes. Some Operating System (OS), such as Android, informs users about the accessed resources at installation time but, mainly, such information is not user-friendly and users can either avoid installing the App or grant unrestricted access to all the required resources, without means to further control permissions or to audit the access to PD. Increasingly this phenomenon is widespread due to wide adoption of the so called *social logins* (i.e. the use of the credentials of a particular social network to log also into third party services) through which, third party service-providers can directly access the plethora of users' information collected through their use of social networks. This further sharpens the incongruity between the information consciously and transparently disclosed by users and the users' personal data concretely accessed by third parties. Nevertheless, the benefits of the usage of personal data are always more imbalanced between the users and, mainly, the world-wide biggest ICT companies.

This is far from the desired scenarios in which PD enable and contribute to the generation of widespread socioeconomic benefits to the collectivity. In order to reach these benefits, we believe that we need a fair PD management, where individuals, empowered with control and awareness over their PD, are enabled to actively and knowingly participate (in)to a PD eco-system. We present the design of *My Data Store*, currently validated in a living-lab: a privacy preserving service that enables users to collect, control and exploit PD generated in mobility. We integrated *My Data Store* into an innovative framework which enables the development of trusted and transparent (in terms of access and use of PD) services and apps: a user can control and audit their behavior. In this way, it is possible to create an eco-system of PD-based trusted apps/ services. The framework, acting as a broker, would also potentially allow users to gain direct economic benefit from the disclosure/exchange of their data.

2 The Context

We are experiencing a rapid change of paradigm in technology and in business, where data are becoming an essential resource for the design of new and better services and products. The amount of data available, generated and processed on a daily basis is so huge and rapidly increasing. "Big Data" has become the keyword around which innovation, competition, and productivity in ICT are orbiting, so as to create a new data-driven society. One of the most interesting classes of data is Personal Data (PD, i.e., any information relating to an identified or identifiable person): they are data about people, their behavior, their preferences, etc. When handled and interpreted such data can describe an individual's actions, behaviors and habits [2].

While so far most of the PD had been static (e.g. socio-demographic profiles), the smartphones, jointly with many other connected personal devices (e.g., environmental sensors, wristbands, etc.), have enabled the collection of highly dynamic PD, describing the behavior of people in the real life (e.g. locations, communication patterns, social interactions, apps usage, etc.). The exploitation of this data is a key element for enabling the design of novel personal services able to improve users' experience. These services, moreover, can generate novel types of PD, becoming also source, not only consumer, of PD that continuously enriches the user's "digital trace". Assuming it is possible to gather all these data from people, we have a perfect example of "Personal Big Data" with enormous potentials. The availability of such a huge amount of PD is an invaluable resource and opportunity for organizations and individuals to enable new applications and businesses. Organizations can leverage on these PD to have a deeper understanding of people's needs and behavior, either as single individuals or communities, and can provide tailored services. Accordingly, people (the actual data "owners") can benefit from the creation of novel personalized apps with an enhanced user-experience that help them measure/track and improve the quality of their life.

The current adopted models of managing PD often do not fully allow a controlled and effective exploitation of these opportunities; in addition, people are currently excluded from the life-cycle of their data, relegated to the role of PD producer with limited ability to control and to exploit them. PD are collected by several services in a fragmented (often redundant) way and then spread in the data centers of a multitude of organizations, which manage them according to the specific agreement signed by people. This results in several limitations: (i) it is not possible to have a holistic view of individuals, as their PD are collected and stored in several independent silos; (ii) there is a limited involvement of people, thus resulting in a scarce possibility for them to understand how their PD have been used; (iii) people cannot manage a copy of their PD, with great limitation on the possibility for them to fully exploit their PD.

In order to overcome the drawbacks of current "organization-centric" approach, a new user-centric model for PD management has been proposed [7, 11]. In general these initiatives promote the possibility for people to have a greater control over the lifecycle of their PD (e.g., collection, storage, processing, sharing) and they recognize the crucial and active role played by a person into a righteous and fruitful PD ecosystem. As mentioned by [1] a user-centric paradigm should complement and not replace the organization-centric one. A key aspect of the PD user-centric model is the right of the user to have copy of all their PD [7]. While this is a first step this right does not necessarily create value for people, if not combined with tools for their PD management and for easily and dynamically control how PD must be accessed and exploited by the services. A Personal Data Store (PDS) platform [4, 10] delivers a set of services enabling the owners of PD to collect, manage, track and control their data according to their wills and needs.

3   The Mobile Territorial Lab Experience

We designed and experimented *My Data Store*, a PDS platform able to manage heterogeneous PD, from those collected by apps and sensors on smartphones or on connected devices (e.g. environmental sensors, etc.), to those gathered from online services (such as social networks) or organizations in relation with their customers/

users to whom they offer services (e.g. network operators, service/utility providers, retailers, etc.). We then devised an innovative framework for a trusted PD management built around the role of *My Data Store*, as far as any other PDS. Its architecture supports developers in building trusted and transparent apps compliant with a user-centric PD management model. Specifically, it provides users with a mobile UI allowing them to dynamically control and audit the accesses, collection and usages of PD by means of the compliant apps. In this way we aim at creating an eco-system of trusted and transparent apps, feeding and exploiting the data stored in the PDS, pushing forward paradigms and common practices in PD management.

In cooperation with other partners, we are currently experimenting [9] the user-centric PD paradigm within the "Mobile Territorial Lab" (MTL, www.mobileterritoriallab.eu), a long-term living lab where a real community (involving about 150 families) experiments this new paradigm in a real living environment: in fact the participants to MTL collect, manage and use their PD while they act in their real life, e.g., by interacting and performing digital activities through their smartphones, and by using ad hoc designed apps exploiting their PD. The project and its objectives have been included in the World Economic Forum reports of the Rethinking Personal Data initiative (pg. 28 of [11]). Participants to MTL are provided with a smartphone empowered with a sensing SW continuously and passively collecting users' data in independent users' silos. The data automatically sensed consist of: (i) call and SMS logs, (ii) proximity data scanning for near-by devices, (iii) locations from GPS and WiFi. Additional PD such as (iv) mood and (v) expenses done by the participants are collected through experience sampling methods by means of ad hoc apps. MTL participants collect also (vi) the air-quality in their surroundings (e.g. CO and other gasses levels) by geo-referencing the values measured by an environmental sensor connected to the smartphone. Each MTL participant is then provided with a private *My Data Store* account, through which they can access, visualize and transparently manage all the mentioned PD collected about them.

4   My Data Store

My Data Store offers a set of tools to manage, control and exploit PD by enhancing an individual's awareness on the value of their PD. The *My Data Store* development has been driven by principles emerging from existing studies on PD management, as in [6, 8]. In particular, the principles followed are:

Participant Primacy: users should be provided with appropriate functionalities that enable them to have complete control over the management of their PD. This includes a nuanced process of permission-granting ensuring that users can easily move through the collection and sharing settings and take clear actions over them (decide which data gather in their space, share/delete sub-sets of them, etc.);

Data Legibility: users should be supported in understanding the meaning and the potential of different kinds of data, as well as the risks and the consequences associated to PD usage (e.g. the data which can be inferred, also from aggregated or anonymous collection of data, when PD are shared with 3rd parties);

Long-term Engagement: it is necessary to provide users with technologies for controlling their data (collection, sharing, visualization, etc.) but it is equally important that the system and the process of collecting and managing PD is perceived to be relevant. Services and tools provided to users over their data and exploitation opportunities can help and enhance such engagement.

While the above general principles inspire the design of any PDS service, the methodology followed during the design of *My Data Store* included a specific focus-group study whose goal was to identify elements and guidelines relevant for users in a real setting, to be used as drivers. The results highlighted the following:

PD Awareness: participants did not really realize the extent of the PD impact on their life and initially struggled to understand the value of PD and thus the need of a technology to manage them. This raised the need of providing support for guiding the users in the discovery of the PD risks and opportunities to make them aware of the meaning, the value and potentials of their data (as in *Data Legibility*). One of the solutions adopted is the usage of visual elements that lower the barrier for non-skilled;

Personally Meaningful Data as Triggers: one goal in the focus groups was to identify the scenarios perceived as valuable by the users and that ensure the *Long Term Engagement* general principle. The scenarios emerged as more relevant to the users are those related to time or cost savings. The design of the system should hence consider personal values to enforce users' engagement with PD and thus must provide relevant and intuitive data management features. The increasing exploitation of PD contextually to the growth of an eco-system of services/apps built on top of PD further foster the effects of this driver;

Social Comparison of users with other users (single, similar or particular groups/communities of users): it can both work as a tool to improve awareness and to stimulate the user engagement.

4.1 My Data Store Services

My Data Store is a Web portal with a controlled access that makes available to the granted users a set of tools for managing their PD, collected from several sources. The design of *My Data Store* was driven by the principles described above. In particular, we focused on three drivers: empowering people with full control over the life-cycle of their PD, improving their awareness on the data and enabling the exploitation and use of PD in accordance to their needs and willingness. The design aimed also at simplifying the user experience by providing people a limited, but clear and powerful set of capabilities.

4.2 Data Regions

In order to increase users' awareness and their ability to control, the data collected in *My Data Store* are organized in Data Regions (DR). Under the principle of Data

Legibility DRs are created by grouping in the same region different data sources w.r.t. their (i) perceptiveness, i.e. considering the information that can be inferred from the data, abstracting from technical details (e.g., both GPS and nearby WiFi AP, bring along the localization concept, etc.) (ii) sensibility to privacy, i.e. data with comparable levels of privacy-risks (e.g., data concerning interactions between individuals, such as calls, SMS, Bluetooth contacts, etc.). Every DR is associated with a brief description of the information brought by the PD and its list of data sources (Fig. 1). At this stage all the *My Data Store*'s features operate in an uniform way w.r.t. the DR, but in future it will allow expert users to customize their settings w.r.t. the single sources or service/ application generating data.

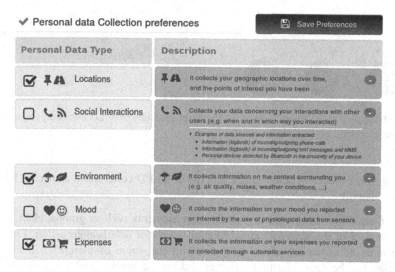

Fig. 1. Example of *Collection Area* (organized by Data Regions).

4.3 Main Functions

My Data Store includes PD Management features to fulfill the *Participant Primacy* principle over the entire PD life-cycle (i.e., from the collection to the deletion of a data record). Its main functions are:

Collection Area: In the Collection Area users can choose how DRs are collected and stored (Fig. 1). Users then have a complete set of controls for tuning the settings the best fit with their privacy concerns, exploitation or usage wills (indeed, the PDS is associate to a collector application, running on the users' devices, which is the responsible of collecting and sending the information desired by users);

Sharing Area: Users can set the disclosure level of the collected data by granting those who can access them and the level of detail. So far the choice concern only the disclosure with the participants of our experimentation community, but further options will be considered in future providing finer granularity;

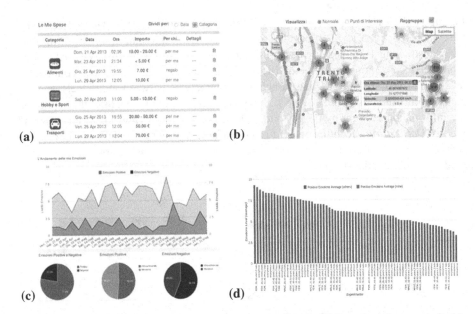

Fig. 2. Examples of *Individual Views*: (a) Expenses (auditing), (b) Locations (aggregated), (c) Mood (aggregated), (d) Expenses (social).

Deletion Area: users can delete single records or all PD collected in a specific DR and time interval.

My Data Store makes use of visualization elements such as graphs, chart, etc. to show the data in the above areas at different levels of details/aggregation. First, this choice aims at increasing users' awareness on the value of their PD, in terms of perception on the data informative power and on the level of risks arising from PD disclosure and exploitation (Data Legibility principle). Second, being able in providing intuitive, interesting and representative visualizations play a crucial role for a *Long-term Engagement* of users and in stimulating users toward the exploitation and use of their PD (Data as Triggers), e.g. by sharing them for apps/services or social comparison. The types of visualizations provided by *My Data Store* are (Fig. 2):

1. *Detailed "Auditing" Views* in tables or maps, where every available piece of raw data for every data source is represented in detail;
2. *Aggregated Individual Views* with aggregations, at different levels, of the PD owned by a single person (e.g. charts, pies, clusters of frequent locations, distance travelled, quantity of contacts, etc.) which aims at increasing his/her consciousness on daily behavior);
3. *Social Views* built from the PD voluntarily shared (with different levels of details) by other users enabling a social comparison of a person's behavior (e.g., *"How much am I social?"*, *"How my spending pattern does compare with others' one?"*) with the ones of similar users (e.g. by gender, age).

My Data Store differs from similar systems, such as [3], for the wide types of dynamically collected PD and for the flexibility and the user-friendliness of its Personal Data Management (PDM) features.

5 Toward an Eco-System of Trusted Personal Applications and "The Bank of Personal Data"

On top of the PDM features provided by *My Data Store* we designed a framework to manage applications (e.g., offered either as online services or as apps on devices) accessing PD in a trusted way. The goal is dual:

1. to provide users with a way to discriminate PD *Trusted and Transparent Applications*, i.e., those compliant with the user-centric approach, and to empower them with a clear description of the potential impact of each of such apps on PD (e.g. the generated/accessed PD, declared granularity/quality) and with tools to monitor/audit PD access at real time;
2. to provide apps developers with a workflow process and architecture enabling them to be compliant with the requirements of a trusted and transparent user-centric approach, easily interacting with solutions for PD collection and control, such as a PDS.

To achieve the goal the applications that want to be compliant with the framework must define (and keep updated) a "Statement", which declares the list of PD types handled by the application and for each of them:

the quality and granularity of the data acquired or generated (type, accuracy, tolerance, etc.);

the terms by which these PD will be handled by the application (frequency, purposes, etc.);

and distinguishing also among different usages:

Dynamically accessed (i.e. required instantly at run-time) by the application (e.g. accessing the current user location in order to provide location-aware hits when searching the Web);
Collected (i.e. stored for future uses into a repository such as the PDS);
Accessed "historically" (i.e. the requirements and usages of historic data accessed from the repository, e.g. for providing maps, charts, or inferences based on long-term analysis of user behaviors);
Shared (i.e. used and transmitted –possibly aggregated and/or anonymized– into applications which are not only personal but also shown or used, for any reason, to/ by other users or third parties).

Potentially the Statement could include further information "describing" the application capabilities that require each specific PD usage, i.e. those that could stop properly working on the chance that the user revokes the grant to perform that action on that particular data (so that the user can be properly informed).

Users are provided with a Mobile or Web UI (the *Apps Area*) allowing them to check the list of enabled (e.g., those installed on their devices) trusted applications (Fig. 3, left) and to control at any time (granting or denying usages) how they can access/use the different PD (Fig. 3, right) accordingly to their Statement.

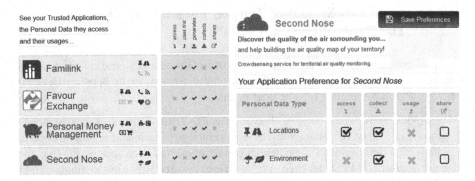

Fig. 3. Example *Trusted Applications*: app list (left); user settings for air-quality app (right).

The framework provides a set of APIs for the development of compliant trusted applications, thus for the run-time access, collection and historical usage of the user PD. These APIs could be provided either server-side by the PDS, or device-side as a layer on top of the device OS or directly ensured by it. These APIs guarantee that any access to the PD is performed (and thus contextually monitored and logged) in compliance with the application Statement and the user settings. Applications could be certified on the basis of their exclusive usage of "trusted and transparent" APIs.

The framework middleware, thus, automatically carries out the retrieval and collection in/from the PDS of the PD for which the user requested/granted the collection (so that the user is empowered with full transparency on the accesses PD, exploiting the PDM features of the PDS, and further put into value/exploit the collected data) and the collection of the auditing information. Similarly (mobile-) browsers and Web applications could provide the same set of APIs enabling the collection and monitoring of other PD (e.g. browsing history, bookmarks, published content, etc.). On the basis of the auditing logs the framework can provide to the user reports on PD collection and usage, on services/applications behaviors and reports if a service/ application behaves in line with its statement.

Interestingly our technology enables a very diverse variety of applications. One specific application scenario could concern the direct monetization of users' personal data, gaining personally an economic remuneration from the disclosure of their personal data. In this last scenario the PDS could play the role of the *"Bank of the users Personal Data"* [5] where, not only the data of the user can flow and be stockpiled from different data sources, but also various exploitation opportunities can be proposed to the users as a data brokerage platform, on the basis of their choices/policies, with all the appropriate protections (e.g. anonymization and/or aggregations of data from large, selected user bases). The framework, in fact, allows for the complete auditing of data accesses and usages enabling, contextually, the automatic accounting and the dynamic user control on data exploitations.

6   Conclusions and Challenges

Introducing *My Data Store* we tried to push further user-centric Personal Data Management, extending the concept of Personal Data Store (PDS) so as to provide users with full control and awareness along the whole life-cycle of their PD from data collection, to data exploitation into added-value services and even data monetization.

In particular we focused our effort in letting the PDS be the core element of a novel framework enabling a new generation of personal apps and services. Our framework provides apps developers a way to access PD in a fully transparent way, consistently with the user choices, and aims at supporting users and developer in the process of PD collection (improving user awareness and widening the set of controlled exploitation opportunities) and in monitoring the apps/services real behavior. This framework could be included, e.g., as middleware of (mobile) platform or OS, while the PDS features could be provided as cloud services.

Even if it cannot prevent from misuses (e.g. illegal copies) of the PD to which the access has been granted and cannot prevent from the coexistence of "non-trusted and non-transparent" applications, our framework shows the way toward the provisioning of transparent, privacy-preserving applications. This solution will fully satisfy the user "right of copy", enabling them to benefit from data reuse, data fusion or monetization scenarios. The main challenges consist of creating the user demand (and thus developer and OS provider availability) towards this kind of applications and to let the PDS-like services become "the Bank of users" PD" [5].

We believe that a change of paradigm in PD management and the construction of a fruitful eco-system of data producers and consumers pass only through such an enhanced transparency and the empowerment of individuals; in particular, individuals should have the possibility of controlling and exploiting their PD, consciously and actively participating in the eco-system, In this way, the value of PD is unlocked and transformed into business and societal value,

References

1. Doc Searls: The intention economy: when customers take charge (2012). www.searls.com/time2grow.html
2. Dong, W., Lepri, B., Pentland, A.: Modeling the coevolution of behaviors and social relationships using mobile phone data. In: Proceedings of the ACM MUM (2011)
3. Hong, J., Landay, J.: An architecture for privacy sensitive ubiquitous computing. In: Proceedings of the ACM MobySys (2004)
4. Moiso, C., Antonelli, F., Vescovi, M.: How do i manage my personal data? - A telco perspective. In: Proceedings of the International Conference on Data Technologies and Applications (2012)
5. Moiso, C., Minerva, R.: Towards a user-centric personal data ecosystem – the role of the bank of individuals data. In: ICIN 2012 Proceedings, pp. 202–209 (2012)
6. Mun, M., Hao, S., Mishra, S., et al.: Personal data vaults: a locus of control for personal data streams. In: Proceedings of the ACM CoNext (2010)

7. Pentland, A.: Society's nervous system: building effective government, energy, and public health systems. IEEE Comput. **45**(1), 31–38 (2012)
8. Shilton, K., Burke, J., Estrin, D., et al.: Designing the personal data stream: enabling participatory privacy in mobile personal sensing. In: Proceedings of the Communication, Information, and Internet Policy (2009)
9. Vescovi, M., Perentis, C., Leonardi, C., Lepri, B., Moiso, C.: My data store: toward user awareness and control on personal data. Proc. ACM UbiComp **2014**, 179182 (2014)
10. Wang, J., Wang, Z.: A Survey on Personal Data Cloud. Sci. World J. **2014**, 13, Article ID 969150 (2014). doi:10.1155/2014/969150
11. World Economic Forum: Unlocking the Value of Personal Data: From Collection to Usage (2013). www.weforum.org/issues/rethinking-personal-data

Security-as-a-Service in Multi-cloud and Federated Cloud Environments

Pramod S. Pawar[1](✉), Ali Sajjad[1], Theo Dimitrakos[1,2], and David W. Chadwick[1]

[1] The University of Kent, Canterbury, Kent CT2 7NZ, UK
{pramod.s.pawar,ali.sajjad,theo.dimitrakos}@bt.com,
d.w.chadwick@kent.ac.uk
[2] British Telecommunications, Adastral Park, Ipswich IP5 3RE, UK

Abstract. The economic benefits of cloud computing are encouraging customers to bring complex applications and data into the cloud. However security remains the biggest barrier in the adoption of cloud, and with the advent of multi-cloud and federated clouds in practice security concerns are for applications and data in the cloud. This paper proposes security as a value added service, provisioned dynamically during deployment and operation management of an application in multi-cloud and federated clouds. This paper specifically considers a data protection and a host & application protection solution that are offered as a SaaS application, to validate the security services in a multi-cloud and federated cloud environment. This paper shares our experiences of validating these security services over a geographically distributed, large scale, multi-cloud and federated cloud infrastructure.

Keywords: Application security · Data security · Cloud security · Multi-cloud · Federated cloud

1 Introduction

Cloud computing provides flexible and dynamic access to virtualized computing and network resources, however, its complexity, especially in multi-cloud and federated cloud environments gives users cause for concern over the security of services hosted in the cloud [1]. Due to the dynamic nature of clouds, new categories of security threat emerge [2]. Hashizume et al. provide an analysis of security issues in the cloud considering the three service delivery models, SaaS, PaaS and IaaS [3]. The major security concerns for SaaS applications include data location, legislative compliance of its data, security policy of the providers and data protection. This obliges the SaaS provider to have additional security mechanisms beyond what is offered by the PaaS and IaaS providers, in order to protect their applications and data.

The emphasis of this paper is on the security and protection of the SaaS applications and user/consumer data. Due to the dynamic nature of the cloud, significant challenges exist in applying the traditional security solutions such as firewalls, IDS/IPS

© IFIP International Federation for Information Processing 2015
C.D. Jensen et al. (Eds.): IFIPTM 2015, IFIP AICT 454, pp. 251–261, 2015.
DOI: 10.1007/978-3-319-18491-3_21

and data protection, in the cloud environment. This paper proposes security as a value added service that forms an additional layer of security for hosts and applications in the cloud and is dynamically provisioned. Specifically, it considers a data protection solution and an application protection solution that are offered as a SaaS application, to demonstrate security services in a multi-cloud and federated cloud environment.

Most of today's existing data protection or secure cloud storage services focus on file-level encryption of the user's data, following one of two approaches: either the data is uploaded to the cloud provider and is then encrypted, in which case the keys are managed by the service provider, e.g. Dropbox, Google Drive, Microsoft Sky Drive; or the data is encrypted at the user end and then uploaded to the secure storage service provider and the keys are managed by the user, e.g. BoxCryptor or the Virtual Cloud Drive [4–8]. Although these approaches are suitable from the point-of-view of online backup and write-once read-many types of scenarios, they become very unwieldy when the data has to be modified frequently and resides on virtual machines in the cloud. This is further complicated when the user wants to take advantage of the growing inter-cloud usage scenarios. The data protection solution considered in this paper is developed to address these issues, however there is a need to validate the functioning in a multi-cloud use case scenarios.

The host and application protection solution considered in this paper is developed to enable cloud providers to dynamically provision the protection functions to cloud service users while allowing them to have full control over the security of their applications and hosts. As this solution is required to be integrated in the provisioning workflow of the cloud service provider and required to be offered to large numbers of cloud consumers, there is a need to verify the automation workflow since it will automatically deploy the protection components in a multi-cloud environment, on a heterogeneous and scalable infrastructure that can host hundreds of VMs.

The validation of these security services is performed as experiments executed over the Fed4FIRE (Federation for Future Internet Research and Experimentation) infrastructure which is an EU funded, geographically distributed, multi-cloud and federated cloud infrastructure [9]. This paper describes the experiments performed for the dynamic provisioning and automation of services, our experiences and findings and provides feedback about the Fed4FIRE infrastructure. The rest of this paper is organized as follows. Section 2 provides the details of the application protection and data protection solutions used in this paper. Section 3 describes the Fed4FIRE infrastructure used for evaluating the solutions. Section 4 provides the objectives of the experiment and Sect. 5 describes the experiments. Section 6 provides the experimental results. Finally, Sect. 7 provides the concluding remarks and the future work.

2   Overview of the Security Solution Used for Experimentation

2.1   Secure Cloud Storage - Data Protection Service

Secure Cloud Storage (SCS) is a cloud security service that provides data protection for public and private clouds and other virtualization platforms. It allows users to protect and control their confidential and sensitive information with a user-friendly file and volume encryption service that keeps their data private and helps meet their regulatory compliance requirements. Secure Cloud Storage can be deployed as a hosted Software-as-a-Service or as an On-Premise software application, but in either case only the user has access and control of the decryption keys, giving them the freedom to decrypt their data on-demand and in real time. It offers users the capability of applying policy-based key management, a means to validate the identity and integrity of virtual machines requesting the encryption keys, and it can specify where and when the encrypted data can be accessed.

Key technical features of this service include:

(1) *Policy-Driven Key Management:* this (a) uses identity and integrity-based policy enforcement to ensure only authorized virtual machines receive keys and access secure volumes (b) automates key release and virtual machine authorization for rapid operations or requires manual approval for increased security (c) enables the use of policies to determine when and where keys were used;

(2) *Advanced Encryption Techniques:* this (a) features FIPS 140-2 certification and FIPS approved AES encryption (b) encrypts and decrypts information in real time, so data at rest is always protected (c) applies file and volume encryption to secure all data, metadata, and associated structures without impacting application functionality;

(3) *Robust Auditing, Reporting, and Alerting:* this (a) logs actions in the management console for audit purposes (b) provides detailed reporting and alerting features with incident-based and interval-based notifications.

Users of the Secure Cloud Storage service can monitor the integrity and protection status of their volumes via a configurable web-based dashboard offered to them over a secure channel via BT's hosted service. Users can define different roles for their cloud administrators, security operation teams and auditors giving them different levels of control visibility and rights to define policies as appropriate. Security administrators with the appropriate rights can define policies for each volume on any virtual machine that has been registered by a secure cloud agent.

2.2 Intelligent Protection - Host and Application Protection Service

Intelligent Protection is a cloud security service that is designed and developed to protect virtual servers and hosted applications on cloud infrastructures [10]. The novelty of this service centers on offering security as a value-added service (multi-tenant security SaaS) while enforcement is delivered via the cloud infrastructure, with minimal integration overhead. It enhances cloud user experience by offering more secure, flexible, auto-mated security management for applications deployed or on-boarded on cloud infra-structures (IaaS) such as BT Compute or other 3rd party equivalents (e.g. Amazon EC2 or V-Cloud enabled IaaS) while placing the users in control of their own security operations though its Security SaaS operations dashboard [11, 12].

Intelligent Protection enables its users to automatically perform the following security functions via an intuitive web interface: (1) *Virtual Security Patches*

(2) *Intelligent Intrusion Detection and Prevention (IDS/IPS)* (3) *Bi-directional stateful firewall* (4) *Anti-Malware* (5) *Integrity Monitoring* (6) *Incident Reporting and Analysis* (7) *Recommendation Scans.*

A user of the intelligent protection service can: analyze their virtual networks, servers, and applications for vulnerabilities; obtain recommendations of missing security patches, and the best security to address the identified vulnerabilities on each system that has been analyzed; continuously monitor for attacks, intrusion, viruses, exploits and any other security incident; monitor performance and scalability; and apply corrective measures updating the security policies accordingly.

Users of the Intelligent Protection service can monitor the health and protection of their virtual machines and servers via a configurable dashboard offered to them over a secure channel via BT's hosted service. Tenants can define different roles for their cloud administrators, security operation teams and auditors giving them different levels of control visibility and rights to define policies as appropriate. Security administrators can define security policies via an intuitive GUI by combining policies from a library or by asking the Intelligent Protection system to analyze a selected environment's vulnerabilities and recommend which security policy rules to apply on that environment.

3   Overview of the Fed4FIRE Facilities

The goal of the EU FP7 Fed4FIRE project is to federate various Internet experimentation facilities to enable an innovative cross-domain experimentation platform, providing researchers with easy access to resources on different facilities. The project currently involves multiple facilities, introducing a diverse set of technologies such as cloud computing, wired and wireless network, software defined networking, Internet of Things and smart cities. Some example facilities are: EPCC BonFIRE (UK), Virtual Wall (EU), PlanetLab Europe (EU), Smart Santander(EU), NORBIT(Australia), KO-REN (Korea), Sanford optical access testbed (USA) [9].

The incentive for using the Fed4FIRE facilities stems, on the one hand, from the scale and heterogeneity that the Fed4FIRE facilities bring to the experimentation, and on the other hand from the likelihood of continuity and expansion of research experimentation by using the FIRE facilities that expose open standards management interfaces. Furthermore it enables the verifiability and validity of the protection services over 3rd party Cloud platforms. These characteristics make Fed4FIRE an appropriate environment for evaluating Secure Cloud Storage (SCS) and Intelligent Protection solutions. Furthermore, the geographically distributed infrastructure of Fed4FIRE, which is connected through the Internet, allows the experiments to be run under real-world network behavior that is not present in a simulation or a single public or private cloud. The comprehensive monitoring infrastructure and services of Fed4FIRE enables the scalability and performance of the security solutions to be easily measured. Additionally, Fed4FIRE provides the jFed tool and Rspec. The jFed tool is a Java based framework that provides an integrated view and interface to communicate with all the infrastructures available in Fed4FIRE. Rspec is the resource specification written in the jFed tool that allows provisioning of VMs on the Fed4FIRE infrastructure.

4 Objectives of the Experimentation

The evaluation of our data protection service and host & application protection service is targeted on the automation, scalability and performance of the solutions. Accordingly, the following objectives are specified for the data protection service:

(a) to be able to automatically deploy the Secure Cloud Storage solution on a hybrid multi-cloud environment within the Fed4FIRE Cloud facilities,
(b) to provide a method for provisioning encrypted volumes to VMs deployed on the multiple cloud platforms, and
(c) to assess and automate the methods for transferring secure volumes from one VM to another and from one cloud platform to another.

The host and application protection service included the following objectives:

(a) to be able to automatically deploy the Intelligent Protection components in a hybrid environment of public cloud, private cloud and physical servers,
(b) to automatically provision Intelligent Protection agents and protect IT assets on a large number of virtual machines emulating real-world scenarios, and
(c) to develop a blue print of a managed security service to apply virtual patches to proprietary applications deployed on multiple virtual machines.

The following parameters of the data protection service were measured:

(a) the complexity of the workflow required to achieve the deployment and configuration of the SCS service components on multiple cloud platforms,
(b) the time-scales involved in the workflow,
(c) the mix and heterogeneity of the cloud platforms,
(d) the time for the creation of data volumes of different sizes on multiple clouds of Fed4FIRE,
(e) the number of volumes attached to the VMs deployed on these clouds, and
(f) the time for volumes to be encrypted by employing the full disk encryption technique.

The measurable parameters of the application protection services are as follows:

(a) the feasibility and speed of deployment of the agents in the hybrid multi-cloud environment,
(b) the maturity of the automation of workflow required to achieve the agent deployment and configuration on multiple cloud platforms,
(c) the time for deployment, configuration and security management of the agents in up to 50 virtual machines on multiple cloud platforms, and
(d) the performance associated with the security management function such as the automatic security patching for standard applications such as databases, Email servers, Apache web servers, and various Windows and Unix operating systems.

5   Architecture and Experiment Set up

5.1   Data Protection

The architecture of the SCS is composed of three main components:

(a) *Key Management Server (KMS):* this is a key server self-hosted or hosted by a trusted Service Provider. It is the only place where the encryption keys are stored persistently.

(b) *Web Console:* this is a console that allows SCS administrators to review and approve pending key requests, check device status and integrity, set up policies, manage devices, check reports and logs, and manage user accounts.

(c) *Agent:* this is software installed on a virtual machine that communicates with the KMS and performs the actual encryption.

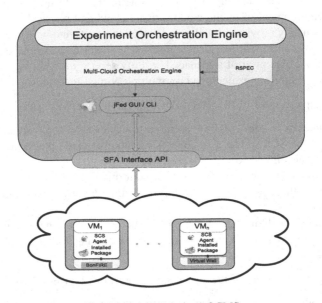

Fig. 1. Detailed design of CMS

The experiment uses the federated tools and interfaces provided by Fed4FIRE to discover, reserve and provision the required resources. The resources required for this experiment are VMs and persistent storage blocks or volumes that can be attached to those VMs. The experiments use Virtual Wall 1 & Virtual Wall 2 and BonFIRE as a multi-cloud infrastructure. To help with the deployment and provisioning of the SCS agent on the Fed4FIRE infrastructure VMs, Puppet is used as the configuration management service (CMS). This allows contextualization of the VMs to fulfil all the dependencies of the SCS agent and also to deploy the appropriate version and build of the SCS agent on the target VM's. To conduct the experiment in a multi-cloud environment, the jFed tool is used, which allow end-users to provision and manage experiments via a GUI and CLI. The design of the CMS in this context is given in Fig. 1. The experiments are specified and orchestrated automatically by constructing a RSPEC file provided to the jFed tool. The Key Management Server and the SCS Web Console were hosted at BT on a dedicated facility and offered as a cloud-based service to the experiment.

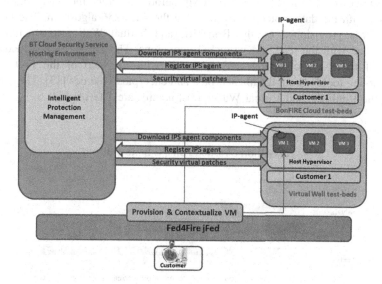

Fig. 2. Intelligent protection provisioning architecture in Fed4FIRE

5.2 Host and Application Protection

The Intelligent Protection architecture comprises of the following to support on-boarding and enablement of application protection elements in the Fed4FIRE infrastructure:

(a) *Intelligent Protection Management Server:* This has a web interface to manage the Intelligent Protection (IP) agents that protect the cloud nodes. The components of the server include: a dashboard, Alerts, Events, Computers, Policies and Administration.

(b) *IP-agent:* This is agent software that can be either manually deployed or deployed using deployment scripts on the VMs to be protected.

(c) *Deployment Scripts:* This is a script, which on execution on a VM, automatically downloads the agent from the server, then installs and registers the agent with the server. This setup requires one or mode nodes in the Fed4FIRE infrastructure to have connectivity to the Intelligent Protection Management Server and an Rspec that is configured for automatic provisioning of an agent. An RSpec document is prepared that contains nodes of Virtual Wall 1 & 2 infrastructures and the deployment script for automatic provisioning of the agents (Fig. 2).

6 Experiment Results

6.1 SCS Performance Experiments

The objective of this experiment is to analyze the provisioning of SCS agents on VMs and assess the data volume encryption overhead on I/O bandwidth and I/O latency. The tests compare file I/O performance of VMs before and after the data volumes are encrypted with the data protection agent using the AES-256 algorithm. The tests are run on VMs provisioned on the BonFIRE and Virtual Wall infrastructures and benchmarked with the read and write I/O operations. The effects on bandwidth and latency of these I/O operations are measured with the help of the FIO storage benchmarking tool for both the unencrypted and encrypted volumes [13]. The volumes used in the BonFIRE and Virtual Wall infrastructures are 1 GB in size.

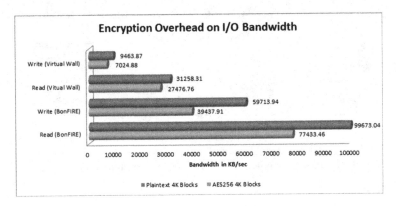

Fig. 3. Encryption overhead on I/O bandwidth

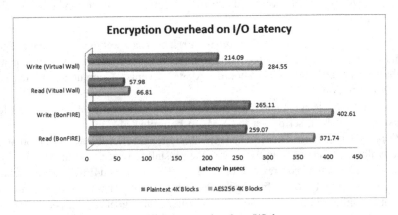

Fig. 4. Encryption overhead on I/O latency

The FIO tool is configured to use whole volumes in the read/write tests i.e. 1 GB of data is written and read in all the tests. All the volumes are formatted with the ext4 filesystem with 4 K block sizes. Figures 3 and 4 show the encryption overhead on I/O bandwidth and I/O latency respectively. The measurements shown in Figs. 3 and 4 demonstrate that the data protection solution enables data security in clouds while maintaining reasonable performance for typical filesystem and database workloads.

6.2 Scalability Experiments

The aim of this experiment is to evaluate the performance of automatic provisioning of protection to the VMs, in a scaled environment. The provisioning of protection includes downloading of the agent from the Intelligent Protection Management Server, installing the agent on the VMs, registering the agent with the server and updating the agent with the security policies. To perform the scalability evaluation, 50 VMs (40 VMs on Virtual Wall 2 and 10 VMs on Virtual Wall 1) are simultaneously created in a multi-cloud environment and the Intelligent Protection Server is hosted in the BT cloud.

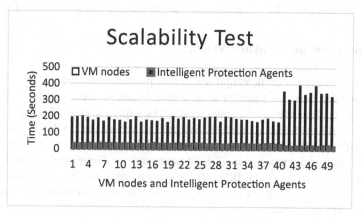

Fig. 5. Agent deployment performance in a scaled federated cloud environment

VM nodes 1–40 are created on Virtual Wall 2 and VM nodes 41–50 are created on Virtual Wall 1. The time durations of booting the VMs and provisioning the agents on the infrastructure is recorded. The observation in Fig. 5 shows that the Intelligent Protection agents are deployed and configured in less than 1 min after the VMs are booted on both infrastructures. Although the VM provisioning performance is different in the two infrastructures, it was observed than the Intelligent Protection agent deployment was consistent even in the scaled environment of 50 VMs. These time scales were obtained for the automatic provisioning workflow without any manual intervention from the user or the administrator of the targeted Cloud platform.

6.3   Feedback to the Fed4FIRE Infrastructure

The various characteristics of the Fed4FIRE infrastructure such as scale, heterogeneity, multi-cloud, and federation are potentially valuable to the experiments and a detailed feedback was provided based on our experience of the experiment. The feedback also included some of the limitations of the existing infrastructure which were the obstacles we experienced while performing the experiments. These were:

(a) The SCS software can only run on recent versions of Ubuntu, CentOS or Windows operating systems, none of which were readily available and required templates to be provisioned on request.
(b) The Intelligent Protection Agent is only supported for Windows and unix, but for widely used variants of these operating systems, such as Windows 32/64, Red Hat Enterprise Linux 6.0/5.0, SUSE Linux 11, Ubuntu 12.04/10.04, Amazon Linux, Oracle RedHat Enterprise Linux 6/5, Solaris 9/10/11 and HP-UX 11i v3 IA-64. However the Fed4FIRE infrastructure only supports Ubuntu 12.04/10.04 and no other widely used operating system for which the agent is available.
(c) The Virtual Wall infrastructures do not provide facilities for creating and attaching data volumes with virtual machines, which prevented the data protection experiment from performing volume encryption and confined it to file encryption.
(d) Some Fed4FIRE infrastructures do not provide an option to create VM templates.

7   Conclusion and Future Work

The paper describes experimentation with a data protection service and a host & application protection service offered as a value added security service in Fed4FIRE environment and presents the experimental results. The experiments verify the provisioning and automation workflow and the results validate the performance and scalability of these services in the Fed4FIRE which confirms the capability of these services to perform in a large scale multi-cloud and federated cloud environments. The obstacles experienced for the experiments on the Fed4FIRE infrastructure were provided as feedback to the operators. As a future work, we intend to perform more experiments after enhancements are made to the infrastructure.

Acknowledgement. This work has been partially supported by the EU within the 7th Framework Programme under contract ICT-318389 – Fed4FIRE (Federation for FIRE).

References

1. Mell, P., Grance, T.: The NIST Definition of Cloud Computing, Sep. 2011 http://csrc.nist.gov/publications/nistpubs/800-145/SP800-145.pdf
2. Ibrahim, A.S., Hamlyn-harris, J.H., Grundy, J.: Emerging security challenges of cloud virtual infrastructure (2010)
3. Hashizume, K., Rosado, D.G., Fernández-Medina, E., Fernandez, E.B.: An analysis of security issues for cloud computing. J. Internet Serv. Appl. 4(1), 1–13 (2013)

4. Dropbox. https://dropbox.com/. Accessed 13 March 2015
5. Google drive. https://drive.google.com/. Accessed 13 March 2015
6. Microsoft Sky Drive. https://skydrive.live.com/. Accessed 13 March 2015
7. Boxcryptor | Encryption for cloud storage | Window, Mac, Android, iOS | boxcryptor.com. https://www.boxcryptor.com/. Accessed 13 March 2015
8. TERENA/CloudDrive · GitHub. https://github.com/TERENA/CloudDrive/. Accessed 13 March 2015
9. Fed4Fire. http://www.fed4fire.eu/. Accessed 13 March 2015
10. Daniel, J., Dimitrakos, T., El-Moussa, F., Ducatel, G., Pawar, P., Sajjad, A.: Seamless Enablement of intelligent protection for enterprise cloud applications through service store, pp. 1021–1026 (2014)
11. Amazon Web Services, 22 May 2013. http://aws.amazon.com/. Accessed 22 May 2013
12. vCloud. http://vcloud.vmware.com/. Accessed 13 March 2015
13. Flexible I/O tester GitHub. https://github.com/axboe/fio/. Accessed 13 March 2015

The Role of SLAs in Building a Trusted Cloud for Europe

Ana Juan Ferrer[✉] and Enric Pages i Montanera

Atos, Research and Innovation, Diagonal. 200, 08018 Barcelona, Spain
{ana.juanf,enric.pages}@atos.net
http://www.atos.net

Abstract. The European commission recognises Cloud potential to improve competitiveness by enabling transformation to better connected and efficient society. However, still trust and security concerns hamper its massive adoption, both in private and public sectors. Towards a establishing a Trusted Cloud Europe this paper stresses the role that Service Level Agreements (SLAs) play by providing the mechanisms that allow both users and providers to establish a common understanding on the services to be provided and enforce guarantees around performance, transparency, conformance and data protection. To this end, the paper explores trust stakeholders and factors per cloud layer in the Cloud computing environment; it analyses the role of SLAs and provides a taxonomy of terms to support more tight and detailed SLA definitions that support users' requirements in order to improve reliability and transparency in Cloud.

Keywords: Trust · Cloud · Sla

1 Introduction

Cloud Computing has reshaped the IT industry, and has the potential to change businesses and the economy by enabling higher IT efficiency and reliability. The European commission through the Steering Board of the European Cloud partnership [1] has recognised Cloud potential to boost growth, innovation and competitiveness in Europe [9] while enabling transformation to more connected and efficient society driving to benefits to citizens, business and public administrations alike.

For this to happen it is fundamental that Cloud services become reliable, trustworthy and secure for all users. The more extensive use of Cloud computing technologies bring to the users concerns on its data security, privacy issues and legal concerns, especially for public Cloud adoption. These concerns, in many cases are associated to intrinsic factors the nature of the Cloud computing model, such as multi-tenancy.

Service Level Agreements (SLAs) play a key role by being the mechanism that users have to enforce guarantees around performance, transparency, conformance

© IFIP International Federation for Information Processing 2015
C.D. Jensen et al. (Eds.): IFIPTM 2015, IFIP AICT 454, pp. 262–275, 2015.
DOI: 10.1007/978-3-319-18491-3_22

and data protection. As cloud adoption increases, cloud users, from both private enterprises and the public sector, will be seeking more tightly defined SLAs as a mean to build up dependable and trustworthy relationship terms with cloud providers.

This document first explores trust stakeholders and factors per cloud layer in the Cloud computing environment. Then, it analyses the role of SLAs. Finally it provides a taxonomy of terms to support more SLA detailed definitions [2], applicable to both private and public sector, aiming to support the development for trustworthy Cloud for Europe.

2 Cloud Computing Trust Stakeholders and Factors

Cloud computing differs from traditional IT security scenarios by its multi-tenant nature. Multi-tenancy refers to the ability for multiple customers (tenants) to share applications and/or infrastructure resources. This characteristic is the factor that allows Cloud providers to efficiently manage resource utilization among several users in a shared environment; and therefore, it is the enabler for providers to achieve economies of scale and commercial benefits.

However, it is the main source of concern for cloud users, if insufficient protection mechanisms are in place to guarantee security and privacy for both data and applications.

In the trustful provision and consumption of Cloud services, there is a difficult balance among confronted actors interests: cloud service providers and cloud users, where none of them can provide an overall solution for the issue at a general level. Depending on the nature of the cloud service offering (IaaS, PaaS, SaaS) providers are not aware of the contents and security requirements for the applications, while users, in the current state of development of Cloud, do not have sufficient vision of the security mechanisms and controls in place at providers facilities neither for detecting security incidents or holes. The following sections analyse specific security and trust factors in each Cloud layer by providing details on the specific issues and relevant research.

Software as a Service(SaaS)

SaaS completely decouples application execution from the users IT infrastructure. In this model, all application services are solely accessed by the user by a Web browser or thin client over the internet. While enterprise data is stored into the SaaS providers infrastructure, which can be based on a PaaS or IaaS provider or in a traditional infrastructure provisioning model. SaaS, despite being the Cloud model in which users information is more exposed to Cloud providers threats, given the complete loss of control from the user, is the lesser explored at security research levels, accounting for only a few references addressing concretely this topic [3,4]. This can be motivated by the fact that SaaS applications are commonly delivered in the form of web applications for which security issues are a well-known and deeply analysed problem.

Platform as a Service (PaaS)

Nowadays, there is a truly diverse array of capabilities being offered as PaaS offerings. A PaaS cloud provides a container platform where users deploy and run their components. Diversities are present in supported programming tools (languages, frameworks, runtime environments and databases), in the various types of underlying infrastructure, and even on capabilities available for each PaaS. Taking the example of Google App Engine, Googles PaaS platform, it provides an execution environment where applications run on a virtualised technology foundation that scales automatically on demand. Google App Engine is often criticized for not providing transparency to the user to control infrastructure and how this infrastructure is used. Developers do not have direct control over resource allocation, because the underlying system and hardware resources are masked by the App Engine layer. Other existing PaaS platforms, such as Cloud Foundry automatize the application deployment to a set of template VMs, with complete and isolated platform stack. Vulnerabilities of these types of PaaS are the same than in IaaS environments.

Infrastructure as a Service (IaaS)

IaaS is by far the most analysed Cloud layer with regards security and data protection. In order to produce a systematic view on the question four different issues will be analysed separately: Security of Cloud APIs, VM repositories security and network issues. It has to be noted that security concerns on virtualisation technologies, are intentionally not further elaborated but in the context of public cloud IaaS implications.

- Security of API and interfaces: Cloud APIs or Cloud control interfaces are the means that the Cloud providers offer to manage VM images in an IaaS environment. They provide the capacities to add VMs, to modify them, as well as to manage their life-cycle (start, stop and resume). Somorovsky et al. [4] analyses the security of these interfaces in a public Cloud environment, Amazon EC2, and a private Cloud management system, Eucalyptus. In it, two different classes of attacks XML Signature wrapping attacks and XSS attacks on browser front ends are demonstrated. It is important to notice that vulnerabilities in this aspect expose important security breaches of providers, given that the attacker get access to all virtual infrastructure of the user, and therefore its data.
- Security of VM repositories: Public VM repositories are a useful mechanism that both private cloud and public cloud providers can offer in order to simplify to users the task of creating their own VM images from scratch. Regardless of the usefulness of the mechanism, research demonstrates it can be a source of security risks both for the publisher or the image, the consumer and even the provider in which an instance of this VM is executed [5] in their work identify that the publisher can release sensitive information inadvertently. From both the receiver and the provider result is that they get VMs that contain

malicious or illegal content. Balduzzi et al. [6] have performed an exhaustive analysis over a period of 5 months for all virtual images publicly available in the Europe, Asia, US East, and US West Amazon datacenters. In total 8.448 Linux images and 1202 Windows images were available. Of those available 5.303 images were analysed. The result of this analysis presented images containing software with critical vulnerabilities and leftover credentials.

– Secure Networking of VMs: Once again, the main source of concern about networking in public clouds is multi-tenancy. VMs from different customers may reside in the same physical network through which data traffic generated by VMs is transported. In order to overcome this issue techniques as network virtualization, through VLAN or other logical network segmentation are applied, so it segregates and isolates traffic among different user groups or subnets. However, some authors claim that these techniques were designed for the context of an enterprise, and therefore not securely applicable in the context of a public cloud due to limitations in the scale e.g. firewall policies ability to support load, or susceptibility to large scale DDoS attacks [7].

3   Users Needs and Requirements

Common concerns with regards cloud adoption; compliance, security, privacy and integrity, rely on the inability for users to measure, monitor and control activities and operations in Clouds third party platform or infrastructure. This is commonly understood as providers lack of transparency.

Improving transparency of Cloud services increases uptake of cloud, and this is beneficial for everyone: users and providers. A few concrete examples will help explain how benefits can be made by a dialogue between the different points of view to establish SLA model terms:

Benefits for Cloud Users:

– Provide mechanisms and a framework through which organizations make informed decisions when selecting a provider, using criteria such as: service availability, performance, monitoring, data privacy conditions, or penalties in case of SLA non-fulfillment.
– Compare Cloud Service levels with on-premise service levels (features and prices are easier to compare).
– Make informed decisions about Hybrid Cloud in the mix between public and private clouds.
– Easier ability for public sector to agree on EU-wide service expectations.

Benefits for Cloud Providers:

– Allow providers to make clear statements of differentiation by offering different levels of service at different prices.
– Open new avenues for innovative business models such as cloud brokerage and cloud aggregation.
– Make clear statements of differing cloud services from best effort to minimum commitment.

In addition, for providers, the benefits anticipated by the development of detailed SLAs are twofold: First, by more concretely describing their services they can extend their usage levels thereby incrementing their customer base and profitability (enabled by economies of scale); Second, it can drive to richer Cloud scenarios by facilitating the development of Bursting, Brokerage or any type of multi-cloud scenarios. In these scenarios Cloud providers do not offer Cloud services themselves, but they rely on a more complex cloud ecosystem, enabling Cloud providers to offer better and more advanced services at a reduced price.

At all levels of its Stack (IaaS, PaaS, SaaS), the requirement of establishing adequate SLAs is to assure that both applications and infrastructure meet the promised performance and reliability benchmarks. This requirement is needed by any type of adopter, being applicable both for public sector and in general by any business environment or particular user.

- Allow providers to make clear statements of differentiation by offering different levels of service at different prices.
- Open new avenues for innovative business models such as cloud brokerage and cloud aggregation.
- Make clear statements of differing cloud services from best effort to minimum commitment.

4   Service Level Agreements (SLAs)

SLAs specify cloud service provider and cloud service user consensus in the services to be provided.

From a legal perspective, SLAs are a binding contract among users and providers. Analysis of current SLAs offered by public Cloud providers performed in the context of the Cloud Legal project from Queen Mary School of Law Legal Studies [10] show clear limitations. It demostrates that many Cloud providers include elements in their Terms and Conditions asserting wide-ranging disclaimers of liability or of any warranty that the service will operate as described. In addition this research also found out that SLAs will often be couched in such terms as to exclude the majority of causes of a Cloud service outage, and will provide remedies only in the form of credits against future service. An additional remark done in the context of the OPTIMIS European research project [8] refers to the lack of clarity on how the layers of contract take into consideration the data subjects interests and rights where personal data are processed due to the complexity of cloud architectures and functions.

SLA terms must be defined in a way that all parties have the same understanding of what is being provided therefore, it is clear that the need for a consistent definitions will only become more important as time goes on.

The following sections elaborate on SLA terms' taxonomy that aims to provide definitions relevant for the EU public and private sectors, based on common outsourcing practices that are applicable also to Cloud services cases.

These are structured according to three main categories: Access, Dependability and Security:

Access

- Availability of service.
- Problem Resolution/Incident Response.
- Reporting and Quality of Service.
- Data Portability.

Dependability

- Auditability.
- Certification and Compliance.
- Limitations.
- Penalties.

Security

- Data privacy conditions.
- Security Provisions including backup and disaster recovery.

4.1   Access

Access parameters refer to service characteristics details.

Availability of Service

It is commonly understood as the degree of uptime for the service.

The ITIL [11] model provides the following definitions:

- A system is available when the customer receives the service stated in the SLA. The measurement and reporting of availability has to be based on a common understanding between the service provider and the service consumer.
- The degree of availability of a component or service is often expressed as the percentage of time for which the service is available. These figures can be determined in terms of downtime over a fixed period.
- Common formulas to calculate availability include:
  - Availability % = Actual Availability/Agreed Availability * 100.
  - Actual Availability = Size of measurement interval Downtime.
  - Downtime = Time to repair or Service restoration time detection time.

ENISA [12] makes important remarks to be taken into account:

- SLA should clearly define when a service is considered available.
- An SLA may define a recovery time objective (RTO), which is measured against mean recovery time (MRT).
- SLA may define MTBF (mean time between failures), which can be useful in the case where long periods of uninterrupted operation are critical.

Problem Resolution/Incident Response:

Using ITIL Terminology [11]:

- An incident is defined as an event which is not part of the standard operation of a service and which causes or may cause disruption to or a reduction in the quality of services and customer productivity.
- A problem is a condition often identified as a result of multiple incidents that exhibit common symptoms. Problems can also be identified from a single significant incident, indicative of a single error, for which the cause is unknown, but for which the impact is significant. The primary objectives of Problem Management are to prevent Incidents from happening and to minimize the Impact of Incidents that cannot be prevented.

According to ENISA [12], the service level of a providers detection and response to incidents is often defined by means of:

- Severity: It has to be based in a well-defined scheme.
- Time to respond (from notification/alerting): the time to implement a remedial response.

Reporting and Quality of Service Monitoring

Reporting refers to make available information in order to provide an overview of service performance and its operational status.

ENISA [12] provides the following classification of parameters:

- Service Availability: Based on services' definition of availability. Examples of means to monitor this parameter are the following: relying on users, relying on providers' logs, by executing service health-checks, relying on providers' monitoring tools.
- Incident Response: Examples of incident data to be provided include: time of first reporting incident discovery time, incident resolution time, incident severity, and affected assets.
- Service Elasticity and Load Tolerance: the main aspect to monitor is the ability of the service to securely provision required resources when they are needed. It is proposed to verify it by means of regular testing. Depending on the nature of the provided service it can include: Number of CPU cores, CPU Speed, Memory size, VM quantity, VM storage, VM storage throughput, Bandwidth, Application response capacity.
- Data Life-cycle Management: It includes aspects such as: back-up test frequency and results, restoration speed, success or failure of operational backups, data recovery points, percentage of response to requests for data export successfully completed, data loss prevention system logs and system test results, data durability.

- Technical Compliance and Vulnerability Management, such as: Information on patches and controls in place vs open vulnerabilities, information on compensating controls applied, data on specific vulnerabilities and trends, such as their classification and severity scores.
- Change Management. Among others it may include: change notice time, change triggers, loss of certification status, changes or extension of jurisdictions in which data processing occurs, patches and major system changes, significant changes in security controls and processes used, time to implement security-critical customer change requests.

For the identified parameters, their reporting, based on the time-criticality of the information, can be provided based on three categories:

- Real-time service level data/feeds, including service level dashboards.
- Regular service level reports.
- Incident reports raised by the provider.

Data Portability

This refers to the users ability to create, copy and/or perform transmissions of data among cloud providers or between users facilities and a cloud provider.

Several initiatives and project are working on developing and identifying common standards or frameworks for cloud solutions to increase the data and application interoperability between different cloud providers, such as the European Telecomunications Standards Institute (ETSI). Current lack of data interoperability standards, leads to significant effort for the customers to port data among providers in a usable format to avoid vendor lock-in.

Usable format to avoid vendor lock-in. Article 18 of the draft Data Protection Regulation [13] specifically addresses this issue, by granting data subjects the right of data portability. So that, e.g. to transfer data from one electronic processing system to and into another, without being prevented from doing so by the controller. As a precondition and in order to further improve access of individuals to their personal data, it provides the right to obtain from the controller those data in a structured and commonly used electronic format. It is expected that this characteristic takes on a relevant role in cloud adoption in the future.

The following parameters are proposed as part of the SLA:

- Data Format: Specification on structured and commonly used electronic formats available for the users to get its data from the provider.
- Data Availability: Mechanisms in with data is made available, potentially including the specification of transport protocols and the specification of APIs, or any other mean, for the user to effectively get its data from the cloud provider.
- Data Sanitation Period: Transition at the end/termination of service: Period in which the data will be available in a usable format when the services are no longer needed or the service has terminated for any reason.

- Data Retention and Deletion clauses: Retention period for the provider to keep the data for the user, the period in which the provider is obligated to delete all personal data (including backups, Virtual Machine (VM) images, etc.) after service termination.

4.2 Dependability

Trust parameters reference parameters that allow determining the providers trust.

Auditability

Auditability refers to the ability of an organization, or defined systems or processes of the organization, to be evaluated on how the cloud computing service provider addresses the control frameworks of the specification.

A right to audit clause in a cloud SLA gives customers the ability to audit the cloud provider, which supports traceability and transparency. The goal of such an audit is to provide cloud service providers with a way to make their performance and security data voluntarily available. Using Audit specifications could provide a standard way to present and share information about performance and security needed by users to evaluate the service. Standardized information, in addition, could make comparison among providers easier.

Three different types of audit and assurance information can be provided by cloud providers to its users and reflected in SLA terms:

- Third-Party Attestations, Reports and Certifications: Reports and certifications produced by third-party auditors which attest to the design and operating effectiveness of the cloud provider environment such as: HIPAA, SOC 1/SSAE 16/ISAE 3402, SOC 2, SOC 3, PCI DSS, ISO 27001, CSA STAR.
- Documentation on procedures, standards, politics as well as configuration information, such as information about standard configurations and documentation for the current configuration of the users systems.
- Continuous Logging and Monitoring Information. See Reporting and Quality of Service monitoring.

Certification and Compliance

Compliance refers to the act of fulfilling the requirements of a regulation.

Cloud providers privacy compliance is a major area of concern. Diverse initiatives are emerging in order to provide independent certification by reputable third parties so to provide a credible means for cloud providers to demonstrate their compliance with data protection principles. Besides, these initiatives could establish an assurance level to potential cloud users to evaluate providers level of privacy compliance. Among others, the following initiatives are highlighted:

- Safe Habor Certification [14], as created under the EU-US Safe Harbor Programme refers to US companies aim to process personal data from the EU. It evaluates compliance with the Data Protection Directive. The certification is renewed annually, and failure to renew this certification implies that the provider directly loses Safe Harbor benefits.
- Cloud Security Alliance (CSA) Privacy Level Agreement [15] (PLAs), aim to define an extension to SLAs for privacy, in which the Cloud provider will clearly declare the level of privacy and data protection that it maintains with regards to relevant data processing. A Privacy Level Agreement (PLA) has a double aim: first, act as a tool for cloud users to assess a cloud providers commitment to address personal data protection and secondly, to offer contractual protection against possible damages due to lack of compliance by the provider with privacy and data protection regulation. The PLA Working Group recently published a PLA outline for the sale of cloud services in the EU that is based on the EU and the OECD privacy principles, and aims to provide a common structure for PLA worldwide.
- European Privacy Seal (EuroPriSe) [16], this certification is offered to manufacturers and vendors of IT products and IT-based services. The certification process is required of the evaluation of the product or service by legal and IT experts, as well as, the validation of the evaluation report by an independent certification body established at the Office of the Data Protection Commissioner of Schleswig-Holstein in Kiel, Germany.

The SLA could include terms to reflect compliance with data protection principles available, similarly to Third-Party Attestations, Reports and Certifications section with regards to Auditability.

Limitations

Limitations define the scope and restrictions of the provided service. Commonly it also defines providers liability terms.

These could include:

- Warranties and excluded warranties.
- Disclaimer.
- Liability.

Penalties

SLA penalties define what will happen in the case that a provider fails to deliver the agreed service.

According to Web Services Agreement Specification (WS-Agreement), Penalties terms when present in a SLA express the penalty to be assessed for not meeting a business level objective. WS-Agreement specification [17] defines a language and a protocol for advertising the capabilities of service providers and creating agreements based on providers offers, and for monitoring agreement compliance at runtime. Violation of guarantee terms during an assessment window can incur certain penalties. The penalty assessment is measured in a specified unit and defined by a value expression, which can be assessed from service monitoring information. The WS-Agreement defines term language and SLA templates to express this parameter. Multiple research initiatives such as SLA@SOI, CLOUD4SOA, OPTIMIS, and others have assessed its applicability to Cloud environments [18].

4.3 Security

Security refers to parameters related to safety and protection mechanisms for cloud users.

Data Privacy Conditions

As reported by OPTIMIS European Research project [8], the Data Protection Directive makes clear that one of the main aims is the protection of fundamental rights and freedoms and in particular the right to privacy with respect to the processing of personal data. In addition, the Directive shall ensure the free flow of personal data between Member States.

The Directive deals with the processing of personal data. Personal data is defined as any information relating to an identified or identifiable natural person. As opposed to anonymous data, personal data is any information relating to persons who can be identified with reasonable effort. Although encrypted by technical means, this data is still considered personal. Anonymous data is data where the data subject can only be identified with an unreasonable amount of costs, capacities and time. This directive applies to the processing of personal data, going in detail through the terms:

- processing means any operation or set of operations which is performed upon personal data.
- addressee of the Data Protection Directive is the controller, this is the body which determines the purposes and means of the processing.

Whether data protection law is applicable depends on the establishment of the controller and the processor.

European Data Protection Directive is rather fragmented with regard to data security measures to be implemented by controllers and processors and the level of harmonization among different EU countries, where often technical and organizational data security measures are low. However, a minimum security requirements for cloud computing can be extracted. All measures mentioned aim to ensure confidentiality, integrity, authenticity and availability of the data. Destruction: Personal data must be protected against accidental or unlawful destruction to ensure integrity and availability as well as business continuity.

- Loss: The Data Protection Directive aims to protect the logical and physical availability of personal data by requiring the Member States to implement security measures against unplanned events (natural disasters, hardware failures).
- Alteration: Protection of personal data against alteration aims to ensure the authenticity and integrity of the data processed.
- Disclosure: One of the cornerstones of data protection is confidentiality of personal data. Therefore, the Data Protection Directive requires controllers and processors to protect personal data against disclosure.
- Access: Access to personal data must be controlled by specific security measures in order to maintain the confidentiality of personal data. Finally, data must be protected against all other unlawful forms of processing. This vague legal term aims to promote the use of privacy enhancing technologies when planning an information system designed to process personal data.
- State of the Art: Security measures have to consider the state of the art.
- Appropriate Measures: Security measures must be appropriate with regard to the anticipated risks inherent in the data processing, as well as with regard to the nature of data and the costs of their implementation.

Based on this it is proposed to include the following terms in the SLA, using the terms provided by OPTIMIS project [19]:

- Data Protection Level:
  - None: when data is not sensitive, and it can be transferred without restriction.
  - DPA: Data can only be moved to countries that have a sufficient level of protection. It specifies whether the data included in the service under consideration is sensitive or not.
- Data Encryption Level: Defines data encryption algorithm to be applied (AES, Twofish).
- Data Breach Notification: In addition, based on the proposal for a new data protection regulation and the obligation to notify data breach, SLA parameters to consider this are also included.
- Eligible Country List/Non Eligible Country List: Specific allowed and not allowed countries to host the data.

Security Provisions Including Backup and Disaster Recovery

ENISA [12] refers to these set of parameters as Data lifecycle management. It considers the group of parameters that measure the efficiency and effectiveness of the providers data handling practices (data export, data loss prevention and services back-up). Based on this SLA terms proposed under this category are the following:

- Back-up test frequency and results availability.
- Restoration speed: the time taken to obtain data from back-up from the time of request.

- Frequency of operational back-ups.
- Data durability: some providers specify a durability parameter which relates to the amount of data which can be lost in a time period.

5   Conclusions

SLA terms and taxonomy presented in this document aim to improve reliability and transparency in Cloud usage for all kinds of organizations. However, as remarked in the European Cloud Strategy [20], the public sector has a strong role to play in shaping the cloud computing market. As the EU's largest buyer of IT services, it can set stringent requirements for features, performance, security, interoperability and data portability and compliance with technical requirements.

Early cloud computing deployments for governmental agencies have demonstrated tangible benefits for both the public administration and the citizens. A very significant example in Europe is UKs G-Cloud Cloud store. This Government eMarketplace enables departments and organisations across the UK public sector to easily access centrally negotiated deals. At the time of writing this paper, it is on its sixth iteration, G-Cloud 6, with numerous accredited suppliers offering a high variety of services [21] to public-sector buyers. Among them, the percentage of SMEs is remarkable. Ovum research reports that the majority if contracts so far have focused on consultancy with Agile and Cloud enablement [22], and it is increasingly becoming the procurement mechanism of choice.

Generic benefits gained from adoption of cloud computing in Government, such as economies of scale, reduced maintenance costs, and the ability to leverage elastic and reliable computing infrastructures, have the potential to provide improved services in terms of reliability, availability, cost-efficiency and security.

In order to make reality of this potential, SLAs are a key tool, as they can provide transparency, assurance and therefore trust in European companies. Well-defined SLAs can offer fair and transparent conditions for Cloud service trading in Europe.

References

1. Commision, European: DG Communications Networks. Establishing a Trusted Cloud Europe, Content and Technology (2014)
2. Mell, P., Grance, T.: The NIST Definition of Cloud Computing Recommendations of the National Institute of Standards and Technology (2011)
3. Software Progress, SaaS Security and Privacy Whitepaper, (2008). http://commu nity.progress.com/cfs-file.ashx/__key/communityserver-wikis-components-files/00-00-00-00-20/SaaS_5F00_Security_5F00_WP.pdf
4. Somorovsky, J., Heiderich, M., Bochum, R., Gruschka, N., Iacono, L.L.: All your clouds are belong to us security analysis of cloud management interfaces, pp. 3–14 (2011)

5. Wei, J., Zhang, X., Ammons, G.: Managing security of virtual machine images in a cloud environment. Cloud Computing Security (Vm), pp. 91–96 (2009). http://dl.acm.org/citation.cfm?id=1655021

6. Balduzzi, M., Zaddach, J., Balzarotti, D., Loureiro, S.: A security analysis of amazons elastic compute cloud service on Applied Computing (2012). http://dl.acm.org/citation.cfm?id=2232005

7. Popa, L., Yu, M., Ko, S.: CloudPolice: taking access control out of the network. In: Proceedings of the 9th (1), 16 (2010). http://dl.acm.org/citation.cfm?id=1868454

8. OPTIMIS project, Cloud legal guidelines final report. http://www.optimis-project.eu/content/cloud-legal-guidelines-final-report

9. European Commission, MEMO/13/898 15/10/2013, What does the Commission mean by secure Cloud computing services in Europe?. http://europa.eu/rapid/press-release_MEMO-13-898_en.htm

10. Bradshaw, S., Millard, C., Walden, I.: Contracts for Clouds: Comparison and Analysis of the Terms and Conditions of Cloud Computing Services, Queen Mary School of Law Legal Studies Research Paper No. 63/2010 (2010). http://ssrn.com/abstract=166237

11. ITIL Availability Management: Beyond the Framework (2003). http://www.cmg.org/measureit/issues/mit33/m_33_1.html

12. European Network and Information Security Agency (ENISA), Procure Secure, A guide to monitoring of security service levels in cloud contracts (2012). http://www.enisa.europa.eu/activities/Resilience-and-CIIP/cloud-computing/procure-secure-a-guide-to-monitoring-of-security-service-levels-in-cloud-contracts

13. European Commission, A proposal for a Regulation of the European Parliament and of the Council on the protection of individuals with regard to the processing of personal data and on the free movement of such data (General Data Protection Regulation) COM (2012). (11 final)

14. Safe Habor Regulation. http://export.gov/safeharbor/eu/eg_main_018365.asp

15. CSA Privacy Level Agreement Working Group. https://cloudsecurityalliance.org/research/pla/

16. European Privacy Seal. https://www.european-privacy-seal.eu/

17. Web Services Agreement Specification (2007). http://www.ogf.org/documents/GFD.107.pdf

18. Cloud Computing Service Level Agreements - Exploitation of Research Results (2013). https://ec.europa.eu/digital-agenda/en/news/cloud-computing-service-level-agreements-exploitation-research-results

19. Barnitzke, B., Ziegler, W., Vafiadis, G., Nair, S., Kousiouris, G., Corrales, M., Wldrich, O., Forg, N., Varvarigou, T.: Legal Restraints and Security Requirements on Personal Data and Their Technical Implementation in Clouds Workshop for E-contracting for Clouds, eChallenges (2011)

20. COM(2012) 529 final, Unleashing the Potential of Cloud Computing in Europe. http://eur-lex.europa.eu/LexUriServ/LexUriServ.do?uri=COM:2012:0529:FIN:EN:PDF

21. G-Cloud raises the ceiling again for government IT procurement. http://www.computerweekly.com/news/2240208076/G-Cloud-raises-the-ceiling-again-for-government-IT-procurement

22. Ovum Research, UK G-Cloud to champion public cloud, http://www.ovum.com/uk-g-cloud-to-champion-public-cloud/

Author Index

Anceaume, Emmanuelle   92
Antignac, Thibaud   60
Antonelli, Fabrizio   240

Basu, Anirban   76
Butoi, Alexandru   177

Caelli, William   149
Ceolin, Davide   134
Chadwick, David W.   251
Cordin, Lorenzo   240
Corena, Juan Camilo   76
Crowcroft, Jon   76

Daniel, Joshua   217, 226
de Vries, Gerben Klaas Dirk   134
Dimitrakos, Theo   215, 217, 226, 251
Dominguez, Nuria Rodriguez   217
Ducatel, Géry   217, 226
Dwyer, Natasha   126, 185

El-Moussa, Fadi   226

Ferdous, Md. Sadek   13
Ferrer, Ana Juan   262
Fokkink, Wan   134
Fotiou, Nikos   47

Gouvas, Panagiotis   217
Gudes, Ehud   3
Guette, Gilles   92
Guo, Jingjing   203

Hussein, Jamal   109

i Montanera, Enric Pages   262

Jensen, Christian Damsgaard   203
Jøsang, Audun   13, 165

Kalaboukas, Konstantinos   217
Kiyomoto, Shinsaku   76

Lajoie-Mazenc, Paul   92
Le Métayer, Daniel   60
Ledakis, Giannis   217

Liu, Vicky   149
Loutfi, Ijlal   165

Ma, Jianfeng   203
Marsh, Stephen   76, 126, 185
Moca, Mircea   177
Moiso, Corrado   240
Moreau, Luc   109

Nakamura, Toru   76
Norman, Gethin   13
Nottamkandath, Archana   134

Oosterman, Jasper   134

Pasolli, Mattia   240
Pawar, Pramod   226
Pawar, Pramod S.   251
Pernul, Günther   195
Poet, Ron   13
Polyzos, George C.   47

Richthammer, Christian   195
Rösch, Artur   195
Rowlingson, Robert   226

Sahama, Tony   149
Sajjad, Ali   226, 251
Sänger, Johannes   195
Sassone, Vladimiro   109
Sirvent, Thomas   92

Tomai, Nicolae   177

Vaidya, Jaideep   76
Van Der Sype, Yung Shin   76
Vescovi, Michele   240
Viet Triem Tong, Valérie   92

Wong, Andrew   149
Wu, Yongzheng   30

Yap, Roland H.C.   30

Printed in the United States
By Bookmasters